Animals and the Afterlife

True Stories of Our Best Friends' Journey Beyond Death

KIM SHERIDAN

HAY HOUSE

Australia • Canada • Hong Kong • India
South Africa • United Kingdom • United States

First published and distributed in the United Kingdom by:
Hay House UK Ltd, 292B Kensal Rd, London W10 5BE.
Tel.: (44) 20 8962 1230; Fax: (44) 20 8962 1239. www.hayhouse.co.uk

Published and distributed in the United States of America by:
Hay House, Inc., PO Box 5100, Carlsbad, CA 92018-5100.
Tel.: (1) 760 431 7695 or (800) 654 5126;
Fax: (1) 760 431 6948 or (800) 650 5115. www.hayhouse.com

Published and distributed in Australia by:
Hay House Australia Ltd, 18/36 Ralph St, Alexandria NSW 2015.
Tel.: (61) 2 9669 4299; Fax: (61) 2 9669 4144. www.hayhouse.com.au

Published and distributed in the Republic of South Africa by:
Hay House SA (Pty), Ltd, PO Box 990, Witkoppen 2068.
Tel./Fax: (27) 11 467 8904. www.hayhouse.co.za

Published and distributed in India by:
Hay House Publishers India, Muskaan Complex, Plot No.3, B-2, Vasant
Kunj, New Delhi – 110 070. Tel.: (91) 11 4176 1620; Fax: (91) 11 4176 1630.
www.hayhouse.co.in

Distributed in Canada by:
Raincoast, 9050 Shaughnessy St, Vancouver, BC V6P 6E5.
Tel.: (1) 604 323 7100; Fax: (1) 604 323 2600

A catalogue record for this book is available from the British Library.

ISBN 978-1-8485-0242-0

Printed and bound in Great Britain by CPI Mackays, Chatham ME5 8TD.

This book is dedicated . . .

To anyone who has ever loved and lost an animal.

To anyone who has ever been told, "It's just an animal."

To all of the animals on Earth and in Heaven.

And especially to June, the little angel in fur who found me when I was lost, put me back on my path, and showed me the way.

Author's Note

ANIMALS AND THE AFTERLIFE is more than a compilation of random stories; rather, it is the culmination of my personal journey—one that has brought me incredible comfort and understanding. My goal in writing this book is to share this comfort and understanding with those who seek it.

I have designed this book to follow a specific order—the chapters build upon each other, and the stories are interwoven with my personal journey and commentary. So, as tempting as it may be to jump around from story to story, I highly recommend reading the book in chronological order, from beginning to end. Reading the stories within the context of the greater whole will lend greater insight to the reader, greater credibility to the stories, and above all, greater healing for those in grief.

Many of you may be skeptical—and a good dose of healthy skepticism is always helpful in a world of conflicting opinions. As you will soon discover, mine has been a journey from open-minded child to grieving skeptic, and ultimately, to comforted believer. Now, I invite you to join me on this journey. . . .

— **Kim Sheridan**

Contents

Acknowledgments

EXPERIENCE HAS SHOWN ME that it truly does take a *lot* longer to write a book than to read one. I would like to express my deepest gratitude to everyone involved in finally making this book a reality. . . .

Thanks to my wonderful family for making it possible for me to step away from my former obligations as I embarked upon this journey. Thanks for your time and invaluable assistance as my projected "six-month project" became a seven-year all-consuming endeavor.

Thanks to Mom and Dad, who always allowed me to chart my unique path, which was often far from your own, and who continue to support me every step of the way. You are not only the most wonderful parents I could have ever asked for, you are the best friends a person could have.

Dad: Thanks for all of your priceless assistance in building and maintaining the Rat Refuge—and so many other important things—as my time grew more and more scarce. Thanks for doing whatever needed to be done, and never complaining. Your grandrats love you, too!

Mom: Thanks for taking over the important tasks that I knew would be safe in your hands. You made it possible for me to finally step away and finish this book, knowing that everything would be taken care of. Thanks for your invaluable feedback on the manuscript all the while.

Thanks to my husband, Jameth, my best friend and dream come true who has helped to make subsequent dreams come true.

Thanks for taking over the business we started together so that I could focus on this project. Thanks for your support, countless hours, and priceless feedback on the manuscript as it gradually evolved into a book. Thanks for keeping me fed as I spent every day—and most nights—in front of the computer. Thanks for doing the dishes, the laundry, and so much else. Thanks, also, for being my amazing computer guru, and for staying up all night with me in front of the computer so many nights during the final year of this enormous project.

Thanks to my brother and lifelong friend, Scott, and my friends, Gina, Demetre, Mike, and Jaye, for helping out with the Rat Refuge during the final weeks and months of this project, when my time became ever more scarce . . . and thanks for caring.

Thanks to Michelle Sass (June's "Other Mom") for trusting me with an angel.

Thanks to Coral Kingwell for connecting me with Michelle on that fateful day.

Thanks to my dear friend Aden Maxwell for always believing in me and supporting my dreams.

Thanks to all of my other friends—most of whom may not even remember me at this point—for putting up with unanswered phone calls and a continual "absence of Kim" for years on end as I gave up any semblance of a social life, weekends and holidays and, instead, toiled away at this seemingly never-ending endeavor.

Thanks to Gail De Sciose and Judith Guggenheim for being so supportive of this project and referring so many people to me over the years. Thanks, also, to Kathy Bauch and Susan Duncan.

Thanks to Wendy Ruiz for doing such a great job transcribing countless hours of interviews.

ANIMALS AND THE AFTERLIFE

Thanks to Helen Weaver, Martha Koelemay, Diane Newburg, Geri Kepler, and Mom for providing five additional pairs of very keen eyes to help with the final proofreading.

Thanks to Richard Mucci for providing the wonderful cloud photo that I knew would be perfect for the book cover the moment I saw it.

Thanks to my Circle of Light buddies for helping create a safe space in which to explore and grow: Cara, Marilyn, Nada, Janet, and Becky.

Thanks to my animal-rescue buddies who do so much for the animals, including the littlest animals who are all too often forgotten: Maggie Houlihan, Fenella Speece, Jan Martin, Jim Martin, and Diane Newburg.

Thanks to the wonderful veterinarians who have provided exceptional care for my loved ones: Dr. Debbie Oliver, Dr. Daryl Mabley, Dr. Carmine Bausone, Dr. Brian Loudis, and Dr. Sue Redpath.

Thanks to my agent, Bonnie Solow, for believing in this book.

Thanks to my wonderful new friends at Hay House. I'm delighted and honored to be working with you.

Thanks to two of my elementary school teachers, Mr. McCord and Ms. Callister, who saw this coming long ago.

I'd also like to express my deepest gratitude to all of the people whose insights and/or experiences helped shape this book, including those who made the much-appreciated effort to put their experiences in writing, and those who took time out of their schedules so I could interview them. This incredible list of people couldn't possibly be categorized in any particular order, so for practicality, it's listed alphabetically:

Alexandra Alba, Barbara Alois, George Anderson, Diane Arend, Rob Armstrong, Debbie Arxer, Maureen Averett, Richard Averett, Azar "Ace" Attura, Wendy B., Lois Bark, Andrew Barone, Barbara Batelli, Dave Bauer, Mary Blaszak, Lorna Blechynden, Tanicia (Neesh) Bodrero, Bette Boswell, Narelle Box, Dannion Brinkley, Chuck Brown, Sharon Callahan, Bebe Carnes, Barb Cash, Peggy Christiansen, Joep Claessens, Tomas M. Claessens, Judith Hipskind Collins, Audrey H. Cornelius, Bé Courtadet, Jeanie Cunningham, Anita Curtis, Rae Daviss, Virginia (Ginny) Debbink, Bob Degenhart, Kathleen S. DeMetz, Gail De Sciose, Carole Devereux, Ginny Devlin, Monica Diedrich, Trish D. Dodson, Donna L. Dodson, Allan Dominik, Yvonne Dominik, Angela Elliott, Carol Everson, George Everson, Regina Fetrat, Karen Fonseca, Arielle Ford, Melissa French, Janine Fuquay, Gwen Gerow, Gloria Glossbrenner, Sue Goodrich, Thomas H. Goheen, Kathy Grady, Carol Gurney, Stuart Hague, Maureen Hall, Jane Hallander, Clara Elizabeth (Beth) Hammond, Trés Hanley, Frank J. Hannaford, Donna Hassler, Dawn E. Hayman, Regina Heynneman, Kathleen Hill, S.R. Hipwell, Marianne Hirschberg, Trisha Adelena Howell, Sarah Hreha, Sananjaleen June Hughes, Gladys Hypes, Denise Isings, Jim Johnson, Morgine Jurdan, Griffin Kanter, Fran Kenny, Geri Kepler, Samantha Khury, Joanne C. King, Martha Koelemay, Joyce Krause, Debbie Kuperman, Karen M. Lambert, David Larson, Joanne Lauck, Betty Lewis, Nicole Lockard, Kimberly Louie, Lisa Ludwig, Cathleen Macauley, Barbara Mariano, Gabrielle Marie, Mary, Jodie McDonald, Steve McDonald, Susan Chernak McElroy, Barbara Meyers, Kate Mucci, Richard J. Mucci, Sarah Mullen, Loretta Laja Muncie, Katharine Lyle Nelson, Joanne Nemeh, Diane Newburg, Brigitte Noel, Shelley Nunemaker, Elizabeth O'Donnell, Gina Palmer, Renee Pastman, Mary Pavlik, Lance Payette, Videha Psuerse, Ingrid Pohl, Nick Pollard, Tracey Pollard, Jojo Pomeroy, Raphaela Pope, April Prager, Patte Purcell, Rae Ramsey, Wendy Reardon, June Reichenback, Kate Reilly, Rebecca Richerson-Farris, Celeste Robinson, Jeri Ryan, Michelle Sass, Mary Lynn Schmidt, Scorpiona, Eliyana Scott, Elaine Seamans, Joanna Seere,

M.J. Shaw, Brenda Shoss, Robert Simmons, Jacquelin Smith, Olive T. Smith, Penelope Smith, Natalie Smith-Blakeslee, Kate Solisti-Mattelon, Angelique Spieler, Jan Spiers, J.D. Stanger, Nellie van der Stappen, George Stone, William Strole, Victoria Strykowski, Patty Summers, Mary Ellen Szwejkowski, Debra Tadman, Tera Thomas, Kendra Thompson, Jill Thornsberry, Monica van den Tillaart, Tricia Timmons, Al Vickers, Teresa Wagner, Myriah Krista Walker, Sherry A. Warrick, Marta Williams, Winterhawk, Fleur Wiorkowski, Nedda Wittels, Glenn Wolff, Sandy Worth, Karen Young, and all those who chose to remain nameless.

If I've failed to mention anyone, I apologize—please do speak up, and I'll make things right in the next printing! I would like to express my heartfelt appreciation to all of you who shared your beautiful stories with me, whether they find themselves on the pages that follow or not. Thank you for trusting me with your words and your tears . . . I hope I've done them justice.

And last, but certainly not least, I would like to express my deepest gratitude to all those angels known as animals who have touched my life in a very profound way. This book wouldn't exist without you.

Introduction

A note to skeptics . . .

IT WAS ONCE BELIEVED that the earth was flat and not round. It was once considered an indisputable fact that women did not have souls. It was once considered absolute truth that those of certain races were inferior. Galileo was once ridiculed—and even considered blasphemous—for proclaiming that the earth was not the center of the universe after all.

Those of us who know better realize how ridiculous—and in some cases, dangerous—such belief systems can be. They are usually based on arrogance, self-interest, or simply, ignorance. Throughout history, there have been those who have risked their reputations—and, in some cases, their lives—to question such proclamations and to make the truth be known.

I herein offer this latest bit of truth, for those who have remained uninformed up until this point. I, too, have a skeptical nature—yet I understand that there comes a time when enough facts have been gathered to overturn former, outdated beliefs. I contend that, in regard to animals having souls, that time is now. This truth has been a long time in coming.

My journey into this realm has been eye-opening, mind-expanding, and very healing. It is my intention that others will be comforted by the overwhelming evidence of life after death for animals; the highly substantiated notion that our loved ones never really die, no matter their species, no matter their size.

— **Kim Sheridan**

A note to those who are experiencing grief
over the loss of a beloved animal . . .

MY DEEPEST SYMPATHY is with you on the loss of your precious companions. I truly understand the depth of the pain and grief you are now enduring. It was that very pain upon the loss of a beloved companion animal in my own life that originally led to this book. Only those of us who have had such sacred relationships with these special beings known as animals can truly understand what you are going through. It is my hope that this book will provide comfort and assistance in getting through this difficult time. May you find support, understanding, comfort, and peace in these pages.

— **Kim**

- CHAPTER 1 -

In the Beginning

*If having a soul means being able to feel love
and loyalty and gratitude, then animals
are better off than a lot of humans.*
— JAMES HERRIOT

"I'M LOSING HIM." The voice on the phone sounded vaguely familiar, but the words were so choked with tears that they were nearly indistinguishable. I heard sobbing.

"Oh God, he's dying," she cried. "He *can't* leave me." I then recognized the voice. It was an acquaintance of mine, whose whole world revolved around her sweet little companion, Sparky. She was divorced, and her children had grown up and left home, so Sparky was her closest companion. Each evening when she came home from work, Sparky was there, waiting for her. Each time she arrived home late because she'd had a date, Sparky was there, waiting for her. Each time she came home distraught over a broken relationship, Sparky was there, waiting for her. She often commented that this sweet little angel in fur was the only guy she could count on . . . and the only one she needed.

"I don't know what I'm going to do without him," she sobbed. Sparky was old and she had known his time was coming, but still the moment was hitting her like a ton of bricks.

"I feel so helpless. What should I do?" she asked, sounding desperate.

1

"Just hold him," I instinctively replied, "pet him, tell him you love him, *be* with him." My response was automatic. It seemed so clear to me what he needed, what *she* needed. I knew because I had been there. Too many times.

"His breathing seems slower now," she said quietly, almost surrendering to the inevitable. The two of us stayed on the phone and wept as little Sparky made his transition.

This was the first time someone had turned to me for support in their grieving, but it wouldn't be the last. As I eventually came to realize, this was a rite of passage for me, a step into a future for which I had been preparing my entire life. . . .

ONE OF MY EARLIEST MEMORIES takes me back to a time when I was about three or four years old. One night, I had a dream. It was so vivid and felt so significant that its memory has remained crystal clear for decades.

In the dream, several large porcupines, who were bigger than me, were just outside the house, trying to get in. I was terrified of them and tried desperately to keep them out. However, they were determined to get in, and eventually they did.

At that point, my intense fear gave way to wonder as they began to communicate with me, sharing feelings of unconditional love and understanding. They spoke to me not with words but with *thoughts.* Looking back, I now realize that it was telepathic communication, although I didn't know what that meant at the time. They told me that I had nothing to fear; they were my friends. They looked different than me, but inside, they were just the same. They needed warmth, shelter, and companionship, just like me. And they were very wise.

In the dream, the porcupines stayed for a long while, and we had a wonderful visit. When it was time for them to go, I was sad. I knew I would miss them but that they would always be my friends. I awoke feeling that something significant had taken place. I had received an important message. And so began my journey with the animals.

MINE, LIKE MANY, WAS A CHILDHOOD filled with a wide assortment of animal friends. I still clearly recall the wonder of attending to newborn kittens at my cousins' house; the joy of feeding the bunnies next door whenever the neighbors were out of town; and the lump in my throat when my parents took my brother and me all around town, searching for our lost dog, Charlie, who never returned. These were important events early in my life, urging me to consider the relevance of other beings.

I grew up in suburban Southern California, a place of dry summers and wet winters. On rainy days, the snails would come out of hiding and gather on the sidewalks and in the streets near my home. It broke my heart to see them get crushed on their journey, so I spent many a rainy afternoon picking them up, one by one, and putting them near the house, where they would be safe. At one point, I had all of the other neighborhood children joining in the effort, and it felt like an immensely worthwhile cause, helping out those small, vulnerable beings. I just *knew* that those creatures had feelings and that their well-being really mattered.

At a very young age, I became known as the "neighborhood vet," often nurturing injured baby birds with an eyedropper feeder and a warm bed. Usually when someone found an injured or abandoned animal, I was the first one they called. Sometimes these animals were dropped off at our front door, and I always did the best I could for them.

When I was five years old, my family went to dinner at the home of my dad's business associate and his wife. The couple had unconventional taste in animals, and their menagerie included, among other creatures, several graceful mallard ducks in the backyard and a large family of pet rats in the living room. The rats had so much personality, and I was so taken by them that I didn't want to leave. It was love at first sight. Noticing my delight, our hosts offered me a baby from a forthcoming litter.

Before long, I was the proud caretaker of my very own little rattie named Queenie. (When I use the term "my" in reference to an animal, I mean it only in the most endearing way, much like one would say "my best friend" or "my beloved," rather than thinking in terms of ownership. I've always thought of animals as individual beings worthy of our respect, rather than mere property that we own. When the word "pet" is used in this book, it means "beloved animal who is a part of the family"; it does *not* mean possession. When we share our lives with animals, we become their guardians; not their owners.)

Queenie was an affectionate beauty dressed in white with a velvety black hood that covered her head and shoulders, then narrowed to a stripe down her back. She was the first of many rats I have loved since then. I didn't find out until much later that society had a less than favorable impression of rats, not that it would have mattered anyway. In my world, rats were friendly, smart, lovable companions who taught me responsibility and compassion.

Due to my painfully empathic nature (I was often called "a very sensitive child"), I couldn't stand to see animals—such as rats, who are extremely active, social creatures—just sitting in cages all day. It occurred to me early on that it was no different than locking a human in jail, despite the fact that no crime had been committed. So, my beloved rat companions led very active lives.

Each day when I returned from school, I headed straight to the rat cage to free my nocturnal buddies just as they were awakening from a long nap. They spent the rest of the day riding around on my shoulders or running and playing freely in my bedroom as I did my homework. On weekends, they joined my friends and me as we played, and all of the children adored them. Back then, I only had one or two rats at any given time, but I proudly told everyone that when I grew up, I was going to have a Rat Room filled with rats who could run and play freely *all the time*.

My rat companions were always returned to their cage at bedtime, until one night when I was awakened by a gentle pressure on my chest. I opened my eyes and was greeted by the pretty beige face of my sole rat companion at that time, Champagne. She was curled up on my chest and looked at me as if to say, "I want to sleep here with you." She had figured out how to open her cage door, and I watched in amazement as she later headed back to her cage to go to the bathroom and get a bite to eat, then returned to join me in bed once again. From that point on, I spent every night with the warmth and comfort of a little companion curled up on my chest or snuggled up against my cheek.

I never actually went to a pet store or breeder and purchased a rat; they always just came into my life, given to me by friends, schoolteachers, or people who just couldn't keep them for whatever reason.

They still come into my life, now as rescues from a multitude of unfortunate situations. (I never breed or buy them, because unfortunately, there are far too many homeless animals in our world already, and this includes rats.) I've always felt good to be able to provide a good, loving home to these creatures in need. Now I realize that they've provided *me* with a far greater gift.

Looking back, I can see that perhaps they've come to teach me, not only about unconditional love, acceptance, and compassion; not only about life; but also about death. Domesticated rats have a very short lifespan, two to three years or so being the average. So, on a regular basis for most of my life, I've been faced with the death of a beloved friend. Over and over, I've had to face the pain and the emptiness, the tears and the questions, which have pushed me ever further to seek answers. By opening my heart to the love of animals whose lives are so brief, I have learned volumes about life and death.

WHILE GROWING UP, my brother and I spent the majority of our summers on our grandparents' ranch, an enchanted oasis tucked away in the pristine mountains of west Texas. Our parents could only join us for short visits, as they had jobs back at home, so my brother and I stayed with our grandmother and grandaddy, and our Texas cousins often joined us.

The Ranch was a place with no television set and a million reasons not to need one. Hundreds of acres of wilderness provided a vast playground, filled with wide-eyed cows, playful chickens, majestic antelope, nervous deer, and an assortment of other amazing animals. In that setting, I found endless entertainment and friends galore.

I'll never forget Buck, the young deer who took a chance and was rewarded with endless back rubs and treats from my brother, my cousins, and me. Somehow, Buck knew that we were different than the big people. We hadn't been corrupted. We wouldn't be participating in the annual massacre known as deer season, one thing I hated about The Ranch.

Buck regularly came right up to the house to play with us, his friends. To commune with this wild, beautiful creature was an experience that touched a deeper part of me than anything else ever had. To look into his eyes and see that great soul looking back at me taught me more than any Sunday-school lesson.

One deer season, a hunter mistook Buck for "just another deer," and I knew I would never see him again. That was when I learned not to necessarily trust grown-ups, and I understood for the first time why animals didn't necessarily trust them either.

As a gift from our grandparents, each grandchild was given our very own cow, and mine was named Bracelet because one day she stepped into a large, round, ring-shaped object that got stuck around her hoof and made it look just like she was wearing a bracelet. One year, Bracelet had a daughter, and I named the calf Daisy. They were both so sweet and timid, and I spent hours petting them and assuring them that I'd always take good care of them.

Duffy, my grandparents' dog, was my other good friend and my protector. He was a large border collie who kept a watchful eye over the yard and accompanied me on long hikes. I always admired how brave he was, but even *he* trembled and hid at the sight of a gun. He knew there were forces greater than himself, and in observing him, I learned about my own limits.

When my grandaddy got sick and had to be moved to a nursing home, and my grandmother relocated to the nearby town, Duffy went to live with my uncle. But Duffy missed The Ranch too much and was last seen trying to make his way back, a journey he never completed. I never had a chance to say good-bye.

That was always the case when animals died during my early childhood. One day they just weren't there anymore. Not only would I miss them and regret all the things I didn't get to say or do, but I had no idea where they went, and no one had any real answers for me.

I don't think life has ever dealt me more than I can handle, although it often seems to reach my upper limits. I think perhaps there's a reason I wasn't there to witness death early in my life. Maybe I wasn't ready to face it head-on. Death needed to present itself to me gradually but repeatedly, giving me a little more each time.

And so loss came to me, time and again, always when I wasn't around to stop it—or to see what it looked like. My first dog ran away from home. My first rat died while my family was out of town and a neighbor was looking after her. My first deer friend was killed in Texas while I was in California. My first cow was sent off to slaughter, and I wasn't told until much later what that meant.

My second rat, a little white angel named Sweetheart, died while I was at school. I discovered Sweetheart's lifeless body when I got home and went to let her out of her cage to play, as I did each afternoon. Following the shock and the tears was absolute wonder. This was a first in my life. Sure, I had seen dead animals before. Roadkill and most of the baby birds I had rescued and tried to nurture back to health—the ones that didn't make it—had taught me a little bit about the permanence of death. However, I had never before seen the dead body of someone I really loved—someone who had been my constant companion for several years.

Sweetheart had been so active, so playful and busy, always wiggling her little rat nose, finding clever ways to steal my Halloween candy, and willingly tackling any maze or suspension bridge my brother and I set up for her.

Now she was so different. So stiff and cold and still. Unlike cartoon characters, she wasn't back to her old self the next day. I made a pretty little coffin for her and observed her body for a day or two before burying her. I invited my friends over to see her body. I petted her and looked at her and cried over her. I think I needed that time to really comprehend what had happened. I had to really look at death and somehow find a way to accept it.

And that was my experience of death for many years, with

many more animals and also with my grandparents and other people, including one of my schoolmates who just stopped showing up one day. Over and over, they died when I wasn't around to see it happen. I always either discovered their lifeless bodies after the fact and knew what had happened; or, more often, I was merely *informed* of what had happened. This was the case with my second dog, a feisty sheltie named Charger. One morning, he wouldn't eat, couldn't walk, and moaned in agony. My parents and I rushed him to the vet, who said we'd have to leave him there for some tests. That afternoon, I cried as my parents told me the vet had discovered an inoperable tumor and had put him "to sleep"; and I knew I'd never see him again. He was only eight years old.

Never any long, drawn-out event. Just instant death. Over and over, I had seen life, and I had seen death, but I had never really seen the part that comes in between: the dying process. Often that's the hardest part, so it seems that life protected me until I was ready to handle it.

That day came during my first year in college. My best buddy was a sweet little guy named Ben, a black and white hooded rat (white with a black "hood" that covered his head and shoulders, then tapered down his back) who shared my room and sat on my lap while I did my homework. He rode around on my shoulder each day, ran around my room each evening, and snuggled up against my cheek each night. His death was a very long, drawn-out process. I became completely absorbed in his care, taking him to the vet almost daily and trying every remedy and treatment available.

My heart ached as Ben's little body weakened. We both suffered. I just couldn't let him go. I made and canceled the euthanasia appointment perhaps a dozen times before I finally went through with it. After the fact, I regretted not having gone into the back room with him for that final visit. The vet had advised against it, knowing how distraught I was. So I sat and cried in the waiting room until Ben's body was brought out to me in a little box. It was years before I would let myself love another animal after that.

WHILE ATTENDING COLLEGE, I had a part-time job. One day while driving to work, the car in front of me hit a beautiful black dog. The car kept going, but I pulled over, devastated. I dragged the heavy dog's lifeless form over to the curb and cried over him. He had no tags. I wondered if anyone loved him. I wondered if anyone was missing him. I wondered why the driver hadn't stopped. I wondered if anyone cared. But mostly, I wondered where the dog's spirit had gone. What was this thing called Death, that could so instantly change an active, carefree creature into a still pile of long, curly fur? A part of me just had to know—but I was late for work and had a time clock to answer to.

After college, my brother and his dog Reindeer (who looked just like a little reindeer) became my roommates. I was delighted to finally have an animal back in my life, and Reindeer and I quickly became quite attached to one another. Shortly thereafter, Reindeer became ill and I found myself involved in her dying process. She was too young to die. Why did this keep happening? Again came the heartache and the uncertainty surrounding euthanasia.

When the day to end her suffering finally arrived, I determined that *this* time I'd be there, right to the end. My brother and I took her to the vet for that final visit. We sat on the floor and held her close as she took her final breath. Instinctively, we both looked up toward the ceiling and waved good-bye as her spirit left her body and traveled on in her journey. We didn't *see* anything, but we just *knew* she had a soul that continued on. I remember the certainty I felt in that moment.

It reminded me of a childhood game my brother and I had often played. We had a large collection of dolls, including many versions of Barbie®, Ken®, Big Jim, and G.I. Joe. One of the dolls came with a plastic life jacket, and we pretended that the life jacket was a "soul." Whenever we decided that one of the dolls was dying, we put the life jacket on that doll. When the doll died, we removed the life jacket (the "soul") and made it float up from the floor to Heaven. Eventually, all of the dolls died, at which time we put all of the dolls up on the bed ("Heaven") and continued our play with them. They interacted just as they had when they were "alive," but they were now in a higher place. It made sense to us. Life after death was a given.

Another favorite childhood game of mine was "Noah's

Ark." I had a little toy ark, little dolls of Noah and his family, and a whole collection of little animals, two of each kind. I always took my job very seriously as I saw to it that all of the animals were safely on the ark before the flood came. I had known and loved many animals, so I completely understood why Noah made an ark large enough to save all of them, and not just himself. I wondered why more people weren't so concerned about the well-being of animals, that amazing variety of beings with whom we share our world. I figured Noah had put forth a tremendous effort to make an ark big enough for them all. I respected him for his selfless compassion and wished there were more people like him in the world.

I guess I always felt in my heart that animals had souls, just like us. I was raised Christian and taught that if I was good, I'd go to Heaven. Every animal I had known was at least as good as me, so *of course* they had a spot reserved for them beyond the Pearly Gates. When I asked the pastor of our church if he thought animals went to Heaven, he responded by stating that if dogs *didn't* go to Heaven, he wouldn't want to go there either. That was a pretty bold statement coming from a pastor, but then again, this was a man who loved his dog.

The older I got, the more I questioned things. That was certainly the case with death. As a child, the afterlife was a given. When I got older, I wasn't so sure. Where *did* they go, really? Was Heaven just a place we invented to ease the pain? Was there any proof of it? I was pretty convinced that ghosts existed, but beyond that, I wasn't sure. Where was the concrete evidence?

I'VE BEEN FASCINATED WITH GHOSTS and the paranormal for as long as I can remember. My interest in the paranormal was perhaps initially fueled by a wide assortment of psychic experiences throughout childhood that left me confused, sometimes frightened, and always fascinated, determined to understand what was really going on.

Somehow, I seemed to know things without understanding *how* I knew them. My earliest recollection of this goes back to when I was five years old and my family moved from Los Angeles to San Diego. My dad had already picked out a rental house, which the rest of us had never seen before the day we moved in, yet as our moving truck entered the new neighborhood, I instantly knew which house was ours. I didn't know *how* I knew, but I was *certain* which house it was, as if I had already seen it; and that was indeed the driveway we pulled into. Such experiences occurred so regularly that I came to accept them as a normal part of life. However, I got the distinct impression that most other people didn't have such experiences, so for many years I kept them to myself. There were times when these experiences literally saved my life, so although I didn't completely understand them, I was grateful to have them.

My dreams were filled with detailed premonitions that usually came true the very next day and always came true eventually. These weren't just vague images that I pieced together later; these were clear pictures and detailed facts about very unique and unexpected situations that always came to pass. To this day, I dream most nights of things to come, and it absolutely boggles my mind to think about it logically when the dreams come true, which they inevitably do. My logical mind simply can't make sense of the ability to see things *before* they even happen. However, experience has shown me that there is a lot more to reality than that which is generally considered "logical."

As a child, my precognitive dreams sometimes involved the death of someone I knew (or knew *of*, such as a neighbor or a friend's parent), which always occurred quite unexpectedly shortly thereafter, sometimes the very next day. These premonitions frightened me. I recall one such dream, in which someone with diabetes had died. In this case, I wasn't sure who the person was—or if the diabetes was even the cause of death—but for some reason, I knew that the person had diabetes, and I was very upset by their death. In the dream, I was sitting on the front porch, crying, and I watched helplessly as the person was rushed away in an ambulance. I knew that the person was going to die and there was nothing I could do about it.

I couldn't get the dream out of my mind the next day as I sat in school. I'd had enough experiences such as this to know that it was going to come true. When I returned home from school, I began pacing my bedroom, trying desperately to think of who I knew that had diabetes so I could warn them. Just then, my dad called out to me from downstairs and said that the lady next door had frantically asked for my parents' help because there was something terribly wrong with her husband, so my parents were heading next door.

I raced downstairs to see what was going on, and as I headed out the front door, it suddenly became clear to me *who* was going to die. I had never actually *met* the man next door and had no way of knowing if he did indeed have diabetes, yet I now knew it was *him*. I collapsed in tears on the front porch and helplessly looked on as the events unfolded just as I had already dreamt. I sat on the front porch, crying, as an ambulance carried our next-door neighbor away, *just like in the dream.*

When my mom returned and explained to me that my dad had accompanied the man's distraught wife to the hospital, I informed her that he would soon be calling to let us know that the man had died; I had dreamed the whole thing the night before, right down to the details of that phone call.

The phone rang. It was my dad, delivering the news I already knew. He said the man had died, and there was some talk of whether or not it had been a complication of his *diabetes*. As it turned out, the man had died of a heart attack, but I now had my confirmation that he had indeed been diabetic, just like in the dream. I asked my mom why I had to know such awful things if I couldn't do anything about them. She did her best to comfort me, but she didn't know either.

When a similar dream—involving a man who attended our church—came true, my mom called the wife of our pastor, who was a good friend. The pastor's wife was genuinely interested in my experiences but, unfortunately, she didn't really have any insights to offer either. I had learned about prophets in Sunday school, so I knew that such things were known and believed by the Church and were by no means the work of the devil. I just didn't understand why such experiences were so frightening, or why they were happening to *me*.

I often got the feeling that there were unseen presences in our home, especially at night, and this terrified me. So, after determining that hiding in a closet or sleeping in my parents' room wasn't going to make the fear go away, I was determined to understand what I was so afraid of. I believe the unknown is often scary just by virtue of being unfamiliar, so in hindsight, I suspect that the desire to understand my own fears was—at least in part— what originally sparked my interest in the afterlife.

While other children were out playing ball or hopscotch, I was often curled up with a book about ghosts, haunted houses, or other unexplained phenomena. I discovered many stories that provided tremendous evidence of life after death, but none of these stories specifically mentioned animals.

After reading piles of books containing photographs of ghosts, I began trying to capture them on film myself. Although I occasionally spotted some interesting-looking lights in the photos, nothing conclusive ever resulted from my efforts.

My brother, Scott, was my closest friend, and he shared my fascination with ghosts and such things. We spent countless hours reading real-life ghost stories aloud into a tape recorder, adding our own sound effects to heighten the drama. We took turns doing the narration and the voices of the various characters in the stories. To my knowledge, audio books didn't yet exist back then, so perhaps those early recordings of ours were some of the original audio books. I like to think so, anyway.

One of our favorite childhood pastimes was to turn the garage into a "haunted house" and then charge a nickel for neighbors to walk through it. I suppose it was our version of a lemonade stand. This was especially popular around Halloween; but in our world, haunted houses happened year round. In the summers, our Texas cousins often joined us in turning Grandmother and Grandaddy's Ranch house into a haunted one; and during holiday visits to Grandma and Pop Pop's house in New Jersey, our East Coast cousins joined us in haunting the spooky cellar and then inviting the grown-ups for a tour. My favorite rides at Disneyland were the Haunted Mansion and Pirates of the Caribbean, both of which revolve around ghosts. I just loved the idea of ghosts having a good time even though they had died.

My other great delight was performing séances for family members. These séances took place at home and also when visiting The Ranch. Early on, my parents and brother had grown accustomed to my unusual endeavors. My grandparents, cousins, aunts and uncles, however, probably thought of me as "the crazy kid from California"; but I think they found my antics genuinely entertaining. I didn't feel that I ever actually made contact with the dead, but I had a lot of fun trying and pretending.

I determined that when I grew up I wanted to be either a veterinarian (or *something* having to do with animals) or a paranormal investigator (a "ghost buster")—ideally, both. However, it would be decades before I finally merged these two interests.

Meanwhile, I grew up and pursued a career in health and nutrition, spurred by some interesting courses I took during my first year in college. I initially took health and nutrition courses out of personal interest and never intended to turn health into a career, but sometimes life just happens and we forget that we had other plans. I did make an attempt at pursuing my two primary childhood interests, but neither one worked out quite as I had planned.

I was fortunate to attend a college that offered several courses in parapsychology (the study of psychic phenomena), and they were by far my favorite classes. However, they were merely electives offered by the psychology department. So, I pursued general psychology for a while but soon grew tired of watching films of people putting rats through endless experiments in hopes of understanding *human* psychology. I did learn some valuable information (from the studies that actually involved humans) and went on to earn a degree in psychology; but by then I had already decided it wasn't the career path for me. Meanwhile, I had become fascinated with the topic of hypnotherapy, so I went on to become a certified clinical hypnotherapist; but I soon decided that a career in hypnotherapy wasn't my calling either.

My interest in veterinary medicine was quickly abandoned when I mourned over a bucket of dead baby pigs slated for dissection in my first college biology class. Interestingly, the name of the course was Human Physiology, so I wasn't quite sure where the pigs fit in, or the other lifeless animals that I was told would be joining us later in the semester. I didn't stay around long enough to find out.

So, nutrition it was. The more I learned, the more passionate I became about all things health related. When I wasn't in class or doing homework, I was attending seminars and workshops— or reading piles of books—on all aspects of health. I majored in both health education and nutrition, and I left all of my other interests behind, at least for the time being.

AFTER COLLEGE, I MET MY FUTURE HUSBAND, Jameth (pronounced "JAY-meth"), at a health conference on the East Coast. I flew cross-country to attend that conference specifically because I somehow just *knew* that the young man who was to be my husband would be there. And he was. The moment our eyes met, we both knew. He later told me that he, too, had a feeling that he would meet his future wife there. Neither of us could afford the price of the conference or the transportation to get there, but we both borrowed the money to make the trip because we *knew* we had to be there. It was an event that, for me, unfolded just like the rerun of a movie, because all of the very specific details of our meeting— right down to his name and where he sat in the conference hall— had already occurred many years prior, in a childhood dream. So, our magical first meeting was literally a dream come true.

I soon discovered that Jameth was pursuing identical career goals to my own in the field of health and nutrition, and we simultaneously became business partners and, more importantly, life partners. Our connection was immediate, and we've been together ever since. We both went on to earn degrees in naturopathy as well as certification in myriad health and healing modalities, and we pursued busy careers in the health field. We gave regular classes, lectures, and workshops; jointly authored a recipe/nutrition book (*Uncooking with Jameth and Kim*); saw clients in our private practice; conducted and compiled research on multiple aspects of health and nutrition; and dealt with the 24/7 lifestyle and headaches of small business ownership as we founded and grew our own company, HealthForce Nutritionals.

Periodically, I felt stirrings that pulled me in other directions. I felt that I was supposed to be doing *something else,* but I wasn't entirely clear on *what.* So, in my "spare time" (which really amounted to reducing my already scarce daily sleep quota), I briefly pursued the arts. I took some assorted art and music courses at a local community college, which soon spurred a brief career as a "starving artist."

For several months, I drew socks and shirts for an organic clothing company, and then I began a series of drawings called "Ratworks," the subject matter of which was, of course, rats. I made the first two editions of "Ratworks" into note cards and began distributing them through various rat-friendly organizations. However, as HealthForce slowly grew larger and my time rapidly grew more scarce, I soon abandoned my part-time art career altogether. It had been time well spent, and I actually felt quite complete with it because, although it had been a very short-lived career, it had become one less "what if" in my life.

I knew there were plenty of other "what ifs" left unpursued, but I was too busy to give them any more thought. Although my years in the field of health and nutrition greatly benefited my own health and enabled me to help others, my other interests remained, for the most part, unfulfilled. For a long time, I didn't even have any animals in my life.

Jameth and I talked of having companion animals *someday,* when our lives settled down. Meanwhile, our only exposure to animals involved rushing injured or neglected animals—who, for some strange reason, regularly crossed our path—to a vet or a shelter for emergency care. Many of these trips were in vain, and I realized that I was now losing animals without even having a chance to love them first.

Despite the pain of losing them, I missed having animal companions and longed for the day when things in my life would be settled enough to let animals back in. Things never did settle down, but thankfully, an animal crept back in anyway.

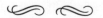

- CHAPTER 2 -

The New Arrival

*Until one has loved an animal, a part
of one's soul remains unawakened.*
— ANATOLE FRANCE

ONE DAY IN THE MONTH OF MAY, a pet rat was tossed out of an open window by humans who didn't want her anymore. They were aggravated that she went to the bathroom on the floor (although they did not potty-train her, nor did they even supply her with a cage or litter box), so they figured the best solution was simply to discard her.

One night in the month of June, a man found the rat searching for food. He trapped her in a pot, put the lid on, and left her in a closet. He happened to be the housing manager of a dormitory building where a young woman named Michelle lived.

"Hey, Michelle, look what I found," he said when he next saw her, two days later, as he knew she loved rats. Michelle took the lid off the pot, and the rat gratefully climbed right up her arm.

Michelle was horrified that this poor rat had been kept in a pot in a closet for two days, and that the man hadn't contacted her *immediately.* After all, she was known as the "rat girl"— *how could he forget?* He told her he thought the rat was "wild." Michelle had known and loved rats before, so she was well aware that this was no wild animal. Rather, this was an animal who had been born in captivity and then abandoned (which Michelle

17

later was able to confirm), who was simply looking for food and shelter and didn't know how to fend for herself. She had been seen foraging and begging for food for quite some time before she was trapped. Because of the time of year, and the fact that this rat was a female, Michelle named her "June."

There was something special about June. She seemed so ancient and wise, so sure of herself and her path on this earth. She had climbed Michelle's arm very deliberately and made it clear that she had no intention of leaving. She was a grayish-black beauty with a wise expression, an adorable white underbelly, and a powerful impact on those around her. Michelle and June formed an instant bond.

Michelle devoted all of her time to June that first day and night. The next day, she had to go to work. Afterward, she ran home as fast as possible. She couldn't wait for another evening with June. Since June was new, Michelle left her in a large cage while she was gone. Michelle didn't like keeping animals in cages, so she was in a hurry to get June out of it.

When she came home, much to Michelle's surprise, June gave birth to a single baby. Rats usually give birth to multiple babies, but in her depleted state, June only had one. Sadly, the baby died. Michelle assured June that she would never again have to suffer due to human negligence.

June soon became Michelle's best friend and roommate, and a very popular resident of the building, where everyone adored her. Each evening, Michelle announced that June would be making her rounds, and the other residents opened their hallway doors in hopes of a visit from the adorable, personable June. June ran up and down the hallways, with everyone calling to her. She ran in and out of their rooms, visiting her friendly neighbors; and whenever Michelle called out her name, she always came running. After her nightly rounds, she headed back to share a warm bed with her devoted human companion.

Whenever possible, June joined Michelle on her outings around town. People often asked about the cute little animal riding around on Michelle's shoulder, and June clearly enjoyed the attention, acting as a little ambassador for ratkind.

Michelle had previously applied for a job she really wanted and had been anxiously awaiting news about her prospective new career, which would take her on the road leading bus tours for international travelers. She'd had high hopes of landing this position, but when she then received the news that she indeed had the job, she was both excited and heartbroken. She was filled with regret and sadness, as she wouldn't be able to take June with her.

She realized that, although her neighbors loved June's visits, none of them was able to provide a permanent home for her, so Michelle began desperately looking for a new home for her little companion. She dreaded the forthcoming separation and was willing to settle for nothing less than an ideal home for June. Michelle posted flyers all around town in hopes of finding such a home, but she worried that she'd *never* be able to find a home good enough for June.

"Don't worry," a friend reassured her. "I just *know* that the perfect home is out there somewhere, and we'll find it."

MEANWHILE, JAMETH AND I found ourselves working all the time, never taking weekends or holidays off, wondering where we had gone wrong. There was no time for "down time," and most of our friends had stopped even inviting us anywhere because we never had the time to go anyway. After many years of this, we were experiencing burnout and wondering when we'd be able to start really living; but we had a growing company that needed us, and customers that counted on us, so we didn't know what else to do. We almost felt as if we were waiting for something to rescue us, but we weren't quite sure what.

We were caught quite by surprise upon hearing a message on our overloaded answering machine. Our good friend Coral shared the news that she had just met a young woman named Michelle who was looking for a good home for a rat, and we were the first ones that came to mind. She left Michelle's number.

I felt an excitement I hadn't felt since childhood as I called Michelle and we arranged to meet in person. Jameth joined me on that first trip to meet Michelle and June.

For me, the first encounter with June was very exciting and significant; it felt like she was opening up a part of my life that had been closed for too long. It was almost as if I were a mere child meeting an elder, not quite sure what to say or do, and feeling a bit inadequate. Jameth had never met a rat before and wasn't quite sure what to make of it all. While Michelle and I were busily discussing all things rat-related, June climbed right up to Jameth and began grooming his fingernails, as rats often do.

"I need some attention here," Jameth said nervously. "I think she's trying to eat my fingers." Michelle and I laughed and assured him that June was doing no such thing; rather, she was mothering him and showering him with affection. June rapidly stole Jameth's heart, and we all had a great time.

By the end of our visit, Michelle felt confident that we were just the people she'd been looking for, and although she'd miss June tremendously, she knew we'd take good care of her. So, arrangements were made for June to move in with us shortly thereafter. As we were leaving, Jameth turned to Michelle.

"June will be my first rat!" he exclaimed, sounding excited at the idea.

"Yes," Michelle replied with a smile, "but I guarantee, she won't be your last." How true those words would turn out to be.

As I prepared for June's arrival, I felt like the child I had been so long ago. I was truly excited for the first time in ages as I cleared a spot for June's cage and "rat-proofed" our home, covering electrical cords and eliminating any other potential safety hazards for a rat. Rats like to explore and they like to chew, which can be dangerous if provisions aren't made. We had no intention of leaving June in her cage all the time, and we wanted to be sure we were providing a good, safe home for her.

I could hardly contain my excitement the day June came to stay. Michelle arrived with June and all of her favorite things. She handed me a bag filled with organic fruits and vegetables, reminding me that "June only eats organic vegan* food." Not a problem, I assured her, as Jameth and I eat only organic vegan food ourselves. I promised her that June would receive the best of care.

I admired June's beautiful dark gray—almost black—coat, and for the first time, I noticed her soft white underbelly, not yet realizing what a comfort such bellies would become in my life. I then set June free to fully explore her new home. Michelle tried to leave before the tears began to flow, promising that she'd come back to visit during her breaks. I assured her that we would give June a wonderful life. And June became part of our family.

At long last, I had an animal to love and care for, and I grew to love June perhaps more than any animal I had known before. It seemed that the older I got, the more I was able to love and the harder it was to lose my loved ones when they died. I had always thought it would be the opposite; that it would get easier. June was already old for a rat when I became her guardian, so I tried not to even think about the eventual outcome.

When June entered my life, my whole world changed. I hadn't had a rat companion since my school days, and June brought with her all of the wide-eyed joy of youth that I had almost forgotten. I was delighted that Jameth had warmed up to her immediately. Then again, who wouldn't? She was a very charming and affectionate little lady. She ate with us, played with us, worked with us, and slept with us. She amused us, comforted us, and taught us.

June helped us get our priorities in order, and she reminded us of the meaning of life, which we had almost forgotten. She was truly our little angel all wrapped up in fur. Friends often asked about her and came to visit her, and Jameth and I soon became known around town as "June's parents." She quickly won the hearts of friends and customers, and most of all, of her new human companions.

Early on, it was June who decided she would sleep with us. Worried that we might roll over on her, we tightened the sheets around our necks and refused to let her under the covers with us. However, June was persistent, and before long, ours was a bed for three. Each night, the scene was the same: two humans and one rat all in a row, lying on our backs in identical positions. When Jameth rolled over on his side, I rolled over on my side and snuggled up to him. And June, without fail, rolled over on *her* side and snuggled up to me. It was a scene straight out of a Disney movie that we looked forward to every night.

Somehow, I felt that taking care of June was the most important responsibility I had ever been entrusted with, so I took my role as June's primary caretaker very seriously. Although I was well versed in vegan nutrition for *humans,* I was unsure of the nutritional requirements for rats and wanted to be sure June received the best of care. So I did my homework and saw to it that June was eating a balanced vegan diet.

To further bolster her health, Jameth and I began mixing various herbs and other nutritious plant foods into a green mush. June absolutely loved the green mush and could hardly contain herself as I mixed a fresh batch for her each morning.

Over time, we experimented and added other herbal ingredients—known for extending lifespan—to the formula. June thrived, and her coat soon grew in thicker, darker (more black and less gray), shinier and healthier than ever before. She became more muscular and strong, and it seemed that she was having a "second youth."

People began to comment on June's amazingly healthy appearance, asking what we were doing to keep her so healthy. They wanted some of this green mush for their own animal companions; so, before long, we were bottling Green Mush™, delivering it to friends, and shipping it nationwide. June tested each new version of the mush to make sure it passed the taste test. We began receiving amazing testimonials from people whose rats, dogs, cats, and other companion animals were thriving on the formula. When they thanked us, we told them we owed it all to June.

I must admit I loved her soft coat, her pretty ears, and her delicate pink hands and feet. But there was a lot more to admire about June than her appearance. She had such *presence.* People could sense it right away. Even those who thought they didn't like rats. Upon hearing that she was a rat, people often initially responded negatively, but upon actually meeting her, they came to know and love her as simply June. She seemed like such a wise old soul, filled with unconditional love for all people, regardless of their initial reaction to her. Once you looked into her shiny, round, soulful eyes, you just knew someone important was looking back at you.

People often commented that June seemed incredibly evolved and spiritual, and they found her presence very healing. When they came by to visit or to pick up health products, many friends and customers seemed more excited to see June than to see *us*. When they called, they often asked about her, and our good friend Aden (a grown man, I might add) always ended each phone conversation with, "Give my love to June."

Because Jameth and I regularly gave lectures and workshops, and we had a published book with our photo on it, people often recognized us around town. One day, while shopping at a local health food store, a grown woman approached Jameth excitedly, clearly recognizing him.

"Aren't you June's dad?" she asked with delight. We soon learned who the celebrity was in *our* family.

June seemed to just *know* who the friendly people were, and from whom to keep her distance. When a friend of ours brought a woman over to our home to discuss our health products, the woman looked uptight and mentioned that she didn't like "the rat's naked tail." Our friend responded, "I can only imagine how June would feel if she saw *my* naked tail—she'd be horrified!" The woman smiled and relaxed, and June's charming presence soon stole *her* heart as well. June managed to change many people's perceptions of rats. She was truly a little ambassador for ratkind.

ONE DAY, I WAS IN A PANIC because I couldn't find June. I searched frantically for her, fearing the worst. Eventually, I discovered that I had accidentally closed her in the closet. She was nestled in a small basket, where she had apparently been enjoying an afternoon nap. She gazed peacefully out at me, obviously enjoying her new haven. She looked at me as if to say, "Relax . . . everything's fine."

Another time, I found June burrowed deep inside an oversized basket filled with crumpled, recycled shipping paper, which we used to ship gifts and health products to family and friends. Unable to resist such perfect nesting material, June had created an elaborate nest in the middle of the basket and began taking her afternoon naps there. From then on, a common sound in our home was that of June shredding paper as she constantly refined her nest. I was worried that we might accidentally ship *June* amid a wad of shipping paper, and I often found myself opening sealed packages to make sure she wasn't inside. So, for June's safety and my sanity, I decided that I must dismantle the nest.

One day while June was out eating her lunch, I removed all of the shredded paper and assorted nesting materials that June had gathered, and I relocated the materials. I figured June, being a rat, would have no trouble constructing a new nest elsewhere. It's what rats *do*.

Later, June headed toward her former nest. She climbed to the top edge of the basket and looked horrified as she stared into the emptiness. She climbed down to the bottom and ran frantically back and forth. I felt horrible as I witnessed this. I'd had no idea she would take it this way, but I now realized that I had violated her personal property. This was her haven, and I had no right to take it away, especially without warning her.

She appeared desperate and furious. Then she climbed out of the basket and just flopped down on the floor like a noodle. I reached for her, but instead of climbing onto my hand as she normally did, she remained motionless. I picked her up and she was completely limp. I felt I understood exactly what she was feeling. She had clearly gone into a depression, and any doubts I may have had regarding the emotions of animals were completely obliterated in that moment.

I began to worry when she didn't snap out of it. I brought her peace offerings, but she refused to eat even her very favorite treats. Then I found her a smaller basket, filled it with nesting materials, and presented it to her. She ignored me. I continually checked on her, until finally, my heart was warmed as I heard the "rip, rip, shred, shred" of June settling into her new nest. It was over, and I had learned a valuable lesson.

June and I became extremely close. For my birthday, Jameth surprised me with a homemade cake (healthful enough for June to partake of); and when I approached the adorable scene of a candlelit cake with June sitting at a distance from the cake, atop of pile of gifts, I instantly knew that June was at that distance intentionally.

"Oh, you poor thing; you singed your whiskers, didn't you!" To me, it was written all over her face, though one couldn't tell from merely looking at her already dark gray whiskers. I picked her up, gave her a kiss, and tried to comfort her. Indeed, Jameth assured me, she *had* singed her whiskers before I had entered the room. No real damage had been done, but it had been just enough to scare her.

"How did you know?" he asked.

"I'm not sure," I replied. "I just knew."

THERE WAS AN UPCOMING MARCH FOR THE ANIMALS in Washington, D.C., which I had been looking forward to ever since the previous one, which I had attended six years prior, so Jameth and I made plans for the out-of-town trip. It is a cause we both feel very strongly about, and June's presence had only strengthened our conviction. At the same time, I felt apprehensive at the thought of leaving June, but I didn't feel it would be safe to bring her with us. I almost decided not to go, but then I thought back to the previous march and regretted not having done more on behalf of animals in the years since then.

We wondered who would stay with June while we were away. Out of the blue, my brother, Scott, called. He worked in the movie business and had just completed an out-of-town project. He would be coming through San Diego and would need a place to stay for a week or so; the timing was perfect. So we arranged for "Uncle Scott" to stay with June.

June somehow knew we were leaving and wasn't happy about it. We wondered how she knew, but she clearly did. On departure day, she ran desperately between us and our luggage and looked me pleadingly in the eyes. As I sat down in the closet to put some final items in a suitcase, June hopped up onto my lap and wouldn't leave. Her eyes began to water, a sign of stress in rats (and people, too, now that I think of it). She appeared highly stressed as she looked straight up at me. I regretted the decision to go without her, but there wasn't enough time to figure out how to safely bring her along.

I *felt* her communicating with me, begging me, *Please don't leave me. Please don't go.* My heart broke, and I felt a huge lump forming in my throat as I held her close to my face, looked her straight in the eyes, and made a promise to her.

"June," I said softly, "I promise you, we'll be back soon."

At first I couldn't find the plane tickets and almost felt relieved that we'd miss our flight. However, I found them just in time, and we departed. While we were away, I missed June and worried about her constantly. I called home daily (at least) to check on her and make sure everything was okay. I got the feeling June was worried about us, too.

When we returned, June seemed upset with us. However, she only remained upset long enough to let us know how she felt about our having left without consulting her first. Then she returned to her happy, affectionate self. I noticed this and realized that human relationships could benefit from this type of clear, in-the-moment expression of true feelings, followed by a rapid letting go. Animals just don't seem to hold grudges (or hide their true opinions) the way humans often do. We could learn a lot from them. Over time, June taught me that expressing emotion is not a weakness; it is a sign of strength and depth.

Jameth and I had made prior arrangements to cat-sit at a friend's house the night we returned home. Mere hours after returning, we left again, and June stayed home with my brother. I'd missed June terribly but reminded myself that it was only one more night.

The next morning, we received a frantic phone call from my brother—June was quite ill. We rushed home and took her to the vet, only to find out that there was nothing physically wrong with her and that all of her symptoms were stress-related. She seemed to be expressing the same stress that I was feeling.

"June," I said as I held her close, "I will never leave you again. I'll never go on a trip without you again. I promise."

And I kept my promise.

She rapidly recovered, and life returned to normal.

Sometimes June got the hiccups, and Jameth and I had learned to put our hands on her body and send her calming, healing energy. We didn't know whether it was a coincidence or not, but the hiccups always promptly disappeared. Early one morning while I was out running errands, June climbed back into bed with Jameth. He noticed that she was hiccupping all the way. She went straight to him and nestled herself right under his hand as if to say, "Please fix my hiccups." She was very deliberate about it. She remained in this position only until her hiccups disappeared, then she promptly got up and trotted away. Jameth had been told many times that he had "healing hands." Apparently June thought so, too.

DURING THIS TIME, my parents were living nearly three thousand miles away. The past several years had been very hard on them. My mom's elderly grandfather's health had begun to fail, and my parents had moved from California to Florida to help my grandparents (my mom's parents) take care of him. My grandparents weren't in the best of health either. My dad's parents had already passed away, and he regretted having left some things unsaid, so he wanted to make sure they were there for my mom's parents.

Dealing with various health crises, first of my great-grandfather and then of my grandparents—as well as the fact that the company my dad worked for went bankrupt and a lot of people suddenly lost their jobs—was almost more than they could handle. On top of it all, they constantly felt torn between taking care of my grandparents and missing us. We had always been a very close family, so the distance took its toll on all of us. However, my grandparents had established a life in Florida, where they had retired after leaving New Jersey, and Jameth and I had established a life in California, where I grew up. My parents were caught in the middle.

Eventually, my great-grandfather passed away with my mom by his side, and things became more stable for my grandparents. Meanwhile, Jameth and I were still overburdened with work and needing some assistance with our growing business but not yet in a financial position to hire any employees, and my parents were hoping to come back to California to help us out. So my dad came for a visit and stayed with us while he searched for a local job and housing. My mom couldn't take the time off work, so she had to stay behind. I hadn't seen her in nearly two years.

During his stay, my dad and June grew quite fond of one another. He and my mom had always been supportive of all the rats and other animals who shared our home in my youth, but now he repeatedly commented, "Of all the rats I've ever known, Juney is my favorite."

We all enjoyed his visit, though he didn't have much luck with housing or jobs. Before long, the day arrived for him to head back to Florida. His bags were packed and he was preparing for his ride to the airport. It had been wonderful to spend time with him, and we were going to miss him. We said our sad, awkward good-byes, and as he turned to hug me, I noticed tears in his eyes. It seemed that, in that moment, all of the pain that had been building up inside of him, for countless reasons, was now bubbling up to the surface. I had never seen him so choked up, and as I searched for words of comfort, I heard a rustle nearby.

We all heard it, and as we looked down, there was June, perched up on the edge of an oversized wicker basket nearby, as high as she could climb. She was looking straight up at my dad and reaching up to him very intently with both of her delicate little arms, which she had never done before. He reached down to pet her, and she very deliberately climbed right onto his hand, up his arm to his chest, and just clutched him and looked up at him. He held his hand up to support her, and she clasped his hand with her own tiny hands and looked him in the eye. It was clearly June's turn to say good-bye.

He then tried to put her down, but she climbed right back up to his chest, clutched him tightly, and resumed eye contact. Of course, June couldn't speak, but in that moment, you wouldn't know it. In her own special way, June spoke volumes. We could all but hear her saying softly, "It's okay, Grandpa. Everything's going to be okay." In that moment, we were all deeply moved. The love and compassion we felt pouring out of that little creature known as June was almost overwhelming.

Not wanting my dad to miss his flight, I reached out for June so that he could go. I was definitely June's "mom," and she always came right to me, no matter who was holding her. But not this time. She looked back at me and all but shook her head as she clearly communicated, "No, Grandpa needs me now." She made it clear that *he* needed her at that moment, to comfort him, and he was touched immensely. She continued clutching onto him, looking right up at him, and communicating in that language beyond words. We all felt it.

"I love you, Grandpa. I'm going to miss you. I really love you," she seemed to say. She stayed there with him, and time stood still as she filled him up with pure, unconditional love. He was deeply moved. We all were.

Once June had completed sending her message of love and comfort, she climbed back down. The whole mood in the room had changed, and my dad left in peace.

I found out later that he had thought about that encounter during the entire flight home, and he had even told the passenger next to him about June, with a smile on his face. Once he had arrived in Florida, he had shared the story with anyone who would listen (as my mom informed me later). To this day, he holds that warm memory, that sweet gift of love and nurturing, in his heart. As do I.

I HAD SEEN SIGNIFICANT EVIDENCE that June was not only able to feel and express her own emotions, but was also able to empathize with others. *So much for the theory that animals don't have emotions,* I thought to myself. I contemplated all of the things I had learned from June, and how much my life had changed since she first entered it. For years, I had put too much pressure on myself and worked much too hard without breaks. No amount of meditation or spiritual discipline had ever managed to bring me into a state of peace the way June could. She taught me to live in the moment, not worrying so much about things that didn't really matter. No matter how busy or stressed out I became, as soon as June entered the room, it all changed. My little three-quarter-pound guru had taught me how to live.

June's devotion had become a priceless gift in my life. I felt blessed by her presence, and I wondered where I'd be without her.

My priorities had changed, and I found it ironic that I had been rescued from the "rat race" by, well, a *rat*. Others had shared with me how June had changed their lives as well. They had previously bought into the societal notion that rats are pests to be hated and exterminated. June had taught them otherwise and opened their minds, and for this they were genuinely grateful.

Looking at June as an example, I began to realize what the animals teach us: total honesty, innocence, and forgiveness; and the importance of expressing anger or hurt, feeling it fully, and then letting it go. Humans tend to hold on; animals teach us how to let life flow. Most of all, animals offer us unconditional love. Through their example, many of us learn for the first time what unconditional love truly is. It's not about being perfect; it's about really being ourselves, and loving each other regardless.

If only I could learn to love half as well as June, I would indeed be an exceptional person.

- CHAPTER 3 -

Conversations with a Rat Named June

. . . soul is the same thing in all living creatures,
although the body of each is different.
— HIPPOCRATES

SHORTLY BEFORE JUNE ENTERED MY LIFE, I had become
interested in the idea of telepathic animal communication. I had
read about it in a local paper and was fascinated. I learned that
"animal communicators" are individuals who have the ability to
communicate telepathically with animals. I wanted so much to
believe it was true, but I was skeptical . . . and at the time, I didn't
have any animal friends to put it to the test.

So, upon June's arrival, I promptly booked an appointment
with a local animal communicator named Brigitte Noel. Now that
I had my own little animal friend, I was anxious to find out if there
was any validity to the idea of telepathic animal communication.

I'd had a lifelong desire to talk with animals. At times, as a
child, I was certain I was doing it. I always felt that I knew what
they were thinking and what they needed, and they seemed to
understand me equally well. Adulthood had taken me away from
all of that, but now June was bringing it back.

On the day of the much-anticipated appointment, Jameth
and I headed downtown with June to meet Brigitte Noel, a very

pleasant and down-to-earth person. Upon Brigitte's request, Jameth and I waited nervously outside while she sat quietly with June for a private conversation in her office; she said it was easier for her to work that way.

After perhaps half an hour, she called us in to tell us what June had communicated. Brigitte had written several pages of messages she had received from June, which she read aloud to us. A lot of what June had apparently communicated made sense to us, based on what we knew about her background, including an incident involving her tail that had taken place just the day before (someone had made a derogatory comment about June's tail).

We then asked June our questions, and she answered them through Brigitte. One of the burning questions was: "Is June lonely? She has *us,* but does she want a *rat* companion?"

She responded with a very decisive "No." This was a surprise to us, as rats are very social creatures and normally crave the company of other rats. But she explained that she was a "rat ambassador" and was here to interact with *humans—not* other rats. In fact, she said she *preferred* it that way. So we agreed to honor her wishes (at least for the time being).

Rather than a rat companion, June informed us that she'd really like some cherries. We had never given her any, but she said she loved cherries. So after the appointment, we got her some fresh organic cherries, and she appeared genuinely grateful as she enthusiastically indulged.

Brigitte gave us our own copy of the written transcripts of her conversation with June, along with a tape recording of the session. Some of the things she said didn't make any sense to us at the time, so we had no way to confirm their accuracy. However, the next time Michelle came to visit June, I told her all about the session, and she understood and confirmed everything June had communicated—including things that only she and June had known. I was impressed.

ONCE I BECOME INTERESTED IN A SUBJECT, I want to know everything I can about it. I was now fascinated with the idea of telepathic animal communication. One day while browsing through the mail, I came across another article on the subject. I called the number at the end of the article for more information and was offered a nationwide list of dozens of professional animal communicators, which I gratefully accepted.

Although I had been extremely impressed by the appointment with Brigitte, I was still skeptical of the idea that there were *so many* people out there who could really do this. I've always considered myself an "open-minded skeptic." It sounds like a contradiction, but somehow, in all areas of my life, both my open-mindedness and my skepticism are very strong, constantly keeping each other in balance. My years in the alternative health field reinforced the importance of both, and I was ever mindful not to allow open-mindedness to become gullibility nor to allow skepticism to become cynicism.

I've never been the type of person who falls for things easily, so I knew this new belief system was going to be a "hard sell" for my logical mind. However, my intuitive mind insisted that there was something real here, something I needed to check out and incorporate, so I listened.

I called several of the animal communicators on the list and discovered that they all offered long-distance phone appointments, so I scheduled appointments with them right away. I then began calling various animal communicators on a regular basis, repeatedly testing them for accuracy. I wanted to be sure I was receiving accurate information, so I never told them anything other than June's name and the fact that she was a rat; and I always made appointments with several animal communicators in different parts of the country, never telling any of them that I also consulted *others* with the same questions. I wanted to see if June's communications matched up, from one animal communicator to the next; and to my amazement, they did.

Still a diehard skeptic, I constantly tested the animal communicators, not telling them *anything* that might influence what they received from June, and they repeatedly amazed me with their accuracy. I often scheduled phone appointments back-to-back, ruling out the possibility that some of the animal communicators might know each other and exchange information between phone calls; and their unrelenting consistency astounded me. Most of them had never worked with a rat before and were quite charmed by June. That part didn't surprise me at all.

I called them somewhat regularly, whenever health concerns or other issues arose during June's life, or when I simply needed further validation that this was real; and I was ultimately convinced that it was.

One time, I called an animal communicator to find out why June was lethargic and didn't seem to feel well. The first thing the animal communicator said was that the back of June's hand hurt. I wondered why that could be; it made no sense to me. Later I recalled an incident that had occurred just the day before, which the animal communicator had no way of knowing about:

June had been on the kitchen counter, where she often kept Jameth and me company as we prepared meals or washed dishes. We always soaked various beans, grains, and seeds in glass jars filled with purified water and covered with plastic lids. June always flipped the plastic lids off of the jars to sample what was inside. However, this time one of the jars had been covered with a heavy ceramic saucer instead of the usual lightweight plastic lid, so when she flipped it up, it slammed back down on the back of her hand.

I watched helplessly as she squeaked and held her hand in pain, looking just like a little person holding an injured hand as if to say, "Ouch!" I felt awful about it and did my best to comfort her. She soon went about her business as if nothing had ever happened, so I assumed everything was okay.

As I NOW RECALLED THIS FORGOTTEN INCIDENT, I thought to myself, *No wonder the back of her hand hurts!* I was continually impressed with the accurate, detailed information I received whenever I consulted an animal communicator.

There were several animal communicators in particular with whom I felt an extra strong connection, so they became the ones I called most often. Even after I had become convinced of the legitimacy of animal communication and no longer needed to make multiple calls, I felt it was good to be in touch with several different animal communicators so that, if an urgent question or crisis arose and one of them wasn't available, I had some backup.

Initially, when I worked with animal communicators over the phone, I had trouble swallowing the notion that they could communicate with June from so far away. However, I came to realize that, unlike verbal communication, telepathy has no distance limits.

I also had trouble understanding how telepathic animal communication could be received in actual *words* (in addition to pictures and feelings), since animals don't speak in words. I came to understand that telepathy is a universal language that, when received, is automatically interpreted in a manner understood by the receiver.

I then recalled one of my favorite childhood pastimes: reading my friends' minds. Of course, I didn't know what the term "telepathy" meant at the time, but that's what it was, I now realized. I really don't recall exactly *when* I began noticing that I understood the thoughts of others before they ever opened their mouths; it seems it was just something I *knew* I could do as a child. I also don't recall exactly when I *stopped* doing it. Somewhere along the way, such things had been educated out of me.

I suddenly recalled the many times in my youth when I had experimented with telepathy. My experimentation had started quite by accident. . . .

One day after school, my best friend and I were playing inside an upright storage cabinet in the garage, trying to entertain ourselves with something new, as children often do. We both liked to draw, so we had our drawing pads and markers with us. We were both quite small and could fit just perfectly in the cabinet in a seated position, facing each other with our knees up. She put her drawing pad up against her thighs and began to draw. I couldn't see what she was drawing, since I was facing the back of her drawing pad.

"What are you drawing?" I asked. She told me it was going to be a surprise, a picture for me, but that she didn't want me to peek until it was done. So, I decided to draw a picture for her, too, and wouldn't let her see it until *I* was done. While we were drawing,

I suddenly felt an indescribable connection to her. We were best friends, we looked a lot alike, and we were seated in identical positions, so I figured that accounted for the connection I felt. I shrugged off the feeling and continued drawing.

When we had finished our drawings, we showed each other our masterpieces. We were both stunned. We had drawn *exactly* the same picture, right down to very specific and unique details. In that moment, I knew it was more than a mere coincidence, but I really wasn't sure what to make of it.

Throughout my childhood, I came up with many "guessing games" which, in hindsight, were actually psychic experiments. The results never ceased to amaze me.

Later, when I was in high school, a new girl moved to town during my sophomore year. She and I had a lot in common, and I soon discovered that she shared my passion for paranormal exploration. On the weekends, we often had "psychic slumber parties"—just the two of us—as we practiced our psychic skills into the wee hours.

We continually astounded ourselves. At first, she would look at various photographs of people I didn't know, without showing them to me. I would focus on her and then describe what I was seeing in my mind's eye. When she then showed me the photograph, it was always identical to that which I had just described.

Then she began drawing pictures or symbols and focusing on them without letting me see them. I would focus on her and then draw what I saw in my mind's eye. When she then showed me her drawings, they were always identical to those I had just drawn. No matter how many times we did this, we were continually delighted and amazed at the results.

We began to wonder if distance would alter the results of these experiments, so we decided to find out. One day at school, we agreed to focus on each other at a specific time that night, when we were each at our own home (in completely different parts of town), and then write or draw whatever we saw in our minds. That night at precisely ten o'clock, as arranged, I went into my bedroom and closed the door, sat quietly, and closed my eyes. I focused on my friend. I soon saw very specific pictures in my mind, so I quickly began drawing on a sheet of paper everything I was seeing.

The next morning we met at our lockers, and on the count of three, we presented our drawings to each other. They were *identical*. We were speechless. We had drawn very specific and unusual things, and everything was the same, right down to the placement of each individual item on the two pieces of paper. In a way, it was unnerving, and we remained silent as we headed off to class, not sure exactly what to say.

AS I NOW RECALLED THOSE INCIDENTS FROM MY YOUTH—and many more like them—it all made sense. *Of course telepathic communication is real,* I thought to myself. *Of course distance and language are irrelevant with telepathy.* I had determined this long ago, but I had simply forgotten. I now realized that telepathy is truly a universal language, one that breaks the boundaries not only of "logic" and distance, but of species.

I looked back on all of the conversations I'd recently had with June via animal communicators. These conversations were often about simple, mundane things, yet it was in their simplicity that I found validity.

ONE DAY, I RECEIVED A PHONE CALL. A friend of a friend had gotten an adorable baby rat for her grandson, but it turned out that the little boy was allergic to fur. So "Susie the rat" needed a home—could we take her? I was delighted at the prospect of having another rat come to live with us, and in my mind I had already moved her in.

However, I had learned the importance of consulting *every* family member when a matter concerned them, and that included our beloved June. So I told the friend that I'd have to consult June first, and I scheduled a string of appointments with various animal communicators.

"No, she does *not* want a rat companion," said the first one. "She's pretty clear on that." I was surprised. And so I tried another, and another.

"I don't need a rat companion," said June. *"You're* my best companions." Over and over again, June made it very clear that this was *her* home, *we* were her companions, and she loved her life just the way it was. She was a rat ambassador and was here to interact with *humans*—*not* other rats.

However, I was worried about little Susie, who needed a home; and I told myself that perhaps June didn't *think* she wanted a rat companion, but if she just *met* Susie she'd change her mind. So I arranged for Susie to come over and meet June.

At first, I was struck by Susie's appearance. She looked just like a smaller, younger version of June. Then I was struck by the difference between them. Though Susie was a very sweet little rat, I didn't feel the instant connection I had felt upon first meeting June. I somehow knew in my heart that she wasn't going to work out.

I brought June out to meet Susie. June's reaction said it all. She had a shocked, betrayed look on her face and immediately ran to a far corner of the room. She kept her back to me and didn't respond to me at all, which wasn't like her. She was *not* trembling in fear of this new rat; rather, she was displaying the same behavior I had seen before when she was upset about something, such as when I had dismantled her nest. I felt terrible about this and told Susie's temporary caretaker that we couldn't keep her. (She found a great home with another couple; they adored Susie and let her sleep with them at night. I was relieved.)

I apologized profusely to June, and things quickly returned to normal. However, the next day, she was very lethargic and didn't want to get out of bed. I felt guilty, thinking she was still upset about the Susie incident. I looked her in the eye and asked her what was wrong. Instantly, I heard her response.

"I hurt," she said, and I immediately understood what she meant: She was in pain—physical pain. She didn't say it verbally, of course, but I definitely "heard" the words telepathically, in what clearly sounded to me like it must have been "June's voice." I was quite startled at this unexpected communication.

Then I began to question myself. I called an animal communicator to find out what was *really* wrong with June, still convinced that she was upset with me, and that she was depressed rather than in pain. I told the animal communicator nothing of my experience, now having dismissed the whole thing.

"She's in pain," said the animal communicator, confirming what June had already clearly told me. I got more details about why she was suddenly in pain—she had hurt herself—so I prepared some natural remedies and June quickly recovered.

IT HAD TAKEN ME A LONG TIME to accept the validity of telepathic animal communication. Over time, I had become quite certain of the reality. However, the idea of *me* being able to do it was another matter entirely. It was one of those things that *other* people could do, but not *me*.

I got past the denial and ultimately felt overwhelmingly grateful for having received my first clear communication from June without the assistance of a professional animal communicator. It wasn't until later that day that it fully sank in.

My God, I thought to myself, *I really am communicating with her.* I stared at June in half disbelief. Until this point, it had been somewhat of a game—a sort of "that would be great if we really could talk with the animals, so for fun, I'll entertain the idea that we can." I had truly wanted to believe, but the skeptic in me somehow couldn't accept it completely. Now I was convinced. This wasn't science fiction; I was a rational human being, and this was reality.

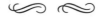

- CHAPTER 4 -

The Next Step

Animals share with us the privilege of having a soul.
— PYTHAGORAS

ALTHOUGH JAMETH AND I had been together for years, we'd never had an actual wedding. We'd had neither the time nor the money for a big wedding when we first met; so we had gone out to the woods and privately exchanged rings and vows, and that was that.

We'd been planning to have an actual ceremony—in the company of family and friends—ever since, but we were always waiting for enough time and financial resources to do so. Now we realized that conditions might *never* be perfect, and we *did* live in an ideal location for an outdoor wedding, so we made our plans.

Sharon Callahan, who became one of June's primary animal communicators, told me about a forthcoming event she was co-organizing: the First Annual Conference on Animals and Spirituality, which was being held at the Best Friends Animal Sanctuary (a huge animal refuge, where over 1,500 animals live "happily ever after") in Kanab, Utah.

I was extremely interested, so Sharon sent me a flyer on the event. Jameth and I determined that we could think of no better place to spend our honeymoon, so we registered for the conference and were given permission to let June join us in the cottage in which we would be staying at the sanctuary, called "The Rock House."

June helped us maintain our balance as we struggled through all of the ups and downs of planning a wedding, including catering it ourselves (which, in hindsight, I wouldn't recommend).

As we prepared for the big day, June met family and friends. Those who had heard of her or had seen photos of her were delighted to finally meet the famous "June the rat" in person. Everything went beautifully, and at the end of the day, Jameth, June, and I posed for some final wedding photos.

Among our wedding gifts was a pair of little white stuffed animals (harp seals), and I brought them out to meet June while she was enjoying a meal in her dining corner of the kitchen floor. The little harp seals were about the same size as June, and I made one of them crawl across the floor toward her to say "hello." June turned and stared at the stuffed animal with a horrified look on her face. She looked upset and betrayed.

Suddenly I realized what was going on—she was *jealous* of the small creature that had joined our family. (What human hasn't felt similar emotions?) I *felt* her reminding me that we had agreed this would remain a family of three. I quickly showed her that it wasn't a *real* animal, and she was visibly relieved.

After the wedding, we packed the car, and Jameth, June, and I headed for Utah. The conference at Best Friends Animal Sanctuary made for a wonderful honeymoon and a much-needed getaway in a beautiful nature setting (in fact, it was our first actual vacation together ever), and we realized we were there because of June. After all, it was June's animal communicator, Sharon Callahan, who had told us about the event. While there, June got to meet Sharon in person for the first time. It was a joy to watch their in-person interaction.

At the conference, many of the attendees told touching stories about their beloved animal companions. I enjoyed sharing some of my own stories about June among kindred spirits, and I felt as though I really *belonged* there. I'll always cherish my memories from that sacred event.

During our honeymoon, I realized that June had slept a lot recently and just didn't get around like she used to. I feared that she might be preparing to leave us. The one question I'd always avoided asking June (her age) now haunted me.

June's walk hadn't been right for a while. I had half-noticed it but had been so busy with wedding plans that it hadn't completely registered. She no longer climbed our pant legs as she used to. She was clearly getting old.

The night after we returned from our honeymoon, I noticed that June had a peculiar hop as she headed to bed with us. The next morning, I discovered her unable to walk at all. Her hind legs no longer worked, and she looked so helpless as she tried to drag herself with her arms. June was crippled. I cried like a child. It was so painful to watch my little angel suffer.

June and I embarked upon a long and desperate journey. I let go of all of my other responsibilities and stayed with her around the clock. Wheelchairs don't exist for rats, so I held her in my arms and carried her everywhere. She pointed her head and indicated where she wanted to go. As I carried her around, our telepathic connection grew stronger than ever. She now relied upon me to feed her and to put her in her litter box when needed.

"It's okay," I told her. "You can just go to the bathroom on me; I don't care." But without fail, she always looked up at me and asked me to set her down in her litter box first.

"We can fix this," I assured her as I frantically called animal communicators, vets, chiropractors, and healers. June patiently put up with poking and prodding, x-rays, and a wide assortment of exams by traditional as well as alternative practitioners. We tried Network chiropractic, herbs, homeopathics, TTouch, Reiki, hands-on healing, and various other healing modalities that are highly beneficial for humans and animals alike.

No one was able to diagnosis any specific health condition, other than old age. (I've since learned that hind-leg paralysis is not uncommon in elderly rats.) No matter what I tried, June continued weakening and losing weight. I knew I was losing her, but I just couldn't let her go. I tried to imagine life without her.

"I don't want another rat," I told her softly. "I want *you*, June. Please stay." She did her best to honor my request as I continued searching for someone who could help her. While some healers flat-out *refused* to help her because she was a rat, others rose to the occasion and expressed genuine concern. The experience taught me a lot about the many faces of human nature.

"Are you sure you want to go to so much trouble?" one healer asked me over the phone. "After all, it's just a *rat*." After a long dissertation from me about how June was a very special soul who happened to inhabit a rat body, the healer was, by his own admission, deeply moved. He then called everyone he could think of who might be able to help.

I had developed an incredibly strong bond with June and had learned to count on going happily to sleep each night with Jameth on one side and June on the other. I feared the end of her life was approaching much too soon. I fought it, all but kicking and screaming, all the way.

Letting go was not an option. She *couldn't* die—I loved her too much. Besides, I was a "health expert" and could surely find *something* to fix her. I suppose a part of me thought that she could be the world's first immortal animal, so I continued my heartbreaking struggle to keep her alive.

A week passed. June was no longer able to clean herself, so I bathed her with a warm washcloth at the bathroom sink. I brought her to bed and set her next to me, as I did every night. Her fur was still damp from the bath, so I decided to get her an extra little blanket to keep her warm. I found a soft piece of fabric covered with pink hearts, which made a perfect blanket for her. I settled her in and stroked her softly, telling her how very much I loved her, as we drifted off to sleep.

When I awakened an hour or so later, June was very still. When I picked her up to go to her litter box, as I always did when I awakened during the night, I knew it was over. As I stood up, my legs weakened and I collapsed to the floor. I held June's vacant body and shed larger tears than I had ever known. I felt as if a part of me had died. The pain that had gnawed at the pit of my stomach since that first morning, when I had discovered she couldn't walk, had never left, and it now overtook me.

Jameth awakened, and he held me for hours as I cried and clutched June's lifeless form. You can never really be prepared for moments like this. Like life itself, you have to actually *experience* such moments to fully comprehend their depth.

As I stroked her soft fur, now soaked in my tears, I *demanded* some answers. I no longer needed to understand what death was, or what the dying process was like. Now I needed to know *why*. Why had she died? What had I done wrong? Of course, I *must* have done something wrong, I told myself, or she wouldn't have died. Death was no longer something I accepted. It was now something I resented.

Early the next morning, I left a desperate message for animal communicator Sharon Callahan. My voice was so choked with sobs that Jameth took the phone and completed the message for me. Sharon had written articles about losing a beloved animal, and I knew I needed help. A little while later, she returned my call and shared a beautiful message she had received from June. She told me that June had been escorted toward the Light by a small dog and a bunny with floppy ears, surrounded by lots of angels. She said June kept looking back, knowing how much I was hurting.

"She told me about something pink that you put around her body," Sharon said. I looked over at the little blanket, covered with pink hearts, which now surrounded June's body.

June's death hit me harder than anything before it. The house felt so empty without her. Nighttime was the hardest; I missed the feel of her warm fur against my skin. We buried her body in the yard, right outside our bedroom window.

Flowers and sympathy cards arrived with words of praise for the beautiful soul known as June, describing how she had touched many lives, and how much she'd be missed. I knew I'd never forget June, and neither would anyone else who knew her. To this day, people ask about her, reminisce about her, and miss her.

For a long time, Jameth and I caught ourselves constantly checking to make sure the toilet lid was closed and automatically doing other things we had done when June lived with us. Little reminders of her brought smiles and tears.

I had always considered myself "a strong, level-headed person," providing words of wisdom and a shoulder for *others* to cry on, but rarely letting my *own* emotions loose. Now the pressure of overwhelming emotions had reached its limit, and I needed an outlet. So, in trying to cope with June's death, I attended a group breathwork session (a form of assisted emotional release facilitated through breathing exercises), in which I could share my pain with a supportive group of people and shed my tears in a safe, nurturing environment.

When it was my turn to share, I told the group about the loss of my precious little companion. A lot of them had, at some point in their lives, loved and lost a dog or cat or other animal, so no one questioned the intensity of my pain.

During this healing process, I visualized sending June to the Light and letting her go, which was a very powerful and therapeutic experience. I had brought photos of June and found great comfort in showing the adorable photos to anyone who asked. Cass, a friend of ours who—along with his wife, Shama—had founded the center where the event took place, hugged me warmly.

"I can only imagine how you must feel," he said. "I don't know *what* I'd do if our dog died." He called the next day and announced that, as a belated wedding gift, he and Shama would like to gift Jameth and me with free attendance at a forthcoming two-weekend emotional-release workshop. It was just what I needed. Jameth was unable to attend due to previous business obligations, so I went by myself.

Opening up emotionally, and allowing myself to be vulnerable in front of anyone, was always painfully difficult for me. Throughout my life, I had swallowed many tears and worn many smiles that hid internal pain. So, my attendance at that workshop was one of the most powerful healing experiences of my life. Finally, it was okay to cry, even though I was all grown up. But equally powerful was the direction in which my life headed as a result of that workshop.

I experienced two life-changing weekends, surrounded by people who understood, releasing the pain of my loss and so much more. June had brought me there, and what a gift it was. Laughing and crying, sharing, really feeling my feelings—the way June had. The most significant part of the event came quite unexpectedly. . . .

During a break, one of the other workshop attendees approached me.

"They come back to us, you know," she assured me. She then told me the story of her beloved cat, who had died and then returned to her in a new body. I wondered if it could be true. During my lifelong exploration of the afterlife, I had heard many quite compelling stories of reincarnation. However, these stories had always involved *humans*. I had never considered the possibility of *animal* reincarnation. I had always felt in my heart that animals have souls just as humans do, but I'd never really found any concrete answers. Something clicked inside of me in that moment.

Later that same day, a man attending the workshop, who was psychic, approached me; he wasn't aware of the conversation I'd had with the woman earlier.

"As you were talking about June," he began, "a very powerful image came to me. While looking at you, I saw a small male dog with long, floppy ears. June will be coming back to you as a dog, and you can call her—or rather, *him—Junior!*" He smiled through sincere eyes. I smiled back, not sure what to say.

What a sweet man, I thought to myself. *He probably thinks that the promise of a new puppy will comfort me. He doesn't realize that I could never love another animal. I'm June's devoted person, and now that she's gone, well, that's that.* I was skeptical about his vision, but I didn't let on, not wanting to hurt his feelings.

Never before had this idea of animal reincarnation occurred to me, and yet, there it was, twice in one day. It's been my experience that whenever something comes up twice in a row like that, there's a significant reason. I wondered what the reason was. Still, I was skeptical and tried my best to get on with life.

The next day, the woman who had approached me before did so again. She told me she'd been thinking about me and got the very strong impression that I was supposed to be doing something important involving animals. She felt guided to share this with me. I felt my life moving in a whole new direction. And I had thought I was just there to cry.

I called and left messages for all of June's animal communicators to let them know that she had died. Somehow, telling people about her death helped me to deal with the grief. It helped me to feel that I was not alone in the experience and that people cared. I didn't tell *anyone* what I'd recently heard about the afterlife or about June coming back. I thought they'd think I was crazy, and besides, I didn't believe it myself.

Shortly thereafter, several of the animal communicators left messages on my answering machine, telling me that June had said she'd be coming back to me, but that it would be a while and she wouldn't be a rat when she returned. For the first time, I felt a glimmer of hope about the possibility of June's return; but I was still very skeptical, and I wondered to myself, *Why not a rat?*

One day I was feeling particularly depressed and lost, and I was becoming doubtful that there even *was* an afterlife. I didn't know where else to turn, so I made an appointment with a professional animal communicator I had never worked with before. I had read that this particular communicator, Gail De Sciose, specialized in communicating with the spirits of deceased animals. I missed June immensely and needed some kind of reassurance that she still existed *somewhere*. I didn't let Gail know that I'd spoken with anyone else, nor did I tell her anything I had heard about June coming back to me.

"June tells me she'll be coming back to you," she began, "but not as a rat next time." *Why not a rat?* I wondered again. I didn't say a word. She continued.

"She's coming back as a dog. A small male dog. It won't be right away, but when the time is right, June will be back."

I was blown away. I had that certain goosebumpy feeling you get when something extraordinary is taking place. Nevertheless, the skeptic in me asked for proof that we'd really contacted June. I wanted June to tell me something only she and I would know.

She then told the story of a small white stuffed animal that she had been jealous of at first, until she realized it wasn't real. I didn't know what she was talking about, but then I recalled the harp seal incident, which *no one* else could have known about. I hadn't told a soul. I then realized that something was truly going on.

Still missing June, and not quite sure what to make of the dog idea, I called yet another animal communicator, again not letting her know I'd called or spoken with anyone else. She proceeded to tell me about a house full of rats (more on that later) and, yes, a vision of a little male dog named Junior.

How could so many people who didn't even know each other, and who had no way of knowing what the others had said, come up with the same story? I was finally convinced that it had to be more than a coincidence.

Weeks and then months passed, and no dog ever showed up on my doorstep. I reminded myself that I was told it would be a while before June's return, but what did "a while" mean? I still don't know. It still hasn't happened. Will June one day return to me as a dog? That remains to be seen, but the possibility made June's departure a little easier to deal with. And it has led me on an extraordinary journey.

SHORTLY AFTER JUNE'S PASSING, I awoke one morning with a "thought" in my mind that I just couldn't shake. I "felt" a voice telling me very specifically that there was something important I was supposed to do. Was this June's voice? It wasn't actual words, but I somehow knew exactly what was being said: I must put this story down on paper. This experience was to become the catalyst for a book that many people would read. I was excited yet overwhelmed at the thought, and I was still very busy, so I put the idea on a "back burner" for the time being.

Periodically, as I worked quietly at my desk, I noticed little rainbow glows around the room. They would just catch the corner of my eye, but whenever I turned to look directly at them, they disappeared. I reasoned that they must be reflections of some sort, yet there were no crystals in the room—in fact, there was *nothing* that could account for these rainbows. Whenever one of them appeared, I felt June's presence, and I began to wonder if these mysterious little rainbows were signs from her. However, I soon convinced myself that it was just wishful thinking, and surely there must be some sort of logical explanation. I never did figure out what that explanation could be, and a part of me always wondered if perhaps I was just beginning to see that which I wasn't quite ready to believe.

AFTER JUNE'S PASSING, the animal kingdom spoke to me like never before. June had opened me up to a world I had almost forgotten existed. . . .

I watched the birds and the bunnies in the yard with a new form of understanding. They were all over the yard now, and they often came right up on the porch. Had I never noticed this before, or had they only just begun doing it?

One day I was out on the front porch and a butterfly landed on the screen door in front of me. The butterfly stayed there for a long time and just seemed to be staring at me. For some reason, I got the feeling that this butterfly was a messenger sent by June, to let me know she was okay. I couldn't imagine why I would think such a thing, but I felt it very strongly.

Shortly thereafter, I had a very unusual encounter with a fly. I asked for a sign (of what, I don't know) and a fly appeared. I asked the fly to land on my hand and talk to me, and the fly appeared to do just that. It could have been a coincidence, but I got the feeling that I was communicating with this fly. Creatures of all types seemed to be approaching me like never before.

One sunny afternoon, I sat in the yard doing some paperwork, and two basset hounds came running toward me (*not* a common occurrence in our yard). They appeared to be a mother and son, and the younger one ran right up to me. He *did* have long, floppy ears, but I didn't think it was June, because even if she did come back as a dog, she probably wouldn't be this big already. Nevertheless, he seemed to have come to me for a reason.

He looked me right in the eye, and I heard, "I'm thirsty." I didn't hear it out loud; but in my head, it was perfectly clear. I got him a bowl of water. He looked at me in gratitude and then lapped it up like a sponge. I called the phone number on the tag and got a recording for the local animal shelter. The dog stayed with me for a while, with his mother nearby; and then when my back was turned, the two disappeared as quietly as they had appeared. I looked everywhere for the dogs, but they were gone. I never saw them again.

During the months following June's death, I sometimes visited a local pet store while running my weekly errands, just to see the rats there. I had no intention of actually taking a rat home, but I just needed to hold them.

NOT DISMISSING THE NEW CALLING I felt from all of these animals, I decided to take action. My parents had finally moved back to California so they could help out with our wedding (thank God—we couldn't have gotten everything done without them). My dad found a local job, and my mom became our first employee, assisting us long before we could afford to actually pay anyone. This freed up some of my time, so I started a dog-walking and pet-sitting business and acquired regular clients right away. I made new animal friends, and I got to know their human companions. I really related to the love these people felt for their animal companions.

Feeling a need to get in touch with children, who are often more connected to animals than adults, I also began baby-sitting, which I hadn't done since my teenage years. I shared photos of June with the children, and they understood; children always seem to understand. I wondered how we might hold on to that understanding, instead of letting it slip away and having to recapture it years later.

I recalled my own childhood interest in and involvement with animals. I recalled the various animals who had touched my life. I now realized the importance of each of these animals and how empty things had been during the years without them, until June had entered my life. I recalled significant encounters I'd had with animals, animal tragedies I had witnessed, animal rescues I had been involved in, regrets and lessons. I shared all of this with the children, and they were fascinated, soaking up everything I told them, as we nestled on the sofa surrounded by their own beloved animal companions.

One day, a woman called in response to one of my pet-sitting ads, and a very special basset hound named Tolie came to stay at

our home while his people were away. I called an animal communicator to help me inform Tolie that his people would be back and
that they hadn't abandoned him. The animal communicator told
me over the phone that Tolie's first reaction was, "What? Who's
talking to me?" I looked over at him, and he was looking up in the
air and all around, appearing quite perplexed.

I began attending workshops on animal communication,
taught by various professional animal communicators. I
was amazed at how similar the telepathy exercises taught in
the workshops were to the exercises I had invented during my
childhood years of psychic exploration. I was equally amazed
at how quickly I seemed to be picking up on the ability. I felt a
strong connection with the other people who were learning
and practicing animal communication, and I felt blessed to be
surrounded by kindred spirits. We shared a common bond, and I
just *knew* we were doing something very important.

ONE NIGHT, THREE MONTHS AFTER JUNE'S DEATH, I had a dream
involving five rats and a guinea pig. In the dream, the five rats
lived in our home and ate out of five little bowls on the kitchen
floor. I wasn't sure where the guinea pig fit in, but I clearly saw
him in the dream. Because my dreams are often precognitive, I
paid attention. The dream really stood out to me, but I wasn't
sure why.

The next day, having forgotten about the dream, I passed an
animal shelter while delivering health products to a local custom-
er. Still missing June, I couldn't stand it anymore. I missed having
a warm, soft creature to love. I had begun to doubt the whole
reincarnation thing, and I realized that our landlords might not
let us have a dog anyway. So, I gave in to my urge to stop and ask
if they had any rats. I couldn't imagine opening up my heart to a
new rat, and yet, I just needed to *hold* one. No, they didn't have
any, but they referred me to someone who might: a woman named
Maggie Houlihan, who rescued and adopted out all types of animals, including rats.

I called her, and as fate would have it, a rat had just arrived: a
young albino male who apparently had either escaped from some-

where or had been abandoned. Having already come up with a name for the rat, I convinced Jameth to go with me, "just to look."

As it turned out, Maggie knew Michelle (June's former caretaker) and had heard of June. She told us that if Michelle had entrusted us with *June's* care, she knew ours would be a great home. We were given a tour of Maggie's home-turned-animal-shelter, and I saw a single guinea pig; I recognized him from my dream. I took this as a sign, and we returned home with Jonathan Livingston Rat.

At first, I felt tremendous guilt. How could I allow another rat into June's home? I felt as if I had betrayed her. The next emotion was grief. Jonathan was very sweet, but he wasn't June, and his presence made me miss her that much more. Sure, they were both rats, but they were opposites in every other way: She was black and he was white; she was female and he was male; she was old and he was young. None of these traits were bad, just *different*. Shortly after we brought Jonathan home, a sad song played on the stereo, and as Jameth and I observed this adorable little stranger who wasn't June, we held each other and cried.

Despite our lingering grief, Jonathan soon stole our hearts and soothed our souls. He became a special member of the family, and we soon determined that, unlike June, he *would* like a rat companion. So I called every animal shelter in town in search of a rat who needed a home. I located three females, so we "just looked," and before long, Katey (white with beautiful black markings), April (black with a white belly), and Cindy (agouti brown) joined our family (we had Jonathan neutered first, so unwanted babies weren't a concern).

Shortly thereafter, a fifth rat joined our family, so we now had our five-rat family, just like in the dream. They enjoyed their meals on the kitchen floor in five little bowls, just like in the dream. After June's death, I had felt compelled to start a Rat Rescue in her memory, so it appeared that this was the beginning.

SAMANTHA, THE NEWCOMER, was a former college lab rat who had apparently been malnourished. She had narrowly escaped being frozen to death in a freezer (the standard way the lab rats were disposed of when the experiments were over), thanks to the sympathy of one of the students who took her home and called me, having been referred by a mutual friend.

Samantha was white with a small patch of black between dark eyes that made her look almost like a little bandit. She wasn't like the other rats. She was a loner, and she had the most peculiar, almost other-worldly facial expression. Un-rodentlike mannerisms were uniquely hers. Although her new home was a veritable paradise for rats (friends have often said that when they die they want to come back as one of our rats), Samantha never quite learned to trust humans or to peacefully co-exist with the other rats in our home. She never was able to warm up to me or anyone else. She always seemed agitated and unhappy. Although the rats had plenty of room to run around in the house, it just wasn't enough for her.

One day, Samantha ate a hole in the screen of one of our windows and disappeared. I had seen her climb up and down that particular screen many times, but it had never occurred to me that she was looking for a way out. Although she was able to access the screen via a sofa that backed up to it, I realized that, once she had jumped down to the ground outside, there was no way she could have gotten back up to return if she wanted to.

I was worried sick about this fragile creature who had already been through so much. I also felt tremendously guilty for not having prevented her escape. After a long search that spanned several days, Jameth and I eventually found her living in a small tunnel under some bushes in the yard. Then a week-long struggle ensued, as we tried to capture her and eventually did, only to have her escape again. It became quite clear that she didn't want to return indoors.

Not knowing what else to do, I set up a huge outdoor hutch in the yard. The hutch was up on tall wooden legs, so I made a small ramp for Samantha to easily get up to it. I propped the door open a rat-width (to prevent predators from getting in) and put a warm bed with lots of nesting material inside, hoping to coax her to safety. I left meals in the hutch for her, and although I never caught her, each morning the food was gone.

Occasionally, Samantha trotted across the porch, almost as if to say "Hi," but she always moved much too quickly to be caught. For the first time in her life, she seemed really content, and the bright white rat was often seen running happily through the yard. I wished I could dye her fur brown so she wouldn't be such a moving target, and I worried about her constantly. I continued to leave meals out for her, and they continued to be eaten.

I worked with several professional animal communicators during the entire saga, and Samantha made it clear that she would much prefer to have a short, risky life outdoors than a safe life indoors. No one could convince her otherwise.

Shortly thereafter, she was attacked by a predator. I found her, still alive, and I held her as Jameth rushed us to the animal hospital. She died before anything could be done.

Extremely distraught, I called Gail De Sciose, one of the animal communicators who had spoken with June after her passing. At this point, I was getting used to the idea of telepathic communication with animals, whether dead or alive, and I needed some sort of comfort. I was filled not only with sorrow, but also with tremendous guilt.

Through Gail, Samantha communicated accurate details of her death, which Gail could not have known, and she expressed that she didn't want to worry me anymore. She said she had loved her freedom outdoors, had no regrets, and in fact, wanted to come back as a small brown wild mouse, much better suited for a life outdoors. I found the idea vaguely comforting but continued to battle guilt and doubt.

SEVERAL MONTHS LATER, Jameth and I noticed something moving at the very screen Samantha had escaped through, the one she had so often climbed up and down. It was just one of many windows in the room, but the movement caught our eyes. The hole she had eaten in the screen was still there, but we had covered it up with a clear adhesive patch.

As we watched, a small brown wild mouse climbed that very screen, up to the top and then back down, just as Samantha used to do (except that the mouse was on the *outside* of the screen).

The window was several feet off the ground. How could a mouse have gotten up there from the outside? I approached the window to get a better look, and to my surprise, the mouse didn't run away. Instead, the tiny creature climbed right next to the patched-up hole and looked me in the eye. Our faces were within inches of each other, and I noticed the most peculiar, almost otherworldly facial expression. I knew I had seen that expression before.

"Samantha?" I asked in disbelief. The mouse just looked intently at me as if to say, "Yes, I'm okay. Look at me—I'm living the life I always wanted." I recalled the session with Gail, the animal communicator, in which Samantha had mentioned coming back as a small brown wild mouse. Now this mouse and I just looked at each other for perhaps several minutes, as time stood still.

When I silently acknowledged that I indeed understood what was being communicated, the mouse then slowly, calmly, turned around and jumped down to the ground. I noticed the mouse's un-rodentlike mannerisms, which were eerily similar to Samantha's. Looking down at the surrounding shrubbery, I realized that the little creature must have worked extremely hard at getting up to that particular window, and I was unable to figure out how she could have done it. The mouse looked back up at me one last time and then disappeared into the bushes.

THAT WAS A TURNING POINT in my life. I realized that the idea of an afterlife for animals was a topic that warranted real investigation. I wanted to know if others had had experiences similar to mine, and I wondered if the possibility of an afterlife could be as comforting for others as it was for me. What I would soon discover was that evidence of life after death for animals is all around us, and that many people have had experiences that are so profound, it's just not possible to explain them away.

As I began the research that would eventually become this book, I thought back on how it had all begun. I recalled the precious moments of June's life and the painful moments of her death. I now realized the magnitude of lessons I had learned from my little angel, both in her life and in her death. I realized that she had opened the door for the new little angels who now shared my life and continued to teach me, and she had opened the door for me to go on and assist others through their own losses.

As I sat at my desk and began writing this book, surrounded by rats, I looked around me, smiled, and sighed.

"Oh, June," I said softly, "look at what you've started."

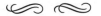

- CHAPTER 5 -

Asking the Animals

Dear God,
Must I bark, or can you hear my thoughts?
— FROM *PETS' LETTERS TO GOD* BY MARK BRICKLIN

MY NEW UNDERSTANDING OF ANIMAL COMMUNICATION, and my conversations with my own beloved animals—both during and after their lives—had brought me tremendous comfort, and I felt confident that it could do the same for others. So when people contacted me for support upon the passing of a beloved animal, I began recommending professional animal communicators as valuable sources of support in handling the grief.

Early on, I discovered that most animal communicators were often sought to communicate with animals who had passed, and that this was just a normal part of their work. I also discovered that they had a wealth of knowledge and experience. So, in researching this book, I interviewed dozens of animal communicators and asked for their perspectives on the afterlife. They generously shared their stories and insights, and they spread the word of my project to their clients. For this, I am immensely grateful. Some of their stories are scattered throughout this book.

Although each of them approached this subject from their own unique perspective, and they came from widely varying religious backgrounds, I found remarkable similarities in what all of them had to say. None of them were merely sharing theories they had read or heard somewhere; they were sharing what they had discovered by communicating with the animals themselves. I found this refreshing in a world often filled with conflicting opinions and confusing conclusions. What they said was congruent, from one animal communicator to the next, and what they said made sense.

When I asked them how they received their information, I found that they all described one or more of the various forms of telepathy that I had experienced in my own life. I was grateful to have had personal experience with telepathy, so I understood firsthand much of what they were describing, and I simply wasn't able to be skeptical in a realm where I otherwise probably would have been.

They all explained that animal communication is the same process, whether communicating with a live animal or one on the Other Side: It is telepathic communication with the soul or spirit of the animal, which lives on even after the physical body has died. Most of them received this telepathic communication in the form of pictures or images, often described as watching a video or film on an ethereal movie screen.

It was also very common for them to hear words, sentences, even paragraphs of information from the animals. They all corroborated my own theory that, with telepathy, our minds are able to translate the information received into words of our own spoken language. That is why animal communicators often give us messages in the form of very specific words and sentences, even though animals don't actually speak our language. Likewise, when we speak to animals, they may not understand all of the words, but they understand the *meaning* behind the words. We receive in our own language, as do they. (It should be noted here that many animals actually have quite an impressive vocabulary of words that they *do* understand, and in some cases, that they can speak as well.) Some animal communicators also described hearing specific "voices" with specific animals, making it clear exactly which animal they were communicating with.

In addition to, or instead of, words or pictures, the communications were often described as spirit-to-spirit conversations, thought forms, or thoughts coming into the mind from outside rather than from within. Sometimes the communication was described as simply a sense of knowing. Many of the animal communicators were also able to receive feelings, either physical or emotional, such as pain or other sensations in specific areas of the body, which were then confirmed. Some felt these sensations in their own bodies, while others had a sense of feeling the animals' bodies. Other forms of receiving included hearing specific sounds, touch, and sometimes even smell and taste (such as the smell or taste of specific foods or remedies that the animal had eaten prior to passing). Such forms of receiving are also relatively common when ordinary people are contacted from the spirit world, as will be covered in subsequent chapters.

I asked the animal communicators for experiences that convinced them—and their clients—of the validity of their work, and they most commonly cited verifiable details that were unknown to the communicator (and often to the other person) until the details were corroborated after the fact. The animals often described very specific things to let their people know that it was really them. There was no way the animal communicators could have known these details. I discovered that an animal will often describe what their human companions have been doing since the animal's death, implying that our departed loved ones are still very present and aware of what is going on in our lives.

I also asked the animal communicators for their views of the death process, the soul's journey, and what the Other Side is really like. Again, the answers were quite similar from one person to the next. I was told that when the animals died, they were greeted and assisted by the spirits of people, animals, and/or angelic beings. They were often accompanied by former animal friends and/or human friends; and when they described these individuals, the very specific, detailed physical descriptions were then confirmed as animals or people who had previously died (unbeknownst to the animal communicator), whom the animal in question had indeed known and loved in life.

A common theme I heard was that, upon passing into spirit, the animals became younger and healthier, as they had been when they were in the prime of life. Interestingly, the people with them were usually (though not always) *also* described as youthful, in good condition, and in the prime of life. Often the detailed descriptions they gave of these people were as they had looked *before* they had grown old and sick. Even though they were in spirit and were no longer actually in their physical bodies, they usually presented themselves in the form their loved ones recognized from when they were alive in the physical world.

The animals always described the Other Side as a very beautiful, wonderful place. They had a feeling of peace and tranquility, and they were very happy and felt very loved. They often described beautiful outdoor scenes, where they were playing and running free. If not outdoors, they seemed to be in whatever environment or situation would make that particular animal the most happy and comfortable. Basically, they were describing Heaven.

The animals on the Other Side often communicated that they felt no real separation from their loved ones on *this* side, and that they were still very much connected to their people here. They described the physical body as merely a temporary vehicle for the spirit. Often, they continued to hang around their former home quite a bit for some time after physical death, as they got used to living in spirit. No matter where they were or what they were doing on the Other Side, they still always had the ability to connect with those of us in the physical world.

These messages from the Other Side have been immensely comforting to many people who have lost a beloved animal. Although I admittedly was very skeptical at first and did put quite a few animal communicators to the test, I strongly encourage people to approach animal communication with an open-minded attitude. If you approach it with a lot of skepticism or sarcasm, this can often make the animal communicator nervous, thereby negatively affecting the accuracy and helpfulness of the session. It's sort of like suddenly becoming unable to type or speak clearly when your boss is looking over your shoulder. We're all human, and we can become nervous (and therefore, our effectiveness can be compromised) when we feel we are being scrutinized. So, for their sake and yours, please bear that in mind when first exploring telepathic animal communication for yourself.

I have done enough research and have had enough experience in this field to feel good about endorsing animal communication as a highly valuable tool, both when our animal companions are alive and after they have passed over into spirit. However, that doesn't necessarily mean I endorse every animal communicator. Just as there are people with varying degrees of talent and skill in any other profession, the same holds true in this one. If you work with one animal communicator and aren't happy with the results, and you feel you've truly given them a fair chance, I suggest trying other animal communicators until you find one you can feel good about working with.

Once a relationship is established with a particular animal communicator, many people find it helpful to stick with one primary animal communicator but to also keep other numbers on file in case the primary one isn't available. That way, you don't have to start from square one for every session, but you're also never left with no one to turn to. Many animal communicators also offer workshops, and I highly encourage people to open up to the possibility that they, too, can learn to develop this valuable form of communication.

Another thing to bear in mind is that telepathic animal communication is just that: communication. As with any form of communication, sometimes intent can be unclear or misunderstood. So, just because it's telepathic, that doesn't mean it's flawless. Often meanings aren't understood at first, and the true value of a session isn't fully understood until after the fact. If you feel an animal communicator is downright wrong about something, let them know. It's possible that something has been misinterpreted along the way. It's important not to dismiss telepathic communication as a whole simply because of a specific miscommunication. If we did that with verbal communication, I think we all would have given up speaking a long time ago!

If an animal communicator isn't included in this book, it doesn't necessarily mean I don't endorse their work. I simply wasn't able to get in touch with all of them or to include all of the wonderful stories of those I did get in touch with. If I had, I'd still be writing, and this book wouldn't be in your hands now. The animal communicators represented here are just some of the many professionals who can assist in communicating with animals who have passed. (For a list of animal communicators and how to contact them, visit **www.CompassionCircle.org**.)

I've received positive feedback from many people who have worked with animal communicators, and the following stories are but a few examples. . . .

Please note: In the stories that follow throughout this book, the names in italics are those of the people telling the stories, followed by their occupations and where they live. If a story is from the United States, only the state is listed, and not the country (to avoid being redundant, since the majority of the stories are from the U.S., where this book was written). As you will see, there are stories in this book from around the world.

Rajah
Lois Bark, Artist
New York

"If I thought that there was a reason to stay, that I could run and I could play, I would stay. I don't see a good end to this. If my family is ready to let me go, then I am ready."

Thus spoke Rajah, our Bernese mountain dog, through Gail De Sciose, the animal communicator whom I had worked with throughout Rajah's illness.

On Rajah's last day, he told Gail that he wanted to be in his bed surrounded by his family. However, that night my husband was coming home late and my son wasn't coming home at all.

So, Rajah was in his bed, but he wasn't surrounded by his family; I was the only one with him. Much to my surprise, in walked Jed and Caleb (my husband and son)—plans had changed and there we were, surrounding Rajah. Just what he wanted!

The next day, Gail told me that the night Rajah died, she was too upset to go to dinner with her husband, and instead went to her room, lit a candle and got into contact with Rajah. At the time, her husband wanted to know what it was about Rajah that had touched her so much. Her answer was, "I remembered Rajah saying, 'Everyone loves me because I love everyone.' I was struck at the time by how simple Rajah made it sound."

Gail later related to me that she could see Rajah (in spirit) playing joyously on our back lawn. She said, "He's running, and he stops and he rolls and says, 'My body would not do what I needed it to do [toward the end of his life]. Now look at me! Being a dog is much more fun than being a human.'"

Rajah also said, "Last night," (after death, when he was watching the house) "lights were flickering on and off." At first I didn't get it. I had no idea what Rajah was talking about. Then, when I later told my very skeptical husband about it, he was able to confirm what Rajah had shared with us. I had installed a new floodlight on the roof that day and when Jed (my formerly skeptical husband) and Caleb went to turn it off, they didn't know how to use it and kept turning it on and off, on and off, and on and off.

Kim's note: This story is an example of the very common occurrence in which our departed loved ones will remain involved in the goings-on in our lives and will report back very specific incidents to let us know that they are indeed watching over us. These are often situations in which the person doesn't understand the message at first, eliminating the possibility that the animal communicator is merely reading the thoughts of the person. Lois, like many, received the message from her departed dog and had no idea what it meant at first. It wasn't until afterward that she figured out what Rajah was referring to: He had seen the lights flickering on and off, and indeed, that's exactly what had been going on when he said it had.

Jokko

*Donna L. Dodson, Legal Secretary
and Founder, Hearts of Gold Pit Rescue
Tennessee*

ONE WORD TO DESCRIBE MY CONTACTS with Joanna Seere, the animal communicator: "Reassuring." I knew she was communicating with my beloved pit bull, Jokko, when she told me he showed her a picture of him licking my face like crazy. Of the four dogs that I had at the time, he was the only one who was a licker.

After receiving IV fluids in the vet's office, Jokko's heart could not pump well enough to distribute the fluids, so he went into congestive heart failure. After an x-ray, he was diagnosed with cardiomegaly (enlarged heart). He got so weak, fighting just to breathe, and did not eat on his own for two weeks. I force-fed him every morsel that went into his mouth. When Joanna and I talked, she sent him some healing energy, and miraculously, he ate the next day, all by himself. Joanna said Jokko was fighting with everything he had to stay on this earth with me. He lived four more months before succumbing to anemia, liver problems, kidney problems, and possible bone cancer.

When he left his body, for the first time in my life I felt totally lost . . . I couldn't function. I called Joanna again, and we communicated with him. He was so excited about his flexible body. He felt like a puppy again. Jokko previously had severe arthritis in his spine, so bad that the vet could not believe he could still walk. When Joanna communicated with him, he kept mentioning his flexibility and the absence of any pain.

He also told me to go outside and run with the dogs. Only I knew what this meant. Jokko's favorite pastime was playing and wrestling and running in our fenced-in acre in the backyard. He would get so excited when I started out the back door, he would yelp in this high-pitched voice. If I hadn't been outside often enough to please him, he would stand on the deck and whine, begging me to come outside. He told Joanna that he wanted me to run with the dogs and that he would be there when I did. I knew this was Jokko. I had no doubts in my mind.

I am still coping with losing the best friend I ever had. Joanna has been there for me, and I don't know how I would have made it through this without her. She understands how deeply a human being can love an animal. She gives me a place that I can honor my feelings and get in touch with those feelings. She is truly a gift.

Kim's note: Again, this is an example of an animal who has given his person a specific message to let her know it's really him. The messages we receive from the Other Side aren't necessarily profound; they are usually about the very common, mundane occurrences from their lives to let us know it's really them. Knowing they're continuing to live on in spirit, and that they're still connected to us, helps us to cope with our grief.

ASKING THE ANIMALS

Wiggie
Debra Tadman, Kindergarten Teacher and Art Teacher
California

I HAD FOUR CATS at the time I called animal communicator Sharon Callahan. My oldest cat, Wiggie, had just died. I'd had Wiggie for seventeen years. Wiggie and I had a very close relationship.

After Wiggie died, I was heartbroken! I knew he'd had a long life with me, though I felt like I had lost a child. He had seen me through a marriage, divorce, other relationships, three moves, and other life experiences. He would always be at home waiting for me to return. And he let me bring in three other stray cats to live with us, without batting a paw. The last of the three condos that Wiggie lived in with me, I purchased. He lived with me there for about ten years.

During the tenth year, Grandmother, whom I loved dearly, took a turn for the worse and died at the age of 93. When she was living, she would always ask how my cats were doing and loved hearing about my cat adventures. A few months later, Wiggie had his last days on Earth and transitioned on.

This is when I called Kim, because I needed support from a fellow animal lover who knows the pain of losing these precious friends. She suggested I call Sharon Callahan. I sent a photo of Wiggie to Sharon, and when I talked with her on the phone she told me the rest. I was amazed at what she said. Sharon told me that Wiggie was sitting in the lap of someone close to me who had just died. This was my grandma; I was amazed. Sharon said that they are my guardian angels and will be helping out in the next few years.

Sharon told me that Wiggie was very concerned about the condo that I am living in. Wiggie told her, "It is a very toxic place for Debra and the other cats, and she needs to do something about this because it is detrimental to Debra's health and the health of the other cats."

About a year later, my niece, Heather, was coming to visit me for two weeks. I decided to paint the inside of my condo and re-move the "popcorn" texture that was on the ceiling. Oh my; I had

69

some of the popcorn ceiling tested and found that it contained asbestos. I had to put my three cats on a patio in cages and have all of the popcorn ceiling removed.

The wood paneling that was going to be painted had to be removed because it had been exposed to the asbestos. When the paneling was removed, there was mold all over the walls. The walls were disinfected from the mold, and parts of it were removed. When parts of the walls were removed, it was discovered that the aluminum wiring needed to be replaced because there were little mini fires that would occur in the outlets. Needless to say, my whole condo went through a major transformation.

Wiggie had said that my condo was a toxic place to live and something needed to be done. To this day I can't believe how accurate and true that reading was. There is no way that Sharon could have known this. *I* didn't even know until I started to have some painting done.

Other things Sharon told me about Wiggie were so true.

One by one, my other three cats have joined Wiggie and my grandmother. Each time, I called Sharon Callahan and received amazing insight. I'll never forget my condo experience. Wiggie knew what needed to be done. I think of my loved ones—who have transitioned—always, and I know they continue to be with me, my precious animal family and my dear human family.

Kim's note: It's not uncommon for our loved ones in spirit to warn us of things we don't yet even know about, indicating not only that they are still watching over us, but that our well-being still matters to them. Wiggie is truly acting as Debra's guardian angel.

- CHAPTER 6 -

Bridging Heaven and Earth: Conversations with the Other Side

The language of friendship is not words, but meanings.
It is an intelligence above language.
— HENRY DAVID THOREAU

OVER THE YEARS while researching this book, I attended presentations given by all of the popular mediums, including George Anderson, John Edward, Sylvia Browne, James Van Praagh, Rosemary Altea, Suzane Northrop, and others. This was before mediums were a regular part of prime-time television. For those who still may not know, a medium is a person who is able to receive information from those who have passed over to the Other Side and deliver messages to those of us on *this* side, thereby acting as a bridge between the physical world and the world of spirit. Like animal communicators, mediums often bring tremendous comfort to those who are grieving the loss of a loved one.

When I first began, I knew that mediums were known for connecting people in this world with *people* in spirit, but I wanted to know their viewpoints on *animals*. So, at each of these group readings (a "reading" is what it's usually called when a medium receives and delivers messages), I sat quietly in a room filled with people who were hoping to receive messages from their departed loved ones, watching to see what took place. At group readings, not everyone receives messages. The medium simply delivers the messages, as they come, to the people they are intended for. However, *everyone* in the room benefits from the validation of the afterlife that they receive by witnessing the experiences of others.

I was delighted (though not surprised) to find that the subject of animals came up at each and every group reading I attended. Usually there was at least one person in the audience who received a message *not* from a *human* on the Other Side, but from a recently departed *animal*. The people were always visibly touched by these messages. Whether or not this happened, there was inevitably someone in the audience who *asked* about animals, and the mediums always stated matter-of-factly that *of course* there were animals in the afterlife. Many of them then cited specific stories of their own on this subject. I had heard what I was looking for.

I never actually received a personal message during these group readings, but something very significant did happen when I went to see psychic medium George Anderson. I brought my copies of the books *We Don't Die* (written about George Anderson by Joel Martin and Patricia Romanowski) and *Lessons from the Light* (written by George Anderson and Andrew Barone), for George to autograph, which he did during a break.

After the seminar was over, I asked Andrew Barone (George Anderson's co-author), who was also at the seminar, to autograph my copy of *Lessons from the Light* as well. At that time, he appeared glad to see me and told me that George had asked him to keep an eye out for me, because he had something for me. My mind was racing as I wondered what it could be.

He then gave me a beautiful framed picture that George had asked him to give to me. It was a picture of a saint with animals, and he told me it was St. Martin de Porres, whom George had seen standing behind me when I had approached him for an autograph earlier that evening. He had somehow felt compelled to bring the picture with him on the airplane to this particular seminar, and as Andrew told me later, "I thought it was odd when George told me he packed it, but after this many years I have learned not to question why the souls [those in spirit] ask George to carry a picture clear across the country—there will always be a good reason."

When I first looked at the picture, I was stunned. There was a dog looking up at the saint, and also at his feet were a cat, a bird, and a *rat* all sharing food from the same bowl. All of the animals in the picture were meaningful to me, as my life has been deeply touched by *all* of these types of animals. However, I was particularly struck by the rat in the picture.

How unusual for a rat to be portrayed so prominently in a portrait of a saint, I thought to myself, *and how appropriate!* George Anderson had never met me before and had no idea who I was (or that I would be at the seminar that night), nor did he have any way of knowing that the animals I've loved and rescued throughout my life have included so many rats (in addition to the other animals portrayed). By the time this event took place, dozens of rescued rats had entered my life, and they now had their own room. I felt a surge of sheer delight and wonder as I gazed at the rat in the picture.

I was equally struck by the fact that I instantly knew where I would hang the picture in my home. In fact, I had left a space open for it and now realized that I had somehow been expecting it. There is a corner in a hallway of my home with a few pictures of spiritual figures with animals. Jameth and I refer to this as the sacred hallway, and this sacred corner is just outside the rats' room. When I originally hung the pictures there, for some reason, I felt compelled to hang them in such a way that there was a spot left open for one more picture. I just had a feeling (though I had no idea why) that an ideal picture would be arriving for that spot, so I should leave it open. As soon as Andrew gave me the picture from George, I knew that was it.

I was deeply moved when I received this most precious gift, and I asked Andrew to thank George for me. I wanted to thank him myself, but by then there were many people crowded around him so I never got the chance that night; but I went away feeling that something profound had just taken place.

I hung the picture that very night and it fit perfectly in the space left open for it. To this day, it hangs right over the hallway where the rats run and play when they joyfully bound out of their room, frolicking and running freely. Interestingly, in the picture, the saint is holding a broom, and he and the animals are standing on a tile floor. The hallway in our home has a tile floor, and a favorite game of the rats is to climb up and down a very similar broom, which is kept nearby.

I really didn't know much about saints when this took place. I knew who St. Francis was (often referred to as the patron saint of animals, and known for his ability to communicate with animals), and I had always delighted in the fact that I was born in St. Francis Hospital, but I had never even *heard of* St. Martin de Porres. When I asked Andrew who this particular saint was, he told me, "The saint George saw standing behind you (that was how he knew you worked with animals) was St. Martin de Porres, who, like St. Francis, believed every thing on the earth that was alive had a soul and was part of God's family (which ran contrary to the Church's stance—and often got him in plenty of trouble)."

He added, "We wish you success with your very important work—it is considered so important to the Infinite Light that St. Martin de Porres took time out of his work to stand behind you at a seminar."

Later, I did more research on St. Martin de Porres, and I was further amazed at what I discovered. He was born in 1579 in Lima, Peru, and at a young age, he joined a Dominican priory (monastery). The son of a Spanish officer and a freed black woman, he referred to himself as a "mulatto dog," but he was known in his community as the "father of charity." He is often called the patron saint of social justice and is a popular saint for those who feel despised or who experience deep suffering. He took care of the poor, the sick, the abandoned, and those who were looked down upon due to race, social class, and even species.

St. Martin de Porres had a vast knowledge of herbal medicines and was known for his amazing cures. He was also gifted with prophecy, clairvoyance, and other such abilities. The startling miracles he performed, which included raising the dead, caused Martin to be called a saint in his own lifetime. Even sick and injured animals came to him for healing, and he set up a shelter/hospital for stray cats and dogs and nursed them back to health (an incredible thing to do back in those days).

To this day he is remembered for his love of animals. He never ate meat, and he extended his love even to rats and mice, whose scavenging he excused on the grounds that they were hungry. As he put it, "The poor little things don't have enough to eat." I was covered in goose bumps as I learned that this incredible saint felt the same love and concern for animals—including rats—that I had always felt.

As great as his healing abilities were, I discovered that St. Martin is probably best remembered for the "legend of the rats." It is said that the prior (his superior at the monastery) objected to the rats, so he ordered Martin to set out poison for them. Martin obeyed, but he also felt deep compassion for them. So he went out into the garden and called softly to the rats—and out they came. He told them about the poison and assured them that he would feed them every day in the garden, if they would stop annoying the prior. This they agreed upon, and forever after, they never troubled the monastery.

Though I certainly don't claim to be a saint, I was amazed at the parallels between his life and my own. I, too, have always felt a deep compassion for the underdogs of our world, including rats. I, too, take in many sick and injured animals, treating them with various herbal remedies; and my home is often referred to as a "rat hospital" where amazing healings take place. I, too, am a vegetarian (a vegan, actually), and although I am now well aware of the health benefits of such a diet, my original impetus to give up meat was my love for animals.

The more I learned about St. Martin de Porres, the more significant his presence became to me. He is also known as the "Saint of the Broom" (for his devotion to his work, no matter how menial), and he called himself "Brother Broom." I now think of him every time I sweep the floor, and every time my beloved "rat children" joyfully climb up and down the broom during playtime. St. Martin is truly an inspiration to me in my own commitment to protecting creation and promoting the sacredness of life in all forms. I am forever grateful to George Anderson for making me aware of this most remarkable saint.

(For more information on psychic medium George Anderson, visit **www.GeorgeAnderson.com**.)

THE CAT'S MEOW

WHEN DEBBIE ARXER, a registered nurse in New York, scheduled a personal reading with psychic medium Natalie Smith-Blakeslee, she had no idea that her recently departed cat would come through.

"When I went to see Natalie," Debbie explained, "I did not expect to hear from my cat, Bijoux. I just didn't think of animals communicating from the Other Side. I went just for a psychic/medium reading. I *never* asked about my cat or told her I had a cat that had died. She brought up a recently departed and very close male spirit. It was a huge surprise that my cat came through. I think he knew I needed to hear from him, and that I had unresolved guilt issues surrounding his death."

During the session, Natalie (the medium) described very specific and unusual details of Debbie's home, explaining that Bijoux, the cat, was describing the house to her—including details of his favorite room. There is no way Natalie could have known these details, as she had never been to Debbie's home, yet Debbie was able to confirm the accuracy of these details.

Natalie delivered other equally accurate messages from Bijoux, including a mention of his collar (which Debbie hadn't been able to find) and his whiskers (which, as Debbie again confirmed, had become "stubby little whiskers" when he got old and sick). Natalie explained that Bijoux was mentioning these things so Debbie would have verification that it was really him.

However, she then began talking about something that made absolutely no sense to Debbie.

"He's also talking about your tires," she said. "Did you do something to the tires?"

"No," Debbie responded.

Natalie asked if Debbie had tires in her garage, and Debbie again said, "No."

Natalie then mentioned seeing a tire off of its rim, but neither of them was able to understand what this could mean. Natalie thought perhaps Bijoux had played inside tires, but this was not the case. Bijoux continued describing tires, and Natalie kept asking

Debbie if the message made any sense to her. Debbie continued saying, "No." She didn't understand this message at all. Neither of them had *any idea* what Bijoux could be talking about. Bijoux was very insistent about getting this message across, but it continued to perplex both Natalie and Debbie. As it turned out, they wouldn't understand the significance of this message until later on.

The session was recorded on audiotape, and no one was expecting what took place when the tape was later played back. On the recording, while Natalie kept trying to explain the message she was receiving about tires, a very distinctive "meow" could be heard on the tape. There were no cats in the house when the session took place, and the sound had *not* been heard during the session.

The session took place at the home of Mary Ellen Szwejkowski, where Natalie stayed while giving readings to clients in the area. Mary Ellen later confirmed, "They [Natalie's clients] all had taped recordings of their readings. In one of the tape recordings, a client's [Debbie's] deceased cat made a distinctive 'meow' on the tape while it was being played back. It was loud and clear. There was no cat in the house during the taped readings. It was phenomenal. This gave much healing comfort to the client who missed her beloved cat."

ELECTRONIC VOICE PHENOMENON, or EVP, is the official term used to describe cases in which spirits' voices are captured by a recording device such as a tape recorder. These voices are not heard at the time of the recording but can be distinctly heard when the recording is then played back. During my lifelong exploration of the afterlife, I had come across many well-documented cases of EVP, in which human voices had apparently been captured from the Beyond. However, this was the first time I'd ever heard of such a case involving an animal.

Although Natalie had heard the voices of deceased *humans* on tape numerous times, this was also the first time *she* had heard the voice of a deceased animal on tape. As she put it, "The tape shows that not only do we live on, but our lovable, adorable pets do as well."

When I first learned of this case, I expected to hear a subtle, muted sound that perhaps could be interpreted as a "meow" by those listening for it. However, when I actually *heard* the recording, I was quite surprised at the clarity of the "meow." In fact, I was stunned to hear it as clear as day, and I was covered in goose bumps as I listened in amazement. It indeed sounded as if the cat were right there in the room with them.

In the recording, I did notice that the "meow" took place when Natalie was trying to impart the message about the tires. I got the impression that there was something important about the tires, so I asked Debbie about this.

"As far as the tires go," Debbie explained, "at first it did not make sense. The reading was on April 22nd. On May 30th, I was in an accident and after the car was repaired, I told the shop the car shook for the past few months. I thought it might be shocks. It turned out that both my front tires were bald on the inside, and if they weren't replaced they would have blown out! Bijoux knew what I didn't."

She added, "I have always thought of Bijoux as more human than catlike; so did everyone who knew him. Natalie told me his presence was stronger than most humans she receives! Once I had a psychic over and he saw the cat and called him 'Psychic Kitty.'"

So, apparently, Bijoux was concerned about Debbie's safety and had been warning her of the dangerous condition of her tires, once again demonstrating that our beloved animals continue to care about us and watch over us from the Other Side.

(For more information on psychic medium Natalie Smith-Blakeslee, visit **www.LoveAndLight.com**.)

OVER THE YEARS, I discovered that many people grieving the loss of a beloved animal had found great comfort in a message delivered by a medium. The following stories are just a few more examples of people who have received such messages of comfort from the Other Side. . . .

Mr. Brow/Browby
Narelle Box, Contemporary Jeweler
Victoria, Australia

AFTER RECENTLY HAVING TO SAY GOOD-BYE to my feline soul mate of fifteen years (his name was Mr. Brow, but we usually called him Browby), I went to a spiritual healer (who is also a medium) in an attempt to ease my pain a little. The medium did not know that I had a cat who had died. When I rang to book the appointment, I spoke to her husband. He just gave me an appointment date, a time, and the address.

Then, when I arrived on the day of our appointment, she opened the door and the first thing she said to me as I walked through her front door was, "Oh, look, there's a black cat at your feet." Those were the first words she said to me and that was the first time we'd spoken. I looked down and saw nothing. Then when I looked back at her, puzzled, she added, "Your best friend that has recently moved on, your cat." What can I say? I was speechless, but it's great to know that they are still looking after us and keeping us company.

Ozu

Trisha Adelena Howell, Author and Publisher
Washington

I WAS A GRADUATE STUDENT at USC film school—taking classes and working a total of about 100 hours per week—when Ozu came into my life. One of my fellow students, Paley, arrived in class one day with a tattered little reddish golden Tibetan spaniel whom she'd found running down the side of the freeway. He was deathly thin, flea-bitten, and with lots of fur missing. As Paley remarked that she wouldn't be able to keep him, I looked into his sad brown eyes and heard a voice say, "I'll take him!" To my shock, I realized that the voice belonged to me!

I'd never had a dog before, but Ozu did everything possible to make it easy for me. (I named him after a Japanese film director whose trademark is shooting from low angles—a dog's eye point of view.) He sat through five-hour film classes in my lap, never making a sound or stirring. He would watch the good films and fall asleep during the boring ones (and, usually, during the lectures). Most professors never figured out that he was even in the class. But he was quite popular with fellow students whom he warmly greeted during breaks outside as he romped among the small grassy hills.

The vet estimated that Ozu was only two, but he'd had a hard life. He'd been homeless on the streets for many weeks before Paley found him and still bore the belt marks of when he'd previously been beaten!

When I took Ozu to an animal communication seminar, the leader tuned in to him and informed me that he'd lived with a woman whose boyfriend beat him mercilessly, so he ran away from home. Ozu said that he'd never known what love is until I came into his life, and his only question was, would he be with me forever? My heart soared with love and joy, and I promised him he would be with me always.

No matter how busy I was, we walked every day. He was always so bright and happy. When I studied, he sat at my feet.

When I slept, he was in his little bed by the side of mine. When I showered, he waited for me on the bath mat.

Ozu and I had a very happy life together. I could never before have even imagined the intense joy a ten-pound creature could bring.

Ozu has been gone for ten years now, and I've never stopped missing him. Yet my grief has turned into joy as the result of several amazing incidents.

Over the years I have had a few psychic readings. Even though I haven't mentioned Ozu to them, psychics have remarked that they see a small dog who loves me very much in my energy field. So he is still with me! Sometimes I have vivid dreams about him in which we cuddle and play together happily.

Four years ago I met a remarkable woman. She radiates a profound calmness, clarity, and joy and is quite a powerful psychic. One day, out of the blue, she started talking about a small, deceased dog I love who had a message for me. The message is that he loves me and will always be with me. He doesn't want me to grieve any longer but to remember all the good times we had together. He knows I love him and did everything possible for him. And someday we will be together again.

I think this message of hope is true for all beings who have deeply loved one another. Neither time nor death can separate us. Our loved one's energy is always nearby, and we will be reunited in some other dimension of life.

Kim's note: Although Trisha doesn't refer to the psychic as a medium, she is clearly acting as a medium in delivering this message from Ozu. Those delivering such messages don't always call themselves mediums, but in these cases, they are indeed acting as mediums, regardless of title.

Geisha
Trés Hanley, Actress/Opera Singer
New Jersey

GEISHA DIED UNEXPECTEDLY. She was at the vet for the removal of a large noncancerous tumor that was interfering with her walking and running. We had been told that the tumor was nothing to worry about, but that if it interfered with her agility we might want to remove it. It had grown, so we decided it would be best to get rid of it, as she loved to run and it was starting to bother her.

She went, happy and healthy (so we thought), to the vet. A few hours later, we got the dreadful call. It was cancer and had spread. The vet asked if we preferred not to wake her up, as she would otherwise face another surgery (which would involve amputating her leg) and then chemotherapy, with an outlook of about six months.

She had never been sick a day of her life, and now this. We couldn't decide what to do, as we were in shock. While we were going over the decision we just couldn't make, she suffered cardiac arrest and the vet was unable to revive her. It was like she knew we couldn't decide, so she did it for us.

Geisha had just turned eleven. She was the youngest of my canine brood of four, and she was just as frisky at eleven as she was at one. We'd had her since she was five weeks old. Right from the start, she was the comic of the family. She was always the baby and the one with the "personality" and mischief that made her the focal presence in the house. Every time my parents made their bimonthly trip to Atlantic City and came home very late, she would take my father's shoes out of his closet and carry them into the bedroom, along with emptying his trash bin in the wardrobe. . . .

This has continued since she's been gone. We have no explanation for it. It can't be the other dogs doing it, as they are now in my brother's apartment downstairs on the nights that my parents make the trip to Atlantic City. There is no explanation. The only reason we have all been able to get through the loss of Geisha is that it seems she *still may be with us*. We still grieve, but there is a bit of comfort in these incidents.

Because of these strange occurrences, I decided to go to a medium. I have always been a "Doubting Thomas," so to speak, about near-death experiences, the afterlife, etc., but I am starting to think maybe *there is* something to it all. So, I went to a spiritualist society to "sift through" mediums. They have "group readings" once a day but limit the audience to about twenty people and have different mediums every day. It is a way for those who don't have lots of money to see if they get lucky that day, as no one in the audience is guaranteed to be chosen for a random reading. I decided to go a couple times a week to see who may *not* be a fake and then book a private reading.

I spoke to *no one* and knew no one there, so there was no way anyone knew anything about me. I was the third person chosen by the medium, and she said a few things that were correct. They were intriguing comments but could have been lucky guesses. Then she said, "I want you to know that dogs and other animals go to the Other Side. I tell you this because you love dogs and there is a very large one standing behind you with her paws on your shoulders right now. You have been talking to her picture every day and weeping. She said she had her own chair in your house, and not to cry; she is with you."

Well, that was it. I broke down and sobbed uncontrollably. The medium went on to read three-fourths of the room, and I was the only one with a *dog* to come through, but then again, I have lost no one that I was close to other than her.

So, I am wondering, what *is* going on? Something must be. There were some other strange things that happened in the house after she died. Things that only *she* would do. Also, regarding the comment about the chair, I realize that perhaps most dogs have a chair they favor, but not most *big* dogs, usually smaller ones. And it was interesting that she noted that she was a large dog.

I still hurt and grieve, but I continue to talk to Geisha in case she can hear me.

Kim's note: An interesting element to this case is the fact that there were already significant signs of Geisha's presence before Trés even went to the medium. Such cases are not uncommon, and the phenomenon of mysteriously moving objects will be covered further in a later chapter.

- Chapter 7 -

There and Back:
The Near-Death Experience

*I believe there are two sides to the phenomenon known as death,
this side where we live, and the other side where we shall continue to live. Eternity does not start with death. We are in eternity
now.*
— Norman Vincent Peale

Throughout history, people of all ages around the world have
reported what are known as near-death experiences. A near-
death experience, or NDE, is an experience in which a person is
clinically dead while simultaneously having very vivid perceptions
beyond their physical body and feeling very much alive in another
realm of existence.

I recall my fascination when I first learned of such experiences in a film called *Beyond and Back,* which I went to see at
a local theater one summer when I was a child. I found the film
more entertaining and fascinating than any other movie or television show I had ever seen.

The accounts of these near-death experiences are often
remarkably similar from one person to the next, regardless of
background or prior knowledge of this phenomenon. Even
small children have reported astoundingly detailed accounts of
such experiences, without prior exposure to the experiences of

others. These children often draw detailed pictures of what they have experienced when they are too young to describe such things with words.

Generally, as the physical body is pronounced dead, the person having the experience finds him/herself floating up above the body, observing what is going on in the room. There have been many well-documented cases in which these people, who later returned to their bodies and were revived, reported very specific details of the goings-on in the room—or even in surrounding rooms—that took place while the physical body was dead. There was no way they could have known such details unless they were, indeed, visually observing from the unique vantage point of floating above the room and looking down at the scene below, dispelling the theory that an NDE is merely a hallucination conjured up within a dying brain.

During an NDE, there is often—though not always—a transition point between this world and the next, which is often described as traveling very fast through a tunnel of sorts, and eventually coming out to a brilliant light on the other side. People sometimes describe this tunnel as a part of the experience; other times they just find themselves at the destination without actually remembering the journey.

The people reporting NDEs often describe the experience as profoundly peaceful. They are surrounded by love and often encounter angelic beings and/or loved ones who have previously died. Usually they don't want to leave such a wonderful place, but they are told they must go back (or they are given a choice, but urged to go back and complete unfinished business); and they then return to their physical bodies, which are miraculously revived.

Another common aspect of an NDE is what is known as a "life review," in which the person experiences a comprehensive yet accelerated review of everything they have experienced in life thus far. Some describe this process as being engulfed in a vision of sorts, in which they reexperience not only all of their actions in life, but the *effects* of their actions (or inactions) on *others*. Despite the content of the life review, the experience seems to have a loving, nonjudgmental tone, as if its purpose is to help us gain greater understanding of the effects of our actions so that we can learn and grow.

Those who have undergone near-death experiences usually find them to be life-altering, to say the least. They sometimes return with prophetic visions, new insights, and/or a new sense of purpose in life. They are no longer afraid of death, and they often radiate peace and love in a way they never have before.

Interestingly, I have encountered a number of cases of animals who have had dramatic personality changes after undergoing major surgery or other experiences resulting in close brushes with death. Much like *humans* who have undergone these experiences and returned with a more peaceful, loving outlook on life, these animals likewise seem to radiate a profound peace and are far more loving than they were before, even those who previously had behavioral problems. I can't help but wonder if these animals have returned from NDEs as well.

Among humans, a very well-known case is that of Dannion Brinkley, who has had more than one near-death experience, as told in his best-selling books. He has been the subject of numerous interviews, documentaries, and a movie about his life and his experiences. Over the years, I've gone to see him speak whenever he has come to town.

I've found him to be an inspirational, entertaining, and warm-hearted man with a beautiful message. He humbly asserts that he was a bully and lived a less than saintly life prior to his first near-death experience. However, as is so common in NDE cases, he returned from the Other Side with a completely different outlook on life, and devoted himself to helping and serving others in need, most profoundly through hospice work. He also came away from the experience with remarkable prophecies and psychic gifts.

While researching the subject of animals and the afterlife, I attended one of his lectures intending to ask for his insights on the subject. At that point, I had seen him speak before, but I couldn't really remember him mentioning anything about animals. So, I was determined to ask him this time. However, before I even raised my hand to ask the question, he said (regarding those who have passed over), "If you think you'll never see them again, you're mistaken." He went on to explain that this was equally true whether the departed loved one was a parent or a pet, and that a lot of people are met on the Other Side by loved ones—*including animals*. Once again, I had my answer.

Dannion Brinkley's authenticity became crystal clear to me when, after his lecture, Jameth and I stood in line for his book signing. There were a lot of people at the event, so the pace was very quick. However, when Jameth and I reached the front of the line, Dannion stopped, paused, looked up as if listening to something that the rest of us couldn't hear, and then said he had just received an important message for us. I knew he'd had such an ability to receive messages from the Other Side ever since his NDE, but now I was witnessing it firsthand.

Although the message didn't pertain to the subject of animals, it did pertain to a very specific situation—an upcoming move—and very specific advice regarding that move that Jameth and I really needed to hear at that time. We took the advice very seriously, and it proved to be invaluable to us in events that followed. The move in question changed our lives in a very positive way. There is no way Dannion could have known any of this information. He didn't even know who we were or that we were even a couple, as he referred to us, while delivering this important message. This experience convinced me of the truth in what he had to say, and I am grateful for both the validation and the beneficial advice we received.

Over time, I discovered that others who'd had NDEs echoed Dannion's view that there are indeed animals in the hereafter. In some cases, animals are viewed at a distance during these glimpses of Heaven. In other cases, the animals actually *assist* the people as they make their journey into the afterlife.

I've found that *many* people who have NDEs are greeted on the Other Side by animals. Two such people are Shelley Nunemaker (who was greeted by her deceased cat in addition to other animals and people) and Sharon Callahan (who was greeted exclusively by animals). Their stories follow.

Obie
*Shelley Nunemaker, Part-time Switchboard Operator
and Volunteer Grief Support Group Leader
Texas*

I HAD MY NDE due to complications during open heart surgery. I do not remember leaving my body or going through a tunnel. I just magically appeared in a pure white room. It was like walking into a room of white porcelain, with white air.

In front of me was a small group of animals. I do not remember what kind, except that I remember a sheep and a goat (I'm a city girl who has never been on a farm). To the right of me were three people all dressed in white robes. They were standing as if waiting in line for something.

To the left of me was my precious cat, Obie, who had died about seven years earlier. Ahead of me was the most beautiful man I have ever seen. He had long white hair and was wearing a long white robe. He smiled at me and looked me straight in the eyes. When he did this, I lost all visual aspect of the experience and was overcome with feelings of joy and safety. I was the happiest I had ever been. I remember thinking, *This is so awesome! I want to stay here forever.* And with those thoughts, I was out of there!

Obie was my favorite cat of all time. I had to leave her with my grandmother because when I tried to move her with me she ran away. It took five days for her to get back to my grandmother's. I promised her she could stay. Unfortunately, I soon had to move out of state. I wanted to take Obie so badly, but feared she would be lost. Several years later when my mom called to say that she had to have Obie put to sleep, I was devastated. I had such guilt for not being there with her. I think Obie was there to greet me to let me know that she forgave me and that she was fine. I can't wait to get back to her.

Kim's note: One thing I really like about Shelley's NDE is that she also saw animals that she hadn't known in life, dispelling the notion that we only see animals on the Other Side if we knew them personally.

Sharon Callahan's Near-Death Experience
Sharon Callahan, Animal Communication Specialist/Author
California

Kim's note: Sharon Callahan is the gifted animal communicator already mentioned in previous chapters, who also has the insight that comes from having had a near-death experience. When I interviewed Sharon about her work as an animal communicator, she also talked about her NDE. The following is excerpted from that interview.

WHAT I HAVE FOUND OUT about the spirit realms is that there are many, many levels that people and animal souls can go to when they cross over, and they all look very different. It is almost like Heaven has different departments, or different levels, and each soul after death seeks its own level. On any given level there will be many, many other animal and human souls because, just as we do when we are embodied on Earth, we seek our own level and we seek friends that are interacting with us on that level and in that area of interest that we have. It's not much different after death.

In my experience, from what I have learned from animals and people that have died is that there is no difference between where animals go and where people go. Once we take off the costume that we call our body, we are simply pure spirit, and we then go to whatever level of the afterlife will best serve our own purposes and our own learning.

When I've been shown the afterlife by animals and by people who have gone there, wherever they happen to reside, whatever level it is, there are always animal souls and human souls together in those places; it's not as if they are separated out and all the animals go one lower place or something. It is very much mixed; the animals are in the same place as the people are. Sometimes the animals are guides for the people in some capacity, and sometimes the people are guides for animals. Sometimes they are simply in the same place because they are learning the same thing.

In my own near-death experience, I actually entered a

realm where I was seemingly the only human soul and there was nothing else but animals. I traveled through a tunnel of light, and after what seemed like a very long time (it was actually only a few minutes), I found myself in what appeared to be an alpine meadow full of animals.

My very first thought was, *Am I in Heaven?* When I thought that thought, the animals answered me telepathically and said, "No, you are not in Heaven; you can't go that far. You are going to have to go back." What the animals in this place told me was that it was the place where the blueprints for everything were kept—the blueprints of the earth and different habitats on the earth. Blueprints that different people make for themselves before they come to Earth.

We all make a plan. We all make a blueprint for ourselves before we come. The animals in this place were guardians of the blueprints. This is an example of the fact that there are all kinds of jobs or assignments that one can have on the Other Side, whether you are an animal or a human. These animals' souls in this particular place were there to guard the blueprints for things. They were like the guardians of the earth.

When I had my near-death experience, one of the things that the animals told me was that many of them were able to see the Divine blueprint of their human companion. They were able to see things about the person's life purpose that they had forgotten. What I find a lot in my readings with animals now is that they have things to tell their people about what they should do about aligning their life more directly with their own Divine blueprint and their Divine purpose.

Often, after an animal dies, they will tell me that they have actually gone to the place where the blueprints are kept to look at their person's blueprint so they can then begin to give that person information that is in that blueprint—so that their person can bring their lives more directly in alignment with it. The level of information that the animals have for us is just absolutely extraordinary. They can't tell us everything even when they can see everything, because part of the reason that we come here is to discover things about ourselves. If we could know everything, then there wouldn't be any reason for us to come in the first place. The animals often are our guides. They are our spiritual guides, and they continue that work after their deaths. They can often guide us in ways that make it easier for us to uncover what our own purpose is. The level of information and help that they have for us is beyond what most people can imagine.

My entire flower essence business, the idea for it and the first original eight formulas, were all given to me by my little cat, Shoji, after he died. He communicated with me for months, giving me all the details of what I should do, what essences I should make initially. He still communicates with me six years later.

Kim's note: Sharon explained to me that most of our Divine blueprint is forgotten after childhood; and by adulthood, we remember just enough to cause us to feel a slight restlessness when we are not in alignment with our original plan. This made sense to me as I recalled the restlessness I felt in my own life during the years when I was not doing what I came here to do. I, too, was reminded of my true path by an animal.

Sharon Callahan is an internationally acclaimed animal communicator, creator of Anaflora flower essences for animals, and author of *Healing Animals Naturally with Flower Essences and Intuitive Listening.* For more information, visit **www.Anaflora.com.**

Beth Hammond's Near-Death Experience

Clara Elizabeth (Beth) Hammond, Law Enforcement
Florida

Kim's note: Although Beth did not actually encounter animals during her NDE, she did receive an important message about them. Following is her story. . . .

I WENT TO THE HOSPITAL for outpatient surgery on my foot. I was afraid to be put to sleep because in the past there had been some complications and they had to shock my heart. I had the surgery, and they put two stainless steel screws in my foot. Off to home I went, feeling okay.

Somewhere between 7:00 and 7:30 P.M., I became really sick. I was vomiting repeatedly till about 3:30 or so in the morning. I was exhausted. The TV was on, and I told my family to just let me sleep on the den sofa. I was so tired I only wanted to go to sleep. I begged, "Just let me go to sleep."

I remember closing my eyes. I was in this long, dark tunnel. I was traveling at the speed of light. As I neared the end of the tunnel, I saw the most brilliant yellow light coming toward me. I was beginning to feel warm. The nearer the light got, the warmer I felt. I could hear myself saying, "Oh God, please let me stay; don't make me go back."

This was the first time in my life that I felt such Divine love. There is no love on Earth with any human being that has this Divine love I experienced. The forgiveness and acceptance was extraordinary. There was so much warmth and compassion that I did not want to return to life. There is no comparison here on Earth. I felt so safe and protected. I never wanted to leave.

I looked more into the light. I saw this amber and green electricity come from it. It became enlarged, and before my eyes I saw my life revealed—every thought, every wish, every desire, and every pain I had imposed on anything or anyone.

I heard a voice say, "Be not afraid, child. It is not your time. You are not through on Earth. Everything has a purpose, and you will have to complete yours before you return. Mankind is doing things the wrong way. Go back and teach humankind that love is what is important. Love one another justly. Help those who cannot help themselves. Teach one another compassion, undying love, and respect. My creatures on Earth, large and small, are here for a purpose. Mankind needs to learn from my creatures. They are here to teach us what is important in life. If you have no love and respect for my creatures whom you have seen, how can you respect me and love me whom you have not seen? Go back and tell the four corners of the earth what is truly important—not which religion. You are but the pure in heart. There will be many wars, poverty, storms upon storms to rage the earth, but will man ever listen? My child, go back and tell."

I AWOKE GASPING FOR AIR—screaming for someone to come to me. I slowly began to relax and began to try to decipher what happened to me. I kept thinking, Maybe I am psychotic or maybe I just dreamed all of this. It was so real. I was shaking. I was afraid to tell even my family for fear of being ridiculed. I began to deny it. I wanted to pretend this didn't happen to me. Why me? I was an ordinary person. Why didn't God pick a priest or religious person? Why me, a nobody?

I went back to my surgeon on the following Monday. I said to him, "Before we get started, I have to talk to someone. I might be losing my mind. I have a story to tell you."

I told the doctor my story. I then asked the doctor, "Has anyone else ever told you something to that effect?"

He said, "I have heard of this before and have been told of such happenings."

I asked him if he thought I was insane.

He said, "No, Mrs. Hammond, I don't. I believe your heart had enough electricity to start back on its own. That was what all the gasping was about. It was not your time."

Kim's note: Beth had never even heard of an NDE when she had her experience, yet it had all of the classic traits described by countless people around the world who have also had near-death experiences. Furthermore, as is often the case, she returned from the experience with gifts she hadn't had before (visions and premonitions that later came true). I was particularly struck by the message Beth received during her NDE. If everyone heeded this message, our world would be a far better place. It is high time that everyone on this planet—including the animals—receive the love, respect, and compassion they deserve. Our animal friends are here to teach us, but it is up to us to listen.

- CHAPTER 8 -

Heavenly Visitors: Feeling a Presence

The best and most beautiful things in the world cannot be seen or even touched. They must be felt with the heart.
— HELEN KELLER

JUST AS WE ARE NOW BEGINNING to realize how common it is to receive contacts from the Other Side upon the passing of a beloved *human,* I've found that the same holds true upon the passing of a beloved *animal.* As I compiled the material that was to eventually become this book, I was amazed to discover that the majority of the stories I gathered were from everyday people who had never been to a medium or animal communicator—and had never had a near-death experience—who had been the subjects of profound, life-changing encounters with the spirits of animals. Many of these people had never before given the afterlife much thought, and they wouldn't have believed in such encounters had they not experienced them firsthand.

Early on, I began putting the word out about my project by placing ads in various publications and posting flyers on bulletin boards everywhere I went, asking if anyone had had experiences that seemed to imply life after death for animals. People soon began contacting me, confiding that they had indeed had such experiences but hadn't shared them with many people, if any, for fear of being ridiculed. In the early days, it seemed that most people who had stories to share were hesitant to use their real names. However, as time went on, I found that the majority of the people were delighted to be included in this project and to disclose their identity.

I also began exhibiting at various animal-related conferences and trade shows, continuing to put out the call for relevant stories. Everywhere I went, people came up to me and shared their own personal experiences. I found that even at unrelated events, such as health conferences, when I put out my flyers and business cards, there was always a handful of people who responded. As the years went on, I found that people from all walks of life had such experiences—cab drivers, teachers, dentists, scientists, you name it. When I put a little blurb about this project on my answering machine, I found that those who called to leave unrelated messages (such as to confirm an appointment) often mentioned that they had, indeed, had such an experience.

Somewhere along the journey, I was connected with a wonderful woman named Judith Guggenheim. She and her former husband, Bill Guggenheim, coined the term "After-Death Communication" (ADC), to describe the experience of being contacted by a loved one who has died. They define an ADC as "a spiritual experience that takes place when a person is contacted directly and spontaneously by a family member or friend who has died." They explain that ADCs are always initiated by the deceased loved ones themselves, without the assistance of mediums or other such helpers or tools.

In their groundbreaking book, *Hello From Heaven!*, Bill and Judith compiled the results of seven years of research in which they interviewed and collected stories from thousands of people who had experienced ADCs. When I first learned of their research, and then went to see Judith when she came to town to give a lecture on the subject, I was delighted—though not surprised—to find that the ADCs they had compiled involving deceased *humans* were remarkably similar to those I was collecting involving *animals*.

Over the years, I gathered stories of people from all walks of life, from around the world, that provide amazing evidence of an afterlife for animals. In some cases, people are contacted by their beloved animal companions in dreams (this is covered in a later chapter); in other cases, their presence is made known in full waking reality, sometimes in the company of more than one witness. These witnesses include humans and sometimes other animals.

Such contacts can take many forms, including sounds, scents, mysteriously moving objects, visual apparitions, and occasionally, fully physical (though temporary) manifestations, which, in some instances, have actually been touched. The witnesses of these contacts are not always loved ones grieving the loss of their own beloved animal companions (and who, according to skeptics, might dream up these experiences as a way of dealing with their grief). Sometimes the witnesses are strangers who don't have prior belief in such experiences and, in some cases, don't even know about the deceased animals they witness until the details are corroborated after the fact.

Many of the stories that follow (in this and subsequent chapters) contain more than one type of contact (such as hearing a sound *and* feeling a touch), so I've categorized them based upon what I feel is the most pronounced aspect of the experience— or where the stories seem to fit best. In this chapter, the most predominant aspect of the stories is what I have categorized as "Feeling a Presence." Now, I'll let the stories speak for themselves. . . .

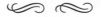

Bo

Al Vickers, Retired Schoolteacher
British Columbia, Canada

IN THE EARLY SPRING, after many wonderful years, my beloved St. Bernard, Bo, died of cancer. My story is about Bo, and is a story that perhaps offers strong evidence of an afterlife for animals.

Before I get into details, I should introduce myself and give you some background information.

I'm a retired teacher who taught high school for twenty-six years in Vancouver, B.C. My wife, Sharon, who is key to this story, is a retired secretary from the Burnaby School Board located in the greater Vancouver area. For ten years, Sharon and I travelled from the rural Fraser Valley to our jobs in Vancouver. Although the daily commute was long and arduous, it was a trade-off that gave us the opportunity to enjoy country living and extra animals (two dogs, three cats, three horses, and two cows).

When the opportunity for early retirement was offered, I left teaching and moved to the Rockies with our two dogs, Sage and Bo. Sage was a twelve-year-old Brittany spaniel and lifetime companion of Bo. Bo was an eleven-year-old St. Bernard and Sage's lifetime companion. Sharon remained on her job for one more year before joining me in our new home.

Shortly after arriving in the Rockies, Bo's health began to deteriorate. Within two months, I decided to return to Vancouver in order to provide Bo with the best possible health care. My heart broke when I learned that Bo had been diagnosed with cancer of the spine. The agony of the situation seemed to outweigh everything, but fortunately did not overshadow my intense desire to embellish her with the unconditional love she had blessed us with during her lifetime. The last few weeks we had with Bo were filled with intensive care-giving and love.

Sage and I were with Bo twenty-four hours a day. What better way to say good-bye to our beloved Bo? Bo died in my arms, with Sharon at my side and Sage close by.

The intensity of losing Bo was indescribable. The years of devotion, love, and happiness that she had blessed us with would now be memories. True, I was left with precious memories, but it was also true I was left with the painful reality that I would no longer be able to hug Bo and tell her that I loved her. Life would be different.

Several months passed before Sage and I returned to our new home in the Rockies. Sharon, who was still unable to retire, would remain in Vancouver for the next eight months.

The following spring, Sage and I were returning home from one of our weekly trips to town. We were driving the last leg of our trip, which was a 37-kilometre stretch of wilderness road. Knowing that a simple lapse of attention on this lonely road could easily have serious consequences, my thoughts were completely focused on driving safely. No other thoughts were in my mind.

As we got within ten kilometres of home, an astonishing event took place. Without warning and within an instant I found myself overwhelmed with intense feelings of Bo. It was as if an external switch had been thrown, a switch over which I had no control. There was no vision, no sound. My experience was a powerful, overwhelming awareness of Bo. It was loving and real and within seconds brought tears to my eyes.

I should point out that what I experienced was not the same as the feelings one can generate when thinking intensely of a loved one. Such feelings come from within. The source of these feelings was *external*, not internal. My experience was comparable to an arrival. My sudden awareness of Bo had come *to* me and had come *from* some place.

Again, it's important to remember that I was not preoccupied with thoughts of Bo. I was focused on my driving. In addition, where this event occurred had absolutely no special meaning to me, our dogs, or any member of my family.

When I got home, I was still upset and emotionally involved. I knew my experience had not been generated by any thoughts I had had of Bo. The events were unsolicited, external, and overwhelming. I have no doubt that communication had been *directed* to me and involved a spiritual "touching" with Bo. What I had experienced was amazing, but events that were to follow were even more astonishing.

As mentioned earlier, Sharon was still in Vancouver. I did not discuss these events with her nor did I mention them to anyone else. I knew that informing others would most likely result in their outright rejection of my experience or they'd render the event as being the product of an overactive imagination preoccupied with Bo. Knowing these possible outcomes, my silence was assured.

Within three months, Sharon was able to retire from her job and joined Sage and myself in our new home. Again, I made no mention of the events to her. Surprisingly, the events were no longer a part of my inner thoughts, something I now recall with near disbelief.

Shortly after her arrival, Sharon made her first trip to town. When she returned, she was clearly overcome with distress. Her face was flushed, and tears were rolling down her cheeks. She was visually shaken and had difficulty talking.

"Did you hit a deer?" I asked, trying to find out what had happened.

"No, it's Bo!" she sobbed. Scarcely able to talk, she continued. "I was just driving along and had this overwhelming feeling that Bo was with me! And it happened very suddenly!"

"Where did it happen?" I asked, recognizing that her story was incredibly similar to mine.

As Sharon began to describe where she had experienced Bo's presence, a surge of emotion, ranging from disbelief to joy, rushed through me. Sharon's experience had occurred *precisely* where mine had taken place. Without giving her any clues, I had to find out more.

"Were you thinking of Bo at the time?" I asked.

"No. I was paying attention to the road. All of a sudden, Bo was there! I *knew* it was her! I didn't see her and didn't smell* her. It lasted for a minute and then she was gone. And I've cried all the way home!"

"What made you cry?" I asked.

"I don't know. It was just the emotions of it. It was a good feeling. Bo was there and she was okay, but then she was gone! It was a good feeling but upsetting because I felt I had lost her again."

I couldn't believe my ears! I had read of unusual stories before but had never heard anything close to what we had undergone. When I then told Sharon what had happened to me three months earlier, she was dumbfounded. It is difficult to dismiss the incredible independent and parallel events that two sane, well-educated adults experienced. With our independent, identical experiences occurring at precisely the same place, we knew Bo had blessed us with the most precious gift of all—her eternal, unconditional love.

Her gift, however, went well beyond that. Our incredible experiences with Bo have made it clear that her life continues, that she is somewhere, and that she is well. If this is true for Bo, it is true for all animals. Additionally, she has shown Sharon and myself that she has an ongoing interest in both of us and has provided me with a strong awareness that she will be waiting for us when it is our time to move on. If this is true for us, then it is true for all who have suffered the loss of a beloved pet.

I SHOULD POINT OUT that while living in the Fraser Valley, the number 26 seemed to reoccur in our lives on a regular basis. I was 26 years of age when I started teaching. I taught for exactly 26 years before early retirement. Our street address was 260, the last four digits of our telephone number were 2626, and our property was located on District Lot 26. Again, when we moved to the Rockies, our new home was located on District Lot 26. But the most amazing 26 of all is located where both Sharon and I encountered Bo. There, posted to a tree, is a sign that reads: "Kilometre 26."

When Bo died, Sharon took Sage for a walk in our back pasture. At that time, and again two months later, Sharon detected a pleasant scent that was "distinctly Bo."

Kim's note: The phenomenon of smelling a familiar scent is a relatively common form of contact from the Other Side. This will be covered in a later chapter.

Shadow

Diane Arend, Project Manager-Systems Asset Management
New Jersey

I WOULD FIRST LIKE TO TELL YOU a bit about me. I am a thirty-eight-year-old devoted wife (twenty years) and a mother of a seventeen-year-old. My mom told me, ever since I was a baby—under the age of two—I was nuts over dogs. I would see a dog—any dog—and go crazy, like other kids might when they see their most wanted toy. My mom always said that my reaction and behavior were rather intense as a child when it came to dogs.

Well, as I matured, every year my Christmas wish list was always the same. (And it often *is* the same.) Anything to do with dogs. Particularly, I loved Doberman pinschers.

Well, my love continued. I now have four Doberman pinschers and a min pin [miniature pinscher]. My very first Doberman, Shadow, was a really sweet dog. My family had a couple of other dogs at the time. We were considering getting a Dobie and there were no puppies available at the time. However, there was a young dog that was a year old who needed a home. He had been with a couple that broke up and now he badly needed to bond with a new family. I was told he was a sweet dog.

My husband was rather concerned at this point. He was worried about getting a dog at a year old . . . and he was nervous about Dobermans. But Shadow changed not only my husband's opinion about Dobies; he also had a great impact on our lives.

When we went to get him, Shadow somehow knew right then and there that we were his new family and he was going home. It was so odd. We talked to his caretakers, while Shadow walked around the room. Then, Shadow came over to us (my husband, daughter, and myself) and lay down next to us. In fact, he leaned on our feet. This dog had just met us for the first time. He really did act like he *knew* he was going home.

Well, he also took very quickly to the other two dogs at home. Within a day, it was like we'd always had him since he was a puppy.

Years went by. When Shadow was about four, we began to notice that he was bumping into things. Shadow went blind. We brought him to every doctor and specialist under the sun and spent loads of money trying to find out what was wrong and what caused his vision to go. No one could tell us what caused his blindness. Many guesses were made, but certainly nothing definite; and more than certainly, nothing that would bring his vision back.

Knowing this, we were sure not to move any furniture in the house or leave anything out in the way to upset him. He lived fine like this for over a year. But then we noticed he had lost his sense of smell and he also had seizures. We felt so bad for him and our hearts broke. We loved Shadow so much. He had his hearing, but he could no longer see or smell. His only sense left was his hearing. When we would go to make his food, he would hear the bowl filling, but when we set it down for him to eat, he couldn't smell for it. We had to guide his head over the bowl so he could find his dinner and eat. He was on steroids for a while because of the seizures, and he began to lose control of his urine.

Shadow became very unhappy and frustrated—to the point of anger at his disability. He began to snap at other dogs, and things startled him. Our boy's day had come to make that step over the Rainbow Bridge.

I brought him to the vet to be euthanized, as there was nothing else that could be done for him and he was suffering. I sat on the floor and hugged him and kissed him as I talked to him. I wanted to be with him to the last minute.

I hugged him, kissed him, and told him how much I loved him . . . and that I would miss him so much. The doctor gave him the medication that ended his suffering . . . and sent him on his way to the heavens. Heaven, where I am certain all dogs go, and all dogs *do* have souls . . . regardless of what some people believe.

After my Shadow was gone, I felt this *tremendous* rip of heartbreak and pain. I screamed and cried like a four-year-old. I was devastated. I hurt so badly. As I struggled to regain my strength to bring my body up from the floor where I had sat next to my boy—my friend—I also struggled for a decent breath that wasn't labored from sobbing. I felt like I had just been stabbed.

I stood, looked at my vet, and said, "Please take good care

of my boy, and thank you for all you have tried to do for him." I walked out of the vet's office, still crying like a child, not caring who saw me—or what they thought. I didn't care, for my grief was so deep and so raw, I could not suppress it, much less contain myself.

I slowly walked to my car, opened the door and got in. I took in another deep breath, waiting to see how long it would be before I should trust myself to drive. I let out another belt of a cry and said aloud in the car, "I miss you Shadow . . . I hate this . . . I miss you so bad . . . I love you," tears just flowing down my cheeks, my shirt already saturated, my nose stuffed beyond air.

It was not more than a few minutes. Then, all of a sudden, I sensed my dog's soul—his being—come to me and pass through me. It was as if his soul left the hospital, and hearing my cries, came to me—and I felt his presence. It was such a real and profound feeling that I was stunned by its impact and reality. It was almost as abrupt as someone snapping their fingers to get your attention.

I immediately felt this overwhelming sense of peace and that all was okay. For I know, am positive—beyond any doubt—that when it is my turn to pass over to the other side of the Rainbow Bridge, I will see my boy again. For I know the depth of a human and dog relationship and the strong bonds that remain . . . long after the two separate.

Kurgan
Mary, Health Care Administrator
Illinois

A FRIEND OF MINE HAD A DOG named Kurgan. Kurgan has always had a special place in my heart, and I spent a lot of time with him before he passed from cancer. I am . . . oh, let's call it spiritually connected . . . I do energy work, crystal healing, and I sometimes see auras and feel and know things that others do not. Many of my visits to Kurgan prior to his passing were spent doing energy work, so I felt very connected to him. The day he was euthanized, the vet said that due to his size, he would likely need three injections. I felt him pass (a great "whoosh") after the second injection, and the vet confirmed his death right after that.

Several times since Kurgan's passing, I have felt him for a couple of seconds, but I had a "knowing" that when he gave us a sign, there would be wind involved. I should also tell you that my friend (I hate to say Kurgan's "owner" because they were best friends) felt great comfort in reading the poem about the Rainbow Bridge where dog spirits play together in a green field and wait for their humans to pass so that they can cross the bridge together.

I had read several accounts of people who saw rainbows in the strangest places after their pets had passed. My first strong feeling of Kurgan involves rainbows. One evening when I was out walking my dogs, I stopped to speak with an elderly neighbor. He kept looking over my shoulder in a strange manner. He finally said, "Is that a rainbow?" I turned around, and in a sky with absolutely no clouds, there was a very pale rainbow. I tried telling myself that it was nothing—a trick of a soon-to-be-setting sun. I brushed it off and kept walking.

About ten minutes later, the wind really picked up. I especially noticed it because my dogs were straining at the leash to catch little bits of paper and leaves that were blowing around. I suddenly "felt" Kurgan, looked up at the sky, and there were *two* rainbows, one inside the other (concentric). I had never seen anything like it in my life!

[*Kim's note:* The subject of rainbows will be covered in a later chapter.]

My second awareness of Kurgan came just this afternoon. When Kurgan passed away, my friend donated some of Kurgan's toys to Pet Rescue, but he also allowed me to give some of them to my dogs. One of Kurgan's toys was on the floor near me (which was not uncommon). I suddenly thought that I felt Kurgan. I would have brushed it off as strong memories of him because of the proximity of the toy, if one of my dogs hadn't done something. My male dog loves to initiate play with anyone that will give him attention, but his favorite "victim" is his sister. When he initiates play, he will set a toy down in front of her and take his nose and nudge it toward her and sit there and look at her, and then nudge it again.

He did that this afternoon, and when she didn't express any interest, I expected him to bring it to me and do the same. What he did instead was set the toy down in front of the place where I felt Kurgan and then nudged it toward the "empty" space next to Kurgan's toy. I knew in that moment that Kurgan was really here.

Casey
Name withheld for privacy

ON A SUNDAY AFTERNOON, our beautiful seven-and-a-half-year-old golden retriever, Casey, died suddenly, running in the yard, of an apparent heart attack. Our family was instantly devastated by this horrible event. Our female golden retriever, Cobey, grieved, and the cat yowled at the door all night. It was one of the worst things to ever happen to our family.

In the weeks after his death, our female golden, Cobey, would suddenly start growling for no apparent reason; the hair on her back would stand up and she would look up in the air at a corner of the family room. This happened a couple times and I didn't pay too much attention. I wondered if maybe it was Casey's spirit coming back to visit. It was kind of unnerving, but something was definitely going on.

One night, I was home alone watching TV and Cobey started the growling thing again for about twenty minutes. This time the cat was there, and he was looking up at the corner of the family room, too. This time I just watched, and I really believe I felt Casey's presence in that room. I know *for sure* that he was there. All of a sudden, Cobey then stopped her growling, walked over, and laid down in the very spot where Casey always slept, and curled up and went to sleep, perfectly content. She has never slept in that spot before or since.

My husband also said he felt Casey's presence on a number of occasions when he was sitting out in the backyard under the tree by his grave. But by far the most compelling instances were the ones in the family room, where my other golden was aware of something in the room with us. I would not have known about these times if it weren't for her reaction. There was definitely something in that room with us. And every time, she looked up at a corner of the room and growled and barked.

Since I feel that night I was given the message that he was "all right" the occurrences have stopped. I think he has gone across to the Other Side, and that night was his way of reaching us. I have felt better about his death since then, and know that we will all be together again someday.

Tassi
Karen M. Lambert, Retired Social Worker
California

MY ELEVEN-MONTH-OLD PUPPY, Tassi, passed away one May. She was a gorgeous and rambunctious half Husky and half Chow. She was with my husband and me all the time—in the car, in the parks—as we are both retired. We bonded so closely with her that she was a member of the family. I even made her "people food" like taquitos. She was my baby. Fifty-five pounds with a glorious red coat, she filled my life. I was newly retired from a back injury, and she made the transition easier.

She was poisoned, unknown to us, by the ivy next to our cul-de-sac. Secretly, the homeowner's association was putting rat poison in the ivy without telling the owners. She loved to run in the ivy, and she would swipe bones and other things that I pulled out of her mouth. She lost twenty-two pounds within two weeks, and the veterinarian was puzzled and assumed it was allergies. When the liver scan came back showing severe liver damage, she had to be euthanized. It was agonizing to do this to a dog less than a year old.

Over the next two to three weeks, she came to visit us from the Other Side.

First, there was a strange occurrence in her play area outside. She had a favorite little rubber blue ball. Just after she crossed over, it moved. It would be on one side of the gate one morning, and on the other side of the gate the next morning. It was as if she were nudging it with her nose from the Other Side.

Next, her favorite chair, a heavy wood piece, was pushed back four feet off the area rug onto the tile flooring. She would play with my husband, Jerry, over and over each day when she was alive, against that chair.

I felt such anger that Jerry had allowed Tassi to run in the ivy, as I knew it harbored unsafe conditions. Every time that I expressed anger at my husband, the chair would be pushed back four feet when I awoke the next morning.

I finally understood that she was telling me from the Other

Side that she loved and adored Jerry, and for me to stop blaming him for the poisoning. I would awaken in the middle of the night, and it would be pushed back, just telling me of her unconditional love for him.

When I called her to me one day, I felt her presence in the room and told her I was no longer angry at Jerry.

The next morning, all the area rugs (used to brighten a home filled with ceramic tile) were pushed up against the sides of the walls. My cat could never have done this, as the rugs were heavy and bulky. I know that Tassi made it known to me that she was joyful at the knowledge I now carried with me. The knowledge, not only that we communicate with our pets on the Other Side, but also that love is all there is. She was so happy that I was filled with love instead of anger.

She never returned to play anymore. She had delivered her message.

Although she does not return for mischief, I can call her to me anytime that I wish. I feel her presence in the room, her sweet fur next to my leg. When I want her there, she is there. I know because my heart feels warm and loving. She comes to me late at night to say, "I love you."

Love continues, no matter what being you are. It endures for eternity.

Buddy

Gwen Gerow, Resource Engineer
New York

MY HUSBAND AND I have been married almost twelve years and don't have any children, but have had the good fortune of sharing our home with three wonderful pets, two cats (Buddy and Rex) and a dog (Mocha). They have been part of our lives ever since we've been married and are truly cherished members of our family. Buddy was the oldest (he would have been thirteen this year) and was the best companion I could have ever asked for. We shared a very special bond.

Buddy was always, always my cat. He followed me everywhere, inside the house or out. From room to room, even across the street to the neighbor's house, he would sit on the front porch looking in the door, waiting for me to come back out. My husband always said he was more like a dog than a cat. He was very social, always wanting to be involved whenever we had company (Rex, on the other hand, would hide). I could go on and on about him; he was so intelligent, he knew things that I have no idea how he learned. But above all, he always wanted to be with me. He couldn't wait for me to sit down (usually in our favorite chair) so he could join me, and at night he always slept on the bed with me, either on my pillow, or in the crook of my right arm with his head on my shoulder and front leg across my neck. Sometimes during the night, or on warm evenings, he would move to the foot of the bed, but as soon as I woke up, he'd be right back at the top. He always had such a strong personality and presence in our house; and was always a huge source of comfort to me during times of stress, sadness, happiness, or any other time.

I have experienced the loss of older family members, childhood pets, and even the death, five years ago, of a very close friend who was thirty-three years old at the time. As difficult as that was, nothing compares to the profound feelings of grief that I experienced with the loss of Buddy. I fell into a deep depression, I couldn't sleep or eat, and my stomach was upset all time. I had huge issues of unresolved guilt (for not taking him to the vet sooner and not being with him when he died), and just felt like part of myself died along with Buddy. I felt like there was no joy left in my life and that I would never be able to be happy again.

I would like to share some things that I have experienced since Buddy's death, things that I considered to be "communications" from him. I have had to be cautious as to who I could share these with, since my husband basically thinks that I'm losing my mind, and my mother thinks that I need to stop dwelling on it. Let's face it, many people don't feel that the loss of a pet should be a big deal, and there just aren't many resources for people like myself who are struggling with this type of loss.

First, I feel I should tell you just a little about myself. I have a degree in mechanical engineering and a master's degree in business administration. It's my nature to always look for logical explanations for things that happen; I'm trained to gather facts and evidence to support theories.

It was about two weeks after Buddy died when things began to happen. All of our pets have made a habit out of coming in the bathroom whenever I'm in there. There is a spot on the wall where Buddy would always go to, reach all the way up, and stretch. Through the years of doing this, some distinct sets of prints can be seen from where his feet wore the paint away. Before Buddy died, I'd been telling myself that I needed to get that wall painted; now I can't bear the thought of covering those paw prints up!

Anyway, one day I was in the bathroom and Rex came in. My heart almost stopped when I realized that he had gone right over to the spot where Buddy used to stretch. My only thought at the time was that Rex was going to do the same thing, which he had never, ever done. In fact, he never paid any attention to it before. There he was, in the exact spot that Buddy would have been standing in to stretch, except Rex had his nose at the base of the wall and was sniffing intently. Then, he lifted his head all the way up and put his nose directly on the first spot, about twelve inches off the floor. Then he turned to his right, still sniffing very intently, then turned around to his left, again sniffing, and stared into the corner of the room. I watched in amazement, not having a clue what could be going on. I couldn't think straight at that time anyway; I was so sick with grief.

After a short time, Rex just turned and walked away. I didn't know what happened, but I felt touched that, at the very least, Rex was thinking about Buddy. It wasn't until afterward that I began to consider the possibility that Rex was sensing Buddy's presence in the room but couldn't figure out for himself where Buddy was.

It was about this time that I had a series of very vivid dreams about Buddy that happened over the course of several nights. I had not once dreamt about Buddy until that time, and haven't since.

One morning, maybe a week after I had the dreams, I walked into the front hall to get something. I suddenly had the strongest sensation that Buddy was there with me, like if I turned and looked down he would have been standing right behind me. This sensation only lasted a few seconds, then was gone. I was confused because I didn't know why that would happen in a place that I didn't really associate with Buddy, and thought that something in the area must have triggered a memory that made me feel that way, although I couldn't figure out what it could have been. There was nothing that should have done that. I kept going back to the hallway and repeating my motions to see if I could get the sensation again, but nothing happened and I guess I just dismissed the whole thing.

I thought about the bathroom incident with Rex, and the sensation I had in the hallway, things that I had perhaps not recognized for what they may have really been. I have some pictures of Buddy on the kitchen counter, one in a frame with some of his fur inside the glass. I jokingly refer to this area as "Buddy's Shrine." I walked over to it and said, out loud (my husband wasn't around at the time), that I was sorry for not recognizing those two times when he may have been trying to get through to me, and I promised, if he ever did again, that I would. This was in the afternoon, and I left the house for a while that evening, basically forgetting about the whole thing.

I came home later that night and went to bed as I normally would. I was alone since my husband was working nights. It was around 4 A.M. when this really profound thing happened. Again, this is hard to describe. I wasn't dreaming; there was nothing leading up to this. It was as if I was just sleeping, and my mind's eye opened up. I looked down at the foot of the bed, between my legs, and there was Buddy, lying on the bed and looking directly at me. I don't know what this was, but it was very real.

I woke up immediately and said, out loud, "Hi, Buddy, hi, baby" (I always called him "baby"). The thing is, when I woke up, I was lying in exactly the same position as when I saw Buddy, flat on my back with my arms to the side, not a normal sleeping position for me. I remember being thankful that my husband wasn't there, since he thought I was losing my mind as it was, and that Rex was lying next to the bed and knew what was happening. I then fell right back to sleep.

When I woke up in the morning, I remembered this "dream" vividly. Replaying it in my mind while in the shower, it occurred to me what I had said to Buddy the afternoon before, that I was sorry for not acknowledging his presence. I don't believe in coincidences and can't help but think that the two things are directly related. All day long I felt so grateful that this, whatever it was, had happened. Of all the things that I have experienced, this was by far the most bizarre. I have no explanation for what it was. It definitely wasn't a dream. Since then, I haven't picked up on any more signs from Buddy.

I miss him so much, but I am so thankful for the signs he gave me, signs that helped me get through a very, very difficult time. I am so thankful that he shared his life with us, and helped open our eyes to the possibility that there is something more beyond a physical existence, although the lesson is a hard one. And I'd also like to add that just writing this story down has helped me immensely. If no one else ever reads it, I'm still glad I did it. I will always remember the things that have happened and their amazing effect on me.

- CHAPTER 9 -

A Touch of Heaven

If I have any beliefs about immortality,
it is that certain dogs I have known will go
to Heaven, and very, very few persons.

— JAMES THURBER

AFTER HIS CAT DOOIE DIED, Thomas Goheen, an electronics repairman in California, had reason to believe that Dooie was still around. On several occasions, he felt Dooie rubbing against his leg as if the cat was really there. When this happened, the sensation was, in his words, "very, very cold—I mean, almost ice cold." It is very common to feel a drop in temperature during a contact from the spirit world. Perhaps this is, in part, why some people feel goose bumps during such encounters.

The first time it happened was the night before Thomas got a new cat, two months after Dooie died. As Thomas put it:

> I went down to the pound and found a new cat, and they had to put a hold on him for a week. Then, the night before we brought the new cat home, I felt the cold rubbing sensation. The day we brought the cat home, I felt it again. The rubbing sensation was very pronounced. I was in the kitchen and I felt him rubbing against my legs (Dooie was very well known for rubbing against our legs); and then the day we got the new cat, I felt Dooie rubbing against my

117

legs many more times. It hasn't happened since—I kind of hope it does.

Perhaps Dooie was checking in on Thomas and giving the new cat his blessing.

Then there was Regina Fetrat, who shared the following experience:

> I once had a rabbit named April. He died after being with me for several years. When he was alive, he would hop on my ankles to waken me and get his ears rubbed at night and early morning. After April died, I felt him on my ankles just like normal, while I was awake. This went on for many weeks.

OVER THE YEARS, I collected many stories very similar to these. Following are more examples. . . .

Boozer
J.D. Stanger, Product Manager (Purchasing)
California

SEVERAL YEARS AGO, my husband and I shared our life with a beautiful yellow (neutered) tomcat named Boozer. Boozer lived with us for almost twelve years. Our darling boy was taken from us when a car struck him at the edge of our driveway. I was heartbroken. For days and nights, all I could do was cry. I missed him so much.

One night I was in bed, lying face down and crying into my pillow. I felt Boozer jump up on the foot of the bed and walk alongside me. He walked all the way up to the side of my face, and I felt his nose touch me. I know it was him; this had been a routine with us when he was alive—he always did exactly the same thing when he was ready to find his spot to sleep. This time he came not to nap but to kiss Mom "bye for now." It brought me tremendous peace, and I was able to start the healing process.

Bindu
*Eliyana Scott, Motion Picture Projectionist
and Holistic Massage Therapist
California*

I'D LIKE TO TELL YOU A STORY about my dog Bindu. I rescued him when he was about three years old, by the vet's estimation, and we lived together for eighteen years after that. Bindu was a very affectionate, intelligent, protective, and loving dog. During our many years together, whenever I stood at the kitchen sink to wash dishes, he would walk over to me and give me one little lick on my left leg, about three inches above my ankle. After that he would turn and walk to my left, circle around a few times, and then sit down with his back against the wall, where he could watch me. Even if he had been asleep in another room when I started to wash the dishes (which was sometimes the case when he was older), he would invariably wake up and come to give me his little doggie kiss on my left leg before settling down to rest at his usual spot against the kitchen wall.

Eventually Bindu died. I was too upset to work that day so instead I went for a walk in the woods, seeking a peaceful place where I could calm my emotions and be undisturbed as I spoke with Bindu's spirit. As I sat on a log at the side of a creek, sunlight filtered softly through the leaves and I began to relax, listening to the soft, peaceful sounds of the water as it gurgled over rocks and twigs. Birds sang out in answer to each other's calls. Tiny insects stopped to drink from the creek, and occasionally a pair of winged maple seeds or a leaf would slowly float to the ground. I was aware of the nurturing presence of all of nature supporting me as I sat there.

I talked to Bindu just as you would talk to a best friend. I spoke out loud, freely expressing all of my thoughts and feelings about our years together. Bindu was my first dog. He enriched my life tremendously. He helped me to more fully experience and understand what love is. It was an honor and a joy to have had the opportunity to live with this wonderful, loving being. I thanked Bindu and all of the nature spirits who were there with me as I

119

spoke. After I finished saying everything that I wanted to say, I felt a sense of completion and inner peace.

About a week or so later, while I was in the kitchen washing dishes and my other dog, Honey Pie, was asleep on a bed in another room, I felt a little lick on my left leg in *exactly* the same spot where Bindu always gave me his doggie kiss. I could physically feel it—a light little kiss. It felt like I was being gently touched just at the edge of my skin's surface. It was the kind of touch that you would feel if you gently touched the hair growing out of your skin, but didn't actually touch the skin's surface.

I was so surprised that I looked down in shock at my left leg and the place where Bindu always stood as he did this. To my delight and surprise, I realized that I could sense exactly where his spirit body was as he turned and walked away from my leg toward his usual place against the kitchen wall, where he circled several times and then sat down to let me know that he was watching over me. This only happened once, but once was enough. Bindu came back to teach me that love lives forever.

Bobby

Mary Pavlik, Homemaker
New Jersey

WE HAD A FAMILY PET—a white poodle named Bobby. We had him for many, many years, and he was adored so much. He died on my birthday. He was hit by a car. He tried so hard to hang on, but we lost him.

About one week or so after his passing, I would actually feel the presence of him around. Now, my mother and brother thought I was nuts...but I could actually point to the spot where I felt he was sleeping.

After a few more weeks, my brother would feel something jumping up on the end of his bed. It would freak him out, and I would tell my brother, "It's Bobby." Bobby loved sleeping on the end of my brother's bed.

Then, more time went by, and my mother would feel something brushing up against her leg . . . and again, I said it was Bobby. So, eventually they started to believe me! Now, they were experiencing the same thing I'd been feeling all along.

I would be outside in the yard, and time and time again, I would see our other dog, Rusty (a large Irish setter), running in the yard, playing . . . and all of a sudden I would see a white flash running behind Rusty. Bobby used to always chase Rusty around the yard . . . always . . . and he still did even after his passing!

The presence of Bobby hung around our home for about a year. Finally, one day, I said to my mom, "Bobby's presence is gone. He is finally gone. He went off to Heaven." My mom was saddened by that, and she said she felt the same thing. No one brushing up against her leg . . . no one jumping on my brother's bed. His presence was gone. But I told her not to be sad; he finally found his way to the Light and accepted his passing.

Still, every now and then, I see that white flash running by . . . and I know in my heart that he will be with us forever. . . .

Kim's note: As this story illustrates, even after our loved ones have gone on to Heaven, they can still come back to visit anytime.

Lil Guy

Patte Purcell, Host, The Next Dimension *Radio Show*
Nevada

MY LIL GUY kitty of seventeen years got very ill and we decided to let him go to sleep after struggling to keep him alive. The day we took him in I told him that I loved him and that I wanted him to come back to let me know he was okay.

The night after he passed, I got his clear signal. He used to sleep on my pillow every night, and in the middle of the night he would tap me on the head until I woke up and gave him some treats. The night after he died, in the middle of the night I felt such a strong tap on my head that it woke me up out of a sound sleep. Shortly afterwards, both my husband and I felt a jump on the bed. He woke up, too, and we both said, "It's Lil Guy."

We got a couple of kittens shortly afterwards, and they both would stare at the hall like someone was coming in. I asked one of the mediums I had on my radio show if Lil Guy was there, and she said it was him. He was just breaking in the new kittens.

I've also been told that there are three spirit kitties around me: one black one (Lil Guy), one orange one (Felix), and another dark one (Smoochie). These are all kitties that have passed. I still miss them, but it's nice to know that they are still around me.

Biscuit

Kendra Thompson, Student
New Jersey

FRISKY, WHOM I LATER affectionately nicknamed Biscuit, was a cat I brought home when I was eleven years old. Though I never had a single year growing up without at least one cat, I considered Biscuit my first cat because she was the first to live with me in my present home and also because she was the first pet I had that would teach me the bonds that surpass friendship . . . that only a pet could provide. Though after her, a few more cats had joined the family, Biscuit was my closest buddy. I could never sit down without her coming over to me and jumping into my lap. If I was lying down on my stomach, she'd curl up on my back near my shoulders . . . as close as she could get to my face, and she always slept in bed with me at night, without fail.

When she was twelve years old, she developed mammary cancer. We decided at the vet's office that surgery seemed the best option. After surgery, she wasn't the same. The incision went from her neck down to her groin, and she lost balance in her back legs. After the biopsy from the surgery, the vet told us the cancer had spread to her lymph nodes and other areas and that lung cancer would probably be what would ultimately end her life. She passed on only three months after that painful surgery that I wish I had never allowed.

Even though she had an incision that practically cut her in half, and her back legs were not working properly (preventing her from jumping), every night even after the surgery, she would stumble to the bed and try to jump up. She would fall down, though; she didn't have the strength to get all the way on top of the bed, so I picked her up and brought her into bed with me. Our best moments over the last few years were at night just before I went to sleep. I called her the "pillow snatcher" because whatever pillow I chose for that night, she had to lie on . . . as long as she was on top of my face. During these times, I would talk to her while she kneaded my face and purred her unique, high-pitched squeaky purr. Then, eventually, after I'd fallen asleep, she'd curl up in between my legs. It felt like she was strapping the blanket over my legs, but she loved to do it, so I let her.

A few nights after her death, as I was lying in bed about to fall asleep, I felt someone jump onto the bed. I checked to see who was there, but I was all alone. So I made myself comfortable under the covers again and shrugged the feeling off. Then I felt, so distinctly, someone curling up in between my legs and the feel of the blanket strapping them. Without the slightest doubt in my mind, Biscuit came to bed with me one last night.

Rest in Peace, PeeWee

*Azar "Ace" Attura, Artist, Photographer, Animal Rescuer
Virginia*

Kim's note: The first part of this very creative story is told from the perspective of the cat, giving us a chance to feel what it must be like to be on the other end of such experiences.

HOW MANY YEARS HAS IT BEEN? How many more kittens will I give birth to? I am so tired! I feel so sick! Wish my beloved would come back for me. . . . At night, I hear her crying and I want to comfort her, but I can't. She asks the Big One if she can come and bring me home; the Big One always says "No!"

The Kind Old Lady feeds me and *all* the cats here in this empty lot, but at night when I lie under these rocks, in the rain, the cold, the snow, with ice under my paws, I hear my beloved crying for me. I want to go to her, but I don't know where to find her!

My fur used to glisten. I was lovingly brushed every morning—like a mama's tongue licking me. My beloved told me how she took me home with her when I was very young. I remember seeing her when my eyes first opened—I thought she *was* my Mama! She fed me with a bottle, taught me how to potty, taught me everything I needed to know about being a *cat*. I'm so proud of her! She fed me tasty food and played with me before she went out the door every day. When she came back, she was so happy to see me—I loved her so!

The Big One was usually kind to me. But she would *not* let me sleep with my beloved! She locked me in the small room with the big tub, where I would cry, and then fall asleep. Sometimes my beloved would sneak me into her bed—that was fun!

Oh, I feel so *very* sick. The night is cold, I feel so alone!

I am getting up now, but I don't see anything. I feel myself walking, but I can't see anything.

Oh! *There is my beloved!* She's awake! *Beloved, can you see me?* I will jump on your bed, I will walk on your legs, I will stand on your chest, I will give you a love bite, just like I used to do! There! *Oh, my beloved—I have found you!* But now . . . I feel so strange!

I WOKE UP at 2 A.M. one cold October, four years after I had to leave my much-loved kitty PeeWee behind in the Bronx when moving to Virginia. (How I cried—Mom refused to spay PeeWee, and the only home I could find was with a kind lady who fed her cats but let them wander! PeeWee! I *never* wanted to leave you, but I was only fifteen years old, and Mom said I had to leave you behind!)

I suddenly felt something jumping on the bed, sitting on my chest, giving my hand a love bite. Was this PeeWee? Nothing was visible, yet I was wide awake! PeeWee had come in spirit to say good-bye to me.

Buster

Renee Pastman, Homemaker
Florida

I RESCUED BUSTER at only four weeks old from a lady who was sick. Her dog was the mother. She couldn't afford the puppies and was sending them to the pound in three days. I immediately bonded with him and took him home. I had only been married for one week and we already had a stray dog named Molly that we had gotten two years before.

Buster was so smart and trained very easily in anything we tried. When I became pregnant, Buster even knew before I did. Molly tried to jump in my lap, which she had done so many times, but Buster pulled her back and wouldn't let her near me. I had always heard that dogs sometimes had a keen sense about these things, so I took a test, and sure enough, I was pregnant. Things were going great; we had a nice house with a huge yard, and I gave birth to a beautiful daughter.

Then we had a job opportunity come up, which meant we had to move a thousand miles away. On the day we were moving, everything changed. Normally the dogs were in the house, especially at night, but we had everything out and were packing, so they were outside. I had gotten a "tie out" [long leash that attaches to a stake in the ground] for each of the dogs because we didn't have any trees for a run. Molly had broken her "tie out" so she had to go into the basement, but I left Buster outside on his.

We had been gone for about four hours to take some things to my mother's house, and when I pulled up in the yard, I saw my Buster just lying there not moving. I knew right away he was dead, but I rushed to his side and tried to get him loose. He was still warm, so I thought maybe I could still save him. It was too late; my Buster was gone. I couldn't bury him myself, so I had to call animal control to come and get him. I have never been so sick with grief.

We still had to finish packing and leave that night as we had planned to. I was so glad to leave that house and the terrible memory.

When we got to our new place, I was in bed trying to relax and go to sleep. Then I heard a bark—not Molly's bark, but Buster's bark—and then I felt a huge indentation in the bed behind my legs. Buster slept that way with me every night. I didn't think anything of it and went on to sleep. It was only when I woke up the next morning that I realized Buster was gone and it couldn't have been him. Molly always sleeps under the bed and weighs about fifty pounds less than Buster did.

Since then, I have still been dealing with the grief, but each day it gets better. I know that just by telling this story I feel like I can find closure.

Pooh
Melissa French, Student
Colorado

WHEN I WAS AROUND SEVEN, my parents got me my first dog, a cute little white cockapoo named Pooh with a tail that reminded me of a pig's. When I think about him, I can remember dressing him up in doll clothing and walking him down the street. I think it might have hurt his pride a little, but he put up with everything I did.

When he was three, he got out of the house and vanished. We looked for him for hours; we went from house to house to no avail. We decided to give up our search until the next day. When we got home, we had a message from a vet. They had Pooh and it didn't look too good for him. Some boys thought it would be fun to run him over with their car. Luckily, a lady saw what happened and rushed him to the vet, to no avail. He died an hour later from a bruised heart and a punctured lung. It hurt to know that I didn't even get to say good-bye.

The next morning, God gave him a chance to tell me good-bye. I woke up with him on my feet. I didn't see him, but I felt his weight on me (and no, it wasn't a dream; I was awake) for a good thirty minutes until he decided to get off the bed.

Later on that day, my mom was cleaning house when he scratched on the door to be let out. When my mom heard this, she opened the door. She didn't see him, but she heard him and felt his presence. Not five minutes later, he scratched again to be let in the house.

That evening when we were all watching TV, he walked in front of the television. My mom, dad, and I all saw him, not like he would look when he was alive, but more of a white blur walking in front of the TV. God gave him a day to say his good-byes.

Kim's note: A compelling aspect of this story is that it involves several different types of contact, including not only feeling Pooh's presence and his touch, but also hearing and seeing him. The latter two phenomena will be explored in later chapters.

Willy
Audrey Cornelius, Retired
California

I GOT MY CAT, WILLY, when he was just six weeks old. Eventually, he got sick and I had to take him into the emergency animal hospital. He was there two weeks, after having two surgeries, then died two days before his third birthday. Needless to say, I was heartbroken.

One week later, I had my first "experience." I was lying in bed and felt a movement and the bed vibrated, then pressure against my legs, which is where Willy used to lie all the time. I did not know what to think of this and wondered if I had imagined it, but two nights later I was lying on my stomach when I felt footprints up my back, then suddenly a loud purring and a face rubbing against mine. I was scared, elated, and excited. I was on a high for the rest of the day.

Several nights later, same thing. He came up and put his face against mine and this time I was not scared and put out my arm and felt *fur!* I talked to him and said, "I love you, Willy." Then he was gone. My bedroom is quite dark, but I did make out a large dark blob, which must have been his head.

I have also heard him meowing in the night beside my bed a couple of times. I did not believe in animals' afterlife, but as you can imagine, now I do!

- CHAPTER 10 -

Music to My Ears

You think dogs will not be in Heaven?
I tell you, they will be there long before any of us.
— ROBERT LOUIS STEVENSON

WHEN THOMAS GOHEEN of Fullerton, California, distinctly felt
Dooie the cat rubbing against his leg even after Dooie had died,
this wasn't his only indication that his beloved cat was still very
much around.

When Dooie was alive, each night he had slept in a chair in
the kitchen until around 4 A.M., when he wanted to be let out.
So, he would walk down the long hallway from the kitchen to the
bedroom. Thomas explains:

> He would look in my bedroom and "meow," which
> meant he wanted to be let out, so I would get up—and then
> he would zip down the hall to the door. If I didn't get up
> quickly enough, he would "meow" again, and a minute or so
> after that he would "meow" a third time, more forcefully. . . .
> Well, a couple of nights ago, it was around four in the morn-
> ing and I heard this "meow" from the hallway. I looked
> down the hall and, of course, there was nothing there, but
> that's just what he used to do and when he used to do it.

As time went on, I gathered more and more stories very similar to this one. People also reported hearing such things as the familiar bark of a recently departed dog or the sound of scratching

at the door just as a beloved animal had done when still alive. There was even the case of a dog who, when alive, loved to drink out of the toilet and could still be heard periodically scratching on the bathroom door, which would then slowly, mysteriously open—seemingly all by itself—just wide enough for the dog to get in, at which point the scratching was heard on the toilet seat.

Another rather unique case involved a man who always rang the doorbell to let his beloved dog know he was home. Several days after the dog died, the doorbell mysteriously began ringing all by itself. The doorbell had never done this before.

Yet another case involved a dog named Ty. After Ty passed, her devoted human, Carol Everson of Washington, continued to hear her bark and whine and actually saw impressions left by her in the carpet and bed. Carol continued to feel Ty's presence and to hear her even after she and her husband, George, got a new puppy named Lily Mae.

As it turned out, Carol wasn't the only one who would literally *hear* evidence of Ty's continued presence even after she passed. One day, the Eversons' grown daughter, Kim Louie, went to her parents' house but found that no one was home. The garage door was closed, and she heard a dog barking and crying inside. So, assuming it was the new puppy, she stooped down at the garage door to tell the pup that her parents would be right back and not to cry. She thought it was strange since they never left the puppy alone at home. In her words:

> I started past the garage door; that's when I heard the crying, so I stayed there for a few minutes talking to her, to try and let her know that Mom and Dad would be home soon. I'm sure I looked strange to the neighbor, talking to a garage door. Anyway, I stayed for about ten minutes, then decided she wasn't calming down with me on the other side of the door. So, home I drove, twenty-two miles with time to think how *mad* I was at my parents for leaving the "poor li'l pup" in the cold garage alone—how mean! Once home, I told my husband how surprised I was by their actions. Within ten to fifteen minutes, in the driveway came my dad's truck; Mom got out and came to the door. As I started to tell her that I was at their house trying to

calm the "baby," she looked at me and said, "What are you talking about? Lily Mae's in the truck with your dad. We just went grocery shopping and he stayed in the truck with her while I had to do the shopping by myself, because he wouldn't leave her alone."

Sure enough, in the truck sat my father with his new baby [the puppy] all content on his lap. We have talked of this often, and the neighbor did tell my mom that their daughter was up while they were away and that I was standing at the garage door for a few minutes, like I was talking to someone. Well, I was . . . I know what I heard! Weird, huh?

Well, perhaps there was a time in my life when I would have thought it *was* weird. However, an experience of my own showed me that such things *do* happen. . . .

Jameth and I have a minivan. One of the reasons we chose this type of vehicle is because our giant "travel cage" fits just perfectly, so we can take our beloved "rat children" with us when we travel. That way, we don't miss them or worry about them when we're gone, and they always seem to enjoy going with us and visiting new places. During long car trips to conferences or to visit relatives, it is common to hear the familiar rattling sound of their water bottle, and occasionally, the distinct high-pitched sneeze of one of our little travel companions in the back of the van.

One night, shortly after several of our beloved rats had died of old age, Jameth and I were driving home from a local errand. The rats were not with us, and the back of the van was empty. Suddenly, and quite unexpectedly, I heard the familiar, distinct, high-pitched sneeze of one of our little travel companions. At first, it seemed like quite a natural sound to be coming from the back of the van, until I realized that the rats weren't with us. I wondered if Jameth had heard it, too.

"Did you hear that?" he asked.

"Yeah," I replied.

"It sounded like a rat sneeze," he said.

"Yes, it sure did," I responded, looking back into the emptiness of the van. "Well, there aren't any rats back there." We looked at each other.

"Do you think it's the spirit of one of the rats?" he asked.

"Well, I'm not quite sure what else it *could've* been," I reasoned, and we discussed the possibility that one of our little travel companions was still with us.

GLADYS HYPES OF WEST VIRGINIA shared the following about her departed dog, Cindy:

> Cindy had very long toenails and did not hesitate to try to bite you if you cut them. As she aged, I didn't bother her with cutting them anymore. She slept in a bedroom with a tile floor and you could always hear when she was ready to get up, as her toenails would make noises on the tile. Several times after her passing, my husband and I heard her walking around in that room. For four to five nights we did not say anything to each other about this, for we both thought the other would think we were crazy (we knew nothing of after-death communications at that time). Finally, I had to ask my husband if he heard that and he said *yes*. We have not heard her since.

Then there was the case of a woman who originally contacted me about my research, wanting to know if my book was out yet because she had recently lost her beloved dog and needed some support. She was absolutely beside herself with grief, and although I didn't yet have a book to offer her, I did my best to console her. Having been there myself many times, I felt a kinship with her during this sensitive time. We kept in touch thereafter, as I wanted to know how she was doing. Then one day, she contacted me with the following:

> I wanted to share something with you—don't know if I'm going crazy or it's wishful thinking—but last week I had to take a drive into the city—it's about sixty miles, and a good portion of the way I kept hearing my dog whining like he always did when he wanted out. That was the only time I heard it. I don't know what to think about it, do you? I want so much to hear from him or see him that it's making me crazy. Do you think I'm really losing it, or have you heard of things like this before?

Her question was not uncommon. We have been so conditioned to believe that we live in a very physical world that works in a certain way, that whenever we experience the extraordinary, we assume we must be going crazy. Now, granted, there are cases of people with genuine psychological conditions causing them to "hear things." However, my background in psychology, coupled with my years of research into afterlife communications, has helped me to discern the difference.

Studies have shown that we can talk ourselves out of the reality of just about anything, if the general consensus is that it did not really happen, regardless of how real the experience is. For example, I recall one experiment from college psychology in which a person who absolutely *knew* what day of the week it was became the unwitting subject of this phenomenon.

The people who were "in" on the experiment repeatedly referred to the date as being a *different* day of the week. At first, the subject of the experiment argued that he knew for certain what day of the week it was, and that they were wrong. However, they didn't back down, insisting that *he* was the one who was wrong about the date. After a while, he began to question his own perception of reality; and eventually, he came to believe that he had been wrong and that, indeed, everyone else was right about the date. And such is often the case with so-called paranormal phenomena. If enough people tell us that such things are not possible, we tend to believe them, regardless of what we have actually experienced.

Although the woman who heard the sound of her dog whining chose to remain anonymous for fear of being ridiculed, she did agree to allow me to tell her story, which didn't end there. . . .

It has happened three times now, and it's only when I'm alone in the car and going on longer trips. And in my home I have a room that is my computer room; and when my dog started to get sick, I moved his cage (which I kept him in when I was not at home) in there. After his passing, I just left it the way it was with his water bowl and food bowl and two toys in there. Then the door was closed and has not been reopened since the night he died. But I have on two occasions heard his toy bones being moved around in the cage like when he used to play with them. And something else I noticed is that sometimes it feels like something brushes against me when I'm just sitting at the computer desk or standing at the kitchen sink preparing the other dogs' food. It feels like a light brush either across my back or the back of my legs.

I did contact an animal communicator and she says my dog is near me all the time and he's worried about how I'm handling this situation. I still cry all the time and I want so much to see him again or touch him. Also, I have some medical problems myself, and one night very recently I had gotten sick and was on the floor not able to get up. It was around 2 A.M. and while lying there, it felt like something was licking my face just like my dog always did when I was sick.

No matter how vivid these experiences are, people do sometimes question themselves or their sanity when such things happen. Of course, skeptics may argue that these experiences are the results of wishful thinking. However, it's not so easy to dismiss these events when witnesses are involved, especially when those witnesses happen to be other animals. Her story continues. . . .

I wanted you to know about a few things that have been going on around my home. That whining I told you about that happens on the road, well, it has happened several times at home the last ten days or so, and when it occurs, one of my dogs will go into the living room and just growl at nothing, at least nothing I see.

This, too, is not uncommon. Often, it's other animals—who experience reality fully and without preconceived notions or fear of being ridiculed—that ultimately confirm the validity of these experiences. As it turned out, this woman had other experiences, both before and after the above, but she never shared them with anyone. Her further experiences will be covered in a later chapter. Meanwhile, following are more stories of people who have heard what, for them, was "music to their ears."

Cubbie
Joanne C. King, Wife and Mother
Florida

MY BELOVED MALTESE DOG, Cubbie, became ill and passed away two days later. I had just lost my grandfather and was dealing with that grief, but nothing prepared me for the passing of my greatest companion and friend. Cubbie and I went everywhere together. He slept in my bed, licked me when I cried, and was never quite comfortable unless his body was in constant contact with mine.

He was a dog, but once you get to know them and you look deep into their eyes, year after year, you no longer see an animal; instead you begin to see the depth of any human capability of emotion. It is given freely, and the wealth of comfort it brings cannot be completely understood until it is taken from you.

After Cubbie passed, I thought my heart would shatter into a million pieces. I didn't want to get out of bed, I didn't want to talk to anyone, and I certainly didn't want to accept this reality.

One night, I was watching television. It was around 11 P.M. I was alone, except for my two cats. I started to get sleepy and rolled onto my side. I was still listening to the TV, as I could hear it clearly, although I was drifting into a sleep state. All of a sudden, I heard a growl . . . it came directly into my ear. I thought, at first, *What an odd sound for my cat to make!* Then it came again . . . a clear dog growl. It was so close to my head, and I could actually feel the pressure of a small animal on the other side of my pillow. I pulled myself to turn over and look. My mind thought, *Cubbie!* When I completely turned around, I looked and there was nothing there. The television set was still on, continuing the same program I was listening to, and whatever made the growling sound was gone.

I absolutely believe this was Cubbie. I had wondered why he would growl to get my attention . . . probably because it is audible and because he had such a high-pitched bark that it used to make me jump out of my skin! Whenever he would bark, I would correct him, but never when he would quietly growl.

I miss him to this day. I keep a picture of him in my living room. He is still adored and loved . . . as love continues and is constant. I know that one day we will be reunited.

Nicky

Martha Koelemay, Registered Nurse, Healing Touch Practitioner
Arkansas

MY BEST FRIEND for almost fourteen years was a wonderful Samoyed named Nicholas. I have shared my life with many dogs and loved them all, but Nicky was that extra-special companion sent to be with me through the most painful, difficult period of my life.

When the heartbreaking time came that he had to leave his physical body, I was desolate. I don't remember now how long he had been gone, but several weeks, I think. I was sleeping soundly one night with my boyfriend beside me (to my right), when I was awakened by the sound of snoring beside the bed to my left. Something felt strange and familiar about that snore. I dropped my hand down and felt only air, so I sat up and looked for the other dogs. They were all sleeping on the floor at the foot of the bed, none snoring. The snore had stopped, though, so I lay back down. Then came a sort of "knowing" that I can't really describe. My boyfriend was also roused by the sound and said, "What's that?" By now weeping with joy, I said, "It's Nicky. He's sleeping in his old place beside the bed." We lay quietly for a while, and then there came a gentle bump and I knew that he had gone again. But I treasure this memory and its certainty that this beloved friend is somewhere and that he still cares for me.

There were other times that I felt Nicky's presence, but this one was the most vivid, and the only one that someone else witnessed.

There was another incident, too, that I "saw his paw in," when he sent me a companion to get me through the first Christmas without him. He was pretty goofy in many ways, and he loved Christmas and Christmas presents, getting as excited as a child. That Christmas Eve afternoon I was out in the yard, and suddenly there appeared a huge Great Pyrenees dog at the head of the driveway.

She just stood there for a minute or two, and then she sauntered slowly down the driveway and right up to me. I knelt down, and she put her head on my chest, right over my heart; then she looked right into my eyes as only a dog can.

She stayed with us for about a month, and then disappeared as mysteriously as she came. I know in the deepest parts of my heart and soul that Nicky sent her to me. As I said, he was a very special dog.

This is the only animal companion I have had to whom I was this bonded, and I'm sure it had a lot to do with the circumstances of my life while he was with me. I know he was sent to be with me during this period. I live in the Ouachita National Forest in Arkansas, on the Ouachita River, and Nicky's grave is on the hill just out from the deck onto which my bedroom opens, overlooking the river. I don't feel him often and am certain he has gone on, but once in a while I get a strong sense of his presence—maybe he just "checks in" from time to time.

Kim's note: It's not uncommon for animals to mysteriously enter the lives of those who have recently lost a beloved animal, almost as if they have been sent to assist them through the grief.

Georgie
M.J. Shaw, Retired Social Worker
Washington

SOME VERY STRANGE THINGS happened before and after the death of my beloved kitty, George Bernard. But before I tell about them, I should probably talk a little bit about my relationships with animals.

Even though I had no pets of my own when I was growing up, I always felt very close to animals, whether they were neighbors' pets, or animals on the farms and ranches of the relatives we visited when I was a child. When I talked to them, they seemed to understand what I was saying, even though I knew they couldn't understand my words the way humans could.

There were many other pets along the way, including my cat Sandy, who died of kidney failure. My grief at losing Sandy seemed unbearable, but one day about a month after she died, I very suddenly had an urge to go to the Humane Society and see the animals. This was certainly not something I had planned to do, but as I drove to that facility I thought that I might get an older cat or dog who had lost their human. I had no intention of getting a kitten or puppy.

As I was walking past the cat cages, a little orange tabby, who was about nine weeks old, caught my eye. He was pawing at me behind the cage and demanding in the bossiest way that I get him out.

He was the same color as a previous cat named George, and they looked very much alike. I decided to name him George Bernard, partly after his predecessor and partly because our last name is Shaw.

We bonded immediately. He seemed to understand right away that I am very hard of hearing and that I did not respond to meows all of the time. He knew that to get my attention he would have to pounce on me or make eye or tactical contact with me. I taught him to wake me up when the alarm went off, but he figured the rest out for himself. He truly became my ears.

People were always amazed at the bond between the two of us. We could almost read each other's thoughts. Our times together were so joyous. He was always on my lap having his tummy and head scratched when I watched TV in the evening, and when I was reading in bed, he would push my book away with his head and climb up on my chest. He then rolled over on his back and I had to sing "rock-a-bye-kitty" to him and pet him under his chin. If I stopped, he pulled my hand back with his paws.

One day, I started having the most horrible sense of impending doom. I have always felt that some people have psychic powers but that I was not one of them. At this time, when Georgie climbed up on my chest to be rock-a-byed, thoughts that I should cherish those moments because I might not always have him with me kept coming to my mind. I had never had thoughts or feelings like this before.

Then one day, shortly thereafter, Georgie chased a neighbor's new cat into the street and was killed by a car. I was in severe shock and wondered how my life could go on. I could not sleep, had difficulty breathing, and spent most of my time crying.

TWO NIGHTS AFTER HE WAS KILLED, I felt him jump up on the bed. He always hit the bed with a thud, and I could always feel it.

The same thing happened the next night, and about four days after his soul left his body I heard him very violently coughing up a hair ball. He had always had hairball problems, even though he was given special food for this condition. When he coughed like this he always got my immediate attention. When I heard this so clearly, I thought I was hallucinating.

Other things started happening within a week of Georgie's death. It seemed that whenever I was gone from the house and I was seized with uncontrollable grief, a cat would all of a sudden appear, look me in the eye, and seem to give me comfort. These cats just seemed to *be there* for me. It was as if Georgie had asked his friends still on Earth to comfort me.

An Animal Lovers' Tail
S.R. Hipwell, Lecturer, Teacher
Worcestershire, England
My Dobermans, Sophie, Merlin and Crystal;
and the cats, Woody and Max, all return to us from time
to time. . . .

A SHORT TALE OF THREE DOGS AND TWO CATS who graced our family with their presence. In order of seniority, Woody the cat came to us first; we found him in a wood, hence his name. He had been dumped, and although the vet thought he was thirteen to fourteen weeks old, he was only as big as a six-week-old kitten. Woody stayed the small, always cautious black bundle, until he was called for the last time nearly sixteen years later.

Sophie came next, a Doberman, wisdom incarnate; she had a vocabulary of some two hundred and sixty words. She was taken very suddenly at only seven years of age. However, Sophie left us with Merlin and Crystal, two of her seven offspring. Merlin, the firstborn, became the strong but silent type; he was thirteen at the final whistle. Crystal was born last, such a pretty little thing who could run like the wind. A brain tumour at the age of eleven was Crystal's demise.

Max, a tabby tom, was adopted from the local cat sanctuary. He grew to be an enormous cat, bold and fearless, much to his undoing. He became an RTA [Road Traffic Accident] at just over the age of three.

How do we know they are still with us?

Often, when we open the side door, we hear a trill, just as Woody made to tell us he was on his way. Occasionally I hear a purring when in my workshop, like Max would purr after jumping onto my bench. Merlin still rattles doors as he did if he was not in the kitchen when the lady of the house was baking. The top of the stairs was Crystal's domain, and she would circle before dropping to the floor with a thump. This is the most often-heard sound of our friends' presence. Visitors have heard some of these noises, but do they really believe our explanations? Perhaps they are too polite to say, "Could it be all in the mind?"

If you are not convinced, Sophie may just have the last bark! Sophie, the canine professor that she was, would not let anyone, other than the immediate family, sit next to the good lady. She would always force her bottom between them, but she kept all four feet on the floor. Even now if someone sits by my wife on the settee, they can feel a pressure on their leg on the same side as my wife is sitting. Now, this includes people who are unaware of Sophie's existence. It occurred so regularly that we had to make a conscious effort to avoid the situation and the subsequent explanation.

Are you convinced? We hear and feel the truth.

- CHAPTER 11 -

HeavenScent

If there are no dogs in Heaven, then when I die
I want to go where they went.
— WILL ROGERS

ONE NIGHT I WAS AWAKENED out of a sound sleep, not by a touch or a sound, but by a scent. It was so intense that it literally pulled me out of my slumber and drew my attention to an area of the bedroom to my right side, a few feet away from me, where the scent seemed to emanate from. Rather than startling me (the normal response when I am so abruptly awakened), it filled me with a sense of absolute peace.

The scent was nothing less than heavenly: the most beautiful floral fragrance I've ever encountered. I did not have any flowers, perfumes, essential oils, or candles in the room, nor do I even know of any that could have emitted such a strikingly beautiful aroma.

The scent then seemed to permeate the room, and I simultaneously became aware of what felt like an angelic presence at my side, watching lovingly over me. I'm really not sure how long it lasted. I just felt completely in the moment when it occurred, and I felt more peaceful than I ever remembered feeling before.

Then the scent suddenly vanished, but the sense of peace remained. I pondered what had just taken place, and I continued to dwell upon its significance the next day and for a long time afterward. At the time, I had no idea that visitations from the spirit world often take the form of a scent. Yet I felt strongly that I had just experienced a mystical encounter. I never figured out exactly *who* it was in my bedroom that night, but there was no doubt in my mind that *someone* had been there.

Then, when we lost our beloved rat Katey, I recall sitting on the sofa one evening. This particular piece of furniture had been Katey's favorite hangout, and she had often run happily back and forth across the back of the L-shaped sofa, stopping periodically to nestle on the shoulders of whoever sat there.

Now, as I sat on what had been "Katey's sofa," I suddenly detected the very familiar, soft scent of her fur, which always took on a delicate, sweet, perfumey scent when she groomed herself. The scent was subtle and brief, but it was definitely there. It lasted only a few seconds, and I got the strong sense that Katey was just "passing through," possibly to say a quick "hello" and run across the back of her sofa once more. I smiled and acknowledged her presence, and the experience took away some of the grief I had been feeling over her passing.

I began to hear stories of other people who had detected a very specific scent in conjunction with what appeared to be a contact from the Other Side. People reported very distinctly smelling their dog's shampoo—or other familiar scent associated with a particular animal—after the beloved animal had passed. Like my own experiences, these events always took place "out of the blue" and not when the people were expecting anything to occur. Like me, the people usually had no idea that such a thing was even possible, until it happened to them.

Years after my first experience along these lines, I had another very similar experience . . . except this time I had a witness. Jameth and I had a few friends over, and we were all enjoying meaningful conversation. Suddenly, I began to smell an otherworldly floral fragrance, accompanied by the sense of an angelic female presence. Before I could even say anything, our good friend Russell (who is quite spiritually attuned) spoke up.

"Do you smell that?" he blurted out quite suddenly. I nodded.

"I sure do," I replied.

"Do you know what I think it is?" he asked.

"Yes," I responded. We simultaneously agreed that we felt a loving female presence in the room. It lasted a short while and then vanished. Although I had never questioned the reality of my experience in the bedroom that night many years before, I felt validated, as someone else now acknowledged the same presence.

As a result of these experiences, I knew exactly what was going on when a similar event later took place. I was home alone one night when suddenly, right in front of me, I distinctly smelled a very strong, masculine aftershave or cologne. This scent was accompanied by what I felt to be a very pronounced male presence right in front of me.

At first it startled me, as the presence felt very *human* (rather than animal or angelic), so I phoned Jameth and nervously asked him to come home right away. The scent had vanished by the time I completed the call, but then it happened a second time a few minutes later, so I turned on all the lights and anxiously awaited Jameth's arrival.

When I told my mom about the experience the next day, she reminded me that my recently deceased grandfather (her father) had always worn fairly strong aftershave, and it then occurred to me that perhaps he had simply stopped by to say "hello." I felt a little ashamed of myself for having been so frightened by the experience, but then I realized that human intruders when we're home alone are simply more unnerving than animals or angels, especially when we don't realize *who* the humans are.

On the other hand, of all of the stories I gathered from people who had similar experiences involving *animals,* no one ever reported being frightened by the experience. Such visitations from beloved animals always seem to bring comfort and peace.

Following are stories of people who have had such experiences. In some cases, the scent is the exclusive experience. In other cases, the scent is accompanied by other evidence that it is indeed the presence of a beloved animal on the Other Side. . . .

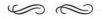

Patchouli
Nicole Lockard, Pet Resort Manager
Maryland

MY GRANDFATHER, the most wonderful man, passed several years ago. I often feel him near me, or more specifically, I smell him! His scent was very unique: a combination of Chesapeake Bay air (he lived on the bay; I do not), Polo cologne, tobacco, and whatever else makes up one's personal scent.

My beloved Dalmatian, Patchouli, passed away last summer. My heart was broken and I missed her so terribly. She was truly an angel with fur. Recently, the scent of my grandfather has been taking on a new hint of Patchouli (the dog, not the herb).

Since she was a puppy, I loved smelling Patchouli's paw pads. They kind of smelled like popped corn. Every so often, out of nowhere, I get that familiar whiff of my grandfather, followed by the smell of my Patchouli's paws. I like to think that they are taking care of each other somewhere, and sending me a little "hello." They never met in life, but they would've been great friends. Maybe now they are.

Sugar Bear
April Prager, Psychic and Animal Communicator
Kentucky

ABOUT A MONTH AFTER my cat Bowie died, I decided to go to the pound to look for another cat. This beautiful tabby point male caught my attention.

He looked like he was getting ill, but I had a connection with him. When I held him, he just purred and purred.

I asked the people there if they would treat him for a few days, and if he got better, could I adopt him. They agreed.

Four days later, he was a little better. He was still running a temperature, but they let me take him anyway.

He was fine for a day. Then he started throwing up and running a high fever. I took him to my vet. We felt like he had distemper. We decided to try to keep him alive with fluids and antibiotics and see if he could kick it. He wouldn't eat and got weaker every day.

I started to feel like he wasn't going to make it, but he just kept hanging in there. He was getting weaker and weaker. I think he was trying to stay for me.

While Sugar Bear was very ill, I kept him in my bedroom. There was a certain smell that permeated the room. It got stronger the sicker he became.

We put Sugar Bear to sleep soon after that. I buried him next to Bowie.

A few days passed. I had a dream in which Sugar Bear came back to life and when I awoke, that same smell was everywhere in the bedroom.

I got up and walked through the house. Only in that room could I smell that smell. It lasted about fifteen minutes.

I was sure Sugar Bear had come to visit and to tell me he was alive and well.

Rex
Gwen Gerow, Resource Engineer
New York

I SPENT THE LAST TWO WEEKS of my beloved cat Rex's life sleeping on the couch with him because he would no longer come into the bedroom, and he had gotten very particular about where he would get water from. He would only drink from the kitchen faucet (he was never allowed on the kitchen counter, but I made an exception when he became sick since it was the only place he would drink from at that point). So, at night I would listen for the sound of him jumping down from the counter and I would get up and turn the water on for him. Several times a night we would go through this routine. The last couple of days he turned away from the kitchen faucet, but I found that he would drink from the bathtub faucet (something he had done in the past when the tub faucet used to drip). He also, at times, would sleep in the bathtub.

Anyway, the time came when we felt that we should have Rex put to sleep, a decision that my husband and I agonized over. Neither one of us had ever had an animal put to sleep before, and this was such a difficult decision, especially for my husband because he and Rex were so close.

After we came home from that last trip to the vet, I walked through the kitchen and I thought I could smell Rex. He had this kind of aroma that I think got stronger due to the B12 vitamin that we had been giving him. But then I realized that the vitamin bottle was on the counter and that must have been what I was actually smelling. My husband had been lying down in bed and came out to the kitchen, so I told him how I thought I smelled Rex, but it must have been the vitamin instead. My husband just looked at me and said that he smelled Rex, too, but in the bedroom while he was lying in bed. The thing is, as I mentioned, Rex had stopped going in the bedroom and hadn't been in there for a couple of weeks.

Then, a couple of days later, we were talking about Rex, and my husband told me that while he was in the bathroom early that morning, he heard Rex in the bathtub. As I mentioned, Rex used to hang out in there at times, and he would startle us by making this sound when we didn't realize he was there. This was the same sound my husband heard that morning. Let me just say that I was very surprised to hear him mention this, and that he actually thought the sound was coming from Rex. My husband is definitely not one to believe in anything like that at all. I told him that I was happy for him, happy that Rex was trying to let him know he's still around and he's not upset with us for having him put to sleep.

The last and most profound thing happened to me eight days after Rex had been gone. I was having a particularly hard time and thinking a lot about him. I was in the bedroom when I heard a sound that stopped me in my tracks. I even said Rex's name out loud. There was nothing in the house that could have made this sound; the radio wasn't on—television, laundry, you name it—nothing was on or running. I knew this sound all too well. I had heard it several times a night for two weeks as I lay on the couch taking care of Rex. It was the sound of him jumping off the kitchen counter onto the hardwood floor. A very distinct sound as first his front feet, then his back feet, made contact with the floor. I walked slowly out into the kitchen and glanced over at the counter. In my mind I even knew which part of the counter the sound had come from, but I didn't walk over to it. I stopped to try and figure out what else could have possibly made that noise, but there was nothing.

About an hour later, I was walking through the kitchen and something caught my eye. I stopped in my tracks because I couldn't believe what I was seeing. From about five or six feet away, standing out clearly on the dark floor, was one of Rex's whiskers. And the whisker was right underneath the counter where only an hour earlier I knew was the spot that I had heard that sound come from. This whisker was right in a spot that gets a lot of traffic. There is no way it could have been there for eight days without my noticing it (even for one day, for that matter). His white whisker clearly stood out in contrast to the hardwood floor; it looked like a big scratch in the wood. And the fact that I heard that sound only shortly before—I can't explain any of this. I suppose someone could say that the whisker was on my clothes or somehow got transported to that spot. But you can't tell *me* that's what happened. Especially since Rex had been gone for over a week. Where did that whisker come from? I was blown away when I saw that whisker lying there, and I believe that, somehow, Rex left it for me as his way of trying to comfort me when I was feeling down.

Kim's note: This is an example of a person who received more than one type of contact, not only smelling her departed cat, but also hearing him and finding his whisker (this latter phenomenon is not uncommon and will be covered further in a later chapter).

Kooter
Gladys Hypes, Homemaker
West Virginia

I'M WRITING THIS IN MEMORY of my beloved schnauzer, Kooter
Dan VonKraut. After fourteen years of love and dedication, that
precious soul crossed over while being held in the arms of my
husband and myself. I'm not sure where to begin with this journey
but I can tell you for sure that it's far from over.

Kooter became sickly with kidney stones at a young age. He
had two operations to remove them and on the third occasion our
vet said he could not do the surgery again. Kooter would need a
special operation that our vet had never performed and needed to
go to Richmond, Virginia, but our vet did not think he would live
that long. Upon my request, our vet did the surgery and Kooter
lived for ten more years.

I must tell you a little about myself here in order for you to
see the whole picture. I have clinical depression, brought on from
an unloving, uncaring upbringing. I am fifty-four years old and
have never come to terms with the whys of my raising. Life has
been very hard for me to adjust to. I have been blessed with a
wonderful husband, three fine children, and eight grandchildren,
but still the void remained. On several occasions I felt the need to
end my life. I knew my family would mourn and probably would
not understand, but they would surely get past it and move on. But
Kooter . . . there would be no understanding for him; and, as he
would not eat or drink if I was not home, I knew he would suffer
to his death if I weren't here. My life was spared so he could live.

Kooter suffered through three strokes, one massive. At the
time of his third stroke I was totally unprepared to survive without him. As he lay unable to hold up his head, I begged God not
to take him, and that very evening he was up and walking around.
Dr. Krese, our vet, was always in awe of Kooter's desire to live.

When Kooter's time eventually came, my husband and I did
not leave his side. I slept on the floor beside him and consoled
him throughout the night. At 3:30 A.M. my husband and I made
the decision to have Dr. Krese relieve him of his suffering when his

office opened. This was unacceptable to me, so at 3:45 A.M. I asked God to please take him home so I did not have to do that horrible thing. Fifteen minutes later, he was in God's hands.

Kooter's presence is everywhere . . . I can't explain it. I don't want to explain it . . . I only want to know and feel it. His scent is here . . . my husband has picked it up twice and two times for me, all at different times. He's simply been passing by. I went to a search engine to search for Websites where I might learn the things to do to bring him closer to us and the first Website I clicked onto brought up a picture of a black schnauzer lying on a rug . . . my Kooter. My heart overflowed.

This is but the beginning of great things to come . . . until the light shines brighter. In spite of the tears, heartache, and loneliness, my life has been changed for the better due to his passing. I have come to realize a magnificent and unexplainable thing that has happened since Kooter's passing. . . .

As I mentioned, I have clinical depression; and along with that there was so much anger inside of me, anger that I had dealt with for as long as I can remember. I never did fully understand where all the anger came from. As Kooter lay dying in my arms that terrible morning, I soaked his coat with my tears. I later told my husband I felt that, because of the tears, Kooter took part of me with him. Little did I know at that time . . .

Since his passing there are no signs of depression or feelings of anger. My heart is very heavy and sad, but there's a difference between these feelings and depression. Somehow, far beyond any understanding on my part, I believe that Kooter took my depression and anger with him, knowing I could not function on a normal level if he weren't here to help me. I owed my life to him while he was here and it seems I will be in his debt forevermore. What a wonderful God we have that is able to accomplish such a task.

Kim's note: Gladys continues to experience various signs of Kooter's presence. She recently shared the following: "My husband has seen Kooter out of the corner of his eye several times. I myself have not but I have heard him in the house three different times. Thinking it was my little Gibby (our youngest schnauzer), I was shocked to find him elsewhere beyond being able to make the sounds."

She then added, "I wanted to share with you what I am now doing in memory of Kooter. I do woodwork crafts and am decorating our groomer's office. A sign hangs in her office that reads: *'Crafts donated in loving memory of Kooter Dan VonKraut.'* It has helped me very much to move on somewhat and yet not leave Kooter behind. . . . I most certainly have found that love never dies. It's been almost a year now since his crossing, and my heart is filled with as much love for him as if he were still with me." Perhaps he is.

Miss Moostache
(A "Debutante" Fishie)

Azar "Ace" Attura, Artist, Photographer, Animal Rescuer
Virginia

MOOSTACHE AND HER BROTHER BUMBLEBEE were two very cute but *tiny* goldfish, swimming in the big fish tank at the pet store. For 89 cents each, I brought them home from the pet store to live with me. Although I had been raising goldfish for twenty years (and many of them lived to be five, six, even seven years old), when I saw Moostache, I was in awe of the responsibility I had of raising her and keeping her alive. She was—at most—six months old, which is still a "baby" for a goldfish, and incredibly tiny—no bigger than the nail on my pinkie. As I watched her and her brother (Bumblebee, who was slightly bigger than her, and had stripes on his fishie-butt, hence his name) wriggling frantically and fearfully in their little plastic bag, I wanted nothing but the best for these little frightened fishes.

I gently opened the bag and poured them and their water into a large fishbowl (already filled with some dechlorinated and aerated water), adapted a small outside filter for it, and then made a screened cover for the top. They were safe from jumping out, and their tank was clean and aerated (goldfish need lots of oxygen), but the two little fishies were so scared, that for the next two days they tried very hard to burrow out of the rear of the bowl by perpetually wiggling their little noses on the glass. I fed them twice a day and talked soothingly to them. Soon they realized that I, the big shape with no gills, was the source of their food and their sweet-talk.

Bumblebee was brash and a little bigger than his sister. Moostache and the Bee soon began to wiggle over to greet me and "yell" at me in goldfish ("silent yapping" is more like it) for their food. Moostache reminded me of a chubby little baby girl in a dainty little dress (her fantail), as she wriggled and impertinently "yapped" at me in goldfish language. Mom called her "The Debutante," because Moostache would yap, cheerfully toss her head, and wiggle her fantail like a queen (see, they *do* have personalities!). I was her loyal subject.

Moostache was female. How did I know? Well, not to sound sexist, but she acted like a little dainty lady. And then as she grew older, I could tell—female goldfish have nonsymmetrical butts. Male goldfish have symmetrical butts and sometimes get "tubercles" on their gills (looks like five o'clock shadow) and sometimes on the edges of their dorsal (front) fins. The Bee was a male fishie.

They were a unique pair. Sometimes I would get up in the middle of the night for a drink of water, or PB&J sandwich, and when I passed their fish bowl in the dim light of the hall light, two pairs of bright eyes would be staring up at me. Wonder if they got the munchies at 2 A.M. too?

She and the Bee got along well, but one day I introduced a sweet little Lioncap Oranda (fancy goldfish) into their tank, whom I named Beauty. Goldfish, being social creatures (they travel in schools) like to hang out together. Beauty was no exception. She swam over to Moostache, who promptly put the equivalent of her fishie-nose into the air, and swam away. Poor Beauty was snubbed! After doing this several times, I guess Moostache felt she had maintained the pecking order, and the two of them coexisted peacefully. The Bee was always a "hail-fellow-well-met" type of fish, so he got along with everybody.

One Fateful Day

When Moostache matured and grew bigger, her ovaries (egg-sacs, whatever) deflated her swim bladder, and she began to have trouble swimming. She'd stagger over to me, just as happy as ever, and would continue to toss her head and yap for her food. But one day as she tossed her little head, she fell over, righting herself just in time to avoid crashing to the floor of the tank. She even looked a little scared after that happened. Sadly, that was the last time she ever tossed her head at me. After several days, her swim bladders gave out altogether, and she would lie on her side on the floor of the tank (she was now living in a five-gallon fish tank—she was still quite small).

A Very Brave Little Lady

Although Moostache was now doomed to a life at the bottom of the fish tank, she still maintained her cheerful demeanor. I kept her in the best of health, even though she was now crippled. My mom lost a great deal of mobility in her legs at the same time (diabetes)—she would drag herself over to the tank to see Moostache (she called her "the Kootchy Kootchy Fish") and Moostache would daintily drag herself over to greet Mom! I think they were very good for each other's morale.

I would medicate her with special aquarium medications for goldfish (or would use goldenseal, which is a powerful natural antibiotic) when she sometimes got the equivalent of "bedsores" from lying on her side on the bottom of the tank. She would heal. I always kept her tank clean, and sometimes I would feed her (in addition to her regular food) a little bit of brownie, which I'd roll up in my fingers and drop in the water so it would fall right in front of her waiting mouth—what a treat it was to her!

The End . . .

One night, I "heard" Moostache calling to me in my mind—it was as though a little child was delightedly calling to its friend or its parent to say, "Come here *quick!* And look at what I found!" I walked quickly to the tank, stomping a bit on the floor with my feet, because she had learned to recognize that those vibrations (which she could feel through the fish tank) meant that I was coming over to her. She had pulled herself to the front of the tank and was looking at me sweetly (they *do* have expressions on their faces!). I "stroked" her nose through the tank glass, and she seemed very happy. When I started to walk away, she tried to wiggle after me, as though she were pleading, "Stay a little while longer, please!" So I did. Then I had to do chores, and I promised her I'd be back soon.

When I came back a few minutes later, I saw that she had turned to face the back of the tank. She had died. But she and I had said our final good-byes—she knew. I had no idea that she was dying . . . I was so sad. A bright light in a beautiful tiny body had been extinguished.

Tears were streaming down my face as I went to pick her up with the net. Her body, which had lost much of its color in death, suddenly became bright again—was she still alive? I left her there in the tank overnight. I didn't sleep much that night.

The next morning, I went over to her tank. Her body was in the same position as I had left it the night before. Her colors were faded; her gills were still. Yes, she was dead. I picked her up with the net, and when I lifted her from the water, instead of dead-fishie smell, I smelled a wonderful fragrance (which I later recognized as oleander!) coming from her body. A "Sweet Odor of Goldfish Sanctity," perhaps? I'm not making this up.

I wrapped her in lace, with some of her favorite red-flake fish food (to sustain her on her journey to the next world), wrapped this little "shroud" in tin foil, and then taped it all so she would remain untouched by multi-legged things. I left home early, before work, and buried her under a wild cherry tree in (what I have now renamed) "Goldfish Park." This park is not too far from where I lived, and it held the little bodies of many of my fish pets (flush 'em? Never!). It was a damp and muddy day. The lilacs were blooming, and I put some over her tiny shroud before I covered her over and tamped the soil back into place (covering everything over with leaves).

I had to go back home to change my shoes, and when I entered the apartment and looked at her tank, there was such a sense of emptiness in my soul—I felt such a great loss! Mom and I had lost a faithful friend. Her brother, Bumblebee, lived to be seven years old, and died from a tumor on his head. I treated him well to his dying day, and I am sure Moostache was very happy to see him once more.

"Only" a fish? No—a wonderful living creature who gave and received joy. I hope that when Miss Moostache daintily swam through the Pearly Gates, God would have been most pleased to place this plump little lady with gossamer fins on the golden flowing robes of His lap.

- CHAPTER 12 -

When Seeing Is Believing: Visual Encounters

As much of Heaven is visible as we have eyes to see.
— RALPH WALDO EMERSON

AS I GATHERED STORIES over the years, I came across a surprisingly large number of people who had actually *seen* the spirits of departed animals with their own eyes, but many of them had never shared their experiences with anyone for fear of being ridiculed. Once I gained their trust, they opened up in a way that was both revealing and healing.

There's something about sharing our stories, and feeling validated that our experiences are indeed authentic, that can provide a healing in and of itself. When I began to ask permission to include some of these stories in my book, most people—whether or not they felt comfortable about this—told me that they had already received much healing just in the telling.

One woman, who had always kept such experiences to herself for fear of ridicule, eventually felt comfortable sharing her experiences with me. In her words:

> My horse, Rusty, whom I had for thirty-two years, developed an inoperable intestinal problem and we had to put him down. He was thirty-six years old. Rusty died on a

Friday, and the next Saturday my mother passed away. So my husband and I had to go to California for the funeral, and on our return home we stopped in New Mexico. Late that night, my husband got up and went to the store, and while I was sitting watching TV, I heard what I thought were hoofbeats outside. I never thought about it again until several months later when we were moving to a new home. I was out in the back yard of the old house and I swear I saw Rusty run across the yard. I just sat there in amazement, and due to the fact that no one would believe me, I just always kept it to myself.

Although she now felt comfortable sharing these experiences with me—and agreed to allow me to tell her story in this book—she still preferred that I withhold her identity. I completely understood and agreed to honor her request when sharing her experiences, which continued. . . .

Something new happened two weeks ago. I had gotten very sick one evening and was having spells of severe dizziness and passing out. My husband had gone to the store, so I was alone. I made my way to the phone to call an ambulance and then passed out again. And when I woke up, I was going down the street—red lights and siren—and the strangest thing happened. I saw my dog [who had previously died] sitting in the corner of the ambulance when I awoke. Very afraid and confused, I then started to feel an overwhelming sense of safety. I turned my head and he was right next to me, licking my hand like he always had when I was sick. At that point my fear was gone, and I knew I was going to be okay. These are the strangest things, aren't they?

In a culture that doesn't readily accept the reality or even the possibility of such experiences, yes, they do indeed seem strange. However, once we open our minds to such possibilities, more and more people will feel comfortable sharing such experiences without fear of ridicule.

When these experiences occur in hospitals, they are often dismissed as drug-induced delusions. Although it is true that drugs can sometimes induce hallucinations, it is equally true that those who have serious illnesses or close brushes with death—and who are *not* under the influence of any drugs—often report seeing loved ones who have previously crossed over, and this includes animals.

Another woman shared the following about her departed dog:

> I got up in the middle of the night once and saw what appeared to be my dog on the oriental rug that he used to lie on. I could have sworn I saw him there, but it wasn't like it was solid him—and I am *not* the kind of person who believes in this sort of thing. I understand there are psychics and so forth, but I'm not an afterlife kind of person. I'm not into New Age stuff. I sort of looked and said, "Well, I think I'll just get back into bed and pretend that I didn't see it." It was a little eerie, but I didn't feel any fear.

Some of the people who shared these experiences did, indeed, express doubt. Either they doubted the reality of these experiences *themselves,* or others around them did. Often embedded within their accounts of what took place were little explanations or rationalizations that almost seemed to negate the reality of these experiences, for fear of otherwise sounding crazy. It seems our minds—or the minds of those around us—are always trying to fit such events within the context of what we have come to accept as "reality."

Elaine Seamans of California shared the following story about her beloved dog, a dachshund named Quackers:

> When Quackers left, we did a really beautiful ceremony with candles and white lights . . . I felt relief.
> It was three days after. I was crying a lot, and missing her, yet I had a bit of peace about it because I knew she was ready to go. I was sick and coughing a lot, and I wasn't able to sleep, so I got up. I had previously done the laundry and had washed her big pillowcase. I had folded it and put it down the hallway, which is where she would sleep sometimes when she was getting too warm.
> I got up at five o'clock in the morning, coughing, and I walked down the hallway . . . I looked down and there she was. I stopped and I thought, *Maybe it's just the shadows of*

the pillow. It was so clear. I was saying out loud, "Quackers? Quackers?" I saw her little ear on top of her head, her skinny little legs (she had had cancer and lost a lot of weight). I put my hand down, a little bit nervously, and my hand went through her image. I didn't know what to do. The reality part of my mind is thinking, *It's just the shadows, the folds of the fabric.* I, like an idiot, pulled the corner of the fabric and she disappeared.

I went back to bed thinking that it was my imagination. Then when I got up later that morning, I thought, *There is no way—even though I knew her the best—there is no way I could have folded the fabric to put her ear on top of her head and one leg on top of the other. There is no possible way.* I know now that was the biggest gift she ever could have given me. I had been crying, saying, "Quackers, if I could just see you one more time." And then she gave me that gift.

THE STORY THAT FOLLOWS is yet another example of the self-doubt that so often accompanies these experiences. . . .

Boots
Steve McDonald, Graphic Designer
Edinburgh, Scotland

WE HAD TO HAVE OUR LOVING CAT Boots put to sleep after being diagnosed with renal (kidney) disease two weeks earlier. As far as cats go, he was old, but only eleven. He was too young for this, so it came as a shock. We decided to have him cremated and receive his ashes to give him a befitting memorial. We have three other cats (Boots's sister, Ivy, and two younger cats, Dougal and Dylan), and they knew. It's strange how animals know things.

Our cats and us are a very strong family unit. There are no children. The cats each have their own personality, and every one of them is extremely affectionate. Boots always looked after one of the younger ones, Dougal, who always looked up to Boots. One day this youngster got lost outside and was gone overnight. Boots went out and found him.

IT WAS A SAD DAY when the other cats realized that Boots was on his way. When he was ill, he isolated himself in the bedroom. The other cats stayed away from him until the last day, when they came through one by one, almost as if to say good-bye. They knew. As soon as we came back from the vet, the cats were extremely upset. They were very down and not active or running about. This has now passed except for his sister, Ivy, who I think still misses him.

AFTER HIS PASSING, after many periods of sadness I could see Boots as he was at his best in places he would always be . . . in the bathroom, on top of the laundry basket, on the windowsill, lying next to me on the bed. I tell myself these are just memories, and I feel it is a case of wanting at such a recent loss, but I believe he is here letting us know he is happy now and we did the right thing.

The sightings continue and are very clear. Usually I see him sitting on the windowsill looking out the window, one of his favourite spots. At times when I am slightly dozing while listening to the radio, I think he is sitting on my lap. Or if I am lying on the bed watching the TV, he will come across the floor and jump up, looking for a cuddle. Maybe it's me still missing him, but it is comforting. I will always remember him, and I hope I continue to see him around the house.

SKEPTICS MAY ARGUE that people have these experiences because they *believe* in them, but many times it's quite the opposite: They believe in them *because* they experience them. I've come across many cases involving witnesses who have encountered the spirits of animals quite unexpectedly.

For example, Robert Simmons of Montpelier, Vermont, shared the following experience.

Robert and his wife, Kathy, shared the love of a golden retriever named Hobbes. Hobbes died of lung cancer a mere ten days after the diagnosis. In honor of Hobbes, they made a "shrine" of photographs of him, which were displayed on the refrigerator.

Kathy continued to feel the presence of their beloved dog, though she did not actually see him. She did see him in her dreams, however, which Hobbes often interrupted (this relatively common form of after-death communication will be covered in a later chapter).

A week after Hobbes died, Robert and Kathy's son, Moe, returned from college. A female friend of his came back from a different college, and she waited in the family's kitchen while Moe was showering, as the two were planning to go out that evening.

When Moe then joined her in the kitchen, she asked him why there were pictures of Hobbes on the refrigerator. He explained to her that it was a shrine, because the dog had died the week before.

"No, seriously, why are the photographs displayed there like that?" she asked again, thinking he was joking when he said that Hobbes had died. Moe repeated his answer, assuring her that the pictures were on the refrigerator because Hobbes had indeed died.

She looked at him incredulously and exclaimed, "That's impossible! He was just in here and I petted him!"

She had no idea the dog had died. Needless to say, she was absolutely stunned.

Experiences such as this cannot be explained away as "wishful thinking" or a coping mechanism of a mind steeped in grief, as the young woman didn't even know that there had been a loss to grieve.

In another case, George Stone of Ontario, Canada, reported the following experience, which convinced him of an afterlife for animals. In his words:

> I would say they live on after death and they come around us. I say this because I have seen a dog. It was night-time, and I was on my way home. I was walking down a road where there were no streetlights when I saw this big white dog come across the road. It was jumping as it moved in slow motion and just went right through the fence on the other side, and on up through the field. I watched as it ran, still in slow motion, until I lost sight of it. So, yes, I believe they have spirits like we do. I think every living thing has an afterlife.

In speaking with professional animal communicators, I found that some of their clients had shared similar experiences. For example, animal communicator Gail De Sciose had the following to say:

> I have had people tell me that they have actually felt the presence of their animals after they have departed. There was one woman in New York City who told me that at times she could feel her cat sitting on her lap purring, even though the cat was deceased.
>
> I also had a client who had moved into a house where she started seeing a spirit animal, a cat. Her own animals saw that spirit animal, too, and everybody was very comfortable with it because the cat had a very nice energy. We later found out that this particular cat had lived in that house twenty or thirty years ago, and the cat's person had since died.

Cases such as this help to further validate the reality of these encounters, as the witnesses are outsiders (including humans *and* other animals) who aren't even grieving the loss of their own beloved animal companions and certainly aren't looking for such things. They witness the spirit of an animal without even knowing who the animal could be, and then are often able to verify the former existence of that very animal after the fact.

Another animal communicator, Elizabeth O'Donnell, shared the following experience involving her own dog, Sarah:

> I had her since I was eleven. She passed away when she was sixteen. We sort of grew up together. She was my absolute best friend, complete soul-mate animal, who lived with me through everything. After she passed over, she would appear to me like you could reach out and touch her. I know it was not my imagination. It wasn't just me; she also appeared to my parents. It was quick, but she was there. I would say it's not as clear as I'm looking at my dog right now; she had sort of an ethereal quality—it was her shape, her fur, her colorings, her markings—but as though she had a dimmer switch on and she was just dimmed down a little bit. The tinkling of her little tags on her collar [was heard]—she had three tags and she was always jingling around. I know she is with me now. Her spirit definitely goes to where my parents live now, and my dad will tell me all the time that he hears her. He hears the jingling.

Another case was shared by Barbara Meyers of New York, a certified grief therapist, human-animal bond consultant and animal behaviorist with the gift of interspecies communication. While interviewing her, I asked her if she could share any experiences that had convinced *someone else* of an afterlife for animals. Here is what she had to say:

> There is one that comes to mind right away, although there are many. When the true skeptic—more than a skeptic, in fact—was confronted with a solid visitation from the afterlife.
>
> For a number of years, I consulted personally with a chiropractor—and I think that chiropractic is one of many wonderful techniques, both for animals as well as people. At that time, one of the canine members of my family was a toy white poodle. Her name was Skila. Skila accompanied me, quite literally, everywhere. If I went to business, she was—in my lap, being so very portable at her size, and highly sophisticated—welcome everywhere. So I took her to my chiropractor as well; and anyplace that we went where she was not welcome, we didn't go. It was that simple. (Just as an

aside, we made many visits to the hospital to see friends and family who were hospitalized, and she was a great comfort. In a simple, heavy-duty shopping bag, we were in every major hospital in New York City.)

As Skila grew older, she had some subluxations [partial dislocations] in her spine, so I convinced my chiropractor to adjust her, and reluctantly, he did, knowing of the complete trust. It was just marvelous. He would do the adjustment, and she would go rickshaw all around the office, run down the hallway outside the exam room and run back and jump into his arms with an obvious "Thanks a lot." He always knew when we were there even before we were in because he could hear her coming down that hall. Even though we were in the waiting room area, she would always go down the hall and look for him. They would say hello; she would come back; we would wait to be called in.

About six months after she died, I received a very agitated phone call from him, and he told me the following: He was in his office at the end of the building, working at his desk, and there were a few patients waiting out front—and the secretary. He heard something in the hallway. It wasn't the footsteps of his secretary or patients coming down. He was compelled to get up, and when he got up and peeked out his office door, Skila was walking down the hallway as she had done so many times before. It was not a feeling or an image or some kind of shadowy sensation. It was what is known as a solid visitation.

He was stunned. He called me, not so much to tell me that Skila had come to visit him, but that he thought he was having a breakdown. You see, he was a person who (since I knew him for so many years and we talked about many things) believed that all of this "stuff," as he would call it, was simply the effect of a grief stricken mind; but that day, everything changed for him.

He was so upset. It was really a frightening experience for him. There was nothing menacing about it; there she was, coming down the hallway to see him. She was there. He thought he was having hallucinations and a mental breakdown. It happened again a number of days later. This time we had talked many times about it and he was okay with it. He had two solid visitations within a short time. Then he would say later that sometimes he would get up from his desk and look out, kind of looking for her. He never saw her again.

Then he fulfilled a wish that his children had had all of their lives, and they were pretty well grown up by then, high school and college. He got them a dog. This is a situation where you can make a real good case for coming back to make a visit to give someone the opportunity to enrich their life. They had never had a dog or a cat or anything. Their dog became the love of his life, as well as everybody else in the family. When she was diagnosed with cancer, how he cried. What he wouldn't have done and did do for her. And this was the man who had never patted a dog on the head.

One of his sons went on to become a chiropractor himself. He and his wife, also a chiropractor, have had built into them from that time such a deep love of animals. Such a deep and abiding love and respect, and their current dog is a wonderful example of the perfect dog's life. One of the things that drew them together when they met at chiropractic school was that she had a dog. Not to make more of it than there is, but there are many forms in which there is a gift; there is a lesson.

EXPERIENCES SUCH AS THIS can certainly be life-changing in many ways. When we come face-to-face with such profound evidence of life after death, it can alter our very understanding of reality. And it can bring much reassurance to those who *thought* that death was the end.

Over time, I was impressed at the sheer volume of people who had seen departed animals with their own eyes. Not only were these encounters highly unexpected, but they often happened to the staunchest skeptics. Then again, perhaps the skeptics are the ones who need these experiences the most.

Interestingly, the one person in my own family who has always been the biggest skeptic about an afterlife is my dad. So he was the *last* one I expected to have an actual visual encounter of his own.

One morning, he left a message on my answering machine and said he had something to tell me. Based on his voice, I got the feeling it was something he really needed to share, something intriguing, so I called him back right away. He explained what had happened.

The night before, in the middle of the night, a voice had loudly whispered his name ("Joe!"), awakening him from a sound sleep. This is not an uncommon form of after-death communication, but my dad really had *no idea* that such things were possible. He knew the *title* of this book, but beyond that, he basically had no knowledge or experience of after-death communication whatsoever. Had I told him anything about it, he probably wouldn't have really believed it, anyway. He was *supportive* of my project—or *whatever* I chose to do with my life—but he really didn't know a thing about the afterlife; and it's not something we had ever really discussed. So he had no way of anticipating what happened next.

Shortly after being awakened out of a sound sleep by the whisper that so clearly spoke his name, he was in utter disbelief at what he saw right before his now-wide-open eyes. He was lying on his back, and sitting on his chest was the dark form of one of our departed rats (one of his "grandrats," as they're lovingly called), looking right at him.

He was in awe. He couldn't imagine how she could be sitting there, looking lovingly at him . . . yet there she was. The room was dim, but not at all completely dark. He couldn't explain it away; he simply saw her, perfectly clearly. He wasn't frightened, just amazed. He reached out to touch her, but she faded away.

My dad had begun helping me out with the care of our ever-increasing family of rescued rats while I was busy working on this book, and he had become quite attached to several of them, some of whom had died. Apparently, they had become quite attached to him, too!

He had always been quite afraid—terrified, really—of death and dying. He didn't even like to talk about such things. Yet, ever since this experience, he has had a newfound openness and a sense of peace about the hereafter.

FOLLOWING ARE MORE STORIES of people who have discovered that seeing is believing. . . .

Garden Dogs
Stuart Hague, Mortgage Broker
Leicester, United Kingdom

I AM A MORTGAGE BROKER in the UK and have been for a number of years. I used to have an office in town. Many clients would come along to obtain help and information when they were looking to buy a new house or remortgage their current one.

I would sit them down, offer a cup of coffee, and usually have a chat to break the ice. Some of these clients became friends, and long after having bought or remortgaged their house, they would often come back into the office for a coffee and a natter.

One day, Mr. and Mrs. Smith and I were chatting about some of the strange happenings we had come across when Mr. Smith said, "Humph! You'd better talk to *her* about strange happenings!" By *her*, he meant his wife.

When I asked what he meant, Mrs. Smith said that over a number of years she'd had a number of dogs who, when they had passed on, she buried in her rather large back garden.

They had not been married all that long, and Mrs. Smith had been living at the property for many years.

After a while, she became aware of a couple of dogs roaming around her back garden and thought they had somehow jumped over the fence. Then, on closer inspection, she recognised them as dogs she'd had a few years earlier *that had died* and had been buried in her garden.

When she excitedly pointed them out to Mr. Smith, he looked blankly into the garden and could not understand what all the excitement was about. Although *she* delighted in watching her old friends, *he* could not see them.

This persisted over a period of time and was made worse for Mr. Smith because his mother-in-law could also see the animals, which were now increasing in number, and still he could not. He soon began to become a little aggravated by the ladies' behaviour and pooh-poohed what they said they saw, sometimes getting quite annoyed.

This continued until one day when Mr. Smith was standing at

the kitchen sink doing what came naturally, the washing up. He suddenly looked out the kitchen window and shouted to his wife in a somewhat irate manner, "Mary, have you seen all those flippin' dogs in our garden? Where the heck have they all come from?"

Needless to say, Mrs. Smith and her mother took great delight in standing there with great big smiles on their faces and body language that spelled out in capital letters: "SEE, WE TOLD YOU SO!"

Kurgan, Part 2

Mary, Health Care Administrator
Illinois

Kim's note: A friend of Mary's had a dog named Kurgan. Although Kurgan wasn't Mary's own companion animal, they were very close. Mary spent a lot of time with Kurgan before he died; and after he passed, she felt his presence many times, as told in her story in Chapter 8, "Heavenly Visitors." Shortly before this book went to press, Mary had yet another experience to share. . . .

YOU MIGHT BE INTERESTED in knowing that I've had another encounter with Kurgan—this time a sighting. This is the first time in my life I've actually seen a deceased animal with my own two eyes. Here is what happened. . . .

Sometimes when I leave for work, my dogs run to the bedroom window to watch me drive away. (Cutest thing you've ever seen, by the way—two little Shiba Inu faces pressed to the glass.) The window has an old screen on it, so when I do see them, they are a little "foggy" looking through the screen. One day a couple of weeks ago as I was backing out of the driveway, I stopped and looked up at the window, and there he was—*Kurgan*. He sat there, looking so proud and just enjoying the warm breeze in the window.

It took me a few seconds to absorb what I was seeing. At first, I assumed it must be one of *my* dogs, but then it hit me that Kurgan, an Akita, was several times bigger than my Shibas. Then I realized that I was seeing him crystal clear—there was no fuzziness from the old screen. In addition, when my dogs look out the window, they are sitting on a daybed, so I only see them from the chest up. What I was seeing was the whole dog—paws and all. He almost appeared to be sitting level with the windowsill, which would have been impossible for my dogs. We made eye contact for several seconds. I didn't feel like he had a message for me or anything—but I could feel the contentment around him. I looked away for a second, and when I looked back he was gone.

175

Cheech
Victoria Strykowski, Wild Horse Mentor and Greyhound Rescue
Illinois

MY FAMILY TOOK IN CHEECH, a German shepherd, when she was about one year old and I was about ten. She was a beautiful black and silver color, looking very much like a wolf. We were inseparable. She slept on my bed every single night that I was home.

When Cheech was nine, she was diagnosed with cancer, and I was devastated. There had been no warning. I brought her in to the vet because she had a sore in her armpit and they said it was an open tumor. This was years ago, before I knew about alternative therapy. The vet said she should be euthanized, and I just started crying hysterically. My friend, Michele, had come with me that day, and thank goodness, because she was the one who had to drive home. I was in such shock, I couldn't even stay with Cheech as she passed.

A few months later, Michele and I went to a local disco where a friend of ours worked. This particular night was very slow and the place was just about empty. There were booths creating aisles that led up to the dance floor, and it was very dark, except, of course, for the disco lights. We got up to dance, and as we were walking down the aisle towards the dance floor, we both just stopped dead in our tracks. I looked at Michele and she had a very strange look on her face. I asked her if she had just seen Cheech. She said she had. We had both seen her following us to the dance floor, only for a second and in the darkness of the aisle.

I've felt Cheech's presence many times, but that was the only time I actually saw her.

Duke

Kathleen Hill, Dog Groomer, TTouch For Companion Animals
Nebraska

DUKE WAS A WONDERFUL COMPANION. My husband and I acquired him while still living in an apartment, soon to be moving to an acreage. He was part German shepherd/elkhound, and he was with us even before our children were born. He was with us during our six years on the acreage; with us on a flight to Phoenix—where we lived for three years; and with us on a car trip back to the Midwest. He went with us always, wherever we went.

He was fourteen years old when we started to see a change. He seemed to be getting weaker, had trouble going up and down the stairs, and wouldn't eat. We tried everything to get him to eat something, anything we thought he might like, but still he wouldn't eat. I knew that he wasn't going to last much longer at that rate. But still we tried.

We were at my in-laws' lake cabin, sitting on the hill overlooking the lake. I could almost see in his eyes that he knew this was the last time he would be there. He seemed so peaceful. I made up my mind that weekend that Monday we would make our last trip to the vet. I just couldn't stand to see him suffer. He was in pain, still wasn't eating, and could barely walk. I knew that it was the right decision. I cried all weekend long.

Monday morning I made that terrible phone call to our vet. That afternoon was set up for us to come in. My husband offered to take him in, but I had to be the one to do this; I wanted to be the one to sit with him till the very end. It was awful, walking into the office; tears just wouldn't stop. Even up to his last moments, people commented, "He's such a beautiful dog!" I remember someone asking why he was there. I didn't have to say anything as I sobbed going into the room. It was one of the worst days of my life.

The next day I was home by myself, crying my eyes out. It was so quiet. When he was alive we had always kept all his tags on him, so he would jingle and we would know where he was at all times.

I was now walking through the dining room into the kitchen and I heard his jingle. I turned around, and Duke was prancing toward me like he always did when he came in from outside. He looked happy and healthy again. (He could barely walk in his last days and had looked just awful.) As he came toward me, he disappeared. I could still hear his jingle for a few seconds. This was during the day, and I was wide awake.

Off and on during that week, my husband and I would hear the jingle of his tags and I would see him out of the corner of my eye. I knew he was there to comfort me and always will be.

Baby
Bette Boswell, Retired
Maryland

SHE CAME TO US ONE COLD EVENING. Our oldest son had gotten her before knowing the work and devotion required of him. He asked my husband and me if we would keep her for a short while. We agreed, not knowing what "a short while" meant. Week followed week, and without knowing it, we became the parents of a beautiful yellow Labrador retriever. We named her Baby. It seemed appropriate at the time, as she was a bundle of yellow fur. When she came into the house that evening, she went to everyone to say hello. Weeks became months, and we became a family.

I had to have surgery on my heart, which caused me to have a stroke. After many weeks of recuperation, I was ready to take a walk to enjoy the beautiful spring weather. I put the leash on Baby to have her join me on my walk, when everybody started to yell, "Don't take the dog," figuring she might pull on me, injuring my incision. But she walked beside me like a trooper, never once pulling or trying to run away. So, as I became stronger, my husband and I would take Baby to the nearby high school to run and play on the athletic field.

The night before I was to come home from the hospital, my husband said he'd had a talk with Baby, telling her to take care of me and to always stay with me, not letting me out of her sight. One day, my son and I went shopping for flowers to plant in the yard, and we took Baby with us. I walked a little too fast, and for the first time in her life she started to howl and cry while pulling on her leash to get to me. She never let me out of her sight again. I guess she really understood what my husband was telling her the night before my return from the hospital.

One day we realized that our Baby was not a youngster any longer. As she lay in her favorite spot, she would look at us as if to say, "Help me, please." So my husband and I knew it was time to say good-bye to our beloved pet. She had become so much more than a pet. When it was time, my husband put his arms around her and whispered, "I love you" as her spirit gently floated away.

Two weeks after Baby left us, we moved into a new house at the beach. Oh, how she would have loved the beach. Water to her was like breathing air to us. I worried that if she ever tried to come back to visit us, she wouldn't know where to find us.

To my surprise, one night, two years later, in our new house, there she was at the foot of my bed. She was turning around in circles as if to find a comfortable place to lie down. I reached out to pet her, but my arm went through her. I tried again, but my arm went through her again.

It is because of her visit to me that I know she lives, still. She survived! I don't mourn for her any longer because I know she is okay. My husband passed away two years ago, and I am convinced they are together. Yes, there is no doubt in my mind that animals have souls and that they live on after they are finished with their lives here on Earth.

Kim's note: People sometimes ask if our departed animals know where we are and can find us when we move. As this story illustrates, of course they can!

Princess

Jodie McDonald, Advisor for State Government
Kentucky

I HAD AN AUSTRALIAN SHEPHERD MIX named Princess. I rescued her from the Humane Society when she was only a week old. I bottle-fed her and bought my house for her. She is so very special to me. I love her so very much.

We had to have Princess put to sleep. It was one of the hardest things I've ever had to experience in life. I planted flowers in her memory. I made a shadow box with pictures, poems, her collar, and the bottle I used to feed her with. I sure did shed a lot of tears making it. I knew she was in Heaven with God; I knew she was okay, but I missed her so much, I would cry myself to sleep.

One night after I prayed and cried myself to sleep, I woke up in the middle of the night and Princess was at the foot of the bed, looking at me. She looked so beautiful. I sat up and reached, wanting to hug her, and she disappeared. I wasn't dreaming; I was totally awake.

I rescue dogs and have a total of seven, and I love them with all my heart and soul. I don't want to say Princess is dead because she's not; she's just living with God now, and I know we will be together again one day. I know she is in peace. Every day I send Princess love. I know that when she came to me that night, she did so to let me know that she is okay and that they do continue living on.

Molly

Frank J. Hannaford, Computer Consultant
Nebraska

MOLLY, OUR MUCH-BELOVED COMPANION DOG, passed away after seventeen years of living as an integral part of our family. Our three children shared everything from baby food to beds with Molly, and she, in turn, loved and guarded them as much as their mother and I.

When Molly finally passed of old age, we were devastated. Our other dog and cats missed her as well. One cat in particular, Claudia, didn't know what to do with herself. Being the "old Mother" and nominal leader, she had spent several of Molly's last years acting as Molly's "eyes and ears" . . . staying close by her side at all times, guiding her outside to our backyard when needed, and leading her back in to her bed.

Soon after Molly passed, however, all of us in the family—human and otherwise—came to realize that Molly often dropped by to check on us. At first, we were not sure what was going on. There would be some stirrings and noises in the area where Molly's bed had been, which Claudia would rush to check out. Then some scratching at the back door, when our other animals were nowhere near it. Finally, every member of the family had a visual encounter of some kind.

I remember, for example, going to let the dogs in (we had acquired a second dog some months after Molly died, as our other dog was just too lonely without her old friend around). It was late at night, and instinctively I held the screen door open as the dogs entered . . . one, two, three. All was well, until, with a start, I remembered that there should only be two. I clearly remember seeing Molly's faun-colored shape loping past me on the way in. Looking around, she was nowhere to be found, but I knew she had been present.

Similar events have taken place on a regular basis over these last two years, involving every family member. At first, it was a little unnerving. Now, we are all glad to know that our companion of all those years drops by for a visit now and then. It is comforting to know Molly is, in some form, still with us.

Demetri
Katharine Lyle Nelson, Speech/Language Pathologist
West Virginia

I SHARED MY LIFE WITH MY FRIEND, a beautiful black cat named Demetri. I found her at high noon while working one summer. She became my best friend for the next nineteen years.

She saw me through many pains and losses. The greatest loss was that of the man with whom I thought I would be spending the rest of my life. It did not happen. This man of my dreams left me with many unanswered questions and tears. Demi was there when there were no words left to say. She purred and chirped to let me know she cared. She even licked away my tears.

She often climbed the bookcase in my bedroom, and would knock over the three small pictures I had placed there.

One snowy December morning, I found her in the kitchen and knew that something was very wrong. I rushed her to the vet, but her body was just beyond recovery. I grieved for her deeply for months.

ONE DAY, as I was lying on my bed, halfway between sleep and consciousness, something caught my eye, or so I thought. I looked over toward the bookcase where Demi loved to climb. In my state of grief and grogginess, I simply thought that I had imagined the black blur as it moved down from the bookcase. I continued to lie on my bed, hurting from the huge loss of my friend, and once again, wishing that I could know she was alright.

Something made me fully wake up and look up to her favorite shelf, where I had the three pictures. When I did, I knew I had not imagined that black blur, because every one of those pictures had been knocked over . . . exactly as she had done many times during her life. I smiled through my tears to know my dearest friend had come to comfort me one last time. I know she watches from that great Beyond, and one day I will see her beautiful face once again.

Mixie
Wendy B.
Connecticut

I'VE ALWAYS BEEN A DEEP-CORE ANIMAL LOVER and have long believed that animals have souls and that they do go "home" to God, as we do. This was proven to me very recently.

I met my cat Mixie when I went to apply for a job at a local manufacturing plant. She was the "yard-cat," and lived in the woods surrounding the company. During the days, she would sleep in the lobby, and someone would usually feed her; and in the evenings she would be put back outside for the night. When I walked into the lobby for my interview, she was sleeping on one of the chairs, and she lifted her head, looked directly into my eyes, and meowed, as if saying hello.

I petted and talked to Mixie while I was waiting for my interview to begin, and that was the beginning of the incredible bond we shared. I got the job, and before long I was Mixie's self-appointed primary caretaker. I fed her every day, took her to the veterinarian for shots, and cuddled and talked to her. She began sleeping on a chair behind my desk rather than in the lobby, wanting to be closer to me.

One day I asked my supervisor how long Mixie had been the company cat. She told me that she had been working at the company for twelve years, and Mixie had been coming around for at least that long, and that she had been a full grown cat even back then. I was awed that at her age, with her rugged lifestyle, she could be in such good health. She had successfully survived hurricanes, blizzards, freezing temperatures, and New England predators year after year, living outside in the woods.

It was the winter several years later that started me seriously worrying about Mixie. It was a particularly bad year for snow and freezing temperatures in New England. I hated putting Mixie outside during those frigid evenings, and prayed constantly that she would be okay. It broke my heart that she couldn't stay inside the building, but the owner wouldn't allow it. And since I was still staying with my parents, I couldn't take her home with me. I had no choice but to let her tough it out. But I cried for days each time, until I saw her again and knew that she was all right.

By the next fall, it was obvious to me that Mixie was getting much too old to survive another winter alone outside. I knew in my heart that her little body couldn't take that strain. So I started thinking about finding her a home. But I couldn't think of a single person who would love her and care for her like I did. One morning as I was driving to work, worrying about this, it suddenly dawned on me that Mixie belonged with *me*. I was making good money—there was no reason why I couldn't get an apartment and take her in. Which is exactly what I did.

At first Mixie was a little unsure about the situation and was terrified of the television and ceiling fan (remember, she never actually had a "home" before, and had never seen that kind of thing), but she soon settled in and showed no desire to go outside again.

She lived with me for four wonderful years and seemed very happy there. Then one day, I came home to find Mixie dead on the couch, curled up on one of my sweaters. I dropped the bowl of food I had been carrying to her, and sobbed my heart out. My little sweetie was gone, and I hadn't even been able to say good-bye. She had lived to be twenty-two years old (at least!).

I DIDN'T NOTICE IT AT FIRST, but after Mixie died, my other two cats stopped going into the living room. Not only did they stop going in there, they *refused* to go in there. If I picked them up and carried them in there, they immediately squirmed out of my arms and ran out of the room. I thought it was odd, but I pretty much just dismissed it from my mind. A few days later as I was getting ready for work, I noticed my cat Cinnamon (who was in the bedroom with me) intently staring from the bedroom door through the kitchen, into the living room. Her body was tense, her ears standing at attention, and her eyes were huge. I turned my head to see what she was looking at, and was stunned to see Mixie sitting in the living room doorway. I blinked and looked harder, but she was gone.

I had a strange feeling come over me but then just convinced myself that my eyes were playing tricks on me. It was dark when I got home that evening, and as I walked into the living room and switched on the light, I again saw Mixie, this time lying on the couch. She picked her head up and looked at me, then vanished. I broke into tears, knowing then what was happening. There was no denying it. Mixie was still with me, either afraid of moving on, or too worried about me to go.

I was almost hysterical, not because Mixie was still with me, but because I thought I might be holding her back in some way. I went into the bedroom to think and pray. I asked God what I should do, and I could feel the words come into me, "Tell her to go." Of course—she probably was just waiting to be sure that I would be okay without her. So I immediately got up and went into the living room, sat down on the couch, and started talking quietly to her. I couldn't see her anywhere, but there was a sense of a presence in the room.

I told her that I loved her, that I would always love her, and that I had loved having her with me for the past few years. I told her that it was time for her to go, and that she could come visit me anytime, but that there was a better place for her, with God. I promised her I would see her again some day, and that we would be together again. I was crying as I spoke to her, and I spoke deeply from my heart. I concentrated on sending as much love to her as I could, then prayed to God to send someone to help Mixie find her way home. Nothing spectacular happened, but it seemed as if the room was suddenly empty.

As the next couple of weeks passed, there were no Mixie sightings, by either me or the cats, and they started venturing into the living room again. But I still had a strong need to know that Mixie was okay. I began praying to God for a sign that Mixie was okay and that she was home with Him.

My request was answered on Halloween night (which, incidentally, I've heard is the night where the veil between the spiritual and physical worlds is the thinnest). I had a dream that night that I was walking in a grassy field. I came upon a group of approximately twenty cats, all playing rambunctiously around the base of a majestic tree. Suddenly one of the cats broke from the group and went to drink some water from a dish nearby. Before she lowered her head to the dish, however, she looked over at me, and I realized it was Mixie.

She looked like she did before her age had started to show: young and healthy and fit. She gave me one of those adorable kitty smiles of total contentment, then took a quick drink of water. She started to run back to play with her friends again, then stopped to glance over her shoulder at me once more. In that one glance, I could see in her eyes that she was well and that she was very happy. I woke up then, crying tears of joy. It was such a powerful dream, so vivid and strong with feeling. I didn't just see Mixie; I *felt* her: her gentle, sweet presence. I could feel her love for me, and I could feel her total excitement at being with her friends. For days after that I had a glow of tremendous happiness in my heart. My little one was okay.

I believe with every ounce of my being that this was not just a dream. It was a message from Mixie, as I had requested, to let me know how well she was doing. Since then I've had only a couple more dreams like that, but none quite as powerful as the first. I think Mixie is just checking in with me every now and then to let me know that she thinks about me, just like I think about her. We shared something special, she and I, and I know that I'll see her again someday and be able to hold her in my arms again and hear her sweet purring.

I think that God purposely led Mixie and me to each other, for one simple reason. Every creature (human and animal) deserves to be loved deeply, selflessly, and completely, at least once in their lives. Mixie and I gave that to each other, and that is a bond that can never be broken, not even by death.

Kim's note: It's not uncommon for our departed loved ones to contact us in dreams. As Wendy discovered, these are truly more than just "dreams." This topic will be covered in a later chapter. Meanwhile, I feel it's important to mention here that if we have a visitation from a departed loved one, it doesn't necessarily mean we are holding them back. It is often just their way of checking in, saying hello, and letting us know they still love and care about us.

It was very appropriate that when Wendy told Mixie it was time for her to go and that there was a better place for her, she also told her that she could visit anytime. Our loved ones in spirit truly can have the best of both worlds.

- CHAPTER 13 -

Visions of the Other Side

Death . . . is no more than passing from one room into another.
But there's a difference for me, you know.
Because in that other room I shall be able to see.
— HELEN KELLER

A VISION IS GENERALLY DEFINED as a supernatural or mystical appearance that often conveys a revelation. Many of us have heard of visions within the context of ancient religious experiences as well as literary and dramatic fiction, but perhaps very few people accept it as a reality in our modern world. Without any tangible evidence, I would undoubtedly have an equally skeptical attitude toward such things. However, a personal experience in my youth opened my mind. Although the experience didn't involve animals, it taught me that visions are very real occurrences.

When I was a sophomore in high school, I was asked to the prom by a senior I didn't know very well. I didn't really want to go with him, but I didn't want to hurt his feelings, so I said, "Yes." One day at school, shortly thereafter, I introduced him to my best friend at the time, the one with whom I shared many "psychic slumber parties."

When I returned home from school that afternoon, I went to my room to put my homework on my desk. Suddenly, I felt very strange, almost dizzy and panicked, so I sat on my bed. With that, a vision appeared to me. It was in my mind's eye, but it was so vivid that it seemed as clear and real as day. It was almost as if a movie were being played on an ethereal screen right in front of me. I don't remember whether my eyes were open or closed, but I was definitely wide awake.

As I watched, I saw a flash of a car crash and then a newspaper with a headline that spoke of a fatal car accident in which I had been killed on prom night. I then heard the distant voices of friends and family discussing what a shame it had been that I had died that way, especially since "she didn't really even want to go." As I contemplated what was taking place, I got the very strong impression that I was being shown a potential future, one that would indeed take place if I went to the prom. I got the equally strong impression that I was being warned of this so that I could avert the outcome, because it wasn't my time to go.

I was then startled by the ringing of the telephone, and the vision suddenly vanished. I answered the phone. It was my best friend, whom I had introduced to my prom date earlier that day at school.

"Kim," she began, sounding panicked, "don't go to the prom with that guy! I just had a vision in which you were killed in a car crash on prom night. Don't go! If you go, you'll be killed."

We were both stunned as I told her that I had just had the same vision. Needless to say, I cancelled my date to the prom and stayed home that night. (I didn't disclose the reason to the young man, as I worried that he wouldn't believe me; instead, I told him that I was only a sophomore and my parents weren't comfortable with me going to the senior prom, which was actually true. My parents had suggested I tell him this, as they had become accustomed to my psychic experiences and knew not to ignore them, yet they realized that others might not understand.) I was actually relieved, as the young man made me nervous for some reason, and I felt uncomfortable around him. However, had the vision not occurred, I would have indeed gone to the prom as planned.

Interestingly, the story doesn't end there. The young man who had asked me to the prom continued to ask me out, and I continued to politely decline. Then he graduated, and I thought that was the end of him. However, for the next year, he continued to call, send me strange letters, and watch my house, reporting his observations about the goings-on in my life so that I knew I was being watched. I became very frightened of him over time and wished he didn't know where I lived.

His letters began to take on a sinister tone as he explained that he loved to drive really fast and, in fact, had been in love with someone once, but the girl had been killed in a car crash with him behind the wheel. She had died in his arms. I shuddered as I recalled the vision that had displayed a similar fate for myself.

One year later, I heard the news that this disturbed young man had died in a car crash. He had been the only one in the car, had been going too fast, and had driven off a cliff. There were no skid marks.

That experience taught me, in a most profound way, the importance of paying attention to visions and never dismissing them as random acts of imagination. So, when I heard of other people who had experienced visions, I paid attention.

OVER TIME, I CAME ACROSS MANY PEOPLE who had witnessed animals on the Other Side, not only in dreams, but also during spontaneous visions while fully awake. Those who have shared these experiences are rational individuals who have nothing to gain from making such claims. In some cases, the animals initiate direct contact and communication with the people they've left behind. In other cases, animals are viewed at a distance during these glimpses of Heaven.

Gladys Hypes of West Virginia, who told the story about her beloved dog, Kooter (in Chapter 11, "HeavenScent"), continued to experience other signs of Kooter's presence. One day, she contacted me with the following:

> Last night as I lay in bed, I so desperately wanted a sign that Kooter was okay and well. As I closed my eyes (still awake), I saw what seemed like a movie screen and I was sitting under a big tree and Kooter was running all around the tree. He looked to be full of spunk and life. I saw a few

flowers and a beautiful rock. It only lasted a few seconds but seemed like a lifetime. I remember falling off to sleep in a very peaceful state.

She asked if I had heard of this type of experience before, and I let her know that others had indeed experienced similar visions. She responded with the following:

> It's really good to know that there are others out there like me . . . helps me to know I'm not stepping off the deep end.
>
> As I told you about the vision of me sitting under a tree and Kooter running all around it, I forgot to mention that a few years ago I had a dream about my [deceased] grandmother, and in that dream she was sitting under that very same tree. I know it to be so because I remember thinking last night, *That's the tree Grandma was sitting under.* Can this be explained?

What I have found is that it's extremely common to receive what I call "glimpses of Heaven" in the dream state, as that is when we are most open to receiving such contacts from the Other Side (explored further in the next chapter, "Sweet Dreams"); and very similar scenes are often witnessed during spontaneous visions while fully awake. Her description of the setting (beautiful outdoor scene) is by far the most common type of description I hear from people who have these experiences, although they have no idea that others are describing the same types of experiences. Following are stories of others who have experienced visions of the Other Side. . . .

Topz

Mary Blaszak, Housecleaner and Specialty Soap Maker
New York

MANY YEARS AGO, when I was in my late twenties, I was lying in bed one night, thinking about the little furry brown-and-white mutt I used to have a few years before. I felt guilty because I had let him outside one night and he never came back again. He was very old at fourteen years.

I was still wide-awake and had just closed my eyes, so I know I was not asleep. I saw something like a very large "picture window" and in this window I saw hundreds of dogs—all kinds, big and small—running, jumping, and playing very happily, and then I saw my dog "Topz" also running and looking very happy just following all the other dogs and having fun. This picture lasted maybe a minute or so, but long enough that I got a close-up look at my dog, and I knew it was really him.

Strawberry Shortcake
Karen Young, Word Processing Specialist
New Mexico

I HAD A BEAUTIFUL WHITE CAT who I kept outside because I am very allergic to cat fur. She adopted me, so that is why I had her. One morning at about 6 A.M., I heard her screaming outside. I ran outside in my nightgown and jumped our back fence. Two big dogs were attacking her. I screamed at them and jumped in between them and grabbed her. My neighbor had come out and was standing there with a big board ready to hit the dogs. The dogs stopped their attack. I took my cat (Strawberry Shortcake) up the sidewalk and looked at her. She was still alive. When I got back in my yard, I felt her die.

This is where people stop believing me, but I saw it so I don't care what they think. I know what I saw. I saw her ghost or spirit lift out of her body. She looked the same, only clear. She had an outline and motion. As her spirit left her body, a sort of clear doorway opened up over my left shoulder about three feet away. The doorway was clear and outlined; it had a shimmering motion. There were two "people" (also clear) there who opened the doorway. They were smiling and seemed happy. It seemed bright beyond the doorway. I perceived sunlight beyond it and a lot of activity. They turned and left. My cat's spirit looked over at the doorway. I screamed at her really loudly, "Strawberry! Don't leave me!" She looked back at her body, which was very dead. Then she turned back to the doorway and started to run toward it. There was a big popping sound, and she and the doorway disappeared. All cats do go to Heaven (or someplace). I know it to be true.

This happened several years ago. It doesn't bother me to tell people. It has given people who love cats a lot of comfort. People can say whatever they want to. But I know what I saw. The doorway was there. I believe because I have seen it.

Mable
Kendra Thompson, Student
New Jersey

I WAS RAISED WITH THE PHILOSOPHY that animal lovers had more compassionate souls. Needless to say, I grew up with many animals.

I always had a dog and at least two cats, but I eventually grew very interested in smaller, more uncommon pets. I was amazed to find such personality and life in little animals the size of my palm. Eventually I got frogs, newts, lizards, hamsters, birds, fish . . . but there was always something missing.

Then one day, I went to the pet shop to look at the small animals. I overheard someone talking about the "snake food" and figured it to be mice or rats and was interested in looking at them (the "snake food" was on the floor hidden by a shelf).

So, a woman pulled out a little six-week-old brown-and-white rat who immediately crawled up my arm and situated herself on my shoulder. I took the baby home and named her Mable.

Mable was my first pet rat. Now, I know some people who have not had their lives touched by a rat would not understand how incredible these animals are, but pet rats are very endearing. They are just like dogs in miniature form. I named her Maple Mable because the brown stripe down her back was such a beautiful color, like maple syrup. Mable was the first to open a new and different door to friendship.

Though she was shy at first, within a week she already knew and responded to her name. She eventually spent most of her time outside of her cage. Mable followed me everywhere, sat in my lap a lot of the time, slept in bed with me, and even got her pictures taken with Santa (Santa fell in love with her and didn't want to give her back to me!).

The bond that I had with Mable was very extreme, like I've never experienced with any other animal. She truly seemed to know what I was saying to her all the time . . . she seemed to understand me even when I didn't say words. We had an incredible, mystical friendship . . . we just understood each other. She was very intuitive and intelligent. Each and every day she amazed me even more.

One funny memory that I'll never forget was when I had to put her in a cat cage temporarily until I bought her a new rat cage. Mable was a big, chubby girl, so I didn't think she'd be able to squeeze through the bars. She seemed to like the cage, and it was plenty of space for her, so she lived in it for about three months. One day, I had the cage on the floor while Mable was running loose, and to my surprise, right in front of my eyes, she squeezed very easily right through the bars of the cage to get back in (even though the door was open). My mouth nearly dropped! For three months, she never ever got loose out of that cage, but the whole time, she was capable of doing it if she wanted to. I know that she squeezed through that day just to show me that she could do it if she wanted to.

Once she was sick with a respiratory problem . . . that same time, I had a bad cold. Another time, I sprained my leg . . . she must have done the same because she was limping, too. These are just a few of the many incredible stories I could tell about her.

She succumbed to pneumonia only one and a half years after I had gotten her. She had a very uncomfortable death; she spent one week literally gasping for air. She had been on many medications two weeks before her death but to no avail. I knew the time was coming that Mable would be leaving me. My mind understood, but my heart could not accept it. I took her to the vet one final time to see if there were any other treatments for her, but after three hours in an oxygen tank with no difference, there was nothing else to be done.

The vet literally begged me to euthanize her, but I just couldn't do it. That would've been the first time I ever would make that decision and I could not bring myself to do it, though I knew it was the best thing for her. I wanted her to pass on in the house that I know she loved, with the person I know she adored. It was a Saturday when the vet told me to euthanize her. He wasn't going to be in again until Monday, but after Monday he was going on vacation. He said that if poor Mable was still alive by Monday, to finally bring her back in that last time. I agreed to that.

All day Sunday I kept checking on her. I wished so badly that she would pass on at home. I told her to stop her struggle to live, that if there was anything I could do, I would do it . . . but there wasn't. I told her it would crush me to have to put her to sleep, to please just go on. Monday came and she was still alive before I went to work. I held her and cried. I was so upset to see her still alive, knowing I would have to take her to the vet after work. But I also didn't want her to pass on without me being there; it was very conflicting. When I came home from work, she was still alive. I picked her up, sat on a chair and talked to her as my teardrops fell on her head. She passed on quietly only five minutes later.

I know that happened for a reason. I know she waited until I got home again, but she also made sure I didn't have to make the decision to euthanize her. Obviously, I grieved for her, feeling that I would never have a pet like her again . . . rat or any other animal. She was only with me for a year and a half, but she was the best friend I ever had.

I have always believed in animals coming back to visit from the afterlife, but after living with a whole assortment of animals all my life, I had never had any overt signs of them coming back. Considering the nature of the relationship I had with Mable, I was certain that she would come back to me. If any animal would ever come back, I just knew it had to be Mable. From Mable's death in March until my twenty-first birthday in November, she never came back. Although my mother would mention that she'd seen something white (Mable was white with brown on her head, neck and down her back) scurry across the floor on some occasions, I never saw or felt anything and I'll admit that I was hurt . . . and disappointed. I knew way before her death that she was my soul mate; she was the friend that I would be tied to forever . . . so why hadn't she come back?

On my twenty-first birthday, I planned to go out drinking with my friends. The plans dissolved because they couldn't make it, but I was determined to go out drinking that day, so I just went to a local bar by myself. Toward the end of the night, I noticed a young woman with a beautiful brown hair color . . . the maple brown color of Mable's. The woman took the next seat down from me where she obviously knew the other two girls that were sitting there. To my astonishment, one of the other girls called her "Mable"! I was utterly shocked. On the way home that night, thoughts of Mable—and my other rat, Kelso, at home—consumed me.

As soon as I walked into the house, I started screaming for Kelso (Kel was my new boy to help me fill Mable's void). My mother got Kelso for me, and I was crying because, as sweet and good as he was, he wasn't Mable. Then I starting hysterically crying that Mable never came back to see me: "She must not have forgiven me for not ending her suffering earlier." After about fifteen minutes of crying, I calmed down.

Then all of a sudden . . . I saw Mable! I saw her in an open field of grass; I was looking at her side while she was walking. My mother will tell you that my eyes were wide open in bewilderment as I tried to reach out and touch her, but she wasn't coming close enough for me to. She seemed oblivious to my watching her . . . but she was okay, peacefully walking in the field.

People could write this off as an intoxicated delusion, but of the many times I'd been out drinking during my twenty-first year, I never had visual delusions; and the woman named Mable who sat next to me in the bar certainly wasn't a delusion.

The next day, my mother told me that after I had left for the bar, she saw something white flash across the living room floor over to the door. She believed, even before I came home and saw Mable that night, that Mable had run out the door after me, to protect me. And she believed that I had very much seen Mable.

It was enough just to see her again. She was quite a chubby girl (I have since had many, many rats and she had to be one of my chubbiest!), but before she died, she'd lost quite a bit of weight. When I saw her, she was happy Mable again . . . chubby and running free without pain. That was enough for me to overcome my grief.

I've never loved anyone (human or animal) as much as I loved my Mable. I know there was and still is a spiritual bond between us. Since then, I've never visually seen her, but I feel her all the time. Mable is watching over me.

Misha
Glenn Wolff, Clinical Social Worker
Connecticut

MY WIFE, CARYN, AND I shared a life of sixteen years with our beloved dog, Misha. She was a Westie terrier mix, weighing only eight pounds. Misha was truly our first child and our best friend. She had a remarkable personality, full of love, life, and oomph! Misha passed over one March. Needless to say, her passing left a huge void in our lives.

Soon after Misha's passing, I went to a healer (a Reiki master) to relieve some of the pain and anguish that I experienced after Misha's passing. The healer, during our session, said that Misha's spirit was still with me and she was present in the room. About one month later, I visited the healer again to relieve pain, sorrow, and grief. The healer said that Misha was again in the room. Misha was concerned that I was so distraught and she was "hanging around" to make sure that I was okay.

During the course of our session, I had a clear picture of Misha and myself at a very bright open space. I kept repeating, "Misha, you can go now . . . Misha, you can go now . . . " I then had a clear vision of Misha running into the light. After the session, I wept and wept, but at the same time I felt a great sense of relief and comfort. I knew that Misha was safe and happy, and she only wanted *me* to be safe and happy.

My wife Caryn and I had been trying for several years to conceive a child prior to Misha's death. Caryn went to a healer (a Reiki master) in May, and she too had a vision of Misha and at the same time a vision of holding a baby in our kitchen.

Caryn became pregnant in November. She had a difficult first trimester, and our doctor was unsure if the pregnancy would last. I was still seeing my healer, and she told me that Misha was our baby's "guardian angel" and always would be. Benjamin Ezra Wolff was born the following July and is now twenty months old.

We have a portrait of Misha hanging in our home. I look at her portrait all the time. I show our son, Benjamin, her portrait from time to time. When I ask Benjamin, "Where is Misha?" he immediately points to her portrait. He also giggles sometimes when he passes her portrait. I truly believe that there is a link between Misha and Benjamin, between the timing of her passing over and his birth. I have a Buddhist friend who believes that, in fact, Misha is reincarnated in Benjamin. And I truly believe that Misha's spirit remains in our home and is indeed making sure that we are all well, cared for, and safe.

Kim's note: As Glenn discovered, the act of letting go can be very healing. It doesn't mean we are sending our loved ones away from us permanently, or severing our connection to them. Rather, it means we are taking a step toward freeing ourselves from the grips of grief and despair, and freeing them to move forward. The desperation, holding on, and worry are released, but the love remains. Having said that, I feel it's important to reiterate here that just because we receive a message or visitation from a departed loved one, it doesn't mean we are holding them back. It is often just their way of checking in, saying hello, and letting us know they still love and care about us—and they always will.

Patty
Janine Fuquay, Retired Silkscreener
Montana

I TEND TO "SEE" PEOPLE I LOVE after they pass on, either as visions when I'm awake or in very vivid, realistic dreams of the Other Side when I'm asleep. When my mother passed on a few years ago, I saw her repeatedly afterwards, most frequently when she took me on visits to the Other Side in my dreams. Each time I saw her, she appeared younger, stronger, and more focused. Finally, the last time I saw her, she appeared to be in her twenties and in her prime. She told me she had tasks to do and obligations on the Other Side, so she wouldn't be visiting me as much anymore. I wished her well on her journey and said I loved her. I felt very good about this, and the wonderful things I saw with her have always stayed in my mind.

The same thing happened to me when my teenage nephew, Lee, passed on about the same time. I saw him on the Other Side as well. In our world, he had cerebral palsy and could barely talk, but he was a master at writing poetry. He had a full scholarship to attend college based on the poetry he had already written. Unfortunately, he died before he could use it. On the Other Side, he was a strong, tanned young man with a beautiful speaking voice and a gentle wit. I didn't recognize him at first! I was talking to this charming young man when I suddenly recognized him and blurted out, "My God, you're Lee!" He smiled and said, "Things are a lot different over here." He also was very dedicated to the project he was working on in the afterlife.

I had to have my beloved little cat Patty put to sleep. I was prepared to sell everything I owned to pay for whatever it took to make her better. She had cardiomyopathy, and fluid surrounded her lungs. Finally, the vet said I was only prolonging her suffering. When I held her and she looked up at me, her eyes told me of the pain and extreme exhaustion she was feeling. She was ready to go. It was the most difficult thing I've ever done, but I told the vet to euthanize her. I cried so much.

After a few days, I started seeing her in dreams and when

awake. Just like the others I've seen, she was sweet and healthy. She seemed to be three or four years old, just as she was in her prime of life. It felt wonderful to see her again! I miss her terribly, but I feel assured that all of my departed loved ones and I will be together again someday.

Kim's note: It's not uncommon for our departed loved ones to visit us in our dreams. This will be explored further in the next chapter.

Shelter Dog

Gail De Sciose, Animal Communicator
New York

I WILL FOREVER BE GRATEFUL to a male sheltie whose name I never even learned. When I took my basic class in animal communication, I was originally very skeptical about the truth of communication between species. I had been motivated to pursue this field because I had been a volunteer at a big city animal shelter for several years. I thought animal communication would give me another way to reach the frightened and often badly traumatized animals who were turned in to the shelter. After the weekend workshop, I began having experiences that convinced me that animal communication was, in fact, true. However, I still had reservations about being able to contact animals who had left their bodies and were now in spirit.

About six weeks after my initial training, I made the acquaintance of a beautiful male sheltie who had been turned in by his owners because they no longer had time to care for him. He had a very bad skin condition and was contagious to the other dogs in the ward. He had to wear a plastic collar so that he wouldn't bite and scratch himself. I had to content myself with just being able to talk to him—both verbally and telepathically. This went on for a period of three weeks, and the dog and I developed a friendship. It was obvious that he really missed his people. He was very depressed and gradually started to pick up kennel cough and other shelter-borne conditions. Nothing that the shelter veterinarians could do would help, as his will was broken.

On the last day that I actually saw him, it was clear that he was dying. He had a vacant look in his eyes and coughed dreadfully. Even in this terrible condition, he would come over to the edge of his cage and look at me whenever I could get back to talk to him. I told him not to be afraid—that he would soon be able to leave this diseased body and be free. I told him how much I loved him and that I was sure he would be fine once he was in spirit. I left the shelter that day with my own heart very heavy. This once beautiful dog was only five years old and could have had a long, happy life if he hadn't been abandoned by the people he had loved.

THAT EVENING I was at a meeting where we did a group medita-tion. In the midst of my meditation, my friend the sheltie came to me. I could see him running in a field, and the sores on his back were completely gone. He looked healthy and happy and I could feel the love in his spirit. I was very joyful to see him in this state, as he had been so pitiful earlier in the day at the shelter.

The next time I went to do my volunteering, I asked when this particular dog had been euthanized. It was approximately the same time that he had come to me in my meditation! I felt certain then that he had come to show me that he was fine now that he was out of his body and in spirit. From that moment on, I have never doubted that we can communicate with departed souls, and it has been my privilege to speak to hundreds of animals in spirit.

Wolf Speak

*Myriah Krista Walker, Residential Counselor
for Developmentally Disabled Adults
Colorado*

SHELBY WAS THE ONLY GIRL in Ayla's litter of four puppies. I had given her away to friends at the wee age of six weeks old. This was the normal age to give a puppy away, once weaned.

But not according to Ayla. She didn't forgive me for a long time. Shelby had been her favorite puppy. When I gave the second pup away to friends, Ayla clutched the remaining two pups to her closely. I allowed her to keep them, watching as they grew and marveling at the ways of a mother who devoted herself completely to teaching them wisdom.

Walking with wolf dogs among civilization is a challenging experience. No matter the hybrid percentage that lies in their biology, their natural hunting instincts prevail. The human in the pack must take diligent care and many precautions to keep their charges at home.

Alas, one evening Ayla broke through the fence in the yard and took her three-month-old pups for a cruise in the ranch lands that surrounded our small town. A rancher, alarmed by the sounds of squawking in his yard, fired shots at the dogs until they fled.

All this was unknown to me as I sat soaking in a hot bath. Ayla and I had always had a rare and beautiful telepathic communication, and so when her face suddenly appeared as though hovering above the waters, I did not think it unusual. She and I could mind-talk, using pictures and images and feelings.

Although I've always been able to communicate with animals, Ayla was the first one with whom I had complete and total communication abilities. We spoke as clearly to each other through silent thought and feelings—as clear as two humans talking audibly did. There was nothing in my heart she didn't know. It was as though she was simply an extension of my soul.

Now soaking in the bath, I sent a wave of love from my heart to her vision and mentally said, "I love you, Ayla!" Pure love emanated from her eyes, filling my heart to the brim. I saw a golden energy emanate from the vision. I held on to it for several moments until it dissolved into the ethers. Still unaware of the events that had transpired, I felt grateful for a companion who could communicate in such a way, simply because she loved and because she could.

My husband had been watching television, unaware that the dogs had escaped. When I came downstairs and opened the back door to check on the dogs, I realized they were gone. The vision of Ayla's love still fresh, I now knew something was terribly wrong. I knew she had come to say good-bye, and my heart lurched.

It was not until the next morning that we learned what had happened. My husband made several frantic calls around town searching for the dogs. Finally, it was the sheriff who gave us our answers. Ayla had led the pups to within two blocks of home before the shots in her body became fatal. The sheriff had found the pups mourning beside their mom, but they were too skittish to be caught. My husband was able to coax them to him and brought them home.

One pup was unharmed; the other had been shot and eventually had to be euthanized. Nikoma was his name, and at the moment of his death he also appeared in vision, linking to my heart.

Eventually we found a home for the remaining puppy. Within two months, however, I received an unexpected gift. Shelby's caretaker had died, and his girlfriend did not have the time to devote to her that she needed. Ayla's favorite pup was returned to me!

Shelby lived with me for six years. Ours was a bond of the heart. She helped raise my children, was a gentle guardian of our home, walked with me through divorce and remarriage, and kept my heart alive and open with her playfulness.

Her golden eyes would pierce through me sometimes. Often were the times she simply wanted to be held while we sat together on the couch. She was an eighty-five-pound puppy that never grew up.

My second marriage began to fail. Due to alcoholism and the growing violent nature of my husband, it became necessary for me to leave my home and move away. At the time I moved, I could not take Shelby with me. The people I was to stay with had no room for a dog. I prayed I would one day be able to have her with me, but feared at our parting that it would not be so. She sat before me on the floor, and I spoke to her from the silent depths of my heart. She whined, and then placed her forehead against mine. We lingered for several silent moments, heads bowed to one another touching. It was the last time I saw her.

Months passed, my husband disconnected the phone and I knew not where he or Shelby was. Then one day, a friend who had lived near them told me that my husband had been picked up for drunk driving and Shelby had been impounded. She was never released, and had been put to sleep.

Oh, my friend! I stood outside my new home and wept. I felt so helpless and angry. I wished there had been a way for her to still be with me, but I knew in truth there had not been.

Suddenly a vision of her came fully into view. There was her face, smiling and happy. Her gentle presence vivid. Something within broke open, and I found myself telepathically howling to her spirit. I heard her howl in response. The depth of my own inner howls rose from our joint sorrow. I was too clutched with tears to give physical voice to this pain, but my heart sang loudly.

Then, in the canyon where I live, an audible sound came to my ears. The sound of coyotes howling. On the inner planes they heard our communion, and sang long and mournful in the afternoon sun. Now the howls of sorrow were heard both within and without.

The vision of Shelby remained until our howls subsided and my heart emptied. The howls of the coyotes subsided as well. Pure love emanated from Shelby's eyes, and I both saw and felt her smile. Around her lay a new paradise, full of color and aliveness.

"Oh, forgive me!" I began to sob again. A wave of forgiveness, understanding, and eternal love washed over me as her smile radiated a golden energy into my heart. She continued to broadcast these feelings until the guilt dissolved within my heart. "There is only Love," I heard her heart speak.

I learned that day there is no difference between the voice of our hearts and the sound that comes through physically. There is only Love, real and full and eternal.

Kim's note: The Animal Safehouse Program at the Rancho Coastal Humane Society in Encinitas, California, provides emergency shelter for the innocent companion animals of domestic violence victims. Because of this special program, women are no longer forced to choose between abandoning a beloved animal and staying in an abusive home. If needed, please check for a similar program in your community. It is my hope that one day such a program will be available everywhere, or better yet, not needed at all.

- Chapter 14 -

Sweet Dreams

Millions of spiritual creatures walk the Earth unseen,
both when we wake, and when we sleep.
— John Milton

THE ROUGHLY ONE-THIRD OF OUR LIFE spent sleeping is much more than merely a lot of down time. This is a time when we seem to be most receptive to mystical encounters, without the "logical" mind telling us that such things aren't possible. True, the subconscious mind does its work and sorts things out in the dream state. However, it's been my experience that there's often a lot more going on. Dreams contain a wealth of information and valuable experience if we only pay attention.

Dreams of departed loved ones are often, though not always, actual visitations. It seems that it's relatively common for our departed loved ones to make contact with us while we're dreaming—and during that magical "twilight" stage between sleeping and wakefulness. Those who experience such events can usually tell the difference between "just a dream" and a visitation.

Many people have experienced these so-called dreams. Some of their stories are included later in this chapter, but first, I'd like to share a story of my own. . . .

ONE THING I LEARNED A LONG TIME AGO is that grief, like love, has no boundaries. It matters not the size, appearance, condition, or status of the beloved. Love is love. And so it is with grief upon saying good-bye to that beloved.

I had just buried my only two remaining beloved animals a week apart and was still trying to make sense of the grief. It's never an easy thing to bury our loved ones, and this was no exception. Jameth and I have no children, so for us, our animal companions *are* our children, and we were now childless. One by one, all of the members of our little animal family had reached old age and died, and the losses had become increasingly difficult to bear. We all know that we will, more often than not, outlive our beloved animals, but the reality of this usually does not fully register until they pass. So Jameth and I, in a heartfelt and tear-drenched moment of conviction, decided not to let any more animals into our collective life for a while, as the pain of saying good-bye was just too much to bear. We felt solid in our decision and certain that nothing could sway us from this.

The next day, while sitting in an office waiting room, I happened to recognize a woman sitting nearby. Our eyes met in mutual recognition.

"How's your little rattie?" she asked. By chance, we had been together in that same waiting room several weeks earlier, when my beloved rat, April, was dying. Knowing that my precious little companion didn't have much time left, I had taken her on all my errands with me, cradled in a little baby blanket. I didn't want to leave her alone, and I wanted to be sure she'd die in my arms when her time came.

Because I've had pet rats for the majority of my life, and because rats have an average lifespan of only a few short years, I've had to say good-bye to more than my share of beloved animals. Some people ask, "Why rats?" My response is, "Why not?" They're as soft as kittens, as playful as puppies, and as charming as little Disney characters who ride around on your shoulders and whisper in your ears like little fairies, caressing your cheeks with their rose petal ears. There's something about communing with a creature so tiny and so vulnerable—yet so trusting and so personable—that leaves an irreversible mark on your soul. When they grasp your finger in their tiny hands, something takes hold of your heart.

Over the years, I've met many people who, upon discovering my love of rats, proceed to tell me their own story of an unforgettable little rat they once loved and lost. More often than not, the story ends with the remark that they could never get a pet rat again because they don't live very long and it's just too heartbreaking when they die. *Amen.*

In response to the woman's question about my "little rattie," I informed her that April had recently died. After expressing her condolences, she asked me if I wanted another rat. *You can't just replace them like that,* I thought to myself.

She then went on to tell the story of a little white rat, crouched in the corner of an aquarium with a large boa constrictor. The rat was supposed to be lunch, but for some reason, the snake just wasn't eating. Meanwhile, the rat was starving, having been in there for nearly two weeks with virtually no food or water. The woman had been entrusted with the care of the snake by a friend who had moved away, and she'd had no idea what she was getting herself into. She was distraught and unsure what to do. It pained her to feed the snake live animals, but she didn't think there were any other options. And she didn't count on *this.*

As the woman told me the story of the snake who wouldn't eat the rat, my heart went out to the rat . . . and to the woman (and to the snake, for that matter). The rat was in danger of either starving to death or being eaten alive; the woman was torn up about having to make weekly trips to the pet store for live, terrified rats in little paper bags; and the snake was probably tired of sitting in an aquarium and worrying about lunch biting back. (The rat had apparently already bitten the snake in the nose; in his shoes, I must admit, I'd have surely done the same thing!)

As the woman headed in for her appointment, we quickly exchanged phone numbers. Worried about the little rat, I agreed to take him off her hands and find an alternative way to feed the snake. In exchange, she agreed not to feed the snake any more live animals.

Since the rat was still in the snake's aquarium, I knew I had to do something fast. So I called everyone I could think of who might know of a less violent way to feed a snake. Sure, snakes eat rats (as well as other animals) in nature, but this wasn't nature. This was a captive animal in an aquarium (a completely unnatural environment for snake and rat alike) where the "prey" didn't even have a chance. No chance to live their life first, and no chance to escape their predator. They just had to sit and await their demise, often with a lot of time to think about it first. I don't think that's what our Creator had in mind. No survival of the fittest or natural selection was going on here; whereas in nature, often the predators go after the prey who are already sick and going off to die, serving as a sort of natural euthanasia.

When some of the people I talked to tried to pull the "snakes eat rats in nature" explanation on me, I politely reminded them that wild canines and felines eat rabbits in nature, but that doesn't mean we should be feeding live bunnies to our family dogs and cats. Part of domesticating an animal involves domesticating their diet, because they are actually no longer a part of the wild. Why should rats be an exception to this rule?

Finally, I got some good advice from a fellow rat lover: packaged snake food (not ideal, but certainly a step in the right direction). I informed Jameth and we jumped into action. He joined me on a search for packaged snake food, which we found at a nearby pet store, complete with instructions on how to get the snake to eat it. We called the woman and headed to her house to exchange the snake food for the rat. In keeping with our decision not to let any more animals into our lives, we were determined to then find the rat a good home.

LIFE HAS A WAY OF BRINGING US the thing we think we want least when, in reality, it's what we need most. There he was, little Henry the Rat, peering out at us from the aquarium. His powder white fur hung loosely over his emaciated, dehydrated body, and he seemed so small and helpless next to the giant boa constrictor.

We quickly helped Henry out of the aquarium and into a travel cage, where we had food and water waiting for him. In almost two weeks, he'd had nothing to eat except an old, dried up piece of garlic bread, which he was choking on when we arrived.

We gave the woman the packaged food and showed her how to feed it to the snake. She was visibly relieved that it wouldn't be necessary to put any more live animals into that aquarium. Upon noticing the wounds on the snake's face, I felt that the snake, too, was relieved at no longer having to contend with meals that bite back. It was a unique sort of happy ending as the snake and the rat parted ways.

Poor Henry was so dehydrated, he drank from the little water bottle almost nonstop during the car trip home; and then he began to eat his first real meal in weeks. Once home, I opened his cage door to give him more food, but instead of eating it, he immediately climbed out onto my hand and up my arm. He paused midway and looked up into my eyes for a long while. I felt him saying "thank you" from the bottom of his heart. He then climbed up to my shoulder and began to softly lick my face and gently groom my hair, the way rats show affection.

"He's tame," I called out to Jameth, heading over to show him what was going on. As soon as we approached Jameth, Henry literally reached out to him with his tiny hands. Jameth put out his hand, and Henry immediately climbed up his arm, paused midway for that same silent "thank you" and then headed up to his shoulder to offer the same gestures of affection he'd already bestowed upon me. Henry made it perfectly clear that he understood *exactly* what we had just done, and his gratitude was unmistakable.

All prior plans of finding Henry a good home were quickly washed away with every lick of his soft tongue. He had already found a good home, and we were parents once again.

Henry quickly regained his health and settled happily into his new home. He was like our very own Stuart Little, and we lived that magical fairy tale for the rest of his life. He slept in a little bed of his own next to my pillow, and I felt like the luckiest person in the world each night, nestled happily between Jameth and little Henry.

One day, we realized that Henry would like a rat companion of his own, so we adopted a beautiful little beige-and-white powder puff at a local animal shelter. We named her Ginger. She had been found in a nearby canyon by a compassionate couple that rescued her but couldn't keep her. When they found her, she was shivering, starving, and terrified, obviously having been dropped off by someone who didn't know (or didn't care) that she couldn't fend for herself in the wild (she clearly was *not* a wild animal). Since people don't commonly adopt rats from shelters, she had been there for many months (this was a no-kill shelter). The day we brought her home, she began chattering happily (the rat equivalent of purring), clearly delighted to finally have a family.

Henry adored Ginger and followed her around everywhere. He assisted her in collecting treats and making elaborate nests each day, and he groomed her thoroughly before snuggling up with her each night. Whenever a vacuum cleaner or other apparent threat entered the room, rather than running away, he stood in front of her to protect her. The four of us became a family, and whenever Jameth and I went on a trip, Henry and Ginger went, too. (We had Ginger spayed before we brought her home, so there were no babies.)

Whenever Jameth and I went out in the evening and left Henry and Ginger home alone (where they had free run of our small apartment), we returned home to find the radio blasting loud music and the two of them prancing together joyfully on the bed. They had figured out how to turn the radio on, but only did so when we weren't home. It seemed they loved to "crank the music and party" whenever they had the place to themselves.

By opening our hearts up at a time when they might well have closed forever, Henry had opened the door for many more homeless rats to find their way into our lives. Over time, Henry and Ginger became the King and Queen of an enchanted little kingdom of very happy rescued rats, which eventually became known as the Rat Refuge.

Days became years, and when Henry's time inevitably came to pass, I wasn't ready to say good-bye. Then again, I wonder if we're ever really ready. He had begun to slow down and then had lost interest in food. When we took him to the vet, nothing conclusive was found—other than old age—so we brought him home to die.

I think those of us who love and lose animals often drive ourselves crazy with guilt over the decision of euthanasia. No matter what we decide, we often beat ourselves up for it, convinced that our final decision was the wrong one. This was no exception. Henry began to have trouble breathing, and his condition rapidly declined. He still wouldn't eat, his body weakened, and he was clearly struggling for every breath. No treatment seemed to help him. I agonized over what to do. I didn't want to let him go, but I didn't want my own pain to force him to stay. I didn't want to give up hope of a miracle by giving in too soon, but I didn't want to cause unnecessary suffering by giving in too late.

I finally decided it was time to assist Henry in his transition, so with Jameth behind the wheel and little Henry cradled in my arms and bathed in my tears, we headed off for that final trip to the vet. However, before we ever got there, Henry granted me the one wish I had held onto from the moment I first realized I was losing him: the wish that I wouldn't have to be responsible for such a decision, and that he would instead die quietly in my arms. And that's what he did.

We buried Henry in our yard and felt his absence in our home. Thankfully, Ginger now had the companionship of other rats to ease the loss, but we all had a period of intense grieving. I was plagued with guilt as I felt that I had let Henry suffer too much before he died.

SEVERAL MONTHS LATER, I had a most profound dream. Actually, I was having an *ordinary* dream when suddenly the dream was interrupted. Almost like a television show being interrupted for an important news release, the dream abruptly stopped, everything went blank, and suddenly, Henry appeared as clear as day. He had a very large presence, and I could see his face—and every detail of him—incredibly clearly. He was approaching me from above and to the left, and as he came close, I noticed how real and beautiful and wonderful he was. I began to sob. I felt a strange combination of intense sorrow at losing him and ecstatic joy at this reunion. It was so real, as if he was really there.

I told him that he was even more beautiful than I had remembered. I told him how much I loved him, how special he was, and how much I missed him. Although he did not speak in words, I felt the same communication of pure love that I had felt that first day, when he had climbed up my arm and looked into my eyes. This encounter felt so *real,* unlike any dream I had ever had. I felt that Henry was *really there,* and I was absolutely overwhelmed.

Beyond him in the distance to the right, I saw someone else—a velvety black-and-white female rat named Allison who had died several months before Henry. However, she didn't seem to see me. It was more as if Henry was showing her to me so I'd know they were together. I then reached out to him, wanting to hold him close, but I suddenly felt myself slip out of the dream and awaken.

Upon awakening, I felt enveloped by a profound sense of peace, comfort, and love. As I lay there contemplating what had just happened, I heard Jameth uttering in his sleep. His utterances were unclear and sounded highly emotional. Thinking that he must be having a nightmare, I reached over and gently shook him out of his sleep.

"Are you okay?" I asked. "Were you having a nightmare?"

"No," he replied, "I was having a dream about Henry." I asked him for more details, not saying a word about my own dream. He went on to describe what had just taken place.

Henry had appeared to him, as clear as day, approaching from above and to the left. *Just like in my dream,* I thought to myself. Jameth described how real it had felt, as if Henry was really there, reaching out to him. In the distance beyond Henry and to the right, he had seen little Allison, just as I had, as if Henry was showing her to him. Again, Henry was the one initiating the unspoken communication of pure love. Jameth had been so overwhelmed by this encounter that he had begun to cry out with all of the same emotion that I had felt.

I then shared with Jameth that I had just had the same "dream," and we both knew that something profound had just taken place. Not only did we still love and remember that precious soul called Henry, but it was now evident that he still loved and remembered us, too. In this we found great comfort.

I suddenly understood that the details of his death didn't really matter. Bodies wear out, but spirits live on. Henry showed us this in a way we'll never forget.

In that moment, we learned that love truly has no boundaries, not in life and not in death. It matters not the size, appearance, condition, or status of the beloved. Love is love. Forever.

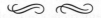

Mandy, Pardi, and Rocky
Denise Isings and Donna Hassler,
as told by Denise Isings, Hobby Artist
Washington

OUR WHOLE FAMILY OF SIX has always been a family of dog lovers. We lost our mother after a long illness, during which time Mom and Dad had the family dogs at their house. The dogs were very in tune with Mom and knew when she was going to have a bad day. They would sit at her feet insistently; sure enough, within a few hours she would always have to go to the hospital.

Mandy was a light brownish-reddish Shiba-looking mix dog that was rescued from the pound by my sister, Dorie. Pardi was my other sister Donna's dog, a parti-colored whippet. When my sisters grew up and left home, Mom and Dad said the dogs had to stay together at their house since they were such good buddies, and they remained there with Dad after Mom passed.

Pardi, the whippet, died first. Years later, Mandy, the other dog, was eighteen years old when my dad had to finally make the decision to put her to sleep. I didn't know he had made this decision. I had a dream in which I saw my mom and Pardi (the one that died years before) running down a hill of clouds. Mandy was running up the hill of clouds to meet them, and then the dogs were all bouncy and licking Mom, and off they went. That day, my sister called and said Dad had to put Mandy to sleep. I knew then that they were all together again and happy.

In the meantime, my sister Donna had gotten a new dog, Rocky. She and her husband never had children, and Rocky was their child. Rocky was a golden retriever mix, same general size and coat and color as a golden, except with longer ears like a cocker spaniel. He was a very big part of Donna's life. He went boating and camping with them and was even in their wedding wearing a bow tie—and walked right in front of her down the aisle.

One night, Rocky woke my sister up and started having seizures. He was fifteen years old and had been having seizures for some time due to a brain tumor. He lost control of his bowels and they rushed him to the emergency animal hospital, where they informed her that he was in a coma and they had to put him to sleep. Just before he woke her up, she had been having a dream of Pardi coming to play with Rocky. She hadn't dreamt of Pardi in years. She was sure Pardi had come to get her friend, Rocky.

Bogart
Kathy Grady, Retired
Florida

WHEN MY DEAR SHIH TZU DOG, BOGART, passed, I grieved so hard until I had what I now know was a visit. I recall it as if it just happened. Bogart's brother, Shadow, was grieving, too, and I tried so hard to hide my sorrow from him.

I was sitting on the sofa with Shadow. I thought I dozed off. Bogart came and sat at my feet. He said in thoughts to me to take care of Shadow and make him happy. I knew his love for me and felt calmness and knew he wanted me to concentrate on getting Shadow through this hard and sad time; he and Bogart were very close. You didn't see one without the other. That is how Shadow got his name: from shadowing Bogart.

Clarence

Geri Kepler, Computer Graphics Specialist
California

CLARENCE WAS OUR FAMILY CAT. Actually, Clarence was our next-door neighbor's cat until he adopted us.

Clarence had to have abdominal surgery. The day of his surgery, I took my daughter to her guitar lesson between 6:00 and 6:30 P.M. While I waited for her in my car, I leaned back in my seat and closed my eyes. In a sort of twilight sleep, I saw Clarence from his chest up, and although his mouth didn't move, I heard him say, "I want to go on." I was startled and immediately opened my eyes. For some reason, I looked at the clock in my car. It was 6:10 P.M.

My daughter and I left after her lesson and arrived home around seven o'clock. The vet called shortly thereafter and told me Clarence had died during surgery. When I asked the vet at what time, he said about six o'clock.

I can't explain how, but I believe Clarence wanted to let me know that not only did he want to die, but that there was somewhere he wanted to go on *to*. I also believe he wanted me to know he would be all right.

The experience made such an impact, I can still see it in my mind's eye more than twenty-five years later.

Dina

Loretta Laja Muncie, Homemaker
California

I LOST MY BELOVED CAT, DINA, by a tragic incident. The night after she died, she came to me in my sleep state. I'm certain it was a real experience and not just a dream. I watched her walking away from me. I saw her whole body as she was heading toward the gate of my yard, leaving to go away. She was showing me that she was crossing over.

Then, right after that, she came to me in bed, at around the same hour she usually did, during the night, to have me pet and massage her. I truly believe she was trying to comfort me, and show me her spirit was still here with me. I can't forget the memory of that experience because it seemed so real to me. I talk to her every day, and I know she hears me.

She still comes to me. She was just here two nights ago in another dream I had. She was alive, even though she was dead. I loved, kissed, brushed, and petted her in this dream, but I know better; it wasn't a dream at all. She was here visiting me, trying to comfort me during stressful times in my life.

Iggy and Milhous
Lance Payette, Attorney
Arizona

I AM A 49-YEAR-OLD ATTORNEY and had the following experience. I have had enough similar experiences involving humans that I am sure it was a genuine contact.

When my wife and I were first married, we got an incredibly intelligent Siamese cat whom we named Iggy. Two years later, we got an extremely good-natured German shorthair pointer whom we named Milhous. Milhous and Iggy never fought, and they grew up together. Iggy would often go over and nuzzle Milhous.

Milhous finally had to be put to sleep after a long and happy life. Iggy was still alive. The following year, we were living in an apartment in Phoenix. Milhous had died before we had moved there and thus had never been in the apartment. One night, I had a very vivid dream where I went out into the hallway of the apartment and saw Milhous sitting in the living room. I said (in the dream), "Milhous, buddy, what are you doing here? You're dead." I then went back into the bedroom and said to my wife (in the dream), "Hey, Milhous is here!" Right then, Milhous walked into the room and stood there. Iggy climbed up onto his back and sat there very solemnly. I said to my wife (in the dream), "Uh-oh, he's come for Iggy." I told this to my wife the next morning.

Lo and behold, Iggy developed kidney failure and had to be put to sleep within the month. We buried him (along with another cat, Bumpus, who had grown up with him) in the same place as Milhous—sort of a "shrine" we had created with rocks, benches, and wind chimes.

Tiger
Regina Fetrat

WE HAD A DOG THAT ADOPTED US from a neighbor's house. He was later given to us to keep as our own. We named him Tiger. He was shepherd/lab mixed (I believe with maybe a little St. Bernard).

We did not have Tiger long when one day he began to limp. He lay by the spring for hours. We had to go out for the day, and when we returned, we could not find him. We are way back in the woods, so we know that he was not taken or anything like that. He had gone into the woods and we did not find him anywhere.

A week or so later, I had a dream. . . .

I saw my young daughter, Angela (then three or so), in the front yard with Tiger. They were playing and he was very happy. I just watched them play.

The next morning, I asked Angela if she dreamed about Tiger. She said yes, they "played in the front yard" and he told her "good-bye."

Daisy
Regina Fetrat

A FAMILY FRIEND HAD A DOG named Daisy who was always tied up—her existence was on a six-foot chain. She was not tended well other than being fed. Her job was to guard the gate and bark at intruders. She smelled so bad that visitors could seldom stand to pet her.

The owner went on a trip, and I was asked to take care of her while he was gone. I bathed her and we had a great time doing things a little differently than normal.

Many years went by and I was no longer in contact with Daisy or her owner. One night, I suddenly had a dream. In the dream, Daisy came to me and thanked me for our time together. She said that it had made her very happy. A week went by and I could not keep from calling her owner. He told me she had died of cancer the week before.

Kim's note: Dogs who are kept on chains and considered by their "owners" to be nothing more than "biological burglar alarms" live a miserable existence because they aren't given the love, freedom, and companionship they need. Regina was perhaps the only human who ever treated Daisy with the care and respect she deserved, so it's no wonder that Daisy came to visit Regina rather than the man who neglected her.

Billy

Angelique Spieler, Retired Wedding Photographer;
Creator, "All Critter" Sympathy Cards (see Resources)
California

IT HAD BEEN A WONDERFUL VACATION. My divorce was behind
me. My newfound "single" freedom was expressed and enjoyed
completely on my first-ever river-rafting trip.

A new romance already pulled at my heartstrings—but a little
fur-bearing "pistol" was about to make his appearance known.

Murphy's Law always rules. Our excursion bus was late
getting back into San Diego proper, thus causing me to enter my
hometown of El Cajon in the "wee" morning hours. As I took my
exit off the freeway, a frightening sight lay before me. A mother
cat and eight or more kittens were trying to cross the mist-filled
road. I dramatically slowed my speed and pressed on my horn,
hoping it would frighten mom and babies back to the safety of the
curb, at least for a while. It worked.

I quickly parked my car and spent the next three hours
chasing mom and kittens back again and again away from the
road. Other drivers had various opinions—some gave a thumbs
up and others, well, they expressed their feelings with obscene
finger language. Despite my best efforts, I was only able to save
one curious, beautiful black-and-white male kitten. I swept him
up and raced home to make him breakfast and put myself to bed,
or so I thought. That first night with Billy, as I named him, was
typical of every day and night thereafter—he was my wild child!
He'd race pell-mell throughout my apartment, chase his tail and
holler whenever he caught it, stop playing abruptly, groom, nibble
his food, and off again to the races. He playfully wore out my two
other very tolerant adult cats who would stare at me with a "Come
on, Mom, give us a break." I'd then banish Billy to the front room
of my small apartment for a short time-out for all.

Billy grew into one of the largest, tallest domestic cats I've
ever seen, long of body and big boned. He never lost his kitten
crazy side, always a teenager. This sweet boy oozed of affection.
He enjoyed being carried around draped around my neck, sitting

on my head or pressed very close to me at night. He followed me everywhere and sat close by quietly, wherever I went throughout my apartment. He made me feel very wanted and loved. According to my neighbors, about half an hour before I'd arrive home (no matter what hour it was that I left work for home), he'd caterwaul, crying for me loudly—he always knew when I was on my way home.

Enter the two-legged love interest of my heart—my future husband Martin. Billy was very sweet to him at first—much kinder than he'd been to other male suitors. He didn't try to stare him down or leave poop in his sneakers. But the closer Martin and I became, the more demanding Billy became of my attentions. After all, he had been the "man" of the house for so long. He'd even growl when things went bump in the night when I'd lived alone.

Martin was always up first so he fed our three cats and our dog, Moca. But one morning Billy didn't come for breakfast. Martin called and called—no Billy. He left me a note telling me Billy didn't come to breakfast. So I called and called and searched, too—to no avail.

Martin came home a bit late that day and said with tears in his eyes that he had something to tell me. I grilled him with, "What's wrong? Is it my daughter? My father?" He shook his head. "Your mother? What then?" I was getting impatient.

"It's Billy—he's gone." I didn't think of Billy. He was too street smart—he always came home—it couldn't be.

"Are you sure it's him?"

"Yes," he replied. "I only left you the note to stall, to tell you myself. I found him and moved his body so you couldn't find him." Billy had died directly in front of our neighbor's driveway. Martin had actually found his body that morning because he was waiting to be picked up by his ride-share directly across the street. How grateful I was for the love he showed me by removing Billy's crushed body from my eyes. Little did I know I was to begin a self-inflicted marathon of emotional torture that almost made me insane with grief and guilt.

THREE DAYS. It took three days for the facts to sink in and the timetable of events to come together. Precisely three days after Billy's death, at 3 A.M., I bolted upright in a sitting position like a bullet leaving a gun. My heart pounding so hard, I began coughing to breathe; I was sweating profusely and wailing out loud, waking Martin. As I clasped my body, arms crossing my chest—trying to hold in the horror of what had actually happened—I cried out, "It was me! It was me! I killed Billy!"

As I'm a professional photographer, I had been out late picking up photos and an order from my processor. I was furious they had botched yet another order. I was very angry and driving too fast. I took the familiar sharp right hand turn onto the street near my house with way too much speed. I temporarily lost control of the car; it swerved way to the left. There was no other traffic at that hour. No one behind me, next to me, or in front of me—so what was that loud crack I heard? I forcibly gained control of the steering wheel, and steered it out of my neighbor's front driveway, not realizing at the time that I had just run over Billy.

It wouldn't stop—the horror of what I'd done haunted me day and night for weeks on end. I'd cry continually and uncontrollably. I'd throw up after eating. I couldn't eat. I couldn't sleep. I had nightmares reliving the event. Sweating, heart pounding. Heart palpitations. Finally, I actually prayed to the powers that be to release me of my torture. Instantly, like a huge gentle hand pushed me to my pillow—instant deep, peaceful sleep and then a wonderful and miraculous dream. . . .

I smelled a meadow. I saw that below the meadow there were gentle rolling hills, where I heard and saw children of all ages playing with animals, all kinds of animals. There were beings in white shimmering robes and shepherds' staffs standing nearby. Then he appeared right in front of me—my wild child running about with his rabbit-like hop, chasing a white butterfly. It was clear. It was real. His shiny black and white coat set off his beautiful gold eyes. And then there was the distinct white stripe running down the full length of his nose. It was Billy, my handsome Billy. Happy, joyful, and whole. He was an arm's length away. He turned and looked right at me, bobbing his head in a gesture of "come and play with me" as he had always done as a kitten. Again, he was distracted by the white butterfly that enticed him back to a happy game of chase. Off he went, bouncing and playing in Paradise.

I woke ever so gently, not ever wanting to leave this peaceful place. I was puzzled but delighted by the distinct aroma of roses that filled and lingered in my bedroom.

Finally, it was over. I realized that I had been forgiven. At last, I had been set free of my never-ending torment of grief and guilt and heartache.

I was finally able to accept that it was a terrible accident and nothing more, and I was able to move forward. I've learned that forgiveness given or received is one of life's greatest gifts, especially to oneself.

- Chapter 15 -

Signs and Messages

Miracles happen, not in opposition to nature,
but in opposition to what we know of nature.
— St. Augustine

I'VE FOUND THAT IT IS QUITE COMMON for people to receive some sort of sign, or message, after the passing of a beloved animal. These signs are often subtle and are perhaps missed by many. When noticed, they seem to deliver the simple message of "I'm okay—and I still love you." It is important to be open to such signs, as they provide tremendous comfort when they occur and are acknowledged; and in my opinion, that's their purpose. I have found that there are certain recurring themes, and I've heard the same stories over and over by countless people all around the world who are unaware that others are having virtually identical experiences.

Many people become aware of the presence of a beautiful butterfly after the passing of a beloved animal, and the butterfly often appears while the presence of the deceased animal is simultaneously felt. Butterflies symbolize rebirth and life after death, as the caterpillar appears to die but then emerges from the cocoon as a beautiful winged being. The theme of butterflies is a very common one in after-death communications. These butterfly encounters sometimes continue on a regular basis for quite some time, almost like little messengers there to assist during the grieving process.

Besides butterflies, the most common signs seem to involve birds, rainbows, and moving or falling objects. Also quite common are cases in which a departed animal's fur, whisker, or other item mysteriously appears in a spot where it wasn't found before. Then there are the more unique signs that are specific to the people receiving them, such as sighting specific or unusual animals in specific or unusual places; or hearing songs—either literally or mentally—that almost seem to deliver a personal message at just the right time.

I found that many of the "signs and messages" reported to me by people from all walks of life were remarkably similar not only to one another, but also to my own personal experiences. As I collected countless stories with the same recurring themes, I was reminded of my own "butterfly encounter" after June's death (mentioned in Chapter 4)—and other such occurrences—which happened long before I became aware that other people were having similar experiences.

I recall an incident that took place when our beloved rat, Melanie, passed away. Melanie was a beautiful Siamese rat who was left in a cage on the side of the road one winter day. Luckily, a friend spotted her cage and called me; and Melanie became a special part of our family, where she remained for the rest of her life. She lived to a ripe old age, and thankfully, died peacefully at home surrounded by the people and other rats who loved her.

After my beloved companion animals pass, I always have their bodies autopsied. (The term generally used for this procedure, when performed on animals, is "necropsy"; but I prefer to use the term "autopsy," since that is the term commonly used for the identical procedure on humans, and I feel that our language should reflect more equality than it currently does.) Afterward, their bodies are returned to me for burial. The reason I have them autopsied is to learn more about their health so that I can be in a better position to help other animals. I began doing this a number of years ago, and as a result I've already learned a great deal that I've indeed found quite helpful for other animals.

When Melanie's autopsy report arrived about a week later, I sat down in my office to look it over. I began reading it thoroughly.

Suddenly, I felt as if something had just happened but I couldn't quite put my finger on it ... almost like my attention had gone somewhere else for just a moment, and then my focus returned to the paper.

I blinked and looked at the paper again, and there was a piece of Melanie's fur. It was right in the spot where I had already been reading, and it hadn't been there just a moment before; but there it was. I was holding the paper somewhat upright and didn't even know how it could stay there without falling off, let alone how it got there in the first place. I was dumbfounded.

I knew it was Melanie's fur, because it had that unmistakable Siamese marking on it (off-white fur with a darker brownish tip), and there were no other Siamese rats in the house. The paper had never been in contact with Melanie's body, having arrived via fax. My logical mind struggled over the impossibility of such an event, until finally, I surrendered to the possibility that Melanie had just given me a most amazing gift. I was so touched by this keepsake of Melanie that I took a small piece of tape to attach it permanently to the piece of paper, where it remains to this day.

SOMETIME LATER, a woman contacted me with the following:

> The day after Leo died, I found some of his fur on my bedroom floor. I know for a fact it was not there before, because I had thoroughly vacuumed the room. The first thing that came into my mind was that it was his way of telling me he is indeed still here with me. Am I crazy for thinking that?

I was amazed at how often I was asked this very question. Thanks to my own experience, no, I don't think it's crazy to think that. I found it interesting that the people who had this type of experience always took it as a sign or message, without even knowing that anyone else had experienced the same thing and had reached the same conclusion.

Thomas Goheen of Fullerton, California, who had both *felt* and *heard* his departed cat, Dooie, also shared the following experience:

In one of our rooms there's a phonograph, an old style console wood one that I keep a blanket on top of to keep the wood safe because it's really old. I'd had the blanket on and off this thing numerous times since Dooie was gone— probably twenty or so times—and I remember one day thinking, *I wish I had one of his whiskers to save;* and when I raised the blanket off, there was one of his whiskers sitting there on the phonograph, just like it had been placed there for me to find.

IN ADDITION TO THE MORE COMMON SIGNS, I've come across a number of cases in which the spirit of a departed animal appears to be captured in a photograph. Such was the case with a special little bird named Raffie.

Judith Collins, a writer in Texas, rescued Raffie, a young, sickly parakeet, from a cold, dark back closet of a pet store where he had been left to die. She nursed him back to health, and the two developed a magical bond. Raffie had free run (or rather, "free fly") of Judith's condo, where he spent the rest of his happy life.

Judith consulted animal communicator Gail De Sciose both during and after Raffie's life. After his death, Gail explained to Judith that, in spirit, Raffie was flying freely in a jungle setting. Meanwhile, Judith had photographed some of Raffie's favorite things as a memorial to him, and she was stunned when the photos were later developed. The lighting in the photos was so unusual that it gave the appearance of a jungle setting, with shadows creating the appearance of jungle plants with sunlight showing through the leaves.

She also took some photos of the cedar box that held Raffie's ashes, and in the photos, hovering in the background above the box, appeared to be a small white bird (who looked just like Raffie, right down to the unique "double tail" he had developed toward the end of his life as his tail feathers separated).

For approximately ten days after his death, every photo that was taken in Judith's dining room (where Raffie's ashes were kept) had the most surreal, mystical light. There was no logical explanation for it.

I have occasionally noticed similar, though less dramatic, inexplicable phenomena in my own photographs. When we buried our beloved rat, Jonathan, I took several photographs of his grave. In two of the photos—one of his box before it was buried, and one of his gravestone after the burial—there appears a white glow in the shape of a rat's hindquarters and tail going off the edge of the photo. I have no idea what could have caused this. There might very well be a "logical" explanation for this, but then again, there might not.

With all that I have seen and learned, it appears that there are no coincidences—that everything happens for a reason. If we keep our minds open, we find that signs and messages are all around us.

Frosty's Mist

Rob Armstrong, Internet Retailer and Web Developer
California

I NEVER THOUGHT that I would see a trace of her beautiful sapphire-blue eyes again after her graduation from this world, but in some form, I believe I did. Frosty had been my sacred cat companion for fifteen years, and as with most people who share their lives with animals, the energy that we shared was extraordinary. Besides the games we would play—tag, fuzzball, hide and seek—every night she laid her beautiful little cat body next to my head, her eyes seeking deeply into my mind and soul, as if she knew me completely. And if she could talk, she wouldn't anyway, because there was not anything to say; it was already being said by the gaze we shared.

I can honestly say that no human relationship has matched the type of love we shared. There is something to be said about being in the presence of another being with no exchange of words, just absorbing all that is there in the silence of the state of just being present. If more people tried this, I think we'd see better relationships.

Frosty and I shared some beautiful times together, and I am sure we both grew from having the gift of each other's company; I know I did. She taught me unconditional love; animals are good at that, you know.

Frosty started showing signs of diabetes a year prior to her life graduation. For over a year she put up with me sticking a hideous needle full of insulin in her neck each day. I look back, and knowing what I know now, I would have attempted to cure her with a more holistic way of healing. I have learned that what kills us humans tends to kill our animal friends as well.

At the animal hospital, I gazed into her vibrant blue eyes for the last time as her pupils dilated and I sensed she was no longer looking out from that venue. Although I did not see her leave her body, I knew she was no longer there. But I still felt her presence.

The next day, my girlfriend April and I took her body to a pet cemetery. We said our good-byes, kissed her, put a flower next to her with a photo, and covered her with my baby-blue baby blanket. We then sealed the casket and wrote loving words with a pen on the outside. When we were ready, the cemetery caretaker lowered the casket into the ground and handed us the shovel to toss in the first bit of earth.

April and I both felt as if we were burying our child, and we were. We put the flower arrangement in the freshly laid grass and proceeded to take photographs of each other with the grave site and flower arrangement. I then said to April, "I wish she could show us her spirit, to let us know she's okay." I then thought to myself, as I clicked off three photos of the flower arrangement, *I wish she would show me her spirit in the photo.*

I had forgotten about my wish as April and I looked at the photos the next day. It caught both our eyes simultaneously; although at first we didn't put it together with the wish, it did not take long for us to remember it the more we analyzed the photo. Although it is quite transparent and light, there is something there. A blue, misty fog. April and I went through all the obvious explanations. Glare? No, it was a very black day, overcast. Perhaps it was something to do with the camera or maybe the film. After debating back and forth, we remembered that I had taken three photos, one right after the other, within seconds of each other, and the camera did not move between shots. We looked at the first two photos and there was nothing; but the third one, curiously enough, was the only one with the blue mist.

We held the possibility that the blue mist was Frosty's energy or spirit, and it comforted us in believing our little friend was saying good-bye and was okay.

Kim's note: It's not uncommon for a mist such as this to appear in a photograph of a grave site (or other location) shortly after the death of a loved one. This misty form has long been interpreted as the ghostly presence of a departed human. As this story illustrates, apparently the same holds true for departed animals!

George
Tera Thomas, Animal Communicator
North Carolina

MY CAT GEORGE WAS THE LOVE OF MY LIFE; it is because of him
that I became an animal communicator. It was his persistence and
his support that finally made me believe that I was truly "hearing"
animals and not just making it up in my head. George was in poor
health the last couple years of his life and he taught me many
things about death. He assured me that even though his body
was going to die, he was not. He told me that birth and death are
both powerful initiations for a soul and that there was life in both
of them. He told me that though grieving would be natural and
cathartic for me, he also wanted me to celebrate and to feel the
joy of freedom he would experience. He wanted me to allow all of
these feelings, the pain and the joy, to coexist within myself.

George chose the spot where he wanted me to bury his
ashes. He said he wanted a gardenia bush to be planted there
because gardenias are my favorite flower and that seeing them
and smelling them would remind me that life does not end. So I
bought a big gardenia bush and set it in its pot by the grave site.
It gave us luscious, sweet-smelling flowers for a couple of weeks.
George and I spent a lot of time sitting on this spot that was to be
his grave. He rubbed his face in the gardenia bush, sat in my lap,
rolled on the ground. Sometimes we would talk and sometimes
we would just sit quietly, enjoying each other tremendously.

Two months later, George left his body, and I was devastated.
As much as I thought I'd been prepared, it hurt more than I could
have ever imagined. The next morning I took his body to be cremated, and when I got home I went to sit by the gardenia bush to
think of him and to cry. There had been no buds on the bush the
day before, but now there was a gardenia in full bloom. I smelled
that beautiful blossom and knew that George was with me. Everyone said, "It's not possible; gardenias do not bloom this time
of year." But there it was. The bush produced one bloom a day for
seven days. I know it was George.

Joshua

*Ms. Lorna Blechynden, Preschool Teacher
and Animal Center Educator
California*

OUR YELLOW LAB, JOSHUA, was twelve years old. He had been very ill for about two weeks and was fading fast.

He was at the vet's office and they called to say they felt it was time to let him go. I asked them to wait until my husband and I could get there. By the time we got there, he seemed to be doing a little better. I sat with him and stroked him for three hours. I now consider that time as a gift I was given.

The next day, they did surgery and found a lot of cancer. Our vet felt the best thing was to let him go at that time, and we agreed.

The following day, I was at work and I was praying, "God, I just can't let go. If only I knew where he was and that he is okay even though he is no longer with us." As I looked up through my tears, my eyes fell on a poster just above me. It was a fawn lying in a beautiful meadow in exactly the position Josh often had. There were little rabbits and other creatures all around and the words read:

> *All things bright and beautiful*
> *All creatures great and small*
> *All things wise and wonderful*
> *The Lord God made them all.*

I said, "Oh, God, can this be true? Are you telling me this is where he is?"

A couple of days later, in church I prayed, "God, if that was really you speaking to me the other day, I need confirmation of it."

That afternoon, we stopped at a friend's house to drop off a candle she had ordered from my daughter. We used to live in that same house but had not been there since we had moved out six months prior. When we got there, our friend said, "Oh, I have something for you that came in the mail." When I saw it was from our vet, I waited until we got home to open it. It was a handwritten note saying how sorry he was about our loss and that he believed that Joshua was now in a beautiful celestial meadow fit for a dog of his stature.

That was my confirmation. If our vet had had our new address, I would have received the card before I had prayed for confirmation, but this way I got it at just the right time. After that I had peace and was able to move on.

Some people would call all of this coincidence. I have had many such incidents over the past years whenever we have lost a beloved pet. I believe it to be Divine comfort.

I now have the poster and the vet's card framed and hanging on the wall along with a photo pictorial of Josh's life from puppyhood on. We have found making these pictorials to be very therapeutic, and it helps us to let go.

Timber

Story written by Kate Mucci.
Accompanying photograph taken by Richard J. Mucci.
Kate and Richard Mucci are authors, television hosts, & musicians:
www.crosswynd.com
Nevada

EARLY ONE JULY MORNING while vacationing in an RV resort in Las Vegas, I was walking with our dogs, Timber and Kayla (pure white wolf/malamute/husky-mix sisters). It was a clear day, sunny, with an incredibly blue sky. We were crossing a street, in the crosswalk, when a young driver, speeding and in the wrong lane, lost control of her vehicle and hit Timber, who was at the time almost ten years old. Of course, both dogs were on leashes, and when Timber was struck, I, too, was pulled down, and my arm was injured.

My poor Timber was screaming and in pain, and I tried to comfort her and calm her down. I tried to use every healing prayer, hands-on technique and everything else I could think of to save her in those few moments. However, she went into shock, and we were rushed to an animal emergency unit. Timber died there, in my arms, about one hour after the accident.

You can imagine the pain that my husband, Richard, and I felt. We have no children—Timber had come to us when we were grieving for a third miscarried baby. She taught us to love, and to hope, and a million other things. When she died, only her sister, Kayla, kept us going.

Later that day, Richard and I forced ourselves to get out of our motor home and go to the area where Timber had been hit. Kayla was with us, although she, too, didn't want to go anywhere or do anything. She kept looking behind to see if Timber was coming.

As we stood there looking at the crosswalk and the stop sign, I happened to look up and, through tear-filled eyes, saw an incredible cloud formation above the intersection. To me, there was no doubt it was an angel with Timber. I told Richard to look up, and he, too, could see it right away. There was no doubt in our minds that Timber was jumping into the arms of an angel. Richard ran back to the motor home and took this photo:

Photo courtesy of Richard J. Mucci

Kim's note: This is the original photo
used for the cover of this book.

That evening, Richard and I walked yet again with Kayla, to the very back of the large resort in which we were staying. There were no RVs in the back section of the park; it had been closed for the summer. I had walked the girls there that morning, and it was on our way back from that area that we had been hit. Timber had loved that area because there were lots of little trees, and the fence that separated the park from the desert was there. She loved to sniff at little burrow entrances and whatever.

That evening, Rich and I just wanted to get away from everybody so that when we cried, we wouldn't make spectacles of ourselves.

I guess I should point out here that Timber hated water. She would freak whenever she got in the stream of a sprinkler. She could hear it when automatic sprinklers were about to come on, and she would run before they would ever get a chance to soak her. Timber was also very independent. When we got her as a

240

puppy, I chose her because unlike all the other pups in the litter who clambered over to greet us, Timber just sat back looking at us—almost saying to us, "If you want me, you come and get me." Timber also was very opinionated and stubborn. She knew exactly who and what she did or didn't like, and she made no bones about expressing her opinion in a million ways. She also made sure she got your attention, no matter what else you might be doing. Of course, we were always delighted to accommodate!

Well, that night, as Rich, Kayla and I were walking along the fence, a little bird hopped from tree to tree in front of us. She would land on a branch in a tree ahead of us, and if we didn't pay attention, she would start singing. We would stop and look at her, and then she would fly away again, to the next tree, stopping at each tree along the way. At the time, I said to Richard, "Do you suppose it's Timber—trying to let us know she's free?"

It just felt like it was her little spirit letting us know she was finally getting to do exactly what she liked—her own thing. We kind of laughed it off as Kayla pulled our attention away from the bird. Kayla had found something interesting under the fence and we had to see what she was into. Just then, that little bird flew right over to the fence and started squawking like anything to get our attention; then she flew back to the tree she had just been on. We laughed and commented that it must be Timber, because she never took "no" for an answer when it came to attention. So, we kept following the little bird, and by now, Kayla was even taking an interest. Finally, we got to a tree in which the little bird was waiting for us. We looked up and started talking to her when I could hear the sprinklers starting under the tree. That little bird squawked, took off, and flew away.

Not to another tree, not to the fence; she just flew away. That convinced us. Timber's soul had come to that little bird and shown us that she was okay, and since we were doubting a bit, she had to prove it with the sprinklers. Anyway, that is our story.

Kim's note: Kate and Richard have a page on their Website dedicated to Timber's memory. In response to the cloud photo, Kate received the following e-mail from a friend of a friend. . . .

"Hi! I'm a friend of Tracy in Scotland. I had a letter from her the other day, and she was telling me about Timber, and your web page. I had a minute yesterday and had a look. I knew it would be sad, but I couldn't resist. I was very moved by the photos and tribute to Timber. She was absolutely beautiful, and I am so sorry that you had to lose her in such a tragic way.

"And she had the most stunning, soulful eyes I have ever seen. My two-year-old daughter came into the office as I was looking at Timber (and Kayla's) pictures and she said: 'Oh doggy, Mom,' and I told her that that was Timber—whom she called Timmer. A few minutes later as I was looking at your cloud-formation photo, she came back into the office and said: 'Timmer fly, Mom,' which totally freaked me right out. I definitely saw a dog and an angel. Maybe that was Timber's way of telling you that she's okay. But out of the mouths of babes!"

Filou

*Bé Courtadet, College German Teacher and Cross-Stitch
Designer
Bressuire, France*

MY NAME IS BÉ COURTADET. I am married and without children.
I teach German at a college in a small French provincial town.
For twelve-and-a-half years, my husband Jean and I had a dog
named Filou whose breed is called Labrit (a Pyrenean shepherd
dog).

Filou died of liver cancer, although no sign of disease had
been apparent then.

We loved our dog very much—especially me, which is why
I insisted on being present on the morning when the vet put him to
sleep. I held Filou very close, his head against mine, when he was
given the injection.

On the afternoon of that same day, Jean and I drove to an
animal crematorium, a two-hour drive from home. I absolutely
wanted to be with my dog every step of the way. We wanted to place
him in the incinerator ourselves, to be there when the cremation
was over to receive his ashes. I did not want to let go of the sight
of his body, to avoid any mix-up. I wanted to be absolutely sure
that I would get back his ashes! (I also refused that his ashes be
reduced to powder, as this would have happened in a room out of
bounds to customers.) Everything took place as we wished, till at
the last minute, I noticed that a small piece of bone had not been
placed in the container with the rest of the ashes. I then thought
that it did not really matter as the incineration was over, so I said
nothing and we drove back home with Filou's ashes, a two-hour
drive back.

On the drive back, I thought again of this little lost piece of
bone and felt very uneasy. I had the impression that something
was unfinished, that I had left something of Filou behind where
it should not be. I mentioned it several times to my husband Jean,
who kept reassuring me and saying that the essential task had
been done: We were bringing home Filou's remains. At first, I felt
reassured, but doubts kept coming back. I was again telling Jean

about the little bone that we had left behind. I was not looking at anything in particular, just at the road straight ahead of me, and suddenly I looked up and saw a rainbow, just in front of us. We both saw it. At first, I did not associate it with an ADC [after-death communication] sign, but then the idea came to my mind and I said, "This is a sign from Filou, who is telling me that the little piece of bone is not important, that he is here with us, alive in an elsewhere where he is whole again, in the serenity of the Light." Otherwise, why would this rainbow have appeared precisely when I could not find peace about this little bone I had left behind? I then felt relieved. An inner serenity replaced the anxiety I had felt about the bone.

The next day, toward the end of the afternoon, we were on the road again. I was driving and asking, "Filou, give us another sign!" Then, ahead of us in the sky, I saw part of a rainbow, near where the sun was (the day before, the rainbow had been in the direction opposite to the sun). At the beginning of the afternoon, a young Labrit dog had crossed our path: He was about two years old, and he looked exactly like Filou at that age. His tail and ears had also not been cut (unlike what is normally done with the breed, but that we had refused to do).

The day after (Thursday), a van cut straight in front of me to make a turn when I was driving back home from college. On the side of the van, in big letters and straight in front of my windscreen was painted a rainbow, the logo of the small company that owned the van.

On Friday, we left to spend the weekend at the seaside. Jean was driving. We always take the same road to go to the seaside resort. I was not thinking about anything in particular when my glance felt attracted to a painted sign on the right side of the road. It marked the entrance of a house on the outskirts of a small village: RAINBOW was written in green capital letters on a white background.

On Saturday morning, we were walking on the beach. At the end of the first lap of our walk, I was looking at the reflection of the sun in the water on the beach when I saw a purple shimmer in a sunlit spot on the wet sand. I looked at the sky and saw just in front of us part of a rainbow near the sun. We looked at it for a long period of time; then we turned back. A moment later, we looked back and saw that the purple shimmer had become paler.

The same happened on Sunday morning. Same walk on the beach. I was looking at the flight of a seagull: first to our right, it was flying low on the surface of the waves; then it climbed to the left toward the sky. Halfway in its flight, in the background of the seagull, I saw another part of a rainbow. Again, it was close to the sun and straight ahead of us.

The following day, on Monday, Jean was alone and saw "his" rainbow: He was driving when he glanced in the opposite direction to where he was previously looking. He saw a billboard. It was the same rainbow logo of the same small company as the van earlier.

What an experience! Seven days in a row since the day when Filou passed on we had had a rainbow: four whole or partial rainbows in the sky and three symbolic or pictorial rainbows.

I believe that Filou has shown us that he is still here, that he wanted to bring us peace and serenity, knowing that we would feel very empty now without him since we had loved him so much!

We scattered Filou's ashes in a place in the Pyrenean mountains where we often went walking with him.

THE STORY GOES ON. . . .

Exactly two weeks after Filou passed on, at breakfast I was explaining to my husband, Jean, what I had been reading the previous evening: that symbolically speaking, the rainbow is a bridge between Heaven and Earth. At the end of the afternoon, whilst I had not been out all day, I drove out to go to my piano lesson, about 30 kilomètres away from home, just like every week at this time. I was singing "Over the Rainbow" from *The Wizard of Oz* and thinking about Filou at the same time (because now Filou's memory is closely associated with the rainbow). I then looked to the left and saw yet another rainbow in the sky. I had to make a turn and found myself directly facing this very beautiful and very bright rainbow, which was shaped in a way that the others had not been: it was brighter in its lower part; it started from behind the trees (so visually exactly on the horizon line close to the earth) and reached into the clouds but stopped halfway in its curve. I immediately thought that Filou was confirming the remark I had made in the morning: "You see, this rainbow really makes the junction between Heaven and Earth." I was able to see this rainbow for the whole duration of my journey because it was exactly in front of me more or less constantly. When I reached my destination, by the roundabout before entering the town, I thanked Filou in my mind for this magnificent rainbow, and I said to him: "Okay, you can remove it now!" And the rainbow vanished in a couple of seconds. . . .

I am now convinced that my beloved Filou lives happily in another dimension and that he hears and sees what we are doing! It doesn't matter if other people don't believe it! I believe it because I saw it!

Since Filou has gone, I continue to "meet" rainbows on the way, when I have thought about him minutes or hours before. I *know* that Filou's life is going on and I am a part of it!

Shelley

Monica van den Tillaart, Homemaker (Former Executive Secretary)
Doorn, The Netherlands

SO THE INEVITABLE HAPPENED. We had been playing on the beach at 4 P.M. and our dog Shelley, a sheltie, was dead at 8 P.M. She started vomiting blood, and knowing her medical history, the vet advised us to let her go. I held her in my arms while she fell asleep. We told her we loved her and that we were grateful for her unconditional love and companionship all those eleven beautiful years. When the vet gave her the lethal injection, I held her and saw the little twitching of the muscles in her muzzle, and I swear I saw her smile!

Shelley was sort of obsessed with mice. In the winter we always have mice come up to the bird feeder, and Shelley would stand in front of the window looking at them. It was difficult for her to choose between going outside for a walk or looking at the mice! And guess what happened. . . . We had brought her to the crematorium, and when we returned home at the summer house, we saw a little mouse right in front of our car! As if it was a sign!

According to ancient belief, the soul stays three days near the body. Saturday was the third day after Shelley's death. We collected her urn on Friday and have her here in the summer house with us. Apart from that, someone sent me a beautiful story about the Rainbow Bridge. When beloved pets die, they cross the Rainbow Bridge to walk to Heaven. And guess what we saw Saturday morning? A beautiful rainbow that reached, like a bridge, from our summer house to Heaven! Isn't that beautiful? Needless to say, I cried, but it was so gorgeous. I am so happy I was able to see this. I will cherish those 'signs' forever!

Kim's note: Monica added the following when I contacted her one year later. . . .

Yesterday it was a year since Shelley died. A lot has happened in that year. We got lots of signs. The most amazing was the following: One day we were walking on the beach, and April and Sunny (our other dogs) were playing around us. We had the feeling that Shelley was there and talked about her being our own little star up in Heaven, when suddenly, I saw something in the shallow waves along the shore. It was some sort of broken toy, with a *star* in it! You'd expect to find anything at the beach, but a star while we were talking about it! It was really amazing . . . and comforting. Little messages from Heaven!

Kim's note: Just before this book went to print, she had yet another experience to add. . . .

We have had another amazing sign. It happened while watching a psychic show on television recently. Before the show started, I lit a candle in front of Shelley's photo. During the show I walked past the candle to get some coffee, when something caught my eye. I just had to look and saw something in the candle that looked like Shelley sitting down [from the side, facing to the left], complete with her large white collar of fur! I extinguished the candle and made a photo of it. Needless to say, I never lit that candle again and I keep it in a safe place next to Shelley's urn.

Shelley   **Candle**

Photos courtesy of Monica van den Tillaart

248

Baby Rat

Wendy Reardon, Papal Historian and Author of
The Deaths of the Popes
Massachusetts

BABY RAT (A BEIGE HOODED) was my first rat, and I had her (and her sister Boo Boo) flown back to America with me when I left England. She and Boo helped me get through a lot of unpleasantness, so they meant a lot to me.

Eventually, Baby Rat died, and I was devastated. I asked her for a sign to tell me she crossed the Rainbow Bridge. Well, the next morning, I got up, bleary-eyed from crying, and made my tea, as usual. Normally, I never look at the tea before I sip it, but I looked and in it the slight foam had formed a *perfect* shaped triangular rat head, with two bubbles perfectly placed for eyes, one perfectly placed bubble for a nose, and perfectly shaped ratty ears.

I didn't have a camera handy, but I couldn't believe it. The foam was also the exact color of Baby Rat. My friends and family said I was just looking for something and I saw what I wanted to see, but those bubbles formed a *perfect* ratty head . . . then it quickly faded away. I have never seen any tangible shape in the form of bubbles in my tea since.

I'm sure Baby was giving me some kind of sign.

God better reinforce His mattresses, is all I have to say, because if He doesn't . . . His mattresses, chairs, and couches will be a lot more holy than they were before Baby joined Him. . . .

Saxon and Blue

June Reichenback, Retired Nurse/School Office Assistant
New South Wales, Australia

WE HAD TWO DOGS, Blue (a blue heeler) and Saxon (a German shepherd), who died within six months of one another, at roughly the same age, ten years, both from illness. After a break of a year, my son decided to get another shepherd pup, and we talked about how the old ones would have felt. Anyway, one night I was home in the lounge room on my own (my husband and younger son were in Austria at the time) when all of a sudden one of the ceiling globes just fell down onto the table but did not break, which was strange, as they were screwed in and could not just come loose; and while I was sitting pondering this, one of the tennis balls our old Blue used to play with just rolled into the room on its own.

I got chills down my spine and asked my other son, who lives in a different part of the house, if he had thrown it but he said no, he hadn't been anywhere near the lounge room. We then decided it must have been our two old dogs giving their approval for the new one. That is the only explanation we could come up with, and it's what we like to think happened.

Kim's note: Our beloved animals in spirit want us to be happy, and they do indeed approve of new animals who come into our lives to bring us love.

Casey

Sherry A. Warrick, Retired Registered Nurse
California

MY BEST FRIEND, a golden retriever named Casey, died from cancer. I was devastated by his passing and was looking for some word from him that he was okay. I never got a chance to say good-bye to him.

My roommate had received some after-death communications from loved ones, and she did from Casey as well. His picture, which was hanging on her bedroom wall, suddenly fell to the floor several days after he died. Other pictures remained on the wall.

I know it was him and that he is okay. I still miss and think about him every day, but it gives me great comfort to believe that he tried to contact and reassure me and is still here with us.

Kim's note: At first, Sherry felt that her roommate had received a sign while she herself hadn't. However, she came to realize that the sign wasn't merely intended for her roommate—the photo of Casey just happened to be hanging on her roommate's wall. It's important that we remain open to signs in whatever form they may appear, and remember to validate them when they come. When I later contacted Sherry, she had received other signs as well. . . .

After Casey's picture fell off the wall in my roommate's room, I put his Christmas stocking (with his name on it) on the fireplace the following Christmas. A day or so later, I found it lying on the floor. It had fallen off the fireplace, while the remaining stockings were in place. It was just like the picture that had fallen!

I have had more contacts with loved ones and from other animals. My second golden retriever, Maggie, died last October. Her death was very different from Casey's, and I was with her when she was euthanized. She visited me that night. I "smelled" her very distinctly, and I know it was her.

Buddi
Kathleen S. DeMetz, Attorney
Ohio

I USED TO BRING MY TWO DOGS, Sammy and Harry, to visit my sister Linda's two dogs, Buddi and Benji, in Minnesota. We had Christmas stockings for them, dressed them up in sweaters, and took pictures of the four dogs. They were all small dogs and looked very cute together. When Buddi and the other dogs were together, we would also have birthday parties if it was one of their birthdays. I loved all four dogs.

When Buddi, one of my sister's dogs, died, she called me long-distance from Minnesota to tell me. I was lying in bed thinking about Buddi, and I said, "I didn't have a chance to say good-bye to you; good-bye, Buddi." Just then I heard a crash in the next bedroom in my home. I found that a picture of dogs had crashed to the floor. That picture has been hanging in my home for fifteen years and has never fallen before that or after that. I believe it was Buddi's way of saying good-bye to me.

Kim's note: Shortly after Kathleen shared this story, her own beloved dog, Sammy, passed. His story follows. . . .

Sammy
Kathleen S. DeMetz, Attorney
Ohio

I GOT SAMMY WHEN HE WAS EIGHT MONTHS OLD, from an ad in the paper that said, "Free to good home: poodle mix." It was love at first sight. He was like a Benji dog, half poodle, half terrier; a little black ball of fur. I just adored this little dog. We had the most special relationship.

I had him before I had the kids. When Sammy eventually died, my kids were twelve and ten. Sammy was almost sixteen. When we took him to be euthanized, we held him and told him that we loved him, and I said, "Sammy, if you can give me a sign that you are okay, I'd really appreciate it."

My daughter said that the night before he died she had a dream, and in the dream Sammy said, "I love you. I have to go now." Then when we were on the way to the emergency vet, my son said he got a message: "I love you. You have always been loyal and kind."

After he died, I was terribly grief-stricken. Sammy died on a Saturday. The following Monday when I arrived home from work, I was in my car and I was thinking, *Oh, Sammy, I hope you are chasing butterflies.* I opened my car door, and a big orange butterfly flew through the open door two inches from my face and out the other side. I haven't seen a butterfly at home since.

Then I went for a walk and I encountered some ladies who also have little dogs that Sammy had played with. One of the ladies said that when her dog died, a butterfly came and landed on her head. At the time, she had no idea about the symbolism of the butterfly, like metamorphosis—from caterpillar to butterfly, like a resurrection. She didn't know what it meant until someone told her. Then this other neighbor lady said to me, "Look at my shirt." She had a butterfly shirt on. She said she was going to wear an old navy shirt to go out on her walk, but something told her to wear the butterfly shirt instead. I took that as another sign.

I brought Sammy's ashes home on his birthday. The next day, I was driving down the road. I had been driving for at least twenty minutes and I didn't have my radio on. A lot of times I don't put the radio on in the car, but something said in my head, "Turn on the radio and put on 90.3." So I put on 90.3 and there was a story on there—I could tell it was the end of the story. I couldn't figure out what was going on—they were talking about the President and some little country, and I'm thinking, *Why am I listening to this?* Then that story ended and the next story that came on was about animal rights. They started telling all these horrible things about the life some dogs have and all these things that happen to these dogs. Then this thought popped in my head: *These dogs had a horrible life. I had a beautiful life; thank you.*

I also received many other signs. All of these things happened within five days. I said, "Sammy, you are giving me an awful lot of messages. I want to thank you. This is wonderful. Why are you giving me so many?" Then I got a thought in my head that said, "So that you can tell other people so that they can be comforted."

Kim's note: One year later, Kathleen had the following to add. . . .

My sister had a little black dog named BJ who looked just like my Sammy, only smaller. BJ and Sammy used to visit each other, and I loved BJ very much, too. When BJ died, my niece told him to come and say good-bye to me. BJ died on a Saturday. The following Monday, I came home from work, and there was a butterfly sitting on my garage door! I couldn't open the door without fear of injuring him, so I went up to him and put my finger by him, and he jumped on my finger. He then flew back to the garage door. I put out my finger again. He jumped on my finger, and then flew back to the garage door again. I then thought, *How am I going to get in the garage?* and put out my finger a third time. He jumped on it again and then flew and landed on the house, next to the garage door.

He remained in that spot from 5:30 P.M. until at least four hours later when I went to bed. When I got up in the morning, he was gone. The butterfly looked like the one I saw when Sammy died, only *smaller,* just as BJ looked like Sammy, only smaller. I am sure that this was BJ's way of saying good-bye to me!

- CHAPTER 16 -

Sweet Reunions

Dear God,
If we come back as humans, is that good or bad?
— FROM PETS' LETTERS TO GOD BY MARK BRICKLIN

WHEN I WAS GROWING UP, one of my best friends was a dog named Charger. My parents had gotten him as a surprise for my brother and me (after our incessant begging, "Please, can we get a dog?"), and he had instantly become a special and memorable part of our family.

Charger was a sheltie, but we called him a "miniature collie" because that's what he looked like. He was a reject from a long line of show dogs because one of his ears didn't stand up "properly," but to me, he was perfect.

Charger and I enjoyed daily walks, and when I was at home going about my business, he often just sat nearby and watched me intently. I sometimes wondered if he felt it was his job to watch over me, and I often got the feeling that he understood my words and thoughts; but more than that, I always got the feeling that he simply enjoyed watching me to see what I was going to do next (much like we humans enjoy watching other animals as they go about *their* business).

When Charger and I returned from long hikes in the nearby canyons, he always had burrs entangled in the long fur on his front paws. So, a regular ritual of ours was to work together on getting them out. He would sit and patiently watch as I separated his fur to loosen each burr, and then he would finish the job by pulling the loosened burr out carefully between his teeth. It was a ritual we both enjoyed, and I always noticed how strong our connection was during those moments.

It was always a challenge for me to get a suntan, because whenever I donned a swimsuit and headed out to lie on a lounge chair in the backyard, Charger patiently looked on as I spread suntan lotion over my skin; then, as soon as I finished and settled down for a snooze in the sun, he climbed up on top of me and spread himself over me, almost as if he was trying to protect me from the sun! I told him I didn't actually *want* any shade just then, but I couldn't help but laugh and thank him for this sweet and very predictable gesture of his. He seemed delighted that I had come to join him for a nap, so I didn't have the heart to turn him away.

Charger lived to be just short of nine years old. It's amazing how quickly the time goes. The last time I saw him was when my parents and I rushed him to the vet for some tests, to find out why he had suddenly stopped eating, could no longer stand up, and was moaning in obvious agony. We were told to leave him there, and that the vet's office would call us as soon as they knew anything.

As it turned out, the vet discovered a huge, inoperable tumor in his abdomen and advised that he not be awakened from the anesthesia. I cried my heart out later that afternoon when my parents informed me that Charger wouldn't be coming home. My biggest regret, besides the fact that I hadn't been able to take away his pain when he was alive, was that I never got the chance to say good-bye, to be there with him, right to the end.

Several years after Charger passed, I was in college and living on my own in an apartment. My brother, Scott, was also living on his own. He had adopted a sweet young female mixed-breed dog from a local shelter, whom he named Reindeer. Scott and I then decided to become roommates, so we found a condo with a nice yard for Reindeer, and we all moved in together.

It was so wonderful to have an animal back in my life, and Reindeer and I bonded right away. We enjoyed daily walks, and when I was at home going about my business, she often just sat nearby and watched me intently. I sometimes wondered if she felt it was her job to watch over me, and I often got the feeling that she understood my words and thoughts; but more than that, I always got the feeling that she simply enjoyed watching me to see what I was going to do next (much like Charger had done before her). I had missed Charger since he had passed, so it was wonderful to have someone back in my life who reminded me so much of him.

Once again, it became a challenge for me to get some color on my fair skin. Whenever I decided to lie on a lounge chair in the backyard, Reindeer patiently looked on as I applied suntan lotion; then, as soon as I finished and settled down for a snooze in the sun, she climbed up on top of me and spread herself over me, just as Charger had always done! This gesture became more comforting to me than I could have ever imagined.

I had always regretted not being there when Charger died. Then, shortly after Reindeer entered my life, I was given an opportunity to do things differently. Within a year, Reindeer began having seizures. After many trips to several veterinarians, no one was able to determine what was wrong with her. However, her health continued to decline dramatically, and my brother and I eventually found ourselves faced with the decision of euthanasia.

Ultimately, we decided it was the right thing to do, and I cried all night on the eve of the appointment, watching helplessly as Reindeer endured seizure after seizure. The next morning, we took her on that final trip to the vet. My brother and I held her tenderly and told her how much we loved her as she drifted peacefully to the Other Side. As we instinctively looked up above her lifeless body and simultaneously waved good-bye to her spirit, which we somehow knew was hovering lovingly above us, I felt surprisingly at peace. Reindeer had given me the opportunity to be with her at her passing, which I had always wished I could have done with Charger.

My experience with Reindeer taught me the importance of opening up to love again, despite having lost before and knowing that loss will inevitably come again. I also learned how comforting it can be to have a companion animal with such similar behaviors as a former beloved animal. However, it wasn't until much later that I began to wonder if, perhaps, these animals with such similar behaviors might, in fact, *be* the same animals.

I had begun entertaining such a concept after June's passing, when I was assured by so many different people that she would be returning to me one day. The idea had been further reinforced on that magical day when I found myself face-to-face with a little brown mouse on the window screen (as described in Chapter 4). Then, as my animal family grew, more magical experiences opened my mind further.

AS A CHILD, I always felt that I, myself, had lived before. This wasn't something I was taught; it was something I just felt inside. I had clear, very specific, recurring dreams of being a different person of a different gender in a different time, and I always felt that these were past-life memories. Though I was, in reality, a child, I was a grown adult in these recurring dreams, and I always relived my own death. The part I found fascinating was the fact that the dreams didn't end at death; in these dreams, I always marveled at how I was able to experience my own death in great detail and then continue on beyond death, as a spirit, still very much alive and aware of what was going on, but no longer feeling any pain or fear.

These dreams felt incredibly real and always contained very specific details that couldn't have occurred in my current lifetime. It felt as though I was being reminded of where I came from, as though I was being shown that death was not the end, but rather, a transition; and I somehow felt that I was supposed to share this with others, though I had no idea why. When I did share this with others, I got the feeling they thought I was nuts, so eventually, I learned to keep it to myself. These apparent past-life memories seeped into my waking life as well, giving me the impression that this was simply the way things were. However, when I asked about this in school and in church, I was told I was wrong, that such things weren't so; and I got the impression that I was doing something terribly wrong by even *suggesting* such possibilities. So, eventually, I figured I must have been mistaken.

It wasn't until my second year in college that I began to entertain such possibilities once again. I came across some thought-provoking, well-documented, and highly convincing accounts of reincarnation, and for the first time I felt validated in my own childhood notions. However, none of these accounts involved animals, so I never even considered that this possibility might hold true for them as well—that is, until my animal friends began to teach me otherwise.

MAGGIE HOULIHAN, the woman from whom Jameth and I adopted little Jonathan (our first rat after June's passing), has become a great friend over the years since then. She is an amazing woman who does a tremendous amount of good on behalf of animals of all types. One October day, she rescued three female rats from the pound, who unexpectedly gave birth to an abundance of babies shortly thereafter. Maggie was heading out of town on business and asked if we could keep them while she was gone. At the time, Jameth and I only had two rats (Henry and Ginger), so our rat family instantly grew from two to twenty. When Maggie returned, she and I worked together to adopt as many of the new arrivals out to good homes as possible, and the rest stayed. So, four of the babies and one of the moms, whom we named Mom (the name stuck), became permanent members of our family.

We only adopted the rats out in groups of two or more (and still do, as rats, like many other animals, are very social beings who generally require the company of other members of their own species for their optimum well-being). I worked with animal communicators throughout the adoption process as we decided which rats wanted to stay together and what types of homes/people would best suit them. The first appointment I made was with animal communicator Gail De Sciose.

At first, Gail said she was a little overwhelmed, as she had never before tried to communicate with so many animals at once. So, we decided to have her connect with just the females. (The males and females were now separated, as they had been weaned and I certainly didn't want to be responsible for any further babies.)

As soon as Gail connected with the female rats, there was one in particular whose spirit she instantly recognized, and she told me that this rat had been with us in the past; she had been one of our former rats, who had died and was now back in a new body. Before Henry and Ginger had come into our lives, we had had our previous family of five rats (Jonathan, Katey, April, Cindy, and Samantha) who had all eventually died. Gail had communicated with them in the past, so I realized that what she was saying *could* be possible. It then occurred to me that this particular rat (the one she said she recognized) didn't seem at all afraid of us, as virtually all of the other new rats were, and she actually acted as if she *recognized* us.

Interestingly, later that same day I watched in amazement as this particular rat, whom we later nicknamed Stinker (and the name stuck because of her mischievous behavior), climbed down from the table on which the moms and all of the other female babies were living in a big cage. (The boys were now living in a cage of their own on a separate table.) The cage doors were kept open because I just couldn't stand the idea of such active animals being locked up. So, I had attached strips of Plexiglas along the edges of the tables, creating a small railing of sorts, to prevent them from accidentally falling off the edge. Most of them would venture out onto the tables, where I had set up little playgrounds with things to climb and explore, but they never dared even *attempt* to climb off the tables into the "great unknown." Like the others, Stinker was still a baby and had never ventured off the table before, yet she now climbed over the railing and down the leg of the table very confidently, as if she knew exactly what to expect when she reached the ground.

She instantly began making her rounds throughout our home, going to all of the exact hangouts that our former rat family had frequented. Many of these hangouts were very unique spots that had to be climbed up to and, in fact, had previously had ladders leading up to them. She just looked up toward each of these spots and then climbed up very deliberately, as if she was already expecting the comfortable haven she would find at her destination.

Our former rat family members had all followed a very specific routine, hanging out in different parts of our home at different times of day, ending up in their favorite nest on top of a filing cabinet next to the front door, and then, like clockwork, heading off to their cage on the top shelf of the walk-in closet in the bedroom at precisely ten o'clock every night (I never could figure out how they knew it was ten o'clock, as my personal routine is not nearly so reliable).

Now, little Stinker (who had never known anything but the comfort and safety of the other rats in her litter) followed this exact routine, hanging out in each part of our home at the same time as the former rat clan had done. Then, at precisely 10 P.M., she climbed down from the familiar nest by the front door and headed off to the walk-in closet in the bedroom, as if she knew where everything was. I was speechless as I observed this eerily familiar behavior. Our current rats at that time, Henry and Ginger, who had come *after* the former rats had all passed, had developed a completely different routine, not even remotely similar to this, so I knew that Stinker hadn't learned any of this behavior by observing *them*. Needless to say, she was one of the babies we ended up keeping.

Two of the male babies (whom we named Cody and Sebastian) displayed a very similar familiarity. (In fact, Cody was the only male to venture off the boys' table and have a very similar adventure throughout our home.) Just as Stinker stood out as different from all the other females, Cody and Sebastian stood out from all the other males. As I held them, I felt an uncanny sense of familiarity that I couldn't quite put my finger on, and they seemed unusually comfortable with us and their new surroundings—completely different than the rest of the babies and even the moms, who all displayed the more usual caution of a rat who isn't yet sure what to make of those giants known as humans.

I recall a priceless moment that took place early on, before I had consulted any animal communicators, when I leaned down next to the boys' cage and little Sebastian climbed up onto my shoulder. As I knelt there with his soft, warm body nestled against my cheek, I felt an indescribable love for this little creature whom

I hardly knew. Somehow, I felt such a deep love for him, and such a comfort at having him there so close to me, that I just couldn't imagine where such feelings were coming from. As I tried to grasp the fullness of what I was feeling, I realized that it somehow seemed as though he and I had been reunited; I almost felt as if my son had returned to me. *Where were these feelings coming from?*

When I later spoke with animal communicator Patty Summers (author of the book *Talking with the Animals*), I didn't tell her any of this. Yet, she immediately keyed in on Stinker, Cody, and Sebastian, and told me they had been with us before. The purpose of this particular appointment was to communicate with the *male* babies to find out what types of adoptive homes would best suit them and which of them would prefer to stay together, so Patty focused primarily on the group of boys. Right away, she stated matter-of-factly that Sebastian had been our former rat Jonathan, and Cody had been our former rat Katey. I hadn't even *considered* this possibility, as they looked completely different, not to mention the fact that Cody was a different *gender* than Katey. I now wondered if it was a coincidence that we had chosen such similar names for them. Interestingly, when I later looked back upon my notes of prior sessions with Patty Summers, I noticed some amazing consistencies.

Before they died, Patty had spoken with both Jonathan and Katey. Jonathan was albino (white with pink eyes) and Katey was white with black patches down her back and the most beautiful black patch over one eye. Everyone always commented on how pretty Katey was. In fact, the first time Patty ever spoke with Jonathan, he told her he thought Katey was very pretty and enjoyed looking at her. Patty had never seen Katey when she told me this.

Then, when Jonathan died, I had another session with Patty. She told me that Jonathan would be coming back to me in the future, but that he wouldn't be albino the next time around. He said he would be male again, but the next time he would have some dark markings. At that point, I was open to the idea, so I asked her how I would find him. She said not to worry; *he* would find *me*.

Now, as I looked at little Sebastian, I noticed his beautiful markings. Not only did he have dark markings, just as Jonathan had said he would, but he looked a *lot* like the subject of Jonathan's admiration: Katey. We had a small mirror in a corner of the cage, which all of the rats completely ignored . . . except Sebastian. He was often seen gazing at his handsome reflection in the mirror, just as Jonathan had once gazed at the beautiful sight of Katey. Could an animal really admire the appearance of another animal so much that he decided to choose a similar body for *himself* the next time around? The idea boggled my mind.

Equally fascinating were the other similarities between the former Jonathan and the current Sebastian (who, according to Patty, were one and the same), including the unique way they both always looked directly up at us with their sweet, knowing eyes. Cody, likewise, displayed many of the same behaviors as Katey had. For example, Katey had always enjoyed "supervising" me as I cleaned cages, and Cody (who, according to Patty, *was* Katey, in a new body), was now the only rat who displayed the identical behavior.

I noticed further similarities once the rats were spayed and neutered and all of them were free to play together throughout our home. Katey had regularly flattened herself out and gone underneath the oven and refrigerator, and now Cody was the only rat doing the exact same thing. We had eventually put blockades across the bottom front of these appliances to prevent Katey from getting into trouble under there, and we had kept the blockades in place until Katey's death. None of the other rats had any interest in squeezing themselves under kitchen appliances. Now, with Cody, we had to put the blockades back in place. *What are the odds?* I wondered to myself.

Katey had always enjoyed climbing up onto my hand and going on "rides" around the house as I held her up to various wall hangings and shelves for her to explore. She had always just stopped for a moment to check out each new destination, and then climbed onto my hand and signaled to me that she was ready to check out something else. Cody now repeatedly climbed onto my hand with the same gestures and enjoyed the same "rides" around the house as Katey had. No other rat expressed the same interest in doing this, and when I tried, they either climbed off at the first destination and headed off to do their own thing, or they headed straight for the security of my shoulder.

Katey's nickname had been Kateydid, which became Diddy for short. Jameth and I used to sing her a song to the tune of "Camptown Races" (with words customized just for her), which we called "The Diddy Song." She always chattered happily when we sang this, as if she knew it was her song. When we now sang this song in front of the new rats, Cody was the only one who chattered happily just as Katey had, acting as if he *remembered* the song.

As I looked back at my notes from a session I had with Patty shortly after Katey died, I was further amazed at the consistencies. Katey died several months after Jonathan, and I called Patty for some comfort. She informed me that Katey, too, was planning to return to me in the future. She went on to say that Katey planned to be male the next time around, as she wanted to have that experience. She also said that she would be returning along with Jonathan, that they would both be white with dark markings, and that they would arrive unexpectedly with a whole litter of other rats. She said that the two of them would make themselves known to me and would stand out from the other rats in their cage.

At the time, I found the idea comforting, but I suppose I didn't entirely believe that it would actually *happen*. In fact, I had forgotten all about it when this litter of rats arrived and I felt an almost immediate connection to Cody and Sebastian, who both stood out so boldly and prominently from the other rats in their cage, just as Patty had said. Once again, they became extremely special members of our family.

SEVERAL MONTHS LATER, another special soul named Allison joined our family. She arrived along with Melanie, the Siamese rat mentioned in the previous chapter. They both had been abandoned in a dirty cage on the side of a busy road. Allison was a beautiful, shiny black rat with a white underbelly and large, beautiful eyes. She looked a lot like June. Jameth and I both felt a connection to her the moment she arrived, and it seemed very mutual.

Allison wasn't with us for very long. She appeared to be older than Melanie; and about six months after she arrived, she began to have trouble breathing and stopped eating altogether. By the time we determined that the cause was an obstruction of the throat (an internal growth) rather than a respiratory infection, her condition was quite advanced. After her first surgery, her breathing was back to normal and she resumed eating, but the vet had seen this condition before and told us that it would most likely recur within a week or two. Unfortunately, the vet was right.

So, we soon found ourselves rushing Allison to another vet for yet another surgery. This time, we went to a different but equally exceptional vet we had recently discovered, who was also very good with rats. This vet was only an hour away, rather than two hours away as our other vet was, but the drive seemed like an eternity as little Allison struggled to breathe and I tried desperately to comfort her.

When we arrived, the vet took one look at Allison and said, "This rat should be euthanized." I knew he was right, but I just couldn't let her go. I had seen such a dramatic turnaround after her previous surgery that I was hoping for another chance. However, Allison's condition had worsened and she was quite weak. I asked the vet to please try his best, and if she didn't survive the surgery, we would consider it "meant to be." He agreed.

Before she went in for surgery, Jameth and I asked for a moment alone with Allison. I held her up near our faces, and she turned her head toward me and looked me straight in the eyes. She looked at me so intently that I knew she was telling me something important. I felt an immense surge of love pouring from her, and I felt a deep gratitude being conveyed. I knew she was saying good-bye. My eyes filled with tears and I watched as she then slowly, deliberately turned her head to face Jameth. I watched as she looked intently into his eyes for a long while, and it was evident that she was expressing the same love and gratitude to him. He, too, felt that she was saying good-bye. But more than that, I felt that she was attempting to comfort us, to let us know that everything was going to be okay. I was amazed at the wisdom and peace of this tiny little being who so clearly knew exactly what was going on. She was the one who was dying, yet *she* was comforting *us*.

As the veterinary assistant then carried little Allison off to surgery, I began to cry.

"She's not going to make it," I told Jameth as he hugged me tightly. He knew. As I played that final good-bye over and over in my mind, I felt that there was something more she was trying to convey, yet I couldn't quite grasp it. I was still just learning to trust my own ability to telepathically communicate with animals, so it remained a mystery for quite some time.

When the vet emerged from the operating room some time later, his face said it all. She had slipped away while under the anesthesia. He knew how special she was to us, and it was obviously difficult for him to deliver the news. We thanked him for doing his best, and for caring so much. He had given it his all, but it was clearly her time to go.

A dear friend of ours, Shirley Marcoux, had become especially attached to Allison, and the two of them had shared many precious moments. Whenever Shirley came over to our house, Allison followed her around, until Shirley inevitably picked her up and showered her with kisses. Shirley often told people that her best friend was a rat. She said that Alli (which was what she always called her) had taught her how truly special rats can be, and that she was a wonderful rat ambassador.

We knew that Shirley was waiting with bated breath to hear the outcome of the surgery, so we determined that we should call her right away. I was too upset to speak, so Jameth offered to make the call. As he began leaving a message on Shirley's voice mail, his voice broke. He choked on his words as he delivered the news. Shirley told us later that, upon hearing Jameth's voice on her voice mail, she had begun to cry before he had even delivered the message; his voice had said it all.

It was about six months later when Henry appeared to both Jameth and myself in that most memorable and comforting dream (as told in Chapter 14, "Sweet Dreams"). Seeing Allison in the background, behind Henry, had brought additional comfort. However, I continued to wonder *why* Henry had shown Allison to us. I had concluded that he simply wanted us both to know that they were together and they were fine, yet I couldn't shake the feeling that he was also trying to communicate something more.

I've noticed various patterns throughout my life. I can't make sense of them, yet I can't help but notice them. For example, I was born on the 29th, met my husband on the 29th, got married on the 29th, and have noticed a lot of other 29s in my life as well. Coincidence? It might very well be, and I would perhaps be the first one to dismiss such a similarity as mere coincidence, or as the observation of a mind trying a little too hard to find some order and meaning in the world where there is none. However, I've also made similar observations that I just can't ignore. For example, I've noticed that the same types of things always seem to happen in my life on the exact same dates of different years, without any preplanning on my part.

In fact, as I was working on this book, the project just kept growing, so I didn't get a chance to transcribe the countless hours of recorded interviews I had conducted until three years later. As I organized and listened to each interview, I discovered with amazement that, *coincidentally*, I was reviewing each interview on the *exact* same date as it had originally been recorded, but three years later.

Also, as I sorted, reviewed, and edited the countless stories that I collected over the years, it seemed that whenever I had a question on something and needed to contact the person who submitted the story, more often than not I just happened to *coincidentally* contact them on the anniversary of the death of their beloved animal companion, unbeknownst to me until they told me how timely it was that I should happen to contact them on that day. This happened time and again. I couldn't help but notice. Again, I couldn't make sense of it, but I couldn't ignore it, either. I still don't claim to have an explanation for it; I can merely report my observations.

Since I began working on this book, many people have contacted me reporting very similar observations in their own lives (such as realizing after the fact that the death of an animal has occurred on precisely the same date as the death of a previous animal, but in a different year) without realizing that others are reporting very similar synchronicities. Whenever people ask me about this, I tell them that I don't have all the answers, but I, too, have noticed such patterns.

One such pattern began several months after June's passing. June had died on October 18th. It was exactly three months later, on January 18th, when Jonathan had entered our lives. Then, exactly two years later, again on January 18th, Henry had unexpectedly entered our lives. Both Jonathan and Henry had been exceptionally special rats to whom we had grown especially attached, not unlike June before them.

Now, here we were, two years later, and January 18th was again approaching. Having seen similar patterns in so many areas of my life, I couldn't help but wonder if yet another extra-special rat would be entering our lives on the forthcoming January 18th.

"I have a feeling an extra-special rat is going to show up on January 18th," I told Jameth. When he asked me why, I explained that I had noticed a pattern. "It seems that an extra-special rat has entered our lives every other January 18th since June died, so I won't be at all surprised if it happens again."

Sure enough, on the morning of January 18th, Maggie, my good friend and fellow animal rescuer, left me a message. She had just gotten a call that a rat was found in front of a local library. Maggie was just heading out of town on business that morning, so she asked if I could pick up the rat. This was the second time Maggie had enlisted my assistance with her own rescue efforts, the first time having been when all the babies had arrived several months earlier.

Later that same day, on January 18th, a beautiful little black and white hooded rat entered our lives. She had been found wandering around in front of the library, looking for food. A little boy had spotted her, and he had begun feeding her. When the librarian had come out to assist, as she had reached out to hand the rat more food, the rat had climbed up her arm, obviously wanting nothing to do with the great outdoors. The rat had apparently been dropped off there by someone who thought she could survive outdoors, even though she was clearly a domesticated rat who had no experience in fending for herself.

The librarian had housed the rat on a bed of wood shavings in a large plastic bin with air holes poked in the lid. I have great respect for that librarian, who cared enough for this little creature in need to take her in to safety and call for help on that fateful day.

As soon as I saw this rat, I felt an instant connection. I've known and loved many animals, and I've had more than my share of rescued rats over the years, but there was something very unique and tangible about this connection, beyond the fact that it happened to occur on January 18th.

Jameth and I named her Penelope, and when we brought her home and got her settled, we both noticed how familiar she seemed. Neither of us could quite put our finger on it, but we somehow felt that we *knew* her, and that she knew us. I scheduled an appointment with animal communicator Patty Summers to check in with this new arrival, as I often did when new rats joined the family, especially if their background was a mystery. All I told her was the rat's name, Penelope.

She told me that the rat seemed fairly young, and this was my sense, too, as she wasn't yet full grown. Patty then went on to say that this rat had a very easy, gentle, sweet, and loving presence; and this seemed quite accurate as well. Then Patty paused as she tried to grasp what the rat was communicating to her.

"I keep getting an 'A' name," Patty said, as she tried to get more clarity on the name she was receiving from this little rat. I asked her if this was the name the rat wanted to be called, instead of Penelope. She said that, actually, this was the name the rat had been called *before*. So, I asked her if she meant that this was the name the rat had been called before we got her. She said, "No," this was the name the rat had been called in a *former life*. She said that the rat had lived with us before, and she was telling us her name. I was speechless as she continued.

"I'm getting something like Alligator, Allison, Alli, Alice . . ." she said as she struggled to make sense of it. She couldn't imagine why she was hearing "Alligator," as she didn't think there was any possibility that we would have called a rat such an inappropriate name. She said she didn't understand it, but this was what she was hearing.

"I don't know why she's telling me this, because you never *had* a rat named Allison or Alli, *did you?*" she asked, absolutely puzzled at this information. She honestly didn't know we had ever had a rat with such a name. I then informed her that we had, indeed, had a rat named Allison the year before. We had only had her for six months, and Patty hadn't known about her. I then laughed as I recalled that we had called her "Alligator" as a nickname, and our friend Shirley had always called her Alli.

In that moment, it all made sense to me. *Of course* she was so familiar. It felt like an awakening as I once again came face-to-face with incredible evidence of a reunion with a beloved animal, a reunion that I once would have dismissed as impossible.

Patty went on to say that Allison was truly "picking up right where she left off the last time around." She explained that it was as simple as going to the store and coming back. She said that Allison had been extremely happy to leave her former body behind, as it was simply worn out and no longer comfortable to be in. While hovering over her body, which had been under anesthesia on the operating table, she had simply chosen to leave . . . and now she was back.

Suddenly, I understood what Allison had been communicating to me on that fateful day as she had said good-bye before going in for that last surgery. I now grasped the final piece of her message that had eluded me for so long. She had not only been telling me good-bye; she had been saying, "Don't worry; I'll be back." And now here she was.

She truly did seem to be picking up right where she had left off, so we decided to call her Allison once again. She displayed all of the same behaviors as before, and once again, she seemed to enjoy the company of humans in her life far more than the company of other rats. As time went on, I observed more and more similarities that I was unable to dismiss as mere coincidence, including her very unique way of reaching out to grab people's faces to express affection, a very specific behavior that I've never observed in any other rat (and I've known *many* rats in my lifetime).

She said she was so happy to be back and that she felt so loved. It was very mutual. She went on to describe the circumstances surrounding her having been set loose, explaining that she had known all along she would find her way back to us. Of course, I had no way of verifying this part of her message, as no one really knew *how* she had ended up in front of the library that day. However, I was able to corroborate the part about the little boy finding her, and her then being put in a large clear plastic bin on a bed of wood shavings (at the library), which Patty had no way of knowing yet described in great detail. When I brought up our friend Shirley's name during the session, Allison had a warm message of love and affection for her as well.

Allison once again became an extra-special member of the family, and to this day she is an incredible ambassador for ratkind. Whenever a new person comes to visit or a new rat comes to stay, Allison is the first one to say hello and to make the newcomer feel welcome. Whenever there is a sick or elderly rat who needs attention, Allison is always by their side, nurturing and showering them with affection. She radiates pure love, and I feel so blessed to have her in my life.

DURING THE SAME CONSULTATION with animal communicator Patty Summers, in which Allison disclosed her identity, I also asked to connect with Henry on the Other Side. At this point, he had been gone for nearly six months. I still missed him and just wanted to check in. I also now wondered if he planned to return to us as Allison had. So, once Allison had communicated all that she wanted to say, Patty then connected with Henry's spirit.

She said that Henry wasn't going to come back, at least not anytime soon, that he was enjoying his job on the Other Side. She then went on to explain that his important mission on the Other Side was to send rats to us. She said that we were helping to heal the relationship between humans and rats, and that Henry's job was to make sure the rats found their way to us. She said that when his mission there was complete, there would be a time when he would be able to "pass the baton" and come back to us, but for now he was happy doing what he was doing. She said that he felt he would be "breaking a sacred trust to come back just yet." She then went on to explain that not very many animals were doing the type of sacred work he was doing and that it was very important work.

As Patty described Henry's presence and the way he appeared to her, I was suddenly reminded of the dream in which he had appeared to Jameth and me. Her description sounded uncannily familiar. She said that he had a very large presence and that she could see his face so clearly. She also said that he was a very evolved soul, and I smiled as I recalled that we had always thought of him as our little "holy man" because he had always seemed so spiritually advanced, so *holy*.

I also recalled that, in the dream, he had specifically shown us an image of Allison; and now, several months later, here she was, back in our lives. This *did* seem to fit in with the notion that his job was to help guide the rats to us. Could it be true? Had he indeed appeared to us to let us know that Allison would be returning? I had always felt there was something more that he was trying to communicate to us in that dream, that there was a specific reason he was showing Allison to us.

I then told Patty about the dream, and she confirmed what I now deduced: that he had clearly been telling us that he was sending Allison back to us. In a strange sort of "out there" way, it all made perfect sense. I felt the arrival of goose bumps as I contemplated the significance of what I was now coming to understand.

Patty also explained that Henry said he had died because he had completed his job in physical form. His job had been to open the door for us to accept many more rats into our home, to open a door that would have otherwise been closed. I recalled that he *did* arrive quite unexpectedly, just after we had buried the last of our prior beloved rats and had decided not to open our door to any more animals because the pain of losing them was just too devastating. He had indeed opened a door that had been closed. There's no way Patty could have known this.

She also said that he had died once he knew everyone was settled in and established as a permanent family. I understood the meaning of this as well. After ten years of working very hard and living in whatever small quarters we could afford at the time, Jameth and I had finally bought our own home, a home in which the rats would have their own room—the "Rat Room" I had dreamed of since childhood.

The first time we looked at the house, we both noticed that the den would make a *perfect* rat room. It had three walls and was completely open on the fourth side, which opened out onto the main hallway. With the addition of a clear gate across the opening, the rats would be secure in their room yet still an integral part of the household. We would be able to see and interact with them every time we walked by, and they would have a place to call their very own. We could build fun things to climb on and play in, and we knew they would love it! And that they did. We now had enough room to welcome many more rats who needed a home, and the Rat Room officially became known as the Rat Refuge.

Henry's health had suddenly and dramatically declined as we were packing and preparing for our change in residence, and he had died the day we moved into our new home, *the day the rats moved into the Rat Refuge.* Since then, many dozens of rats have come to live out the rest of their lives in this safe haven for rats. Henry had opened the door; he had seen to it that this haven was established; and now, apparently, he was seeing to it that the rats found their way here.

AS I LOOKED BACK UPON the various animals I had loved throughout my life, I wondered if my new understanding might shed some light upon the inexplicable familiarity I had often felt upon first meeting certain animals. I then recalled an incident from childhood that I had long forgotten.

After my first rat, Queenie, died, my second-grade teacher—who had pet rats—quietly took me aside toward the end of the school year and asked me if I would like a baby rat from a recent litter. I got permission from my parents, along with a brand-new cage; and on the last day of school, after all the other children had gone home, it was time for me to choose my new baby rat.

As soon as I laid eyes on all of the rats, I just *knew* which one was supposed to be with me. I had been worried that I wouldn't know which rat to choose, but as soon as I met them, I instantly felt drawn to one rat in particular. I actually felt as if I *recognized* her, though I couldn't imagine why. She looked just like all the other rats in her litter, yet I felt there was something different about her, something *familiar.*

Then, when I reached into the cage, she was the only one who climbed right up onto my hand, and she didn't want to climb off. I took her home and named her Sweetheart.

Even at the time, I was amazed at how effortless it was to decide which rat was destined to become my companion. I was usually a *very* indecisive child, but in this situation, there was absolutely no doubt in my mind which animal was supposed to come home with me. I felt as if I already knew her. Perhaps I did.

WHEN I INTERVIEWED professional animal communicators, virtually all of them shared stories of animals who had died and then returned. Many of them had never believed such things were possible until they began communicating with animals and learned of such things from the animals themselves. Animal communicator Gail De Sciose shared the following:

> I have often gotten details in communications with animals in spirit where a dog, for example, will say, "Don't throw away my red bowl, because I may be back and I will want that bowl." Then the people later confirm that the dog did have a red bowl.

Gail has had dozens of cases of animals who have returned to their people. She explained:

> Some of them were able to give a lot of direction about what their physical bodies would look like, or where we would find them, or the actual circumstances of their birth.

In other cases, the return came as a complete surprise. In Gail's words:

> I had a client in the film industry who, while on location for a shoot, found a stray kitten. Although the kitten didn't look anything like her former cat, my client had the sense that it might be him. She asked me to check with him

telepathically and he confirmed that he was her former cat. In this case, the cat found *her*, but it felt to her as though she had just stumbled into him.

In a similar case, Jojo Pomeroy of Colorado, who runs a dog day-care and homestyle boarding business called Noah's Bark, consulted Gail when her beloved cat, Cooter, passed. Jojo explained:

> My very first cat companion was a calico kitten I named Cooter. She and I shared a special bond for twelve wonderful years. When Cooter passed away, I spoke with her in spirit through Gail De Sciose, my animal communicator. She said she would not come back to live with me for some time because she really loved it where she was in the afterlife. I agreed to whatever she wanted as long as she was happy.
>
> About seven years later, I heard the loudest crying I'd ever heard outside my office window. Being concerned, I went out to investigate. Just under the window in the bushes stood a small calico kitten demanding to be noticed. She definitely got my attention. There was something so familiar about her that it was frightening.
>
> I knelt down to speak with her; she came to me immediately, climbing up my leg to wrap herself around my neck. At first contact she stopped crying and started purring. I detached her from my neck so that I could get a good look at her. The way she looked right into my eyes jolted my heart.
>
> I brought the kitten inside the office to show her to the other ladies. I wasn't planning to add any more animals to my current animal family. The other ladies didn't want a kitten, so I put her back outside. I went inside again to prepare to go to lunch and the crying was louder than before. This kitten was not going to be ignored.
>
> I went outside again with a friend following me to see the kitten. As I knelt down, the kitten hissed and spit at my friend and then flared her tail. At this point, I was no longer doubtful whether this kitten and I knew each other. I knew who she was. The kitten again wrapped herself around my neck.
>
> I made an emergency panicked phone call to Gail, since I felt I needed permission from my other animals to bring the kitten home.

Not only did Jojo get their permission to bring the kitten home, but Gail confirmed that the kitten was indeed Cooter. Jojo recalled:

> When I drove home with her, my heart was singing. When we arrived, all three of my cats were waiting at the top of the stairs to greet us. There was no hissing or spitting from anyone. It was as if she had always lived with us. However, she decided that just in case I wasn't convinced she was really Cooter, she would show me all the old habits of Cooter's. Then I wouldn't be able to deny that she had returned. I had a crash course that weekend of Cooter revisited.

YET ANOTHER CASE involved a dog named Mack. When he passed, his devoted humans, Allan Dominik (a government auditor) and Yvonne Dominik (an artist) of Manitoba, Canada, consulted animal communicator Gail De Sciose as well. In Gail's words:

> The story of Mack is wonderful because Yvonne and Allan regularly spoke with Mack in spirit. He gave us a lot of direction about how we would find him and what he would look like. They did, in fact, find him at the time of year when he said he would come back and exactly the way he said he would come back. He has the same characteristics and does a lot of the same things that Mack did that were sort of quirky things.

When I spoke with Yvonne Dominik about Mack's return, she shared the entire magical story. She and her husband, Allan, had never even considered the possibility that Mack might return to them—that is, until they sought the assistance of animal communicators to help deal with their grief. In addition, Yvonne learned to communicate with Mack's spirit directly and kept a journal of these communications. She explained:

> I remember him saying to me over and over, "I will come back and bring you lots of love and joy," and he sure has. He wanted to help me on my spiritual path and he wanted to teach me to trust. He said that love is everything and not to ever fear losing anyone. He told me not to worry. He said, "Stop worrying about my return; things will work out perfectly." I basically had to start trusting that it was going to happen at the right time.

Via these communications, Mack expressed that he would be unique, but Yvonne and Allan did not understand what this meant at first. Then, at the time of year when Mack had said he would be returning, they received an unexpected phone call about a litter of rescued puppies that needed homes. They were all black except one, who was *uniquely* tan with black markings. That was exactly what Mack had looked like. He, too, had been born in a litter of rescued black puppies in which he was uniquely tan with black markings. Allan and Yvonne knew they had found Mack. He had returned to them with the exact same personality as before and is now called Shiloh, which means "gift from God."

DIANE NEWBURG, a legal secretary in Southern California, explained that her rat MacGregor had actually been with her *four different times;* he just kept coming back to her, and she kept the same name for him each time. (There was a time in my life when I would have perhaps written her off as a nut for even *thinking* such a thing. However, I happen to know Diane personally. She is a very levelheaded person and has considerable evidence upon which to base this assertion.)

MacGregor's latest return came quite unexpectedly, via an acquaintance of Diane's named Celeste, who also has many companion rats. When Celeste scheduled a routine appointment with animal communicator Patty Summers to communicate with her rats, she had no idea that she would receive an amazing request from one of the new baby rats under her care. Patty told her that this particular baby said he needed to get back to the woman he had been with before (in other words, *before he had died and been reborn*). He told her that, in his former life, he had lived with a woman in a house full of rats living in open cages on tables. He then described a woman with curly blonde hair and glasses, and said he needed to get back to her because he had returned to be with her again.

Celeste thought for a moment, wondering what this rat was talking about. Then it dawned on her—that description fit Diane Newburg *precisely!* Not only does she have curly blonde hair and glasses, but she also has a house full of rats living in open cages on tables. There's no way Patty Summers could have known this, as she had never met or spoken with Diane Newburg, and in fact, didn't even know she *existed*. She had simply delivered the message as she had received it.

Celeste then consulted another animal communicator, Sue Goodrich. Sue confirmed that this baby rat was indeed Diane's former rat, *MacGregor,* who had been with her three times already and was back to be with her again! Needless to say, Diane adopted him, renamed him MacGregor, and they lived happily ever after.

THE ANIMAL COMMUNICATORS I INTERVIEWED told me that their clients sometimes asked if their departed animals planned to return to them. These animal communicators stressed the importance of not being too attached to outcome or trying to *force* the animal to come back before either the animal or the person is ready. They explained that everything always works out in proper, Divine timing, so there is no need to worry. They also emphasized that they got this information *not* from any specific belief system, but from talking to the animals themselves.

Animal communicator Jeri Ryan, Ph.D., shared the following advice:

> There is one thing that I really want to share with people, and I've heard this across the board. When an animal says, "Yes, I do want to come back to you and I will be a cat again," or, "I will be a dog again," or, "This time, instead of a cat, I'll be a dog," or something like that—the people will say, "Oh, what color will you be? When are you coming? How will I make sure that I don't miss you? I don't want to miss you." It's an honest concern. They love them so much, they don't want to miss them.
>
> The animal will say, inevitably, "Don't worry about it; I'll find you." What this means is that it is the spirit that decides what it needs in a given lifetime, so the spirit then chooses to be with certain people or certain life situations. So, if they make the decision to get to their former person, they are going to get there. We don't have to worry. Usually what happens is that the people will one day start thinking,

Oh, I think I'll go to the shelter, or they will start looking at ads in the paper, or a dog turns up on the doorstep, or a friend calls and says, "Guess what! I have found this incredible animal and I kept thinking about you." Something that we call serendipitous will happen, but it really came from the animal spirit and the intention to get back to this place.

IN ADDITION TO ANIMAL COMMUNICATORS, I found that ordinary people had plenty to share on this subject. As I talked with people from all walks of life and varying religious backgrounds, I compiled a surprising number of stories of animals who had died and then seemingly returned to be reunited with their loved ones, often completely unexpectedly. They usually returned as the same type of animal, but sometimes they returned as entirely different species. The one thing that remained constant was their essence, their soul.

The animals often seemed to retain past-life memories (remembering their people, other animals in the household, their favorite toys and hiding places); and when they returned, they usually had the same unique behaviors and interests as before. They often (though not always) had very similar appearances with the same unique, distinguishing markings. Along with the stories, many people submitted photographs of the animals in both their previous and current incarnations, and their appearances remained strikingly similar, beyond just the usual colors and markings for a specific breed. Perhaps this was their way of letting their people know that it was really them!

The thought-provoking and often heartwarming stories that I've collected over the years are, at times, extremely convincing, providing evidence that goes beyond chance or wishful thinking. Some of the stories that follow are taken from the files of professional animal communicators and their clients, and others have been submitted by ordinary people whose lives have been touched by seemingly extraordinary events. So, it appears that cats may, indeed, have nine lives after all!

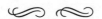

Moritz
Ingrid Pohl, Psychotherapist
Burgwedel, Germany
As told by Gail De Sciose,
Animal Communicator

I WAS CONTACTED one October by a woman named Ingrid Pohl in Germany. Her beloved cat, Moritz, had died the previous July. He was only three years and four months old when he passed on. He had been a white cat with some gray tabby markings, unusual markings on his back and around his head. They found his body in a field close to their home. Ingrid was very upset and wanted me to ask Moritz if he wanted to come back into another body and rejoin the family.

He said that there was another cat in the household, an old male cat named Paavo, who didn't like him very much, and he felt that he probably shouldn't come back as long as Paavo was around because he didn't want to antagonize him.

So Ingrid had me talk to the two remaining cats in the household, Paavo and Toni. Toni, who had been Moritz's very great friend, said he would be delighted to have him come back as soon as possible because he was his playmate. Paavo said that he didn't really like Moritz so much when he was in his body, but he appreciated the fact that Moritz would be willing to wait until he wasn't there anymore. So, it really didn't matter that much to him. He said that if Moritz wanted to come back, let him come back, and to thank him for his consideration. I thought that was incredible, since these guys hadn't been friends.

So, a little time went by and Ingrid had me get in touch with Moritz again to ask him to reconsider coming back. He said he *would* come back—probably fairly soon—in a few months. He also said that he would be a kind of orange tabby type cat, and this would be the way we would know to recognize him.

Over the next couple of months, we tried talking to him again to ask him, "How will we know it's you? How will we find you?" He said, "Don't worry about that; I'll take care of that part." We asked, "Will you show up at an animal shelter? Will you come through the veterinarian's office?" He said, "I will handle it; don't worry." Apparently, there aren't that many orange cats in Germany, and I thought, *That might be a good thing because if he shows up we will have a better clue that this really is him.*

Ingrid and her husband, Jorg, went to Italy on a holiday and they were staying at a farm. I got a phone call from Ingrid in Italy, who said, "You know, the mother cat on the farm had a litter of three kittens. One of them is an orange-and-white cat and he always looks at us in a very touching way." She said, "Could you check with him to see if it's Moritz?" The mother cat's behavior was apparently very odd because she usually kept her kittens hidden from the farmer. In this case, however, she allowed her kittens to be seen.

I asked the kitten if he was Moritz, and he said that he was, that he had indeed returned. This little ball of fluff, who could hardly walk because he was only three or four weeks old, then came up to Ingrid and her husband and looked at them in a "very touching way." That made everybody very happy, but it also created a problem because Ingrid and Jorg had to go back to Germany and the kitten was too young to be taken away from his mother. The farmer wasn't terribly attached to the cat, so he allowed Ingrid and her husband to take the mother and the three kittens back to Germany.

Moritz has grown into a very gentle, lovely cat. Ingrid feels certain that he is Moritz because he does the same things that the former Moritz did. She even gave him that name again. Most people don't do that, by the way; when their animals come back, they give them different names.

What I find to be tremendously remarkable in this case is that Ingrid sent me a picture of the reincarnated Moritz and he has a white body with orange tabby markings, but his markings are almost identical to the former Moritz's, whose markings were gray and white. This doesn't always happen; sometimes the animals don't look anything like they did before, but in this case, he does.

Kim's note: When I spoke with Ingrid Pohl several years later, she added the following updates. . . .

We were absolutely surprised, my husband and I, that all this happened to us. After spending another three years and four months with us [the exact same lifespan as the first time], Moritz died again, this time by a car crash, and we were absolutely desperate. After eight months, he came back again as an orange tabby female cat, and her name is Sonja.

Lil Guy, Part 2
Patte Purcell, Host, The Next Dimension *Radio Show*
Nevada

Kim's note: It turns out that Patte's story about Lil Guy, in which he came back to visit during the night (as told in Chapter 9, "A Touch of Heaven"), was only the beginning of the story. She later had the following to add. . . .

WE LOST OUR LIL GUY after seventeen years. My husband wanted us to go out and get another kitty right away to heal the loss. We got a beautiful white Persian with blue eyes. I picked him up and he started purring. I looked back in the cage and saw his little red Persian brother who looked at me like, "Hey, me too!" I fell in love, and we brought them both home. We called them Boo Boo (the white one) and Bubba (the orange one). We had great fun. They played, and we enjoyed them so very much.

At about eighteen months, Bubba started losing weight. We had the vet out, but she couldn't really find anything. Over the course of the next few months, he continued to deteriorate. Even though we went to three different vets, no one could figure it out. He got worse and worse. They thought it might be the heavy fur he was ingesting, so they shaved him and he was wearing a sweater to keep warm, as he was anemic.

The night before he died, he was sleeping on my pillow, and I had a dream that he had taken off his sweater and was running around. I woke and told my husband that Bubba had just told me he was going to pass. He died that night. We were devastated. Boo Boo was devastated. Before he died, Boo Boo and Bubba touched noses as if to say good-bye.

My husband immediately wanted to get another cat. I told him I needed some time to grieve for Bubba. I do a metaphysical radio talk show, and I have mediums as my guests on a regular basis. I decided to call Dennis Jackson, one of the best ones I've ever seen, to see if I could talk to Bubba. He came right to the phone. I told him what had happened and he said, "Well, there is a black cat here (Lil Guy was black). He wants you to know that he helped Bubba over and they both want to come back!" I was amazed to hear that this could happen very quickly. I asked him how to find them and he told me, "They will find you!" He mentioned looking on the Internet. My husband immediately started looking. We kept looking but nothing really hit.

About the second week in December, I had a dream that I was holding Bubba in my palm; he was on his back and he wrapped his soft little paws around my finger. I woke up and told my husband that Bubba was back! We sent out e-mails looking for any new kittens born after November 1st (the day Bubba passed), and a woman sent us an e-mail saying her Tortie had a litter of two brothers, one a red Persian, the other a gorgeous cream. We rushed right over. The red Persian rolled over in my arm and wrapped his little paws around my finger, just like in the dream. I *knew* it was Bubba.

As for Lil Guy, I thought I was still looking for a black Persian, but this little cream-colored one made it clear that he was coming with us! I checked with the psychic to make sure. Guess what; it was Lil Guy! What is so amazing is they have the exact same personalities as before. The really cool thing is that when we brought them home, Boo Boo and Bubba ran right up to each other and touched noses. Boo Boo looked at us like, "Thank you, thank you!" He loves both of the kittens, washes them, plays with them, sleeps with them, and hugs them! I've never seen a cat so loving towards new family members. He loves them as much as we do! It's a miracle!

Bimbo
Angela Elliott, Homeopath
California

MY CAT, BIMBO, was poisoned and he died a rather tragic death. I knew that he would always be alive in my heart, but never dreamed that he would come back to me!

Last September, I found two very tiny kittens in my laundry room. I instantly fell in love with one of them; we bonded right away. I looked into his eyes and I knew it was him. He is the spitting image of my old cat in every way. He came back to me! I gave him a different name (Frisco) even though I knew he was my former cat.

I wanted to test my theory. I called him by my original cat's name, Bimbo. He didn't hesitate for a second; he came straight to me and kept nuzzling me. Every time I said his old name, he got even more affectionate. He was trying to tell me something! I know for a fact it is him. I haven't a doubt; I know it like I know who I am.

I have received many messages in my lifetime and I have been there to assist many animals in their passing. I know animals return to us.

Kim's note: As this story illustrates, we don't always need outside assistance or a spectacular chain of events to convince us that a loved one has returned. Sometimes, we just "know."

Cody

Debbie Kuperman, Phone Company Service Representative
Texas

TO GIVE YOU A BRIEF HISTORY of my relationship with Cody (my dog), I got him when I was about eighteen. Shortly after, I went into an awful spiral of drug addiction and alcoholism that lasted several years. Needless to say, living that lifestyle, Cody and I went through hell and back together. He was my best friend through it all. Years later, when I was almost twenty-five, I found myself living in a tent on my mother's property in the woods of Arkansas. I lived there for about two months when I discovered I was pregnant with my first child.

I decided to move to the Dallas/Fort Worth area to straighten up my life and get a good job (which I did). Cody loved the woods and the freedom he had at my mom's, so, while it broke my heart, I left him with her. When I was leaving, I couldn't bear to say good-bye to him, so I asked him to go for a walk while I left. He, as always, understood what was happening and he took off down the path. He stopped once to look back, and then continued on until he was out of sight. I quickly got out of there before he came back. I went to visit once or twice after the baby was born and he was always happy to see me.

About three years later, he was hit by a truck while chasing it. (He always loved to chase trucks, and I told him several times that would be the way he would die.) Something told me to call my mom that day and, sure enough, he had been hit about fifteen minutes before I called. She buried him on her property under a dogwood tree where several other family pets are buried. I went up there one time to visit his grave. I could feel that his spirit was living on in the woods and the river that he loved so much, so I was at peace.

Now I have another baby, and my older child is five. I just got them a Great Pyrenees puppy. Her name is Cassie. She is almost four months old and (being such a large breed) is about the size Cody was full grown. Last weekend, we all went up to my mom's for a visit. Cassie (my new puppy) has never seen big trees, a river, or any type of wilderness whatsoever.

The first time we went to the river, she walked right in and swam to the other side (this was something Cody did on a daily basis). Then she swam back and got out. When she started walking, she had his walk, she held her tail the same way he did, and even her face had changed to resemble him. All of us that were there who knew Cody (five people) recognized him immediately. We marveled at it a while and went back up to the house.

That night, Mom cooked spaghetti (which was Cody's favorite—he always got his own plate). Through all the cooking Mom had done thus far, Cassie had never paid attention. I looked over at Mom while she was cooking, and there sat Cassie right at her feet, staring at the stove, slightly shaking with the anticipation of the spaghetti. Cody always did this. I brought it to Mom's attention and, sure enough, there were Cody's facial features again.

Later, Cassie and I went for a walk in the woods. She started to go off down a path. I called her back to me, and she acted as if she didn't even hear me. I called her several times, when I noticed she wasn't walking like herself. She was walking like him. I said, "Cody, come here, boy!" She (or he) stopped in her (or his) tracks and came trotting back down the path to me immediately. I told everyone about it when I got back to the house.

The next day, once again, she trotted down to the river, and Cody went for his daily swim. My sister was down there and called Cassie to come up to the house with her. She, as I had done, called and called. Then she remembered what I had said. She called Cody's name, and he/she came running. There were several other subtle times when Cody would come and go over the weekend, so none of us were sure what to really call her/him at times.

There were five of us there that knew Cody when he was alive who can verify this. There were others there, but I wouldn't count them as valid witnesses since they didn't really know Cody or the way he acted, walked, etc. It was amazing.

[*Kim's note:* Debbie thought that Cody's spirit was using Cassie's body as a temporary host. She did not consider that Cassie might be the reincarnation of Cody, but is now beginning to wonder. Perhaps it was simply more apparent when she visited her mother's home, since that was the home that Cody had known, so therefore, those were the surroundings and activities that were familiar to him.]

There have been other times that she resembled him. I would look into her eyes and swear Cody was looking back at me.

The funny thing is that Pyrenees are usually all white, occasionally having what are called "badger markings" around their face and ears. Cassie has these markings, but she also has two brown spots, one on her back and one by her tail. They are exactly the same color brown that Cody was all over. My mom pointed this out.

There were also some strange circumstances to me getting Cassie. I won't go into those details, but I can assure you that I was destined to have her and no other dog.

I hope this brings people who have loved and lost a member of the family (since that's what our pets are) some comfort in their grief. I know it brought me comfort. To just be able to hug him and see the loving look in his eyes again meant more to me than anyone will ever know.

He was (and still is) so special to me.

Bubbles

Dawn E. Hayman, Animal Communicator/Co-founder,
Spring Farm CARES
New York

A PONY WE NAMED BUBBLES arrived here at our facility when she was in her thirties; she was probably around thirty-two or thirty-three. She got the name Bubbles because she had no teeth and we had to feed her her food mixed in water; she would stick her head down in the bucket and blow bubbles. She also had a very bubbly kind of personality. She was a little Shetland pony—incredible character. Kids adored her. She was very effervescent. One of her favorite things was eating glazed doughnuts, believe it or not, and there was a volunteer that used to come here once a week with a bag of glazed doughnuts. When Bubbles saw that doughnut bag come in through the door she would start nickering and twirling in circles. She would go nuts to have her piece of glazed doughnut. Every Saturday morning, without fail, that was her routine.

Bubbles died of old age. About six months after she died, her spirit announced to me that she was coming back. This was an incredible message because I usually don't get things in time frames about when they are coming back. She was very specific that on April 21st she was going to arrive on our farm in utero and she was going to be born here. I immediately said, "Forget it; the chances of this happening are so slim." She told me she would be a Shetland pony again. We don't do any breeding here; we are a rescue facility. There aren't very many pregnant Shetland ponies that are running around as strays out there. So I immediately thought, *It's never going to happen.*

Nevertheless, I asked if there was anything that we needed to do. And she said, "No, but you may want to tell your friends that if they ever found a Shetland pony in need of a home that you would be interested." So we said, "Okay, we can do that." We did that. April started ticking away, and all of a sudden on the 19th of April I got a phone call from a friend of ours. And she said to me, "There is this very strange situation; there is an elderly woman who is not taking care of her horses—she has a whole bunch of Shetland ponies and a lot of them are pregnant, and I'm looking to place them. Would you be interested in taking one? We have to get these ponies out of there because they are starving." I couldn't believe it.

"You have to be kidding; yes, we are interested, we will come and take one."

She called me back the same day and told me she had been slightly mistaken; all of the foals were born already and they were a couple of months old and would we take a foal? I asked Bubbles, "Would you have been born already?" and the answer came back so strongly, "No, I'm going to be born in the barn. I'm going to be born in the same stall that I died." I thought, *Well, this isn't it. This isn't the one.* It was a roller coaster, but on the 20th of April the friend called back again:

"You aren't going to believe this. I just went over there. There is one mare who hasn't foaled yet, and she's due to foal any day, so we've got to get her out."

We went over to the place and, interestingly enough, the mare had never been handled. She had never had a halter on her; she had never had anything done with her. As soon as she saw us come in the door, she walked right up to us. We put a halter on her, and we led her out to the trailer. She got right on.

We brought her home. It was April 21st, the date Bubbles had told me she would arrive on our farm in utero. As it turns out, the mare was put in the same area where Bubbles had died, which was in an area in our indoor arena where we put up temporary corral gates, and totally by coincidence that is where she ended up again; it was the only place we had available. So here was the pony ready to foal any day now. We were sleeping out in the barn with her in case she had problems foaling because these mares were all starving, and they were in really bad shape.

To add more to this story, our barn manager, a lady, had a small child whom she would bring to work with her every day. To backtrack just a bit, the original Bubbles used to babysit for her, and our barn manager would actually put the baby in a little rocker in front of little Bubbles's stall. When the baby woke up,

Bubbles would reach out and rock the rocker, and rock the baby back to sleep. This little girl was about a year and a half old when Bubbles died. When the new pony came and was getting ready to give birth, they happened to be here, and the little girl was with her mom. Her mom said, "Do you mind if I let her watch the pony be born?" I said, actually not, that would be wonderful for her. As we were watching the birth, our barn manager said to her little daughter, "Who is that? Who is that?" as the foal came out. The little girl, clear as a bell, said, "It's Bubbles, Mommy, it's Bubbles." The little girl and the pony were so connected when she was an infant. Nobody had talked in front of her about Bubbles coming back.

What clinched it for me was the day after this pony was born. We named him Mr. Bubbles. He had that same personality again. We were having a garage sale as a fund-raising event, an open house type of thing. It was a Saturday morning and people were coming to take tours of the barn. Our volunteer came in with glazed doughnuts for the staff—*not* for the horses. We had a table set up with refreshments on it, and it was in front of where the newborn foal was. The volunteer had put the doughnut bag on the table there. All of a sudden, I heard one of the people on the tour yell, "Look, Mom! Look at what the little pony is doing!" I turned around and Mr. Bubbles was squeezing through the bars of the corral gate to reach for the doughnut bag. Newborn foals just don't do that.

TeeJay
Jeanie Cunningham, Songwriter/Producer
California

BACK IN THE EARLY '80s, I had a beautiful black Great Dane named TeeJay. She was my pal and we adored each other. One day when she was a puppy, she accidentally fell in the pool. I jumped in and pulled her right out, and from that day forward, she *hated* the pool.

When she was about two, we would chase each other around the pool, and I'd run to one end, she to the other. I'd tease her and say, "Aw, c'mon TeeJay, you *know* you want to go swimmin' . . . in the pool!" And she would bark ferociously back at me (*most* disrespectfully), and then race around to wherever I was, stick her head between my legs and pretend to snap at my hands as I'd try to grab her front legs. As we played, she let out the most ferocious growls. We *loved* this game. It went on for another eight years until she had to be put to sleep at the age of ten.

I was devastated. Her back legs had given out on her, she'd stopped eating, and the dreadful day that I'd always put off in my mind had finally arrived. She died on her favorite blanket, surrounded by my friends and hers (two other dogs included), underneath "her" lemon tree, as she was gently put to sleep. In spite of the presence of the other two dogs, TeeJay's absence created a *huge* void in me. I grieved and grieved over her.

Finally, after about two months, my best friend Ayn had seen enough of my teary red eyes, so she bought a book about Great Danes and gave it to me

"I think it's time you thought about getting another one," she said. After my initial horror that she could even *think* that TeeJay could ever be replaced, I started to leaf through the book. About a week later, in total agreement with her, I began to hunt for another black Great Dane.

Somehow, none of the puppies that I went to see really *did* anything for me. By the time I visited a third litter, I had almost lost hope. And then, one day, someone told me that a litter had been born less than five miles from my home. So, after a few weeks, I decided to go over and take a look.

I walked in to a litter of seven puppies. Three were black. Two were female. All were adorable. After allowing them to climb all over me, and smelling the sweet fragrance of their puppy breath, I noticed that one stood off by herself. The mother dog came into the pen, and all the puppies headed for her, except this one in the corner, watching me carefully. When the other pups went for their mother, this little pup wriggled over to me. I picked her up. Snuggling her close, she just seemed to . . . *fit* . . . I can't exactly describe it. So I lifted her up to my face to smell her puppy breath, and the little cutie proceeded to suck my nose. This was a bonding moment, strange as it could be, perhaps, but a bonding moment.

I took her home and named her "Ebony." And I introduced her gently to the pool so that she knew the parameters of it by the time she was two months old. She tolerated it well and didn't show much fear or interest either way.

Two years later, I was on one end of the pool, and she on the other. Though her markings were different from TeeJay's, from the angle at which I was viewing her, I felt a sort of "deja-vu." Out of the clear blue I decided to tease her about going into the pool. "Ebony! Whaddya say? Let's go sa-wimmminnn! In the *pool!*"

She proceeded to bark at me in a *most* disrespectful manner, then raced around the pool to where I was, thrust her head between my legs, and let loose with the most *awesome* ferocious growl, all the while pretend-snapping at my hands as I tried to grab her legs. . . .

"TeeJay? TeeJay, is that *you?*" She responded with another enthusiastic growl and thrust with her head, almost launching *me* into the pool!

I then exclaimed, "You dawg! *Come here leedle dawgie— where's your baby?*" (TeeJay used to have this squeaker toy that was "her baby," and she'd go grab it and squeak it merrily, while driving the rest of us crazy with the noise.) Ebony then went racing into the house, searching for something. She acted as though she wanted to go into the front yard, so I let her into the front, where the lemon tree is. She jumped up (just like TeeJay used to) and picked a lemon from the tree, then placed the slimy treasure in front of me for me to throw. She had never done this before, and yet, it was one of TeeJay's favorite pastimes: picking her own lemons, tossing them around the yard, then chewing off the peel underneath the shade of her lemon tree. And now, here was Ebony, doing the *exact* same thing.

I'm beginning to think that one option for the tremendous glut of animal souls (and I *do* believe that *all* animals have souls) leaving this planet after their brief lives, is for them to return to their people if they so choose. Ebony, with the exception of her markings, is/was TeeJay.

Miss Ebony died last year, at the age of ten.

I haven't felt the same compulsion to seek out another dog just yet—I still have two remaining. But I'm keeping my eyes peeled *just in case* TeeJay decides to come back to chase me around the pool again.

Sil

Lisa Ludwig, Telecommunications Circuit Designer
Utah

ON MARCH 23, 1979, the little stray cat I had adopted a few weeks before gave birth to five adorable kittens. One of the kittens was a calico, beautifully colored with red, white, and black. I decided to keep this kitten, along with the mother, and find homes for the others. Unfortunately, the mother disappeared after the kittens all went to their new homes.

The calico kitten grew into a gorgeous Maine Coon cat with long fur. I called her Sil, which was a nickname—short for silly because she would play the silliest games with her toys. Her official name was Calamity Jane. We bonded like mother and daughter. She thought she was human and understood everything I'd say.

Sil was always in excellent health until one morning, July 8, 1994. As I was packing to go out of town for a business seminar, she began throwing up again and again. When I called the vet, he said he was booked until 2:30 P.M. I explained that this was an emergency and I had to be at the airport by 1:00 P.M. He said to drop her off before I left and they would contact my mother when they could look at her to report the problem.

When I dropped her off, she was in terrible pain and it broke my heart to leave her there alone, but I felt like I couldn't do anything else. I told her I'd be back, and they whisked her away from me before I was really able to say good-bye. I kept praying that she'd be okay . . . that this wasn't anything too serious.

At 4:00 P.M. I was still on the airplane and said a prayer to God that she could be at peace. I was hoping the vet would be making her as comfortable as possible, whatever the problem was.

When I got to my destination that evening, I called my mother to get the prognosis. She informed me that Sil's liver and kidneys had been shutting down and she had been in the dying process. They said they had given her something to stop her from throwing up, but she was in so much pain, it was inhumane to let her suffer and they recommended she be put to sleep. They did so at 4:00 P.M.

Needless to say, I was devastated. Even though we all know we will outlive our pets, it is never something we're ready for. So there I was, out of town, stuck in a seminar, fighting back the tears all day long because I felt I should have been there for her but couldn't be. She had always been there for me, through thick and thin, and now I had deserted her in her greatest time of need and left her alone in the place she hated the most.

I had a dream the next night that Sil came out of the grave, shook off the dirt, and walked away, perfectly fine. *That was a strange dream,* I thought as I awoke the following morning.

My mother brought her home and buried her in her favorite place in my yard before I got back. We mourned her passing as much as losing a daughter or granddaughter. We'd had fifteen wonderful years together.

The first morning I was back, when I was just beginning to wake up but not yet totally awake, I heard Sil at the foot of the bed (in her favorite spot) doing her little snoring-purr. (She actually snored as she got older.) Since I was not totally awake, I just thought, *Oh, that's Sil, as usual, snoring on the bed.* Then I remembered, *But she's gone.* The sound was so loud and clear, and I had to open my eyes to confirm what I'd heard. Of course, I didn't see her, but I then *knew* she had been there and was trying to tell me she *was* okay and at peace.

I continued to mourn anyway because it felt like someone had ripped my heart out, and I felt so guilty. My two other cats also missed her and felt my pain. One of them would bring me all her toys every night in an effort to comfort me.

One night, at the end of August, I was lying in bed, missing Sil terribly. Suddenly, a wonderful peace flowed over me and a thought came to my mind: *Don't worry about it; she's coming back.* My logical mind dismissed that thought as wishful thinking. But I couldn't get over how I suddenly didn't feel the pain in my heart and was so peaceful. I went to sleep.

The next day, I had a psychic reading for fun. The woman seemed to be very accurate about me and made several predictions. At the end of the reading, I asked her if she could access information about our animals.

"Like a lost animal?" she asked.

"No," I replied. "Like an animal who has died. Are you able to communicate with them? I had a cat that died six weeks ago and I was wondering if you could find out if she's okay, if she understands what happened when she passed, and why I couldn't be there for her." (That was all I had mentioned about her the entire time. I didn't even mention her name.)

"I don't know," she said. "I'll ask my guides." She closed her eyes and paused very briefly, then said, "They said not to worry about it; she's coming back." The *exact* same words I had heard the night before. I just about fell off the chair.

I then asked, "Does she forgive me, does she . . . "

The woman interrupted me and said again, "They said don't worry about it; she's coming back. She will be the first animal that crosses your path and will look like she did before."

With that I left, and as I was driving away, a sudden feeling of forgiveness, peace, love, and the sensation of an immense burden being lifted came over me. It was so strong that I had to pull over and began to cry uncontrollably.

A moment later, the thought came to me, *She's coming back in November. My brother will find her as a kitten and will give her to me.* Again, my logical mind said I was just imagining this, but yet a little voice told me not to disbelieve it totally. I began to feel a lot better then.

November 1994 came and went. December came and went. January came and went. There was no kitten yet. By then I deduced that I had just imagined the feeling earlier and maybe she was happy to be where she was and wasn't coming back. I put the idea out of my mind.

At the end of October 1995, my brother called me.

"Lisa," he said, "I have something for you. It's your birthday present. And it's alive." I thought he had a plant for me.

"What is it?" I asked.

"It's a kitten that looks just like Sil," he replied. "She even acts like Sil. She doesn't like me, just like Sil didn't. We found her with her litter mates in the road, dodging cars, and brought them home. You really need to come and see her. I know how bad you felt when Sil died, so I thought you'd like to have her." I just about dropped the phone and fainted.

When I went to see her, she was so little. We figured that she and her sisters were only four to five weeks old. I told my brother I thought she should stay with her litter mates a little longer for security development and I would take her home a couple of weeks later. So it was the first week of November 1995 when she came home. She immediately went to Sil's favorite spot on the bed. She started to play with the same kinds of toys Sil liked. She acted eerily like Sil. The resemblance was amazing. I named her Calamity Jane, but I call her C.J. My other two cats accepted her right away, and they are all good friends.

C.J. was the first animal to cross my path, as was predicted by the psychic. I've talked to four different psychics since then, who have all said in their readings that C.J. is Sil. None of them knew anything about the story. The only way the subject came up in their readings was that I asked them what they could tell me about my current three kitties, one of which is C.J., of course. That's all I said. One of the psychics was a pet psychic who described each of them perfectly. I then asked him about Sil . . . as to how she was doing in Heaven, etc. He immediately replied with, "She has come back as C.J."

I believe animals often come to us as guides, teachers, or other higher beings to be with us on Earth. I believe they are from a higher place. I know Sil/C.J. is supposed to be with me for a long time. I know that my other two cats selected me as their human, also, and it was arranged that we get together. I love them dearly as well.

So we are living happily ever after.

- CHAPTER 17 -

The Journey Continues

*Everything science has taught me—and continues to teach
me—strengthens my belief in the continuity of our spiritual
existence after death. Nothing disappears without a trace.*
— WERNHER VON BRAUN

"WHO'S JOEY?" Patty asked as soon as she picked up the phone,
before she even said hello. I had scheduled a phone consultation with
animal communicator Patty Summers and was now phoning her at
the appointed time. We had several new arrivals at the Rat Refuge,
and I just wanted to check in with them, as I often did with newcomers.

I had previously given Patty the names of the rats she would
be communicating with during our appointment, and Joey *wasn't*
one of them. I had never even *had* a rat with that name. Yet, she
told me she had awakened earlier that morning with the name
"Joey" in her head, accompanied by the image of a male rat who
bore this name and was waiting to speak with me during our
appointment. Apparently, he felt it was *very* important that we
speak with him first, before we did anything else.

I thought for a moment, and then it occurred to me who Joey
was. He had been one of the babies from the big litter of rats that
had arrived several years prior. I had called him Owen when he
was a baby, but when he was adopted out, his new family had
changed his name to Joey. He had been adopted, along with five
of the other babies and two of the moms, by a woman named

Sarah Mullen. Sarah had driven all the way down from Northern California to adopt the rats and had given them a wonderful home. We had kept in touch ever since and had become long-distance friends.

By this time, the babies had reached old age, and Sarah had just recently left me a message to let me know that Joey had died. And now it seemed that Joey had a message for Sarah, which he wanted *me* to deliver.

According to Patty, Joey said to tell Sarah that he didn't feel as if he had left her with a full understanding of his appreciation for her, but that he had indeed appreciated her very much. He said she had made him very happy and had touched him deeply, and that he had a special place in his heart for her. He also confessed that he hadn't been "gushingly affectionate," but that didn't mean he didn't love or appreciate her.

"It was my time," he said regarding his death, explaining that there was nothing more she could have done. He wanted to assure her that she had taken very good care of him and that it was ludicrous for her to think otherwise. He emphasized that it was *very* important that she hear this. He also wanted her to know that he was happy and he was okay.

Neither Patty nor I knew any of the details of Joey's death or even of his life and his relationship with Sarah, but he said it was very important to get this message to her, so I did just that. As soon as Patty and I got off the phone, I left a message for Sarah and told her what had just taken place. I told her everything Joey had said, and I described the image of him that Patty had described to me. He had shown her an image of himself relaxing, waiting for her to scratch him; and then an image of a little "smile" on his face to indicate contentment at being rubbed.

Later that same night, Sarah left me a message. She had received *my* message and wanted to share her reaction. She said that, at first, she was somewhat speechless and didn't know *how* to respond. She had been somewhat skeptical of telepathic animal communication and even of an afterlife, yet his message had been quite accurate—and quite unexpected.

Regarding Joey not being overly affectionate, she said that was true; she could definitely see that. She said Joey had always been somewhat independent, and in fact, it had always been hard for her to get him back in the cage when he didn't want to go back. (This was a *huge,* multilevel cage that could fit several humans, which Sarah and her friend Mario had built just for the rats.) She said Joey had always been very indignant about going back in the cage after running around, and he seemed to run his own show, so to speak.

She went on to say that, when Joey got older, it was quite clear that he really liked it when she rubbed his head. That seemed consistent with the image of him showing contentment at being rubbed. She also said that, after he died, she wondered if she had done *enough* for him and worried that she hadn't, so she *really* needed to hear what he had to say.

The other part that really got to her was the fact that she had just recently, within the last few days, been thinking a *lot* about how much she wished Joey could communicate with her from the Other Side and tell her he was all right and that he was happy. So, much to her surprise and mine (and Patty's, for that matter), he had done just that.

INTERESTINGLY, DURING THAT SAME APPOINTMENT with Patty, after Joey had delivered his message for Sarah, another unscheduled rat began pushing his way in. We were *trying* to communicate with a rat named Patrick, as planned, but Patty said she kept getting the image of a *different* rat trying to get our attention. At first, we thought it was a rat named Luther, as he was the only rat in our household who fit the description: a male rat with a commanding presence.

His message was apparently very important, and he continued interrupting as we continued trying to communicate with other rats. Patty felt somewhat frustrated that the message was unclear yet seemed so important. As she struggled to make sense of the message she was receiving, she said that he seemed to be describing a previous *life.* She said he had been male, had lived with other rats in a *different* household (not mine), and that his name had begun with an "M." She also said I knew the person he had lived with.

It was then that I first started suspecting that this particular rat who kept interrupting us wasn't Luther at all. Luther was alive and well, and I got the feeling that this particular rat might very well be making contact from the Other Side, just as Joey had done before him.

Almost ready to give up on this unclear message, Patty then asked me if I had any friends who had rats, and if so, had she ever spoken with any of *their* rats, because this rat told her she had communicated with him before, but he had lived with *someone else* (other than me) when she had done so. Furthermore, she said that I had met this male rat with an "M" name. Patty had no idea what any of this meant, but she said to remember the "M" name, as it seemed to be very important.

I immediately thought of Diane Newburg, a longtime friend in Los Angeles, who also takes in rescues and has a house full of rats. Diane had never had an appointment with Patty. However, Diane had adopted some of her rats from another woman, Celeste, who *had* consulted with Patty before. I had never been to Celeste's home, but I *had* been to Diane's. Therefore, it was possible that Patty had communicated with one of Celeste's rats who was then adopted by Diane, and who I could have then met at Diane's house. So, I told Patty I'd ask Diane if she had ever had a male rat with a name that started with "M."

When I asked Diane about this, she told me that she had only had *one* male rat with an "M" name. His name was MacGregor, and he had *just recently died*. Diane confirmed that I had indeed met MacGregor during a past visit to her home (she had so many rats that I hadn't kept up with all of their names), and that she had gotten MacGregor from *Celeste*. He had been the baby rat who found his way back to Diane via a phone consultation that Celeste had with Patty Summers several years prior (the rat who had said he was trying to get back to the woman with the curly blonde hair and glasses, as described in the previous chapter). Patty did not know that Diane was the woman with the curly blonde hair—or that she had named this rat MacGregor.

And now, several years later, through Patty, MacGregor was contacting *me* from the Other Side. It appeared that he just wanted to say hello and to keep in touch with his beloved human, Diane; and he knew that I would get the message to her. So, it seemed that my appointment with Patty that day had become a "hello from the Other Side" session quite unexpectedly. Needless to say, I was both amazed and honored that the recently departed animal companions of two friends both came to me during that appointment, trusting that I would pass their messages on to their beloved people. And, of course, I did.

As it turned out, that was only the beginning of things to come.

OVER THE YEARS as I had researched the subject of life after death for animals—almost as if to convince me of the validity of other people's experiences, which I might have otherwise doubted—one by one, very similar experiences to those that I was collecting from *others* had begun happening to *me*.

Up until this point, these experiences had always involved my own departed animal companions. But now, just when I thought my research was complete, *other people's* beloved animals began contacting me from the Other Side. From this point on, they no longer even required the assistance of a professional animal communicator; they began coming to me *directly,* with ever-increasing regularity. At first, I didn't know what was going on, but I certainly knew *something* was.

It seemed that these unexpected and spontaneous contacts from the Other Side, which had originally been initiated by the animals of friends, were now being initiated by the animals of people I had *never even met*, who happened to contact me after the fact, inquiring about the progress of my book. It was almost as if the animals *knew* what I was up to and that they could rely on me to deliver their messages, which I always did.

My first clue that something was going on took place during an afternoon nap. I had been working long hours in front of the computer and was suffering from severe eyestrain, so I decided to lie down for a little while and rest my eyes. Soon I was fast asleep.

I had been sleeping for perhaps twenty minutes when I was suddenly awakened by a very distinctive growl/whine in my left ear. It was as clear as day. I was lying on my right side, and it literally sounded as if a dog had approached me from behind or above and had whined *directly* into my ear, startling me out of a sound sleep. I looked around, and of course, I didn't see a dog. I don't *have* a dog, yet I had clearly heard one. To this day, I can remember with crystal clarity the sound I heard that day. It wasn't an aggressive sound, but rather, the sound a dog might make when trying to get one's attention without barking.

I immediately sat up and began to wonder *who* was trying to get my attention. Shortly thereafter, I was contacted by a woman who said she had begun hearing her recently departed dog's whine, and she wondered if I had ever heard of such a thing before. Well, not only had I *heard* of such a thing, I had just *experienced it myself.* What she described sounded exactly like what *I* had heard. It was then that I first began to wonder if perhaps *her* dog had contacted *me* so that I could validate her experience.

As it turned out, that was only the first of a number of mysterious "dog experiences." Early one morning, I awoke to the distinct sound of a dog sniffing, almost as if there was a dog on the bed next to me, sniffing my face. Startled, I instantly opened my eyes and looked around—no dog.

Another of these mysterious events took place when Jameth was out of town on business. I needed to get up early for an important appointment, but I forgot to set the alarm and was still in a deep sleep when it was time to get up. Suddenly, I was startled out of my sleep by one loud, clear, distinct dog bark. It sounded as if there was a dog right next to me, and the tone of the bark was firm and urgent, as if the dog wanted to be sure I awoke.

I instantly opened my eyes, leapt out of bed, and realized there was no dog in the room. All of the windows were closed, so there was no possibility that the bark had come from outside; it had sounded like the dog was *right there with me*. I looked at the clock. It was exactly the time I needed to get up, so I thanked this mysterious, unseen dog for awakening me.

AROUND THE TIME of my initial "dog experience," I began a meditation circle with a small group of people I met at a workshop given by psychic medium Hollister Rand. (Interestingly, during that workshop, Hollister commented that there seemed to be an unusually large number of animal spirits in the room; she knew nothing about anyone in attendance when she said this.)

We began meeting at my home once a month; and early on, we unexpectedly began sensing the presence of departed loved ones in the room with us during our meditations. A few of us found that we were often able to describe the loved ones of other members of the group with amazing clarity, though we had never met them.

Interestingly, though not surprisingly, the majority of the departed loved ones who appeared to *me* during these meditations were *animals*. Over time, it seemed that the animal kingdom was showing up at every gathering. Whenever I described an animal who appeared to me, there was inevitably someone in the group who had once had a companion animal who fit that description *precisely*.

I recall one incident in particular. As usual, we were meditating, and I spontaneously began receiving images of very specific animals. As I began describing a dog who appeared to me in great detail, one of the women in the group recognized the description as fitting a dog from her past. So, in an effort to determine if this was indeed her departed dog, she began asking me questions, such as what was this dog's favorite thing to do, etc.

All of sudden, I felt *very* "on the spot." For the first time, I felt that I was in the position that professional animal communicators had been in whenever I had asked *them* such testing questions. *What if I'm wrong?* I thought to myself. *What if this isn't real? What if I'm just seeing random images in my mind that happen to sound familiar to these people?* I did my best to ignore these concerns, and I simply asked this dog the questions that had been posed to me.

Much to my surprise, I began receiving very detailed information and seeing very clear images of this dog doing very specific things, such as jumping through hoops and playing in water. These images surprised me, as I had never known of a dog who jumped through hoops; and all of the dogs in my *own* past had been terrified of water. Nevertheless, this was what I was seeing.

So, feeling somewhat awkward and embarrassed, I hesitantly

and self-consciously began telling her what the dog was showing me, half expecting her to tell me that this made absolutely no sense whatsoever, that I clearly *wasn't* being contacted by her dog at all. On the contrary, she confirmed the absolute accuracy of each and every detail; I was, indeed, describing her departed dog.

Of course, the skeptic in me wondered if perhaps I was simply reading this woman's mind and *that* was how I knew all these details about her dog. However, the dog had appeared to me in great detail *before* I had said anything, when the woman's mind was somewhere else entirely. She hadn't been thinking of the dog at all, so at least initially, I *couldn't* have been reading her mind. If I *had* been, I would have received very different information that had nothing to do with this dog from her past. I continued to search for "logical" explanations and continued to come up empty-handed.

During another monthly meditation, I began seeing a very clear image of a gray striped cat. The image wouldn't go away, so I asked if anyone in the group knew who this cat might be. One person did, and she happened to have a photograph of the cat; so she showed it to me. It certainly *looked* like the cat I was seeing, but then again, there are a *lot* of gray striped cats in the world— and the lighting was very dim—so I couldn't be sure. She told me that this cat had been missing for some time and was presumed dead but had never actually been found.

We continued meditating, and the image of the cat wouldn't go away. Like a detailed motion picture, I saw a vision of this cat who seemed to be underneath a house. The image remained for quite some time, and I felt that this cat was trying to deliver a very important message, but I wasn't clear on what the message was. All I knew for certain was that I was seeing the cat underneath something. I didn't actually see a house; I just saw the cat underneath something that I felt was a house or something *like* a house. I didn't know how the cat had gotten under there or if there was even a way out.

This image really bothered me, as I wondered at first if perhaps the missing cat wasn't actually dead and was stuck underneath a house somewhere, asking me for help. So I asked the person with the cat photo if there were any houses in her neighborhood that had crawl spaces underneath. Crawl spaces are not very common in modern Southern California homes; I've only seen them in some older neighborhoods. I knew that she lived in a very modern part of town, so it seemed highly unlikely that there was such a building anywhere near where the cat had been lost; but this was what I continued seeing, and again, it seemed very important. She told me she didn't know of any such areas offhand. Somehow, I got the impression that hers might not be the cat I was seeing, anyway.

Shortly thereafter, I was contacted by a woman in New Jersey who had accidentally come across my Website while looking for something else on the Internet. Upon reading about my work, she felt compelled to share the story of her own deceased cat, whose body had been found underneath the wood deck attached to her house. The deck was quite long and had lattice all around it, and when her husband spotted a cat underneath the deck against the house, he had broken the lattice and crawled under the deck to get the cat's body out. He was shocked to discover that it was *their* cat.

I immediately recalled the persistent image of a cat underneath a house or in some sort of crawl space. Could *this* be the cat I had seen in my vision? I asked her what the cat looked like. She described a gray striped cat who fit the description of the one I had seen. I was intrigued. I then told her about my vision, emphasizing the fact that I had no idea if there was a connection or not.

I then recalled the patterns I had so often observed throughout my life regarding dates. It was currently mid-April, and I felt it would be somehow significant if it turned out that the cat's body had been found during the same time of year, but in a previous year. So, not telling her my suspicions, I asked her if she recalled the date her husband had found the cat's body.

"I don't know the exact date that my husband found her underneath the deck," she told me, "but I know it was mid-April." She had given me the answer I was looking for, though I had no idea what it meant, if anything.

At the next monthly meditation gathering, the cat again appeared to me. So I asked the cat who she was. I then saw the image of a young woman holding the cat. It wasn't completely clear, but I did get a very specific description of the young woman. The image of this young woman was somewhat blurry, and I interpreted this to mean that this was something the cat was *showing* me, rather than an actual person on the Other Side. The image of the cat was clearer, on the other hand, implying (or so I deduced) that it was an actual visitation by the cat. I got the feeling that the cat was answering my question by showing me the person she wanted to contact.

The image of the cat remained for quite some time, and I got the strong feeling that this cat was showing me how much she loved this young woman and to please let her know. Then the cat seemed to communicate, "I swear this is true."

So, I contacted the woman in New Jersey and told her what I had seen, including the description of the young woman. I had never seen her in person and had no idea what she looked like or even how old she was, but she confirmed that I was indeed describing *her.* At that point, I felt that perhaps the message had been delivered.

ANOTHER WOMAN, JILL THORNSBERRY, a producer in California, contacted me via e-mail for support upon the death of her beloved dog, Little Bear (nicknamed Bear Bear, or simply, Bear). As is so often the case, she was absolutely beside herself with grief. In her words:

> I feel so lost. I recently lost my dearest friend very tragically. . . . Bear Bear was my constant companion and went practically everywhere with me. . . . He was patient, kind, understanding, loyal, selfless. . . . He was mellow and very, very wise. He was a golden husky chow mix. He looked like an Alaskan wolf. He was and is so regal. . . . He was my guardian angel. My gift from God. . . .
>
> I need to know that he is with Charlie [her other dog who had previously died] and happy and free. And with me in spirit. I have lost a furry child and part of me has died with him. I feel like I'm in a nightmare and can't wake up. He brought me so much love, joy and happiness, and now

it's gone and I feel that I let him down. You see, I have had a lot of loss in my life and I had no inkling from the doctors that it would go down this way. They knew of the special relationship Bear and I had and even talked about it and how special Bear was to them. He was magical . . . I love all my other special friends dearly, but Bear Bear was very special and came into my life when I was so alone.

I just want to talk to him and know that he understands where he is and is not sad without his mommy. . . . He and I are a part of each other. . . . Bear Bear loved life so much, no one could believe he was older, and he never complained. So my message to everyone is, you just never know. One day we're here and the next we're gone. Cherish every moment. . . .

If you could help me talk to him and find some peace I would be grateful. . . . Some people probably think I'm crazy, but until they walk in my shoes and share the special love with a different creature other than man, they will never know what truth and unconditional love is about. . . .

As soon as I read her e-mail, I immediately felt Bear Bear's presence right there in front of me, a little bit above and to my right. In my mind's eye, I saw an image of a dog with the most amazing, loving eyes, and the most incredible fur. He was so clear, direct, and present. It was as if he knew she had e-mailed me and was just watching and waiting for me to respond. I felt him communicate, "We are still connected. I am still here. She need only listen." I was amazed at how clear this message was. I continued to feel his presence until I replied to her e-mail, almost as if he was making certain I did my job.

Jill and I continued to correspond, and I did my best to be there for her during her time of grieving. Interestingly, she told me that, the night before she first found my Website, she had been shopping at the health food store and had come across the product Green Mush™ (the nutritional supplement for animals that Jameth and I formulated for June originally). She had picked up the bottle and wondered who the people were who produced that product. For some reason, she felt that she wanted to know more about the people behind the product. The next day, when she happened to come across my Website, she was amazed to find that I also happened to be the co-formulator of Green Mush™. It was almost as if she was being guided to connect with me.

She asked me if I could communicate with Bear on the Other Side, and I told her I didn't actually do that . . . but that I *had* apparently begun receiving messages from animals who had passed. I explained that it was usually spontaneous and not really something I initiated, but that I would be happy to *try* to connect with Bear and would let her know what happened. (I also suggested that she contact a professional animal communicator.) I then told her about having felt Bear's presence when I received her initial e-mail, and that it seemed he was very much in charge of our communications.

When I then tried to tune in to Bear, he appeared to me just as he had the first time. In my mind's eye, I saw his image in front of me and to the right, his face a little bit higher than mine but looking right at me. Again, I noticed his incredible fur and his amazing eyes. The image wasn't as clear as day or a literal manifestation of him, nor was it a dream. My eyes were open and I was typing at the computer, and I just sort of "saw" him looking straight at me. It was almost as if, for a few minutes, I was perceiving both physical reality and the spiritual realm simultaneously, so his image was bleeding through—like when an image is superimposed on a photo, but it was less visible than that. I could almost, but not quite, literally see him with my eyes; but my mind saw him and saw exactly where he was.

Again, his presence felt very strong, and I felt that he was communicating to me and watching over me as I was typing an e-mail to Jill. As I looked up at his image, I felt that I was looking directly into his eyes, which were full of wisdom, and then I saw the image of a star. This image remained for a while. I had no idea what this star meant.

In my mind, I also heard what sounded like the word "circus" or maybe "circles." I couldn't be sure of which, but when I listened again I realized it sounded more like "circles." I did my very best to pay attention, and I heard "circles in the grass." I had no idea what this meant.

I told Jill about my experience and asked if it meant anything to her. I did think the word I had heard was "circles" and not "circus," but since it wasn't totally clear, I mentioned them both, just in case. I also let her know that when Bear appeared to me, the two features of his that stood out to me were his fur and his eyes . . . such wise, bright, loving, deep eyes. And I told her about the star I had seen.

"I don't know about *circus,*" she responded, "but he would turn in *circles* like every dog does before he sat down on the grass."

Oh, duh, I thought to myself. I hadn't thought of that. It didn't occur to me that dogs did that, as the dogs in my own life really hadn't. However, I figured I must have subconsciously known about this common behavior in dogs, so I dismissed the whole thing as a lucky guess, at best.

However, she then told me the following:

"I think something Bear is trying to communicate has to do with him eating grass. When he got sick he ate a lot of grass." She added, "It's funny you talked about Bear's fur. It was beautiful! I have had other furry babies and they were precious, too, and cute and cuddly, but I have never seen a dog or had one that had fur like Bear's."

This did sound consistent with what I had seen, but I figured it had probably been my own imagination making another lucky guess. She continued. . . .

"You made mention about Bear's incredible eyes. Yes, they were gorgeous. His eyes were brown, but his left eye was incredible; you see, he had an outline of a blue star like the sky around his pupil. And then to top it off his eyes were permanently outlined with a black/brown liner. Like someone put makeup on him. Just incredible!"

The star! I thought to myself. I wondered if the star in Bear's eye, around his pupil, was the star I had seen . . . or if it had all been one big coincidence combined with an overactive imagination on my part. I had always said that skeptics are hard to convince of *anything;* that if they don't believe in something, they still won't believe it even if it looks them right in the face. Was I talking about *myself* when I said that?

One afternoon shortly thereafter, I had been working at the computer for many hours and felt that my eyes needed a rest. So I went out on the patio to sit in the sun for a fifteen-minute break. Shortly after I settled back on the lounge chair and closed my eyes, I heard someone make a vocal sound behind and above me. It was an unusual sound and it startled me, as I thought someone was there but couldn't imagine *who*, since I was supposedly alone. So I nervously looked up and back, and there was a bird up on the roof ledge directly over me, looking straight down at me, just staring. I stared back, captivated by the bird's gaze.

Then, quite abruptly, the bird flew straight over me—swooping down alarmingly close as he went by—to a tree in front of me. The bird just stayed there and started squawking loudly, looking directly at me. Actually, it sounded more like the bird was *barking*. It was unlike any bird noise I've ever heard. It lasted for perhaps a minute, and when it stopped, I regretted not having recorded it.

Then everything became quiet. So I took a deep breath, leaned back on the lounge chair, and closed my eyes. As soon as I did, the bird suddenly flew straight toward me in a flurry (the flapping of his wings was *very* loud and startled me) and then he swerved up to land back on the roof edge above me, where he had started. My heart was racing. I sat straight upright.

"WHAT?!" I yelled, as it was quite evident that this bird was trying to tell me something. Just then, the bird again flew overhead back to the tree, and as I watched, a hummingbird flew straight across in front of me, between myself and the other bird. If the other bird hadn't so adamantly commanded my attention, I would have been resting with my eyes closed and, therefore, I wouldn't have seen the hummingbird.

I felt certain that the birds were trying to give me a message. For some reason, I also felt quite strongly that the message was from Bear. *Perhaps that would explain the "barking bird,"* I thought to myself. I was absolutely astonished at the whole experience, as I had never experienced anything quite like it before. The birds remained nearby until I went back inside, and I had the most eerie sensation that they were watching me.

Still trying to register what had just taken place, I went back inside to the computer. I suddenly felt compelled to check my e-mail, even though I had already checked it earlier that day. The first message that popped up was from Jill, and I was amazed at what she had to say:

> Today I was out watering the tomato plants and a beautiful hummingbird came to me and hovered about one foot away for about twenty-five seconds. I didn't want to move, but the water was running over and so I moved and off he flew. I felt that he was trying to get close to me and if I stayed still he would have. I don't think it was Bear Bear, but a spirit friend of his telling me he's around. I do believe that Bear Bear has brought us together, and I feel in my heart that you have a special attunement to the animals more than you're aware of, but Bear knows that and he picked you to communicate with me for him. Please tell him I miss him terribly, and I am trying to be still and listen.

I immediately replied to Jill's e-mail and told her what had just taken place. I was amazed at how my bizarre experience co-incided with her own hummingbird experience.

"Your bird story is incredible," she responded. "That sounds like Bear. If he wanted someone to really understand—like me—and I wasn't getting it, he would bark and talk to me. Since I wrote to you about the hummingbird, every time I walk outside they come right around me. They have never done that."

Several days later, I awoke in the middle of the night to the sound of a very unusual bird. It was so loud that it sounded like the bird was in the bedroom. I was having a dream when it began, and the noise kept interfering with the dream, so in the dream I was trying to interpret what was being communicated to me. Just *after* I awoke completely, the sound stopped, and I realized that it had sounded very similar to the "barking bird" I had heard in the yard.

That same night, Jill had an experience of her own, which she informed me of the next day:

Last night around midnight, the front kitchen window, which is pretty big—all of sudden something slammed into it, and it was so loud the windows in the living room shook. For an instant I wanted to believe it was Bear, but then I thought, *No, it's just a bird and I'd better go check because, God forbid, it might be dead.* They have done this before, but never this loud. They see their reflection in the window and think it is another bird. So I went outside . . . and nothing. I was thankful there wasn't a life cut short, but then I started thinking what it was and I remembered that when it happened I had an image in my mind that Bear had jumped up and hit the window. He used to jump up and look out the window, but maybe he was trying to get my attention.

Jill and I kept in touch via e-mail and phone, and we continued to inform each other of our experiences, which continued to coincide quite amazingly.

"I don't feel his presence like that right now," I told her one day, "but I get the feeling he's off doing something very important and will continue checking in on both of us from time to time."

"It's funny you would say you feel he is doing something important," she replied, "because that is what I have also been feeling." She said she had been meditating and trying to contact him but couldn't really concentrate and wasn't getting anywhere. She figured it was more difficult, anyway, because she was still in grief. She then told me about a dream she'd had the night before:

Last night I had a dream or vision. A dog came to me, but I'm pretty sure it wasn't Bear or any of my other friends I had here. It's hard to remember, but I do remember he was three different colors or tones, and I was pretty sure he was telling me Bear Bear was okay but couldn't come right now, but would later. . . . I also got the impression I was supposed to leave him alone. . . . I won't be satisfied until it is clear and my sweet boy actually comes to me. It is so hard to wait and be patient. . . . What do you think about my dream or whatever you call it?

I did think her dream, or vision, was significant and contained a real message. I knew she was wanting a very *literal* and *direct* contact from Bear. I suspected the messenger in the dream may have been telling her not to try so hard to *force* such a contact. Perhaps she needed to let go of him, at least temporarily, as a part of healing her grief and letting him do whatever he needed to do in spirit. Meanwhile, it did seem that he was *already* sending messages to both of us to keep in touch, to let her know he was fine, and to make sure *she* was okay, too.

Around that time, a very large dog came running through our yard, right past the window where I was sitting and working at the computer. I had never seen the dog before, and I've never seen him since. It's *not* a common occurrence to see dogs run past the window, as we have a front gate, so I figured this dog must have run up a steep hill to get around the gate. He just ran by, and then he was gone. I'd had experiences like this before, with strange dogs appearing in the yard shortly after a beloved animal had passed over, and I had heard of similar occurrences from other people.

That night, while still working at the computer, I repeatedly saw something flashing by out of the corner of my right eye . . . but every time I turned and looked, there was nothing there. This got me thinking about something odd that had been happening ever since Jill and I had been in regular contact regarding Bear: Sometimes when I went into the rats' room, they seemed startled, acting as if they saw someone with me, someone I *didn't* see. Several of them seemed to be running and hiding from something, but again, I didn't see anything. They don't normally do this, unless there is a stranger with me, someone they don't know. I wondered if there *was* someone with me—someone whom I couldn't see but who they *could* see. *Was it Bear?*

Jill and Bear had had a very strong telepathic connection when Bear was alive, and Jill had had various past experiences indicating that she was quite in tune with the spirit world already. As a result of Bear's passing, Jill now had a renewed passion for her own spiritual development, and she began meditating regularly. Her motivation, initially, was specifically to open herself up to contact Bear in spirit. However, her spiritual practice now had the unanticipated benefit of pulling her out of her grief and despair. In her words:

With Bear's crossing, it has really made me want to learn and grow. I always did, but we get caught up in this world and forget about what we're really here for. . . . I am ready to experience more and delve into the unknown. . . . I wasn't [previously] ready, experienced enough in this life, nor mature enough with my soul and mind to proceed to the next stage. I feel very strongly now I am. . . . Oh, I am so excited! I haven't felt this way in years.

Jill experienced the normal ups and downs of healing grief, but her newly ignited spirituality greatly assisted her with this process. Meanwhile, I continued to feel Bear's presence on a regular basis.

Over time, Bear began appearing directly to Jill in dreams and visions, and interestingly, as soon as this started, all of my own experiences with Bear stopped. Suddenly, I no longer felt his presence around me. I got the feeling that I had been a bridge between them until she was able to let go of her own grief enough—and to trust enough—to receive contact from him directly.

And so it was with others who, over time, found their way to me during times of overwhelming grief. They—and I—always came away from these experiences uplifted, intrigued, and expanded. The "coincidences" continued to amaze me, and as I observed the never-ending synchronicities, I began to see a Divine order to the universe, a universe that animals are very much a part of. It seemed that the animals on the Other Side were well aware of the work I was doing, and they continued to somehow make their presence known to me just before their devoted people contacted me for support.

It was never something I planned; it just happened—and continues to happen. It has now become a part of who I am, and as I learn to trust the process more completely—to let go of my skepticism and self-doubt, I suspect it will continue and increase. I feel honored to be in such a position, and grateful that the animals—and the spirit world—are assisting me in assisting others. I couldn't do it without them.

- Chapter 18 -

The Hard Part Is Letting Go: Handling Grief

Nothing in life is to be feared.
It is only to be understood.
— Marie Curie

"Wow, he really loves you," said the veterinary assistant as she carried little Jonathan away while he desperately reached out to me with both arms, clearly not wanting her to take him away from me. Jonathan was old for a rat, but his symptoms had come on quite suddenly, and we knew something was terribly wrong. His breathing sounded awful, his white fur was standing on end, and he wasn't eating at all. He was so weak he could hardly move. Jameth and I had rushed him to an emergency animal hospital in the middle of the night.

"I love him, too," I cried as she whisked Jonathan away to an oxygen tank in the back room, where non-employees weren't allowed. I had been torn as to what to do. I wanted what was best for Jonathan and I knew the oxygen might help, but I also knew the separation would devastate both of us. So I stood in the hallway and cried as Jameth tried his best to comfort me. Every time someone came through the door from the back room, I asked for the status of the little white rat in the oxygen tank.

After what seemed like an eternity, Jonathan was brought to a room where Jameth and I met with the vet on duty. He told us he had very little experience with rats and suggested we take Jonathan to our regular vet the next morning. This would be no small task, as our regular vet at that time was two hours away. We took Jonathan home and spent the rest of the night trying to keep him as comfortable as possible. We did everything we could think of to help him, but he continued to weaken.

Early the next morning, we headed from San Diego to Los Angeles, Jameth behind the wheel and me cradling little Jonathan in my arms. As the miles went by, I felt that Jonathan's time was running out. It felt as if we were running a race we couldn't win.

When we finally arrived at our destination, I rushed inside with Jonathan while Jameth searched for a parking space. I anxiously paced in the waiting room, gently rocking Jonathan and assuring him that everything would be okay. Jameth soon joined us as we were quickly ushered into an examination room. I stroked Jonathan's little body and told him everything was going to be okay. The vet, Dr. Debbie Oliver, entered the room as I gently set him down on the table. Just then, his breathing changed dramatically and I knew he was leaving.

"You *can't* die!" I cried, begging him to stay. "You *can't* leave!" I told him how much we needed him, how much the other rats at home needed him. A moment later, he was gone. Just like that. Before anything could be done. I began sobbing and blaming myself out loud for not having gotten help sooner.

"Now, I don't want to hear any of that coulda-woulda-shoulda nonsense," Dr. Oliver said gently as I continued sobbing. Being a highly sensitive and compassionate person, she understood all too well what I was going through. I can only imagine how many times a veterinarian must witness such a scene, and I doubt it ever gets any easier. She did her best to comfort us and then left Jameth and me alone in the room with Jonathan's body.

"Take as long as you need," she said softly as she closed the door behind her. We were devastated, and her sensitivity and compassion made a world of difference in those first moments as we faced our loss. Jonathan was our first loss after June, and we hadn't gotten any better at it.

While we were still in the room trying to come to grips with Jonathan's death, we heard sobbing in the next room. A woman was simultaneously facing the loss of her beloved dog. We soon found out that there was a third loss that morning as well. It was a gloomy Monday morning that none of us would ever forget. Soon, virtually everyone in the building was crying.

We requested an autopsy and spent the next hour or two in the waiting room as Dr. Oliver faced emergency after emergency that morning. In between her duties, she consoled those of us in grief with soft words and a gentle, loving presence.

While the autopsy was in process, I headed out to our vehicle to get some paperwork. I needed something to take my mind somewhere else for a while. As I then headed back toward the animal hospital, I passed the woman who had just lost her dog. Our eyes met, and it was almost as if I were looking in a mirror. Our souls met, and we embraced. The two of us had never met and yet, in that moment, we were one and the same. We had everything in common. It was as if we had the same history, one of overwhelming love and overwhelming loss.

We stood there for a long while, hugging each other tightly, offering simultaneous condolences, and sobbing. I felt such love for—and from—this woman, and I didn't even know her name. Somehow, I think our shared grief brought shared healing. There was no question as to whether or not our grief was understood; we were right there in it, together. I've perhaps never felt greater understanding from a fellow human being than I did in that moment.

Long after she and I had offered our final words of comfort and said our good-byes, that encounter left a lasting impression on my soul. It brought a much needed healing, and it also brought me some incredible insight into the importance of grief support. We don't just need to be hugged; we need to be *understood*. Those who lose a beloved companion animal don't always have that level of support. In fact, more often than not, we don't. Many of us are surrounded by well-meaning people who just don't know how to comfort us.

"Don't cry," we're sometimes told. This is usually said with sympathy and concern, but it is truly the last thing we need to hear during these times. We *do* need to cry. Sometimes we need to cry long and hard and loud, and we need a safe space in which to do it. We need to know that it's okay to cry, and we need those around us to know that it's okay. It's part of the healing. Bottled up grief hurts us emotionally and it hurts us physically. It also prevents us from being able to fully heal and move forward in life.

"It's just an animal," some say. "You can just get another one." For those of us who have loved and lost an animal, it's difficult to even *imagine* saying such a thing, but people do. First of all, an animal is not an "it." Secondly, "just an animal" implies that our grief is somehow less significant just because our loved one didn't happen to be *human*, and this is a comment based in speciesism and not reality. It's the bond of love that makes death difficult, and the stronger the bond, the more difficult the loss, *regardless* of species.

Thirdly, we *can't* just get "another one." The animal we loved and lost is a unique soul with whom we've had a unique relationship. Sometimes, having other animals around helps us to get through the pain, but other times, we need a certain degree of healing *before* we're ready to love someone else. This is really an individual thing, so it's important that we listen to our hearts and not follow advice that doesn't feel right to us.

It is important to validate the very real emotions of those who have lost beloved animals and who require the same support as those who have lost beloved humans. It's time we dispel the notion that grief over the death of an animal is somehow lesser, or that it is merely a rehearsal for "the real thing." It *is* the real thing! Many people are actually closer to the animals in their life than the *humans* in their life; and love is love. Grief is not species-specific. It's okay to feel the way we feel and, in fact, it's important to find appropriate avenues for expressing these feelings.

If a person is unable to find adequate support among family or friends, it may be helpful and even necessary to seek outside assistance. There are grief counselors, support groups, and even grief-support hotlines. If seeking such assistance, it's important to ascertain that they are animal friendly and treat grief over the loss of an animal with the same respect as grief over the loss of a human. If they aren't and they don't, it's best to keep looking. Ideally, we should seek such support from a counselor, group, or hotline that specializes in *pet* loss.

I can't emphasize enough the importance of seeking support among people or institutions that acknowledge the existence of animals in the hereafter—or are at least open to the idea. Many people have turned to people they trust—or institutions they have faith in—thinking they'll find the support and comfort they need, only to be fed the outdated notion that animals do not have souls. Countless people have come away from these experiences totally confused and devastated, and more in need of grief support than ever.

I always encourage people to send sympathy cards to those who have lost beloved animals, just as we send cards when *humans* die. I recall a time when a business associate told me that his dog had just died. He was torn up with grief, as this dog had been his best friend for many years. I recalled how much it had meant to me when others had sent me sympathy cards on the loss of an animal in my own life, so I sent this man a sympathy card.

Shortly thereafter, he called to thank me for the card and to let me know how very much it meant to him. He said that none of his friends or family had offered any gestures of sympathy whatsoever, even though they all knew how special this dog was to him. They all just expected him to "get over it." He confessed to me that he had been crying over the loss, a confession that he dared not disclose to anyone else. It broke my heart to hear this, yet this is all too often the case. Real men *do* cry when they need to, so our culture needs to make it okay. Grief is neither gender-specific nor age-specific (nor species-specific, for that matter). It is a universal emotion.

JUST AS WE NEED TO TAKE CARE to validate the grief of grown-ups, it's important to take into consideration the grief of children.

Very often, the loss of a pet is a child's very first experience with death. That was certainly the case for me. Compounding the grief is the confusion that often surrounds this early experience of loss. Parents often battle their own personal grief over the loss of a family pet while simultaneously trying awkwardly to explain death to a bewildered child. I encourage parents not to hide their grief from their children, but rather, to explain *why* Mommy or Daddy is crying. This sets a good example for the child that it *is* okay to feel and express emotion.

I was once contacted by a woman who was very concerned about her young daughter. The family had recently lost their pet hamster, Max, and the daughter was devastated by the loss. The family had Max stuffed and kept his body in the cage he had lived in. However, the little girl didn't understand why Max wouldn't eat or play with her, despite the fact that her parents had explained to her numerous times that Max was in Heaven. The daughter was having a lot of trouble sleeping due to the loss, and she spent hours just staring into the cage repeating, "Max, why won't you play with me?" She was even caught playing with him shortly after he had been stuffed. The mother had exhausted all ideas on how to make her daughter understand that she couldn't play with Max anymore, so she was seeking my advice on how to help her daughter.

I suggested that the family hold a funeral and perhaps bury Max's body, involving their daughter in the ceremony as much as possible. I wasn't sure whether or not the little girl should be involved in the actual burial, as it might be too upsetting for her; but it seemed to me that the body did need to go away so that the little girl could better grasp the reality of Max's departure from the physical world. Regardless of this detail, I suggested they do their best to make it a positive and educational experience for their daughter, enabling her to truly let go of Max. I don't know if that's what the woman wanted to hear or if she took my advice, as I never heard back from her. I could be entirely wrong, but I suspect that keeping Max's body around wasn't doing her daughter any favors.

Humans have held ceremonies to mark various rites of

passage for ages, perhaps since the beginning of time. Without a ceremony—in this case, a funeral—there is no clearly defined transition from one life experience to the next. As far as the little girl could tell, her beloved friend was still very much around, but something dreadful had happened to him, rendering him unable to eat or play or even move. From her perspective, he was cold and stiff and paralyzed, so it must have been difficult for her to imagine how he could possibly be in Heaven when he appeared to be suffering right here on Earth. I am certain that her parents had the very best of intentions in having Max's body stuffed, and they never intended any emotional harm whatsoever to their daughter.

(It should be noted here that I'm not condemning taxidermy. In fact, I'm in no position to comment, as I've never had it done with any of my own companion animals and I don't know very much about it. However, in the case of a child, I can certainly see how this might add to the confusion of facing death for the first time.)

When my niece, Monica, lost her first guinea pig at around the same age as the above-mentioned little girl, she, too, was confused as to why her little friend was so stiff and still. So, her parents took her out to a beautiful setting where they buried the guinea pig and explained that his body was being returned to the earth but his spirit was being released to Heaven. Monica cried as they buried his body, and she asked why they were leaving him there when they turned to leave; but then, in the act of leaving, she began to understand. She knew that if his spirit was still in his body, they certainly wouldn't be leaving him there. They were leaving his body behind, just as *he* had done, because he no longer needed it. He was now able to soar in spirit without it. And Monica was able to move forward, to let go, and eventually, to love another guinea pig just as much as she had loved the first one.

I think we all need that ceremony, that point of reference that clearly defines for us that our loved one has moved on to the spirit world. They no longer need their body, and that's okay. I don't think there are any rules that clearly define what this rite of passage should look like. Some people bury their beloved animals; others have them cremated; others perhaps make choices I'm not even aware of or don't know enough about to comment on. People have asked my advice on this subject. I feel that it is a very personal choice, and I suggest that people do whatever feels right for them and their beloved animals.

I was once contacted by a man named David, a foreign language translator from Maryland, who told me he had been troubled for a long time by the fact that he'd had all of his beloved guinea pigs' bodies cremated, but he didn't feel that he could really talk to anyone about it. He was really bothered by the idea of having his special little friends' bodies destroyed and reduced to ash. However, he just didn't know what else to do. He'd had guinea pigs for years and, since guinea pigs have relatively short lifespans, had lost quite a few of them already. He didn't want to bury them in his yard because he figured he might move eventually and wouldn't want to leave them behind. He knew there were pet cemeteries, but this wasn't something he could afford.

So, cremation seemed the only option. He felt guilty every time he took one of their bodies to the crematory, and he told me he hoped the spirits of his precious pigs understood why he had to do this. He did appreciate that the people at the crematory were very nice and compassionate. He said they did everything in a dignified way and tried to make it all as nice as possible under the circumstances. With cremation, he figured that eventually the ashes could go with him when he someday died, too. He had the ashes in separate little boxes with name plates, and he kept them on a special table in his living room. That way, he told me, he felt that they were still close by. He still had such love for each of his precious guinea pigs and said he felt they were still around even though they were cremated. I couldn't agree more.

I have so much respect for people such as this man, who are so incredibly loving and compassionate toward animals that their compassion and concern continue even after the animals have died and returned to spirit. I feel that the way he chose to handle their remains and to honor them was absolutely perfect and beautiful, and he had no reason to feel guilty whatsoever.

GUILT IS AN EMOTION that those of us who love animals seem to feel quite often, especially surrounding the death and dying process. I've always felt that guilt is a very important and necessary emotion, as it helps us to distinguish right from wrong, and when we make genuine mistakes, it helps us to make better choices in the future. However, guilt is also a highly misused emotion, and it seems that those with the highest level of compassion most often tend to aim it at themselves unfairly. I find that those who do the most good in the world often blame themselves the most when something goes wrong.

When guilt is *justified,* it's important to honor the guilt, learn from it, and vow to do things differently the next time we're faced with a similar situation. However, once we've acknowledged the guilt and truly learned from it, it's time to release the guilt and move forward. Usually there's a lesson in it so that we can make better decisions in the future, or else the tragedy is turned around by becoming a catalyst for something positive. We always get a chance to "make things right" in the end.

When guilt is *unjustified,* which is usually the case when we lose a beloved animal, we need to quit being so darn hard on ourselves! If we choose not to euthanize, we blame ourselves for letting an animal suffer too long. If we do euthanize, we blame ourselves for giving in too soon and we wonder after the fact if perhaps something more could have been done. If we don't take an animal to the vet and feel after the fact that we probably should have, we beat ourselves up for this; if we do and they die, we blame ourselves for not keeping them at home. I've lost many dozens of beloved animals in my lifetime, and virtually every time, I've absolutely tormented myself with unnecessary guilt somewhere along the way. I think perhaps we all do that to a degree.

It's important to remind ourselves that hindsight is perfect and foresight is not nearly so reliable; and that we truly did the best we could at the time, even if it doesn't seem that way after the fact. Meanwhile, our departed companions are very much alive and well in spirit. It was only a body that gave out. It was their time to leave the physical form, and that is something we ultimately don't have any control over. They know we love them and did the best we could in each moment. We always second-guess ourselves after the fact. It seems our minds almost try to *invent* ways to blame ourselves for the passing of a loved one. However, it's not based on reality, and we should all learn to be more forgiving of ourselves.

Along with caring and caretaking comes extreme responsibility. Sometimes, along with responsibility comes agonizing decision-making. In decisions of euthanasia, sometimes we genuinely don't know what to do. It's the animal's life, so we feel that the decision is ultimately up to them, but sometimes we truly can't discern what they want. In this situation, it is often helpful to seek the assistance of a qualified animal communicator who can help to check in with the animal and determine what he or she truly wants. If this isn't possible, all we can expect from ourselves is to make the best decision we can in each situation. As long as we come from a place of love and compassion, we have no reason to feel guilty after the fact, *regardless of outcome.*

"If only I had known, I would have held him/her to the end." I often hear this comment spoken by those in grief, and I've certainly said it myself. Very often, our loved ones die just after we leave the room, even if we're only gone for a moment. Then we torment ourselves with "if onlys." We feel that we've let them down in some way by not being there. Very often, we're not there because we've left the room to get something that we hope will make a dying animal more comfortable; or we have to go to work; or we've gone to take a twenty-minute nap because we're utterly exhausted after sitting up with them day and night, *and that's when they leave.* This can be devastating. It's important to remind ourselves that we had no negative intention in not being there at the moment of death. Truly, if we *had* known—and *could* have been there—we *would* have been there.

I've come to understand that, actually, animals will sometimes intentionally leave when we're *not* there. If we're so distraught over their approaching death that we beg them to stay (whether verbally, telepathically, or with our body language), they have a very difficult time leaving us; so they sometimes wait until we step away, and then they leave. Rather than feeling guilty over not being there, it is helpful to acknowledge that perhaps we've assisted them in letting go of a worn-out body that they were no longer comfortable in.

I recall when our beloved Julian made his transition. He was an extremely affectionate and handsome black rat with a white underbelly and a sweet expression. He looked like a little otter. During his final days, I held him almost nonstop. During his final hours, I carried him around and told him how special he was. I felt compelled to hold him in front of a mirror, and as the two of us gazed at our reflection, I said softly, "That's you, and that's me." He just stared into the mirror and turned his head as he looked from my face to his own reflection.

Then Jameth entered the room and showered Julian with affection. Shortly thereafter, Julian began to stir uncomfortably, so I got the feeling that I should put him back in his little bed in the Rat Room. I settled him in and gently told him once more how much I loved him.

When I went in to check on him a short while later, his body was still. He had died. I beat myself up for not having held him *just a little bit longer.*

Then it occurred to me that I had put him back in his bed because he had *asked* me to. He had died the way *he* wanted, not necessarily the way *I* wanted. I was beginning to realize that there is sometimes a difference between the two. As I cried over his lifeless body, I suddenly looked up. I felt his spirit hovering above me and I said softly, "That's you, and this is me."

DEATH IS TRULY ONLY PAINFUL for those of us who are left behind. Death, which is often a *release* from pain, is actually a beautiful experience for those who return to spirit . . . and it is certainly not the end. It is simply a transition. We need to remind ourselves of this. If we wish we had just said "I love you" one more time, it's never too late. We can speak to them in spirit, and they *will* hear us and understand. (This can sometimes seem incredibly difficult to believe for those of us who are left behind and feel so alone, but experience has repeatedly shown me that this is absolutely true.)

We need to do our best to release the pain and guilt—not to cover it up or suppress it, but to truly face and come to grips with it—so that we can then focus on the love and happy memories instead. Sometimes it is necessary to seek outside help in doing so. If we know of others who are grappling with overwhelming grief, it is important to offer our support and assistance, and if necessary, encourage them to seek outside assistance as well. This assistance can take the form of a qualified grief therapist, pet loss support hotline, animal communicator, medium, friend, support group, workshop, or even a book, tape, or CD.

JUST AS HUMANS FEEL GRIEF over the loss of a loved one, so too do animals. If there are other animals in the household, it's important to acknowledge their grief as well. Although they don't always show grief the same way we do, they very much feel it. I encourage people to give the other animals in the household plenty of TLC (tender loving care) and to work through the grief together with them. They need to mourn, too, and the process of mourning together can be very healing. It can be extremely helpful to have a "heart-to-heart" with them—to tell them what happened, to cry with them, and to reminisce about the departed animal.

It may be helpful to seek the assistance of a professional animal communicator to check in with the remaining animals, to help them understand what happened to their friend, and to assist them with their own grief. I recall that when Jonathan died, the remaining rats in the household went through a period of deep mourning. For the first few days, they looked all over the house for him. After they realized he was gone, they moped around for a time, clearly upset at the realization that he wasn't coming back. So I worked with a professional animal communicator to help them through the grief, and this made a world of difference for them.

Now, whenever there is a loss among my beloved animal family, I take the time to tell the remaining animals what happened and to reassure them that everything is going to be okay. I let them know I understand that they are hurting—and that I'm hurting, too—but in time, the hurt will heal. This is something we can all do, whether we enlist the help of a professional animal communicator or not.

Many professional animal communicators offer workshops, and they assure us that telepathic communication is something we *all* can learn to develop, whether through professional training or diligent practice on our own. It's extremely helpful to learn to connect with our beloved animal companions in this way. Basically, it involves clearing the mind and focusing on the animal. We can ask them questions (in our mind) and then listen (in our mind) for answers.

At first, we may not get anything, or we may get something that we dismiss as obvious or that we feel we are making up. On the other hand, we may actually receive valid information, so it's important not to ignore anything that comes. With practice, we can learn to discern which thoughts are our own and which are truly telepathic communications. As with anything else, some people have an easier time learning this than others. For some, it's an inherent gift, and for others, it's a skill that must be learned and refined.

BECAUSE OF MY WORK IN ANIMAL RESCUE, and because the majority of the animals in my care have been rats, who only live for a few years, I've been given many opportunities to face loss. Since pets are often abandoned or relinquished when they become old or ill, the Rat Refuge has been called a "rat hospital" or a "nursing home for rats." I do try to find good homes for the young, healthy arrivals, but the old and ill rats always stay. In a sense, it's like running a hospice for rats.

Many of the words in this book have been written with a dying animal on my lap or at my side. Since I began writing this book, I've experienced dozens of losses. Since I began writing this chapter, I've had three new losses, three days in a row. Perhaps this Divine timing is further assisting me in covering the topic of grief and loss. Each loss has given me additional insight, and I'm still learning. Experience truly is the best teacher, as painful as it often is.

I recall that Jameth and I, before June entered our lives, had often commented on how silly it was that people took such elaborate measures when a loved one died. The expensive and extensive funeral ceremonies, coffins, flowers, and the like often seemed like "overkill" in honoring someone in spirit who was really no longer attached to physical form.

Then, when June died, our perspective changed instantly and dramatically. We doted over her body and took great measures to prepare for a ceremony in honor of our precious June. We even made a little stuffed "June doll" (made out of biodegradable natural fibers) to bury with her. We wrapped her body in a beautiful cloth and placed it in a box that we decorated extensively, customized just for her. We put little notes in the box with her body, telling her how special she was to us and how much we would always love her. And we prepared all of her favorite foods to bury with her. The very behavior that we had once considered "overkill" was now a very significant part of our healing process. Like never before, we truly understood the importance of ceremony.

We buried her body in the ground outside our bedroom window. Then we wrote her name (in nontoxic, biodegradable ink) on a large stone and placed it over her grave, along with beautiful flowers and more of her favorite foods. We stood over the grave and wept and told her how much we loved her. We smiled through our tears as we recalled the happy and funny memories from her lifetime, and we pondered how different life would be without her. Every step we took in that ceremony was a part of our own healing process. It was a way of saying good-bye, of paying tribute, of letting go, of working through our grief.

That set the pace for handling the loss of each animal that followed. Over time, more stones joined June's in the little area behind a tree beneath our bedroom window. When we eventually moved to our own home, we brought the stones with us and placed them on the ground in what has become our own ever-expanding animal cemetery.

Not all of the ceremonies have been as elaborate as June's. Over time, as we became more at peace with the necessary transition of death, we stopped putting the bodies in boxes and began wrapping them in a simple biodegradable cloth. Now we simply place their bodies directly in the earth, on a bed of fragrant flower petals or leaves. Each evolution of our personal burial ceremony has reflected an evolution in our personal acceptance of death. As the number of stones in the cemetery increases, so too does my understanding of the seasons of life.

Of course, I still feel that familiar sinking feeling—that feeling of dread in the pit of my stomach, the lump in my throat, and the feeling of helplessness—whenever I see the signs of forthcoming death in my own companion animals. I now know they'll still be around in spirit, but I also know I'll miss their soft, warm, familiar physical presence.

And when they do pass, I still grieve deeply and cry intensely, and sometimes—when I find myself in the pit of despair—I wonder if I can continue to handle so much loss with the rescue work I do and the love of animals who have such painfully brief lifespans. Then I commune with my beloved animals who are still with me. I look into their eyes; stroke their soft, warm fur; and think to myself, *Of course I can.* The love they give is always worth the pain when they leave.

SOMETIMES WE NEED A PERIOD OF GRIEVING *before* we can accept other animals into our lives; other times, it is other animals that *help* us through the grieving. This is a very individual thing. We know in our hearts when we're ready to love again. When I lost June, I honestly didn't think I could *ever* love another animal again. Then, when I finally *did* allow another animal into my heart, I felt guilty. I felt that I was betraying June. Of course, I wasn't. Our loved ones on the Other Side truly want us to be happy. They want us to be able to love again. Now that I have a house full of animals, I find that the presence of the remaining animals helps me to get through the grief of each passing. Just their presence helps me to feel that much less alone and to find comfort.

I FIND THAT CREATING A MEMORIAL is often a very important part of the healing process for many people. A memorial can take the form of a grave, an urn or box filled with ashes, a spot in nature where the ashes are sprinkled, an altar, a poem, a photo album, a scrapbook or scrapbox—something meaningful, whatever it may be, to represent our loved one's passing. This physical expression of their passage from the physical world into spirit can help us to integrate this transition into our own life experience. It can be one of the most helpful steps in the grieving process—especially in helping us to accept the reality of our loved one's passing.

Perhaps equally helpful in dealing with grief over the loss of a loved one is committing to do good in their honor. So many wonderful organizations and causes in our world were initially sparked by those in grief who wanted to do something positive in honor of a departed loved one, especially if the loss was a particularly tragic one. I call that "creating a silver lining." It's like facing a gray cloud and looking for a silver lining—and if we can't find one, we create one. For me, starting a Rat Rescue in June's honor was a way of coping with her loss, honoring her memory, and turning a devastating loss into something wonderful. This has very positively affected both the rat kingdom and myself, and I am eternally grateful for this "silver lining."

I encourage those who have lost a beloved animal to watch for signs and "coincidences." Our departed loved ones often will make their presence known to us in one way or another, if we only pay close attention. The signs and messages may be subtle, so we could easily miss them if we don't remain open to the possibility. It takes a while for us to adjust to our loved ones being in spirit. Of course, we'll always remember them, and we miss being able to hold and hug them. However, in time, we will come to accept and understand the transition and develop a renewed sacred relationship with them. This relationship lasts forever. We love them and they love us very much, and this connection will never die. We can continue to talk to them just as we did when they were alive in physical form. Whatever we say to them, whatever we feel about them, they hear and they feel.

When I am contacted by those grieving the loss of a beloved animal, I suggest they pay close attention to their dreams. It's helpful to write them down, as even the act of writing them down helps us to remember them more clearly. As discussed in an earlier chapter, "Sweet Dreams," our departed loved ones often try to contact us in our dreams, as that's when we're most in touch with our spiritual (non-physical) side. Not all dreams are contacts from the spirit world, but those in spirit do tend to try to contact us while we are dreaming, as that is when we tend to be most receptive to such messages. If we pay close attention, we can learn to discern the difference between "just a dream" and an actual contact.

I feel that it's a good idea to keep a journal to record not only our significant dreams, but also our feelings and experiences as we go through the grief process. Just the act of writing often helps us to get in touch with what we're truly feeling. It often takes a long time to get through the grief, so it's important to be patient and gentle with ourselves.

It is especially important that we take good care of ourselves during our time of grieving. Physical exercise is not only essential for our health, but it can also be extremely helpful in balancing our emotional state and overall well-being. Many studies have found that exercise can actually trigger happiness, tranquility, and euphoria. I agree. Going on a long walk in nature, working out with weights, or dancing along with an exercise video can do us a world of good. I find that a combination of vigorous physical exercise, yoga, and meditation is a helpful prescription for maintaining a healthy body and mind—and healing a wounded heart.

(Important: Always use common sense and proper safety precautions when embarking upon any exercise program, and make sure the exercise chosen is appropriate and approved.)

IT IS NOT UNCOMMON FOR PEOPLE to contemplate suicide during periods of intense grieving. Some feel that they simply can't go on without their beloved companion, so they'd rather join them in spirit. This is *never* the answer. Life is sacred and must be treated as such. If a loved one has returned to spirit before us, there is a reason. If we have been left behind, we still need to be here. If a person is having trouble accepting this, I strongly encourage them to seek outside help *immediately.* This might even mean calling a close friend in the middle of the night. Any good friend would much prefer the inconvenience of being awakened from their sleep over living with the knowledge that their friend was afraid to ask for help.

It's important for us to respect that our departed loved ones have their own path, which requires that they be in spirit at this time; whereas, our path requires that we remain in physical form. These two paths are different, but not separate . . . so the bond of love and special relationship will truly continue. They may even plan to return, so it is important to stick around and to be open to *anything*, but not to try to force anything. We love them, so we must respect their path and trust that they are still connected with us, regardless of form.

We must remember not to take it personally if an animal companion doesn't come back; it has nothing to do with how much they love us.

Sometimes they have important work to do on the Other Side. I remember how hurt I felt many years ago when Henry passed and I was told by an animal communicator that he was planning to remain in spirit. *Why doesn't he want to return to me?* I thought to myself, taking it very personally at first. I later came to understand that he did, indeed, have important work to do in spirit, and I now realize that we are still very much connected. I was told that his job was to help other animals to find their way to me, and many special animals have, indeed, found their way into my life—and into my heart—since then.

I can't emphasize enough that whether or not we feel we've made contact with our loved ones in spirit has nothing to do with how much they love us. Why do some people see fully physical manifestations of their departed loved ones and others see nothing? I can't answer that question, but I suspect it's like asking why some people have 20/20 vision and others are nearsighted or color blind. We all may be looking at the same exact thing but may perceive it very differently. The fact that we may not be able to see something doesn't necessarily mean it isn't there. Our world is made up of multiple individuals having multiple experiences, and no two are ever exactly alike. Even in identical everyday experiences, there are always varying perspectives of that experience, whether it be physical vantage point, interpretation, or some other factor.

Rather than asking, "Why not me?" regarding the amazing experiences of others, it is more appropriate to look at those experiences as validation that such things are indeed possible. I feel that the more open we become to such things, the more likely they are to manifest in our own lives.

Then it becomes our responsibility to acknowledge these experiences as real and not just try to explain them away or let someone else talk us out of them. And if they don't manifest—or if we are simply unable to perceive them, which is more likely the case—it can be extremely helpful to work with a professional, such as a medium or an animal communicator. Many mediums and animal communicators regularly work with those who have lost beloved animals, and they are often extremely helpful in getting through the grieving process. Perhaps that's why God created mediums and animal communicators!

ONE DAY I WAS CONTACTED by a man in England named Nick Pollard. His wife had recently lost her beloved horse, Ella, who had been her companion for nineteen years, and Nick was looking for some information to help his wife cope with the loss. He also shared something that had taken place at the time of Ella's death.

"The night Ella was put to sleep," he explained, "Tracey (my wife) and I were with her. Tracey experienced what can only be described as a life bonding experience with Ella in the final moments of her life. She described seeing her relationship with Ella from when Ella was young to the present day. It flashed past in an instant but she felt that both Ella and she experienced it. It was extremely moving."

I instantly knew exactly what Nick was describing. I had experienced the same thing several years earlier when our beloved Cindy had died. Cindy was a rat with agouti coloring— that speckled brown fur coloring so often seen in wild animals. Her spirit was just as wild as her coloring. When I knew the end of her life was drawing near and there was no longer anything that could be done for her, I brought her to bed to spend one last night with Jameth and me. She could barely move, so we settled her gently between us and told her how much we loved her.

As Jameth drifted off to sleep, I stroked Cindy's fur and admired her beauty in the moonlight that seemed to fill the bedroom that night. I didn't want her to go, and I wished there was something I could do to make her stay, but I knew there wasn't. Suddenly, I felt very peaceful and began to experience a mental review of Cindy's life with us. It was incredibly detailed and seemed to last for a long time, although it was probably only a few minutes. Parts of it made me laugh, and I felt surrounded in love as I surrendered to the process. I closed my eyes and watched as her lifespan unfolded before me. I savored each moment as I reexperienced our time together. I felt that Cindy and I were completely connected telepathically and that she was simultaneously experiencing the same thing.

Then our shared "trip down memory lane" began drawing to a close as it brought us to the current moment, with her lying beside me in bed. The moment it ended, I felt a genuine completion of a life fully lived. I opened my eyes and looked at her. Just then, she sat upright like a little sphinx and seemed to be staring intently at something I couldn't see. With that, she let out a unique sound, almost like a "call of the wild," and she was gone. I was in awe. I knew I would miss her tremendously, but I was amazed at what had just taken place. I was convinced it was more than a coincidence that she had left at the exact moment the experience had ended.

I was equally convinced—and still am—that this is something we can *all* experience during the final moments of a loved one's physical life. If it doesn't happen spontaneously, I feel it is something we can initiate with our thoughts . . . and it can become a final farewell, a way of sending our loved ones off to the spirit world filled with the memories of a life well lived.

Of course, not all endings happen so peacefully. That was the only time such an event occurred spontaneously in my own experience, so I now do my best to initiate a similar experience, if not during the final moments of a loved one's life, then shortly after their leaving. Often, the final moments of a life are filled with panicked decision-making and frantic desperation. This has certainly been the case with many of my own departed companions.

During the final moments of Jonathan's life, as I begged him to stay, I recall telling him that he *couldn't* die because April was waiting at home for him; she was *counting on him*. She was his closest rat companion, and the two were inseparable. When they snuggled up together, Jonathan often put his arm around her, and those who witnessed this repeatedly declared, "Aw, look—they're in love!" I knew how much she'd miss him. How much we'd all miss him.

APRIL WAS BEAUTIFUL. Her shiny black coat was soft and silky. She had a fluffy white underbelly with matching white socks; an incredibly sweet face; and soft, gentle eyes. Her official name was April, but her nickname had become Tinkerbell, or Tinker for short, because she only had half a tail (no one at the pound knew what had happened to the other half), and whenever she ran, her little half-tail bobbed and wagged behind her. Somehow it looked like it should have a little bell hanging from it. Hence, the name Tinkerbell.

I recall the day she entered our lives. As soon as we got her home, she began kissing me with her soft, velvety little rat tongue, as if I was her best friend. She seemed so grateful and happy to finally have a home. Before long, she spent every night snuggled up against me just like a miniature cat or dog. Every morning, she would shower my entire face with kisses, and then she'd head over to Jameth to do the same. Every chance she got, she'd nurture the nearest rat or person, and the other rats would literally line up for a grooming session from April. It was as if she were everyone's mother.

"I had no idea rats were so beautiful," said a friend upon meeting April for the first time.

"Wow—they're gorgeous," said another, again upon being introduced to April. And the story was the same whenever someone met April, always the rat ambassador. (Of course, we would have loved her no matter *what* she looked like, but her beauty definitely helped to break the ice among people who were unfamiliar with rats.) Several friends just didn't consider a visit to our home complete without a shower of kisses, April-style. No matter who they were, young or old, male or female, they were full of delightful giggles as sweet April kissed their face, whispered in their ear, tickled their neck, and groomed their hair.

When rats are happy, they make a delightful chattering sound with their teeth. It's the rat equivalent of a wagging dog tail or a purring cat. (Technically, it's called "bruxing," but I call it "chattering" because it's cuter and that's what it sounds like.) Sometimes a rat's chatter is so enthusiastic that their entire face wiggles. Well, April was the queen of chatter. All we had to do was gently scoop her into our hands, or softly tell her how wonderful she was, and she'd chatter away. She was a joy and a true gift in our lives. Right from the start, I knew I would have a hard time letting her go when she eventually reached the end of her life. She was already quite old for a rat when we adopted her. The short lifespan of rats is always the hard part . . . but always worth it for the love they give in that short time.

It seemed April always had some sort of health crisis going on. One morning, she awoke unable to walk, and I thought it was the beginning of the end. I was nearly in tears. However, after a chiropractic adjustment from a holistic vet, she was back to normal. Another time, she choked on some food, and I tearfully said my final good-byes, thinking it was the end. Again, she snapped out of it. Twice she developed benign mammary tumors, and twice she recovered. She overcame infections, old injuries, and days when she just didn't feel well. Each time, I was faced with her mortality. Always, she recovered.

Looking back, I realize that all those little false alarms were preparing me for the real thing. It was just too much to deal with losing a being that special all at once. So I had a lot of practice over several years. In fact, she had an exceptionally long life for a rat (as do many of the rats here at the Rat Refuge, who enjoy a very healthy diet; but, of course, it's never long *enough*). Eventually, April became a little old lady, just as sweet as ever. She had trouble getting to some of her favorite places around the house, so I put up ramps to assist her. She got around a little more slowly, and with a lot more effort, but she never lost her zest for life.

Several months before Christmas, I knew that the end was near. The false alarms were becoming more frequent, and she was clearly aging. Jameth and I were planning to go to my parents' house for Christmas, and to bring April and the other rats along, as we had done the previous year. April was my parents' favorite "grandrat" and they were really looking forward to including her in the celebration. They always asked about her and had photos of her all over their house.

We were all looking forward to spending one more Christmas with our precious April, our sweet little Tinkerbell. So I kept telling her, "Grandma and Grandpa are counting on seeing you at Christmas. Don't let them down! We're all looking forward to spending Christmas with you, Tinkerbell. It just wouldn't be the same without you." I then reminded her that Gram's (my mom's) birthday was the day after Christmas, and what a great gift it would be to have her there to help celebrate. And every time I told her this, she would look me in the eye and listen like she really understood.

Much to everyone's delight (and surprise), April *did* spend Christmas in my arms, at my parents' house, surrounded by the people who loved her most. She was old and weak, and her life force was slipping away, but she was with us. Throughout the day, I noticed that her breathing would periodically stop for several seconds too long; then she would lift her head, and with whatever effort she could muster up, she would literally force herself to start breathing again. I realized she was keeping herself alive for *me*. I had wanted so much to spend one more Christmas with her, and she had gone the extra mile to grant me that wish. She no longer had the strength to walk or groom herself or even eat without assistance, but she was there.

I had always prayed that April would die happy, literally chattering right to the end. Now, here was this weak, dying rat in my arms, and I felt as if I had put too much pressure on her to stick around. So I tearfully wished her a Merry Christmas, thanked her, and told her I would let her go now, that I was sorry I had asked her to stay long after her body could keep up. But she looked up at me as if she had made up her mind. She was staying for Christmas. All of Christmas. And stay she did. That night, she curled up in bed with Jameth and me, and we spent one more night with our little angel. Once more, we told her how much we loved her and said our tearful good-byes.

The next morning, I awoke to find that April was still with us. She was barely breathing, but she was still there. As if fulfilling a promise, April was there for my mom's birthday, the day after Christmas. She was there for the cake, the singing, and the presents. Then, to finish off the day, the whole family watched two rental movies, *Dr. Dolittle* and *Jack*. April was still cuddled in my arms. And she was chattering all the while.

Fate must have guided me to choose that second movie, *Jack*, as I didn't even know what it was about. None of us did. We had never even heard of it. I had just grabbed it as an afterthought on the way to the front counter of the video store, where we had gone (along with April) to rent *Dr. Dolittle*. Soon I realized *why* I had felt guided to rent that particular movie. It was about a boy named Jack who had been born with a disorder that caused him to age four times as fast as normal. So, as a young boy, he had the body of a grown man, and by the time he graduated from high school, he was a very old man.

As the character Jack in the movie was nearing the end of his life, having enjoyed it to the hilt despite the accelerated aging process, I looked down at April, my little Tinkerbell, cradled in my arms. I realized it was the same with animals, except that most of them age even faster than that. As the movie (and Jack's life) was coming to a close, April's contented chattering finally stopped as she drifted off to sleep for the last time. No more tearful good-byes. No more begging her to stay. Just acceptance and peace. I had been prepared many times and in many ways for this moment, and now I could handle it. And as a final answer to my prayers, she had indeed been chattering right to the end. Of course, it doesn't always happen this way, but at least this once, it did.

Like Jack, little April had made the most of her short time

with us, and I suddenly realized how precious—how truly precious—all life is, no matter how long, how short, how big, or how small.

I also realized for the first time that perhaps I'd been selfish in always putting so much pressure on my beloved companions to stay with me. As difficult as it is to let them go, I swore that I would never again beg an animal to stay. So, from that point on, I committed to approach the final hours of each animal's life with only their *own* well-being in mind. I began checking in with them each step of the way, asking if they were suffering, asking if they needed assistance in leaving—or if they preferred to stay. In the early days, I always called an animal communicator to ask these questions. As time went on and I learned to really listen, I asked the questions directly. Over time, I learned volumes about letting go.

Of course, I wanted *all* of them to die peacefully in my arms, in familiar surroundings, in their own time, but some were truly suffering and needed outside assistance. Then there were those who died suddenly and unexpectedly, before anything could even be done. I feel it's important to reiterate here that no matter *where* their final days or hours are spent, they *know* we love them and are doing the best we can for them. As long as we come from a place of love and compassion, we have no reason to feel guilty after the fact, *regardless of outcome*. We are usually far more in tune with our beloved companions than we realize, and they understand that we want what's best for them. They also understand that we have a hard time letting them go.

For every peaceful passing I experienced along the way, there were countless "learning experiences"—times when things didn't end so smoothly, when I vowed to do things differently the next time around. Times when, in hindsight, all of the warning signs seemed so clear. Times when I felt that I should have spent more time with an animal than I did. Times when suffering seemed to be a direct result of decisions I had made. These were moments that haunted me long afterward.

Time and again, whenever a beloved animal passed, I absolutely tormented myself day and night with "what ifs," "if onlys," and absolute certainty that I was the sole reason they had suffered and died; and that if I had made different decisions, somehow, things would have been better. With each new loss, Jameth lovingly asked, "Okay, how is *this* one your fault?" Of course, he knew it wasn't. I think those final moments of suffering become frozen in our minds, and long after an animal has passed, we're still living in those moments. We need to remind ourselves that the animals *aren't*. They've moved on and are doing absolutely fine. Whether we feel that we should have assisted them in leaving but didn't, or we *did* assist them in leaving and now regret it, they truly understand how difficult it was—and still is—for us. And they certainly aren't upset with us. They are in a place of unconditional love and understanding. When it's their time to go, it's their time. All the rest is just "details."

OVER TIME AS I EXPERIENCED MORE LOSSES, I came to accept the eventual inevitability of death. Rather than fighting and begging the animals to stay, I tried to focus solely on *their* needs. I told them that it was okay to go if it was their time, and that they had nothing to fear. I told them that they were welcome to return if they ever chose to come back, but there was no pressure. I've finally learned that part of loving someone is wanting whatever is best for *them*, rather than focusing on our own wants and needs. This has perhaps been the hardest lesson of all.

I wanted to *be there* for them and to assist them in going to the Light, continuing their journey in spirit. I began calling in the assistance of spiritual helpers on the Other Side, including animals who had gone before, to assist at each passing. It really seemed to make a difference, and over time, there were fewer tragedies and more peaceful passings. Of course, each passing is unique, and all we can do is make the best of each situation as it comes. If we can't be there with them physically, for whatever reason—if they're in surgery or we're out of town or whatever the situation may be during those final moments—we can still be with them in spirit, even after they've passed, sending them our love telepathically; and they *will,* indeed, receive it. It's never too late.

As the years passed, I always did my best to make it okay for my own beloved companions to go when it was their time to leave. I tried to let go, for *their* sake. However, I didn't usually succeed, and in those final moments, I often found myself screaming, "No!" and begging them to stay.

Just recently, when yet another exceptionally sweet rat, Samson, was dying, instead of begging him to stay, I felt that he *really* needed assistance in leaving. He was gasping for breath and was clearly suffering. I held him close and did my best to comfort him, praying that he be relieved of his suffering. It was late at night, so Jameth called an emergency animal hospital and inquired about having Samson euthanized. At that hour, there were no vets available for a house call. The woman on the phone said we could bring Samson in to be euthanized. When Jameth asked what method they would use to euthanize a rat, she said they would administer an injection in the heart; so Jameth asked if we could have Samson gently anesthetized first, to ease his passing.

"There will be an extra charge for that," the woman said coldly.

"I don't *care* how much it *costs*," Jameth replied. "I just don't want him to suffer." He then asked if we could be there with Samson until the end. The woman said she didn't think so but would ask the vet on duty. I had an uneasy feeling. I prayed for guidance. I checked in with Samson, who was still gasping and struggling for breath. Suddenly, it was perfectly clear what we should do.

"We're not going anywhere," I told Jameth as I headed over to the living room. I turned on some soft, soothing music and sat down on the sofa with Samson. Jameth joined us. We stroked Samson's soft fur, comforted him, and told him how much we loved him. I asked St. Martin de Porres to please help this precious little rat. I asked the other rats who had gone before him to please join us and escort Samson to the Other Side. I told Samson he had nothing to fear; that he could simply jump out of this painful, worn-out body and he would be free in spirit. He would be welcome to return to us anytime if he so chose. I emphasized that his body was merely a vehicle that was no longer serving him, and that he could simply leave it behind and he'd be fine.

"Go to the Light, Samson." I told him. "It's okay to leave. You don't have to suffer any longer. You can just leap right out of your body, and you'll be fine. Just jump out!" And with that, little Samson literally jumped forward with all his might . . . and he was gone. Just like that. I felt his spirit leap out and up, and I felt nothing but peace and love from him. Of course, I still cried over his vacant body, as good-byes such as these are always bittersweet. But I came away knowing that something good had just taken place. Samson had joined his friends in spirit, and I had finally learned how to say good-bye.

- CHAPTER 19 -

Making the Leap

*Each being is sacred—meaning that each has
inherent value that cannot be ranked in a hierarchy
or compared to the value of another being.*
— STARHAWK

ONE OF THE HIGHLIGHTS of each day in my home is what has come to be known as Happy Hour. Each evening shortly before bedtime, all of the rats anxiously line up just inside the gate to their room. I open the gate, and out they come, running playfully up and down the hallway, while I tidy up their room and put out recycled paper towels for them to make nests with overnight. I then take time to sit and commune with each of them as they climb onto me to deliver rattie kisses.

The ending of Happy Hour is signaled by the arrival of a large bowl of organic fruit or other treats—usually sliced bananas sprinkled with various herbs. As soon as I call to them to come and get their treats, they all run excitedly back into their room and up the long ladders and ramps to their dining table, where their favorite snack awaits them. They enthusiastically dig in. Some stop to eat, while others collect and stash their evening goodies in various parts of the room.

As soon as everyone is back in the Rat Room and their gate is closed, I stand just outside the room and watch their antics, always amused and cheered by this nightly ritual, regardless of what the day has brought my way.

One evening as I looked on, I noticed that Madeline was having trouble getting her share of bananas. Madeline was an ancient Siamese rat who was blind and partly crippled. Old age had been coming on for quite some time, and it now hit me that she didn't likely have many days left in her worn-out body. Many of the younger rats were running off with all the banana slices, while Madeline was having trouble getting to the bowl for her fair share. I feared that the other rats would steal all the food and Madeline would be left out, so I moved to go in and help her out.

Before I even got inside the gate, I watched in amazement as one of the younger rats took a banana slice, headed over to Madeline, and put the banana right in front of her. The younger rat then headed back to the bowl, got another banana slice, and again placed it in front of Madeline.

The youngster continued in this manner until Madeline had a pile of banana slices all to herself, which she began eating with vigor. Then her young caretaker found a fresh paper towel and placed it gently over Madeline and her stash, protecting her from the other rats who might be tempted to steal the remaining bananas. The little hero then sat in front of the concealed Madeline and stood guard, ensuring that Madeline and her stash were left undisturbed until she had enjoyed every morsel.

I then realized that Madeline didn't need my help at all. She already had a friend who was looking out for her. And I was reminded once again—as I had been so many times before—that animals are indeed capable of selfless acts of compassion. In fact, it occurred to me then that I had witnessed such acts of compassion initiated by *animals* far more often than by *humans*. I contemplated the notion of a spiritual hierarchy and found little support for the theory that humans are at the top.

I recalled the countless stories of all types of animals—dogs, cats, horses, rats, and others—who had engaged in thoughtful, and sometimes daring, acts of service on behalf of those in need. Most of these acts had nothing to do with instinct, but rather, with the deliberate effort of someone who understands and wants to help another. These acts of compassion often cross the species barrier, with animals helping not only other animals of their *own* species, but also animals of *other* species, including humans.

Many of these great acts are witnessed in wild animals as well—dispelling the notion that animals learn such behavior from humans. When I hear people proclaim that animals are able to commit such commendable acts—or even to develop souls or earn a place in Heaven—*because of the love of a human*, I realize how limited humanity's thinking still is. Perhaps we're afraid to admit that we humans are not the sole heirs to the universe after all.

As I look back throughout history, it seems that humans have never taken kindly to theories that make us anything other than the center of the universe. In my opinion, that is why some people continue to hold fiercely to the idea that animals do not have souls, without ever having actually investigated this subject for themselves.

> *I care not much for a man's religion*
> *whose dog and cat are not the better for it.*
> — ABRAHAM LINCOLN

I COME ACROSS SO MANY BELIEF SYSTEMS that are still based on human ego. Perhaps the cause is insecurity, but the effect is tremendous unnecessary suffering. I feel that the biggest lesson here on Earth is to learn unconditional love. To love without conditions. It is simple to love that which is similar to ourselves, because we can identify with it and know firsthand what it feels like to be *us*.

To love that which is *different* comes naturally to *some* people, but for humanity as a whole, this has been perhaps the hardest lesson of all. Human history demonstrates this in a most dramatic way. Slavery; the Holocaust; so-called holy wars; and the oppression of Native Americans, women, and countless other groups are but a handful of examples of this. The ongoing and often widely accepted oppression of nonhuman animals in our world is evidence that we have a long way to go yet. We as a species still have a lot of growing up to do.

Perhaps the animals are here to teach *us*. What better examples of unconditional love do we have than our companion animals? Humans are capable of tremendous acts of hatred, so perhaps it is *we* who must learn to commit commendable acts of love—and even to develop our *own* souls and earn a place in Heaven—*because of the love of an animal.*

Interestingly, many of the wisest teachers, philosophers, geniuses, and gurus throughout history have made compassion toward animals a very core element of their teachings. Unfortunately, this is very often overlooked or downplayed, but it is there loud and clear, whether we choose to pay attention or not.

> *The greatness of a nation and its moral progress*
> *can be judged by the way its animals are treated.*
> — GANDHI

Many great spiritual leaders have promoted compassion for animals. In fact, a vegetarian diet is often considered a logical step on the spiritual path. Gandhi, St. Francis, and Jesus were all strongly opposed to animal "sacrifice." St. Francis and Jesus both actually *rescued* animals from "sacrifice," and they certainly didn't gain any popularity by doing so. (For more information on this, I highly recommend the book *Peace to All Beings: Veggie Soup for the Chicken's Soul* by Judy Carman.)

SPIRITUALLY INCLINED PEOPLE often proclaim that we are *not* human beings having a spiritual experience, but rather, we are *spiritual* beings having a *human* experience. I wholeheartedly agree with this statement. However, in the next breath, many people often go on to say matter-of-factly that humans are superior to other animals and are the only ones who have souls. Why? Because we're *human*. Wait a minute—I thought they just said we were *spiritual* beings and *not* human beings; we're simply having a human *experience*. If we are indeed spiritual beings having a human experience, then it could equally be said that animals are spiritual beings having an *animal* experience. The logical conclusion: We are *all* spiritual beings.

I find it interesting that we humans often like to put ourselves at the top of a spiritual hierarchy, claiming that we are the most evolved beings of all. First we're told that we're spiritual beings and that our human aspect is only temporary; then we're told that we're superior by virtue of being *human*. Not only do I find this to be conflicting, but I have difficulty swallowing it. A quick glance at the daily newspaper or the evening news gives us but a mere clue as to the acts of cruelty that humans are capable of. There-fore, if humans are the most evolved and are at the top of some sort of spiritual hierarchy, I'd say our world is in big trouble!

ANOTHER COMMON THEORY I've heard is that animals don't have individual souls at all—that they are simply part of a "group soul" at best, and nothing more. Once they die, they merge with an animal group consciousness, and their individuality—their unique personality—is gone forever. Countless people have come to me in tears after being fed this "fact" by someone they turned to for support while grieving the loss of a beloved companion, a companion who they have just been told doesn't really exist anymore.

Not only is this notion extremely upsetting to those in grief; it is simply not the case. Rather, it is an outdated theory based, once again, on human ego and *not* real life experience. I find that some of the people who preach this theory are actually well-intentioned and honestly believe what they are saying. They themselves were fed this "fact" somewhere along the way, and unfortunately, they adopted it without even questioning its validity. Sometimes people even claim to be receiving this information from a "higher source" when, in reality, it is a belief system that has been adopted by their own psyche based on the common belief systems—or perhaps the collective consciousness—of humanity at large.

All actual *evidence* suggests that animals are not merely part of a group soul any more or less than humans are. We are all individuals, and based on all of my research in this realm, our individuality remains even after we leave our physical bodies behind. Sure, we are all "one" in the sense that we are a part of the greater whole—and there do appear to be groups of souls that share a common bond—but each of us is on our own journey that is not based upon such temporary physical factors as species. The universe is much grander than that. It is a universe filled with endless possibilities and experiences that help us to grow, to understand, and most importantly, to learn how to love.

> *By ethical conduct toward all creatures, we enter*
> *into a spiritual relationship with the universe.*
> — ALBERT SCHWEITZER

WHEN I'VE SPOKEN WITH professional animal communicators about the idea of animals having souls and how this concept fits into their own spiritual belief systems, they've all told me that their beliefs do not come from any book, theory, or teaching, but rather, from what they've learned from the animals themselves.

Animal communicator and psychologist Jeri Ryan, Ph.D., had the following to say:

> I have believed for a long time that animals have souls. When you think about soul as the life force—the vitality in us—why wouldn't they? Animals are similar to us anatomically and physiologically. Not totally, of course, but they have many similarities to us, and why would they *not* have a soul?
>
> My first real solid recognition of this was when I rescued a big malamute dog named Simon. In those days, I wasn't doing any kind of professional communicating with animals. I was just sitting on the floor across from him; I was looking into his eyes and something struck me—I had an "aha" experience. I said silently to myself, *There is a soul in there.* As soon as I said that, he came over to me and put his head on my shoulder. That was a doggy hug and I felt that was an acknowledgment of what I had discovered.
>
> My own belief in hierarchies has changed a lot. As a psychologist, I understand the vulnerability of the human ego, and it's not just the human ego that's vulnerable; there are other animals with vulnerable egos, too. Since we happen to be the ones in charge of the world, ours really stands out more than any. That has made us really want to set up hierarchies of value. So, we see ourselves as the

most intelligent and the most needed and the most valuable species on the planet.

From hearing what the animal spirits have to say, I have come to the understanding that there *has* to be a spirit inside those animals. If you relate to animals and you look into their eyes, you can see the soul—you can't miss it unless you are very shut down. I have no question that there is an afterlife for *all* spirits, no matter what kind of a body they have been in.

OFTEN, IT SEEMS, humans argue tirelessly over philosophical reasons as to why animals do or do not have souls. If we would ask the *animals,* rather than each other, perhaps we would receive more straightforward answers. In addition to animal communicators learning the answers from animals, people from all walks of life have had similar experiences.

Regina Fetrat shared the following story about a beloved parrot:

> I had a parrot named Passion until she flew away in a park on Long Island. I loved her very much and still miss her.
>
> While Passion was with us, my husband and I used to discuss the soul existence of animals. He argued that proof of animals not having souls (and the alleged proof humans do) is that humans have the mental capacity for abstract thought and that art is the proof of this; animals do not produce art and humans do (of course, bah humbug!). Well, we would discuss this in our little bathroom. Now, there was another occupant in the bathroom. I had given Passion a towel cabinet with a few towels for nesting, and she liked to dance on the shower curtain and watch herself in the medicine cabinet mirror while she did. She loved it when we ran the shower.
>
> So . . . right around the time when these "soul proof" discussions began, Passion began carving in the wall at the end of the shower curtain rod. It was weeks after Passion was lost and gone before I realized what she was doing: a self-portrait. I cut the piece out of the drywall and still have it and photos of her just as she saw herself in that mirror. **[See photos, next page.]**

Photos courtesy of Regina Fetrat

Passion's Self-Portrait

Passion

Shown here is a photo Regina took of Passion's self-portrait, along with a photo of Passion herself. (Incidentally, Regina's husband noticed the portrait first but didn't say anything until Regina later noticed and mentioned it!) The thing I find so interesting about the picture that Passion carved in the wall is that it does, indeed, strongly resemble the side of Passion's face as she would have seen herself in the mirror (her eyes are on either side of her head, so she wouldn't have seen her face head-on as a human would). Although the proportions aren't completely accurate, all of the major details are there—the curve of the beak, the white circle around the eye, and even the pupil. Mind you, this was done with her beak! I know a lot of *humans* who can't draw that well with a pencil—and certainly not if they were holding the pencil in their mouth!

> *"All truth passes through three stages. First, it is ridiculed.*
> *Second, it is violently opposed. Third, it is accepted*
> *as self evident."*
> — ARTHUR SCHOPENHAUER

After researching this subject for many years now, I feel that the incredible amount of evidence of animal souls provides long overdue reassurance to those of us who love animals. But more than that, it sheds light on the necessary leap that must be made, from a purely logical standpoint, from a belief system that accepts the existence of *human* souls to one that includes all living beings. (Interestingly, the Latin word for soul is "anima.")

So, what does the idea of animal souls really mean? It is extremely important that we use this new understanding *not* to justify animal abuse (just as the promise of a better life in Heaven was once used to justify the enslavement and abuse of other humans here on Earth), but rather, to hold animals in the same light as we hold humanity. They are, after all, our spiritual brothers and sisters, and once the costumes are removed, we are all of the same essence. I feel that this understanding holds the key to furthering our spiritual progress and to co-creating a more harmonious world.

> *Our task must be to free ourselves by widening our circle of compassion to embrace all living creatures.*
> — ALBERT EINSTEIN

OVER THE YEARS, I've discovered that I can tell a lot about a person based on how they feel about animals—not necessarily whether they rescue animals or have companion animals themselves, but rather, their *attitudes* toward animals. I spent many years in the nutrition field, and although I met many wonderful people along the way, the overriding climate of that industry, like so many, was one of self-interest. It was a mentality of "What's in it for me?" I watched as large groups of people flocked from one trend to another, never paying any mind to the impact of their new fad diet or supplement on the environment or on the animals who suffered in the process.

Over time, Jameth and I discovered quite unexpectedly that we could actually tell a lot about the work ethic, honesty, commitment, and quite often, the long-term outlook of any prospective employee based on their level of compassion toward animals. We have found it to be a valuable clue as to their overall integrity in *all* aspects of life.

> *If you have men who will exclude any of God's creatures*
> *from the shelter of compassion and pity, you will have*
> *men who will deal likewise with their fellow men.*
> — ST. FRANCIS OF ASSISI

When I transitioned from my career in nutrition to my work on this book and other animal-related projects, I was delighted yet not surprised at the level of compassion of this new group of people I now surrounded myself with: those in the fields of animal care, animal welfare, animal rights, and animal rescue. The overriding climate of this group of people is one of caring, and their ethics spill over into all areas of their lives and their work. I find that this group of people, as a whole, refuses to run from trend to trend based on self-interest, but rather, remains steadfast in their principles and their commitment to helping those in need, *regardless* of species.

I have come to understand that those who dedicate themselves to making a positive difference in the lives of animals are taking part in extremely important work in our world. This field of work does not hold a very high ranking in our world's current list of priorities, but it is looked upon *very* highly in the spirit world, more so than most people probably realize. I feel honored to surround myself with those who are taking great strides in making our world a better place for *all*—including those who speak a language most of us do not yet understand.

One such person is Brenda Shoss, a wonderful woman who directs Kinship Circle, an international mail list and Website. The Kinship Circle mail list generates letter campaigns to legislators, businesses, and media to provoke social, political, and ethical reforms for all animals. Brenda has also written many wonderful articles, including the one that follows. I felt it appropriate to include here, and she graciously gave me her permission to do so.

Inner Landscapes: The Emotional Voice of Animals
by Brenda Shoss, Director, Kinship Circle
Letters for Animals, Articles & Literature
Missouri

9/11/01: AT 8:45 A.M. American Airlines Flight 11 smashes into the north tower of the World Trade Center. Fifteen minutes later United Airlines Flight 175 shatters the south tower and irrevocably seizes a nation's invulnerability. Amid a frantic tangle of survivors and rescuers, Salty leads Omar Rivera from the 71st floor to safety. On the 78th floor, Roselle steers Michael Hingson toward an emergency exit. Another dog shepherds his blind guardian down 70 flights of stairs, as glass fragments rain from the crash site above them.

If Roselle, Salty and roughly 300 other courageous canines at Ground Zero could speak, they might have explained: "It's our basic nature. Bravery? I don't know . . . How about a treat?"

Anyone who has witnessed an animal's selfless valor knows firsthand that nonhuman beings exhibit an elaborate range of psychological, perceptual, behavioral, personal and communal initiative. "It is clear that animals form lasting friendships, are frightened of being hunted, have a horror of dismemberment, wish they were back in the safety of their den, despair for their mates, look out for and protect their children whom they love," writes Jeffrey Moussaieff Masson in *When Elephants Weep: The Emotional Lives of Animals*. "They feel throughout their lives, just as we do."

And sometimes they organize. Consider, for example, the thirty monkeys that raided a police station in India to emancipate an orphaned relative. The baby, found clinging to a female langur shot with an airgun, continued to suckle his dead mother in captivity. Meanwhile monkeys atop the station's roof dispatched several liberators to claim the orphan. "It was as if the monkeys had made up their minds to take charge," Inspector Prabir Dutta said. "The monkeys impressed us with their show of solidarity. Human beings have a lot to learn from them."

Scientists and philosophers have long debated the issue

of consciousness in animals. Descartes viewed them as automated entities limited to involuntary instinct. Voltaire argued that animals share our emotional fabric and experience fear, pleasure, rage, grief, anticipation, hope, and love. In 1872 Charles Darwin refuted the 19th-century code of human superiority over animals in his groundbreaking work, *The Expression of Emotions in Man and Animals.* Darwin found that the ability to vocalize is merely one form of communication.

Some animals purposefully inflate hair, feathers, and other appendages when afraid or angry. To intimidate intruders, an apprehensive hen ruffles her feathers and reptiles puff their bodies into jumbo proportions. A dog's assorted ear angles articulate curiosity, surprise, or concentration.

Does body-talk prove that animals speak and feel through myriad channels? Darwin searched for confirmation that animals weep, but found inconclusive evidence that elephants cry under great duress. Still, Masson contends, "tears aren't grief; they're only symbols of grief. We have to look at animal expressions of feeling on their own terms."

Grief and an awareness of loss are regarded as human trademarks. Yet when a mother witnessed the brutal drowning of her three-week-old calf on the banks of the Elk River in Missouri last summer, she frantically guarded her dying child until authorities removed her. The traumatized cow grew paranoid around humans. "We may have to put her down if things don't change," her caretaker reported.

A mother's love crosses the species barrier. Darwin recorded the unceasing calls of parents in search of lost or abducted young ones. "When a flock of sheep is scattered, the ewes bleat incessantly for their lambs, and their mutual pleasure at coming together is manifest."

Kinship brings comfort and joy. When ties are severed, humans encounter sadness and a sense of their own mortality. So do chimps and elephants. In the PBS Nature series, *Inside the Animal Mind: Animal Consciousness*, both animals display grief when relatives die: "Elephants even linger over the bones of long-dead relatives, seeming to ponder the past and their own future."

If animals value interconnected lives, how do we reconcile their systematic isolation and "murder" inside the slaughterhouse, fur farm or research laboratory? This is an odd conundrum that contemporary scholars seem more inclined to embrace than biologists. Plainly, the pig who confronts his killer is terrified. He trembles beneath the crushing blast of an imprecise stun gun and screams with human likeness when the knife enters his flesh. The pig's squeal of anguish differs from the grunt of pleasure after a good meal or roll in the mud. He wants to live; "the only difference is that [animals] cannot say so in words," Masson asserts.

In August, 2000 a six-month-old calf escaped from a Queens, New York slaughterhouse. After hundreds of pleas to save the bewildered runaway, "Queenie" arrived safely at Farm Sanctuary, a non-profit shelter in Upstate New York. Enterprising and decisive—what some might call a "tough broad"—Queenie had made an independent decision to flee a bleak situation.

The emotional voice of animals is astonishingly vast, an inner landscape shaped with perception and inclination. "The warmth of their families makes me feel warm," writes scientist Douglas Chadwick in reference to his time among elephants. "Their capacity for delight gives me joy. If a person can't see these qualities, it can only be because he or she doesn't want to."

ANIMAL ANTHOLOGY: ASTOUNDING STORIES
by Brenda Shoss

IN THE WORDS OF KOKO

When Koko's cherished companion Michael succumbed to cardiovascular disease last year, the grieving 230 lb great ape clung to her dead friend's blanket and signed: "sorry, cry." Michael and Koko shared a unique bond. Their use of words to impart wit, empathy, ingenuity, and a vast range of human emotions has been the theme of Dr. Penny Patterson's Project Koko since 1972.

Dr. Patterson teaches lowland gorillas American Sign Language. Koko uses over 1,000 words. As a three-year-old, she eagerly signed "you, me, cookie" or "hurry, drink." By age six, she challenged authority with child-like gusto, referring to others as "you nut." At ten, she vocalized basic sentences with an Auditory Language keyboard connected to a voice synthesizer.

Along with the rest of the country, Koko watched TV footage of [the World Trade Center destruction] and detected apprehension among her humans. Every time she heard a siren or low-flying plane, she grew anxious and signed "trouble." . . . Koko and her new friend Ndume will soon occupy a more native environment in west Maui, Hawaii, where construction is underway for a gorilla preserve.

UNLIKELY IN LOVE

Perhaps unaware that felines generally ambush mice, seven-year-old female cat Auan lovingly licked the face of Jeena, a three-year-old male mouse. The unusual couple, who reside at a farmer's house in a province near Bangkok, became media sweethearts after their guardian released photos of The Kiss. Auan became Jeena's ally and angel after finding him three years ago—even shielding mouse from dog on a few occasions.

Meanwhile, in Fonfria de Alba, Spain, a disheartened mama dog adopted four piglets to offset the loss of a litter that died shortly after birth. "Linda" enthusiastically nursed the tiny piglets as if they were her own children.

RATS TO THE RESCUE?

Rats have a bad rap. Notorious for inhabiting sewers, cellars and trash cans, these vagabonds of the animal kingdom are seldom acknowledged for their loyalty and courage. Then there is Gerd, the companion rat of Birgit Steich's son in Stuttgart, Germany. When armed burglars invaded the Steich's home, the wee warrior waged a sneak attack from his bookcase stronghold, sinking all four feet and teeth into the face of one crook. Gerd then darted up the pant leg of the second man to land upon a tender portion of the thief's anatomy. "The would-be burglars turned out to be suspects in a series of robberies and murders, but thanks to Gerd the hero rat, the Steich family were not among their victims," Dorothy Hoffman writes in *Heroic Rats*.

Fido, the Gumbley's eight-month-old companion rat, saved his family from fire inside their Devon, England home. At 2 A.M., the odor of smoke from an electric heater roused the sleeping rat. Fido fled his unlocked cage, but rather than scamper to safety the righteous rodent climbed a steep stairway to scratch out an SOS to his sleeping family. Fido's urgent scratching awoke Megan, age nine, who alerted her family to the blazing carpet and furniture below. Thanks to Fido, everyone evacuated safely.

WISE DEER

A no-kill policy prevails within the bounds of Algonquin Park, a large animal reserve in Ontario, Canada. Every November, at the onset of deer hunting season, local deer migrate in significant numbers to the more secure confines of Algonquin Park. Wise deer.

IF ANIMALS COULD TALK

From *When Elephants Weep: The Emotional lives of Animals* by Jeffrey Moussaieff Masson and Susan McCarthy: "Our glorious uniqueness, many philosophers have claimed, lies in our ability to speak to one another. It thus came as a shock to learn that a simple African gray parrot not only 'parroted' human speech, but spoke, communicated—the words used meant something. When animal psychologist Irene Pepperberg turned to leave her parrot, Alex, in a veterinarian's office for lung surgery, Alex called out, 'Come here. I love you. I'm sorry. I want to go back.' He thought he had done something bad and was being abandoned as punishment. Imagine what would happen if an animal addressed us on its imminent murder. If, in a slaughterhouse, a pig cried out: 'Please don't kill me.' If, as a hunter looked into the eyes of a deer, it suddenly broke into speech: 'I want to live, please don't shoot, my children need me.' Would the hunter pull the trigger? Or if a cat in a laboratory were to cry out: 'Please, no more torture,' would the scientist be able to continue? Such speech did not stop concentration camp inmates from being murdered during the Holocaust; there, humans, it was said, were lice and rats."

KINSHIP CIRCLE MISSION STATEMENT:

Kinship Circle Letters For Animals, Articles & Literature is a 501c Nonprofit organization that hosts an international mail list and Website with the primary mission to generate letter campaigns to legislators, businesses and media that provoke social, political, and ethical reforms for all nonhuman animals. The Kinship Circle Website is an information clearinghouse with fact sheets, articles, photos, apparel, and sample letters to expose animal cruelty and promote compassionate choices. When animals are viewed as "things for human use," and thus denied the primary protections humans enjoy, they are victims of speciesism, a discriminatory benchmark similar to race, religion, gender, sexual preference or age. Kinship Circle encourages those with a voice to bear witness, speak out, demand change, and act on behalf of the speechless who suffer in food, fashion, research, entertainment and other industries.

The previous article was reprinted with permission from Brenda Shoss. In addition to directing Kinship Circle, Ms. Shoss is also a journalist who currently writes a monthly column for *The Healthy Planet*. She is a contributing writer for *VegNews, AnimalsVoice Online, Family Safety and Health Magazine,* and many other publications and Websites. Please visit the Kinship Circle Website: **www.KinshipCircle.org**

The animals of the world exist for their own reasons.
They were not created for humans any more than black people
were created for whites or women for men.
— ALICE WALKER

Happiness is never better exhibited than by
young animals, such as puppies, kittens, lambs, etc.,
when playing together, like our own children.
— CHARLES DARWIN

DO ANIMALS HAVE EMOTIONS? *Of course they do* is the resounding response of those who share their lives with companion animals. While some scientists poke and prod lab animals, looking for evidence of emotion (how about *fear?*), those of us who have them in our homes already know the answers. Those who say otherwise have never seen it or felt it, or perhaps they're running away from it out of their own guilt or fear. Fear that humans will somehow become less important if it is discovered that we're not the only ones who *feel*. It is a common human trait to belittle others in an attempt to make ourselves appear more important. Perhaps it's time we understand that the true path to greatness is not in putting others down, but in bringing them up; not in focusing upon their weaknesses, but in acknowledging their strengths.

Animals express themselves with myriad modes of communication. They are able to sense things that we cannot. Humans tend to think of our own verbal language as a superior method of communication, when in reality, it has its limits. In fact, even human communication experts tell us that nonverbal communication is much more powerful and significant than we realize. They are referring to body language. In reality, it goes beyond that.

Animals have a number of highly developed senses that humans cannot even relate to, including complexities of smell and hearing that go way beyond our own abilities. Animals are able to hear sounds that humans cannot hear. Rats, for example, communicate with many unique sounds (related to various experiences and emotions) that we cannot even detect with the naked ear, but that can be picked up when using an electronic device designed to enable us to hear these sounds. One such sound has been equated to laughter, clearly implying that animals feel and express emotions, a fact that those of us who share our lives with animals have known all along.

"Do they know their names?" people often ask, upon meeting my rat family for the first time.

"Of *course* they do," I respond, "and they come when I call them." I then call to a specific rat, who promptly comes running toward us just like an enthusiastic little dog. All of the rats in our family have very unique personalities (as do we all), even when they come from the *same* litter and have *identical* upbringings. Some are more outgoing and friendly; some are more athletic and playful; others are more serious and contemplative. This indicates that these are very individual souls who are not merely products of their environment, instincts, or genes.

Shortly before our beloved rat April died, I repeatedly observed as our other rat, Katey, *literally* hugged April, much as a human would hug another human to say, "I love you; I'm really going to miss you." This wasn't a random behavior. It was something Katey only did with rats she really loved. I had previously observed her doing the same with another rat, Cindy, whom she clearly admired and adored.

I have frequently witnessed similar gestures of love and admiration among other animals. For example, some of the rats at the Rat Refuge become inseparable, like best buddies, doing everything together and clearly preferring each other's company over other rats. I've even observed what would best be described as "romances" between pairs of rats who bond for life. Very often these are rats who arrive with different companions (similar to "arranged marriages," I suppose), but when given the freedom of an actual community, as I've tried to create with the Rat Refuge, they *choose* their partners much as we choose ours. Two of the current residents of the Refuge, Kelly and Donovan, are known as the "lovebirds" and have even set up their own "love nest," separate from the others. Donovan originally arrived with a different rat companion, but as soon as he met Kelly, it was "love at first sight."

One might argue that these pairings are based upon an instinct to reproduce. However, besides the fact that these rats are spayed/neutered and no longer hormonally driven in that way, many of these pairings of buddies occur among rats of the same gender who simply enjoy each other's company.

I have also observed behavior that would best be described as jealousy, anger, and myriad complex expressions of emotion that simply cannot be dismissed as instinct or anthropomorphism. One might argue that I'm merely projecting my own interpretations onto the behavior of the rats; however, the person making such an argument would likely be one who has either never observed rats at all, or who has only observed them under the completely artificial conditions of a small cage or aquarium.

Just as a human being wouldn't be able to blossom fully if they spent their entire life in a small jail cell, so it goes for animals. I believe that one of the reasons I'm able to observe such complex and multifaceted personalities in the rats in my home is because they are living freely in an environment where they have space to truly blossom as individuals and make their *own* life decisions. And they are treated with respect rather than domination.

DR. CHRISTIAAN BARNARD (1922–2001), best known for performing the world's first human heart transplant in 1967, had the following to say about his observations of a chimpanzee:

> I had bought two male chimps from a primate colony in Holland. They lived next to each other in separate cages for several months before I used one as a [heart] donor. When we put him to sleep in his cage in preparation for the operation, he chattered and cried incessantly. We attached no significance to this, but it must have made a great impression on his companion, for when we removed the body to the operating room, the other chimp wept bitterly and was inconsolable for days. The incident made a deep impression on me. I vowed never again to experiment with such sensitive creatures.

I've witnessed countless acts of compassion and concern among the residents of the Rat Refuge. For example, whenever one of the rats in a bonded pair dies, the remaining rat goes into an obvious state of grief. Without exception, our little resident caretaker, Allison, immediately takes over, snuggling with and doting over the grieving rat around the clock. She doesn't leave their side until they have clearly healed their grief. Then, when another death occurs and another grieving rat is left behind, Allison once again steps in. I have observed this time and again. I have seen these same gestures of compassion directed toward *humans* as well.

Somehow, no matter how many times I witness such deliberate behaviors, I am touched at a core level—not only by the acts of compassion themselves, but by the fact that they are taking place among a species that my own species generally considers valueless. I feel honored to be a witness to such boundless expressions of compassion in a place where most don't even look for it and wouldn't expect to find it. I am equally touched when such boundless compassion is expressed by my fellow humans.

> *I could not have slept tonight if I had left that*
> *helpless little creature to perish on the ground.*
> — ABRAHAM LINCOLN

ONE DAY A MESSAGE WAS LEFT on my answering machine by a man who was looking for a home for a young female rat. He had been referred to me by a local veterinarian who knew I rescued rats. When I returned his call, he told me the story of how he had ended up with this rat.

He had discovered a small black rat living in his home, so, being a compassionate soul, he had set a humane trap. Upon catching the rat, he had then driven several miles away from his home to set her free in a safe area.

Shortly thereafter, the rat returned. So, once again, he set the trap, and upon catching her, he took her on a drive even farther away and set her free. As soon as he opened the trap that spelled freedom for the rat, instead of running away, the rat turned to him, stood on his foot, and looked up at him as if to say, "Please don't leave me here. *Please.*"

Staring down at the desperate and determined little creature who stood on his shoe and continued looking pleadingly up at him, he was deeply moved and unsure what to do. As he looked down at her, she stood up and continued looking straight up at him. At that point, he noticed her white underbelly. He didn't think wild rats *had* white underbellies, so it suddenly occurred to him that this might *not* be a wild rat after all, and perhaps she didn't know *how* to fend for herself in the wild.

Unable to turn away from this tiny creature who was clearly asking for help, he took her back to his home and settled her safely in a borrowed cage. He told me that he had talked to some of the other residents of the brand-new housing development in which he lived. The same rat had been spotted by several neighbors, who claimed the rat seemed to be just hanging around and looking for help. Apparently not all of the neighbors had shared this man's level of compassion or choice of traps, as evidenced by the rat's cropped tail, which appeared to have been chewed off midway in order to release herself from the painful grip of a more traditional trap.

My schedule was becoming increasingly hectic, so my dad was now helping me out with the ever-growing number of rats under my care. He proudly called himself the "Rat Chauffeur" and often picked up new rescues and took the rats on vet trips as needed, so we arranged for him to pick up the new rat the next day. When he arrived at the man's house, both he and the man were *quite* surprised at what they found in the cage with her: three *tiny*, pink baby rats. *No wonder she had been asking for help.*

Unfortunately, two of the babies appeared to be dead and the third one seemed quite weak. There was no nest, and the babies had fallen partway between the bars above the floor of the cage. No provisions had been made for the babies because no one knew the mama rat was pregnant in the first place. So, when my dad arrived with the rats, I opened the cage door and placed it in front of a new cage I had set up, complete with a nesting box. The mama rat desperately checked each of her babies and seemed visibly agitated by the fact that two of them were indeed dead. She then reached for the living baby and delicately picked him up. She carried him into the new cage with her and settled him into the nest waiting inside.

I was concerned about both of them, as the mama seemed quite small and thin and her baby seemed quite tiny and weak. I wondered if she was too young to have babies, or if she had been poisoned or malnourished, or if the stress she had endured during her pregnancy had just been too much for her and her babies. I provided her with plenty of fresh water and food so she could regain her strength. I kept her cage in a quiet area and left her undisturbed so that her maternal instincts could do the rest. I quietly checked on her regularly to make sure she and her baby were okay.

The mama rat, whom we named Danielle, did her best to take care of her one remaining baby. She groomed him and nursed him and kept him warm. However, sadly, he died less than a week later. When I later saw what newborn rats normally look like, I was amazed that he had lasted as long as he did. He was much smaller and more fragile than newborn rats normally are. His fur had just barely begun coming in when he died, and I noticed he had the familiar pattern of a human-bred rat. This was no wild rat. This was the product of human irresponsibility. I was saddened by the loss but determined to make it up to Danielle.

Although saddened by her loss as well, Danielle seemed genuinely grateful for what we had done for her. With plenty of tender loving care, she soon learned to trust us. She regained her health and joined the other rats in our beloved rat family. Today she is a full-grown healthy rat with a soft, shiny coat and a playful spirit. She has lots of rat friends and has become a very special part of our family. Whenever I hold her and look her in the eye, I see an expression of gratitude and a remembrance of how she ended up here at the Rat Refuge. I massage her and tell her how much I love her. I then set her back down, and she trots off happily to run around and frolic with her buddies, her little half-tail bobbing back and forth all the while.

If a man aspires towards a righteous life, his first
act of abstinence is from injury to animals.
— ALBERT EINSTEIN

NOT ONLY DO OUR ACTIONS hold extreme power, but our words do as well. As much as we would all like to believe otherwise, words do indeed have the power to hurt or to heal.

"Ew, I *hate* rats!" I've heard these words on more occasions than I'd like to recall. These words particularly sting when spoken by someone sitting near me in an animal hospital waiting room, as the life of one of my precious companions is slipping away and my heart feels like it's breaking into a million pieces. I know that the people speaking these words are merely reflecting a cultural stereotype that goes back a long time, but I also know that they probably wouldn't even *think* of saying such a thing if they had any idea what a powerful blow their words could deliver on an already fragile heart.

We've all said things we regret, things we would take back if we could. Rather than wishing we could go back and un-say them, I feel we can do a world of good by resolving to choose our words more carefully henceforth. Withholding unnecessary or hurtful comments, while being generous with positive words of comfort and support, can benefit both the sender and those on the receiving end. Perhaps if we can learn to see everyone as an *individual,* we'll stop making hurtful blanket statements. My own experience at fielding negative comments toward rats has assisted me in being ultra-aware of the power of words.

There was a time quite a few years ago when our rat April didn't seem to be feeling well. I called an animal communicator to find out what was wrong, and I was surprised at what she had to say. She told me there was nothing physically wrong with April, but rather, April's *feelings* had been deeply hurt. She said April told her that we had recently had a houseguest who had made some derogatory remarks about rats, and April had taken them very personally.

I confirmed that we had indeed had a houseguest the day before who had made just such comments about rats the moment April had entered the room (despite the fact that we had told this person in advance about the rats, and that they are a special part of our family). April had come out to greet us and our guest, as she always did, and she was accustomed to receiving a warm reception filled with comments on her beauty and loving disposition, to which she always responded with overflowing affection.

As soon as the insulting commentary had begun, April had

left the room. I hadn't thought about it much at the time, as I was too busy defending my "rat children." However, now as I looked back, I realized that April's demeanor had changed ever since that moment. We did our best to reassure her and to let her know that humans sometimes say very hurtful things, but not to take it personally. And Jameth proclaimed, "Anyone who hurts our children is not welcome in our home."

This incident reminded me of a time many years earlier, when I was in high school and our family dog, Charger, had an appointment with a groomer. After many long hikes in the nearby canyons, his long fur had become quite messy and tangled, and our brushing and bathing routine just wasn't doing the trick. Being a sheltie (or, as we often called him, a "miniature collie"), Charger was very proud of his beautiful coat, so as a holiday treat, my mom scheduled a visit from a mobile groomer. We figured Charger would prefer a groomer who came to our home, rather than having to go somewhere else.

After assuring me that she would take good care of Charger, the groomer escorted him inside the grooming van parked in our driveway. I went into the house to do my homework.

When the doorbell rang an hour or two later, I knew it signaled the completion of Charger's beauty appointment. So I headed to the front door with the check that my mom had already written for the groomer. As I opened the door, I was shocked at the sight before me. I was basically speechless as I handed the young woman the check and escorted Charger back into the house.

The best way to describe the scene is "Lassie joins the military." Charger had a crew cut, his beautiful, long fur all shaved off. He looked like a little pig with the face of a collie. Even the flowing mane that once surrounded his face had been cut very short and angular, making the poor little guy look like the helpless victim of a very bad joke. The young woman *had* told me she would have to do a *lot* of grooming to get rid of all those tangles, but I'd had no idea *this* was what she'd meant.

My mom called the grooming company and expressed how we felt about Charger's haircut, but of course, that didn't bring his coat back. So Charger, the formerly outgoing, very popular, proud, and beautiful little dog was now anything but beautiful. His whole personality changed. He acted shy, insecure, and often ran for cover when anyone came over.

During a holiday party in our home, he shrunk in humiliation as each guest arrived and laughed out loud, commenting with brutal honesty on his appearance. He did look funny, but he certainly wasn't laughing. We did our best to comfort him, but the damage had been done, and his normally confident disposition did not return until his coat did many months later. I felt so sorry for him, and being a self-conscious teenager myself at the time, I felt I really understood what he was going through.

Animals may not know words (or at least not *all* of them), but they certainly understand the meaning *behind* the words. I think we forget that sometimes, because they don't just say, "Hey, that hurts my feelings." Maybe that's why we hurt other humans' feelings as well. In my experience, the feelings of animals are every bit as fragile as the feelings of humans. The more time I spend with animals, the more I realize we're really not so different after all.

- Chapter 20 -

Holding Animals
in a New Light

I have developed a deep respect for animals.
I consider them fellow living creatures with certain rights
that should not be violated any more than those of humans.
— Jimmy Stewart

One afternoon several years ago, Jameth and I were driving between our office and our home when we noticed the motionless body of a cat in the middle of a busy road. Cars were whizzing by at a frenzied pace. We watched as half a dozen or so drivers ahead of us drove over the cat's lifeless body, not so much as slowing down to take a look. Although the cat's body was in the *middle* of the lane so the tires didn't actually run *over* the body, but rather, *around* it, I couldn't help but notice the complete lack of respect for that pile of fur that was once a cat. I knew that if it were a *human* body lying on the road, the pace would be much different.

"That cat deserves some respect," said Jameth as he pulled over to the side of the road and put the hazard lights on. I agreed. We always keep emergency rescue items in our vehicle, so I reached for our cat-sized makeshift stretcher as Jameth motioned to the oncoming traffic that we intended to retrieve the cat's body. We figured we would pay the cat our respects, apologize on behalf of humanity, and then find a more dignified resting place for his body.

371

Seeing what we were up to, a thoughtful driver put his hazard lights on and slowed down, allowing us to safely collect the cat's body. We smiled and waved in gratitude as we hurried back to our own vehicle, cat in tow. As we ran, Jameth looked down at the cat and then up at me.

"This cat is *alive!*" he exclaimed, and I then noticed the cat's side moving up and down to the rhythm of breath. The cat opened his eyes and looked up at us with an amazing combination of fear and gratitude. I noticed blood coming from his mouth. I wondered how much time he had left.

With Jameth behind the wheel and me in the backseat doing my best to comfort the terrified, bleeding cat, we headed to the nearest animal hospital. I offered soft words of comfort and stroked the cat gently, wondering if this would be yet another heartbreaking, futile rescue attempt.

Once inside the animal hospital, we explained what had happened, expecting the staff to spring into action to help the cat. Instead, one of the women behind the counter began casually asking us who was going to pay, explaining that they wouldn't do anything for the cat unless they had payment up front. They obviously assumed we didn't want to take on any financial responsibility because this cat wasn't our *pet,* as if an animal's life only has value when they're the "property" of a human.

"Of *course* we'll pay for the cat!" we exclaimed simultaneously. "Just *help* him!" We then scrambled for a credit card with enough available credit and filled out the paperwork that would determine whether or not anyone would help the suffering cat. After what seemed like an eternity, we offered some final words of comfort as the cat was whisked away to the back room. We were told that the outlook was dim.

During the cat's hospital stay, we paid regular visits, delivering herbal remedies and words of comfort, as our new little friend made a remarkable recovery. We put signs up all over town hoping to locate the cat's home, but the fact that he had no collar had already prepared us for the fact that no one would likely come forward. And no one ever did.

Having a house full of rats, we knew we couldn't offer a home for this lone hero. So I called Maggie, our good friend and fellow animal rescuer. She already had more rescued animals than any one person should have to care for—and she took good care of them all (and still does), in addition to working full time, serving as a City Council Member, and engaging in countless other humanitarian and community efforts—so I certainly didn't *expect* her to take yet another animal. But of course, she did. She took him in and named him Boris. She gave him his daily medications, remedies, and healing foods, and assisted him in completing his healing process. We kept the signs up around town, but no one ever called to claim a missing cat.

To this day, every time we go over to Maggie's house, a very happy and well-cared-for Boris is there to greet us. I'm grateful that in his second chance at life, living with that incredible woman named Maggie, he is seeing the good side of humanity, certainly something worth sticking around for.

Nothing is more powerful than an individual acting out of his conscience, thus helping to bring the collective conscience to life.
— NORMAN COUSINS

PERHAPS ONE OF THE MOST sobering things a person can do is visit an animal shelter filled with the innocent victims of human irresponsibility. Jameth and I recently spent a Sunday afternoon visiting several local shelters where the majority of the animals will remain unclaimed and unwanted, and will have to be "put to sleep." As we solemnly walked from cage to cage and pen to pen, looking into the soulful eyes of these abandoned animals, I realized that it was no different than visiting Death Row, except that these inmates had committed no crime . . . and they had certainly done *nothing* worthy of such punishment. They looked so sad and lonely. It broke my heart to know that we couldn't help them all.

From disposable goods to disposable companions, we live in a world of excess and irresponsibility. Unfortunately, animals are often the ones who pay the price. According to the most recent statistics I've come across (as of this writing), there are forty-five cats and fifteen dogs for every human born. Furthermore, only one out of ten dogs born (10%) and one out of twelve cats born (8.3%) will find a permanent home. That means that 90% of all dogs and 91.7% of all cats will end up homeless, either dying in the streets or ending up in shelters. According to the HSUS Pet Overpopulation Estimates (**www.hsus.org**), three to four *million* dogs and cats are euthanized per year in the United States because they are not adopted or placed into homes. (This includes purebreds, who account for 25% of dogs in shelters.) That's roughly 10,000 cats and dogs per day, seven days a week, which amounts to approximately 400 *per hour*. (This doesn't even include all of the other types of homeless animals who share a similar fate: rabbits, guinea pigs, rats, and other animals.) That's a lot of lives.

Ultimately, building more shelters isn't the answer. These animals don't need ever more cages in which to live out their lonely lives; they need *homes* and *families* to give them the love and companionship they deserve.

When I've spoken with professional animal communicators about this, they've told me that the shelter animals they've communicated with feel deeply hurt and betrayed by humankind. I couldn't agree more. So, how did this happen? Again, we live in a disposable world. Unfortunately, excess usually begets neglect, and neglect usually begets suffering.

Sure, there *will* be a place for them in the afterlife, but that doesn't excuse the fear, sorrow, isolation and rejection they experience in the here and now, in a world where humans have bred them for our own wants and needs and then failed to take responsibility when things have gotten out of hand. In my view, every moment counts. The promise of a brighter tomorrow, while comforting, does not excuse the abuse or neglect of a gloomy today.

Every moment counts. That's why I feel it is so important for each of us to do whatever we can, no matter how small or insignificant it may seem. Just *being there* at the side of a lonely or frightened animal, adopting our next companion from a shelter or rescue group (for those who really want a specific breed, there are many breed-specific rescue groups to choose from), or simply offering our prayers and our support—these are acts that may go unnoticed in our society at large, but they never go unnoticed by those whose lives they touch.

> *Not to hurt our humble brethren is our first duty to them,*
> *but to stop there is not enough. We have a higher mission—*
> *to be of service to them wherever they require it.*
> — ST. FRANCIS OF ASSISI

I look forward to the day when we all think twice before breeding our family pets, and the day we stop allowing unspayed/ unneutered cats and dogs to roam our neighborhoods without considering the ramifications. I am hopeful that, as time goes on, we as a society will no longer neglect the importance of spaying and neutering as part of the responsibility that goes along with keeping animals as our companions.

I encourage those who are passionate about a specific breed to rescue their next companion from a breed-specific rescue group or, if they have the capacity, to start a breed-specific rescue group of their own. That way, they're still involved with their favorite type of animal, but in a whole new capacity. The difference is, now they're contributing to the solution rather than the problem.

We must encourage pet store owners to sell only supplies and *not* live animals—to use pet adoption, perhaps, as a humane way to get people in the door, and then to earn their living through the supplies that people buy. I applaud the stores that are already doing this.

As with most dilemmas in our world, it comes back to education. Most people simply don't realize the magnitude of this situation. Many animal welfare organizations have powerful educational materials available. We must get them into as many hands as possible. People need to know. People need to visit the shelters and hear the cries, and look into the eyes of these abandoned animals to really *get* what's going on. My heart goes out to those who work in shelters and face this reality day in and day out.

One of the most rewarding things we can do is volunteer to walk the dogs or cuddle the other animals at a local shelter.

Although it's not possible for any one individual to provide a loving home for *every* animal in need (and God knows, many of us have tried), each of us can take little steps that make a *big* difference.

> *Never doubt that a small group of thoughtful,*
> *committed individuals can change the world.*
> *Indeed, it's the only thing that ever has.*
> — MARGARET MEAD

"WHY DO YOU HAVE SO MANY? You *can't* save them all," I was once told by a houseguest who had decided not to like rats and certainly didn't approve of the growing number of rats under my care. Between the lines, the comment implied that because I couldn't save them all, I shouldn't even bother—that it was a waste of time and there were more important things I could be doing.

"I do my part," I responded. I then shared the parable about the person who was throwing beached starfish back into the ocean to save them. There were countless starfish that had been washed ashore and were littered all over the beach. When the person was told by an onlooker that it was pointless, that there were so many starfish on the beach that they couldn't *possibly* all be saved—and that these efforts wouldn't make a difference—the person tossed yet another starfish into the ocean and responded, "It made all the difference in the world to that one." I love that story. The way I see it, we must not use what we *can't* do as an excuse for not doing what we *can*.

Upon hearing of my work in animal rescue—and specifically rat rescue—another houseguest abruptly began talking about all the starving children in the world. Between the lines, this person was saying that my work in animal rescue was menial and unimportant, that there were more important things I should be doing. Again, this goes back to human arrogance and blatant disregard for the other beings with whom we share this incredible planet. I explained that I do what I can to make the world a better place for *everyone*—to help humans *as well as* animals. To me, it's not an "either/or."

I am in favor of animal rights as well as human rights.
That is the way of a whole human being.
— Abraham Lincoln

Compassion, in which all ethics must take root,
can only attain its full breadth and depth if it embraces
all living creatures and does not limit itself to mankind.
— Albert Schweitzer

I find that those who are doing rescue work on behalf of *animals* are often doing all they can for their fellow *humans* as well. Somehow, compassion toward animals seems to have a ripple effect that expands outward to all areas of life.

On the other hand, I find that the people who make such comments to negate the efforts of those doing animal rescue work are usually doing *nothing* themselves on behalf of animals *or* humans. Perhaps seeing the kind acts of others threatens these people in some way, and that's what compels them to make such comments. Perhaps it is their own guilt in doing nothing themselves that compels them to downplay the selfless acts of others. Perhaps they have received only criticism in their *own* lives, so that's all they know. I can't really say *why* people say the negative and hurtful things they do. One thing I know for sure is that we must never let such comments get us down or cause us to lose hope. Every action makes a difference, and no act goes unnoticed. Those of us who have been deeply touched by the love of an animal often feel compelled to give back in whatever way we can, and when we do, the heavens rejoice.

Always hold firmly to the thought that each one of us
can do something to bring some portion of misery to an end.
— from a poster by Bonnie Acker in Tools for Change,
the catalog of Syracuse Cultural Workers

Rats as Mirrors

I am often asked to speak to groups of people about rats, rat rescue, or other animal-related issues. I am always honored to speak on behalf of my wonderful animal friends who have taught me so much. I have spoken to many groups of children and adults alike, and I find it fascinating that, every single time, the children are completely open and receptive to rats. (Of course, I always educate them on the importance of rescuing homeless animals and on responsible animal caretaking.)

The derogatory comments about rats are always delivered by the *adults*, the so-called role models. Perhaps the adults were once open-minded children themselves, but their own role models told *them* who to love and who to despise. I suppose I'm simply one of the lucky few who have been personally touched by these magical little beings.

When I ask the people who make these comments *why* they hate rats, they usually tell me they hate the tails. When I ask them *why* they hate the tails, they tell me it's because the tails are *naked*. I then pull up my sleeve, exposing my naked arm.

"Like this?" I ask, displaying my arm. I find it so interesting that the part people hate most about rats is the part that is most like *us*. Hmmm . . .

The more time I've spent with rats, the more I've come to see them as mirrors of humanity. No matter what we find to despise in them, if we look closely enough, we find that perhaps it's something we could just as easily despise in ourselves . . . perhaps more so.

Many years ago, when Jameth and I lived in a small rental on someone else's property, the landlord showed Jameth some destruction caused by rats. Wild rats had begun building a nest inside the landlord's pool shed, and he wanted to get rid of the "pests." Jameth suggested humane live traps and prevention rather than traditional traps or poison, thinking of the well-being of those creatures who were simply building a home.

Later, Jameth described the destruction to me, and I realized that it was *nothing* compared to the destruction humans cause whenever we build *our* homes. We don't merely cause a little damage in a pool shed; we destroy entire habitats of many animals. In fact, we destroy entire species. I began to wonder who the *real* pests were.

I noticed that the same people who said they detested rats were often quick to defend the use of rats in research. Why? *Well, they would say, because we need to learn from them . . . to help us.* In other words, the same people who claimed we needed the rats to *help* us also claimed to *hate* them. Talk about a slap in the face.

When I learned that rats (as well as dogs, cats, bunnies, monkeys, guinea pigs, and other animals) were (and still are) repeatedly force-fed cosmetics and toxic household cleaners—or gassed, injected, or blinded with *known* toxins—to "see what happens," it occurred to me that, if anything, *they* should hate *us*. Tolstoy once said, "What I think about vivisection [animal experimentation] is that if people admit that they have the right to take or endanger the life of a living being for the benefit of many, there will be no limit to their cruelty." How true his words have proven to be.

> *Mercy is a universal duty, and it cannot*
> *be withheld from any of God's creatures.*
> — Reverend Henry Primatt, D.D.
> (16th-century Anglican priest)

As I contemplated the human-rat relationship, I looked at rats from many different perspectives: the origins of the Year of the Rat (the rat is the very first animal on the Chinese calendar and is also considered a symbol of prosperity in both China and Japan); the way rats are revered and even hand-fed in a temple in India (and other parts of the world, past and present); and the image of rats here in America, where, ironically, we engage in behavior most similar to that which we say we despise in rats.

I thought about the "rat race," which would more accurately be called the "human race," and I explored the other slang terms involving the word "rat" (for example, the term "ratty" is often used to describe that which is unkempt, whereas rats are actually meticulous about their grooming).

I looked at the overcrowding of wild rats in some areas, not unlike the overcrowding of our own species in the same areas. I thought about all the human litter and leftover food that often entices wild animals into our habitats in the first place. I noticed the way we tend to point fingers at rats (which often should be pointed at ourselves). I looked at the intelligence of rats, their social order, and their will to survive.

I recalled a true story I had read somewhere, about a beautiful scene observed by a man who once despised rats. He was preparing to kill some of these "pests," but then he witnessed a wild rat helping another rat, who was handicapped, across the road. He was a changed man.

As I contemplated all of this, I began to formulate a theory. If humanity could only learn to see rats—who usually symbolize the bottom of the barrel, the most despised of all animals—as worthy of our respect and compassion, then perhaps respect and compassion for all other animals would follow. And perhaps if we as a society can learn to deal more compassionately with the animals, we'll learn to deal more compassionately with *each other.*

> *If man is not to stifle human feelings,*
> *he must practice kindness toward animals,*
> *for he who is cruel to animals becomes hard*
> *also in his dealings with men. We can judge the*
> *heart of a man by his dealings with animals.*
> — IMMANUEL KANT

ONE DAY THERE WAS A MESSAGE on my answering machine from a young woman who said she worked at a local preschool and was wondering if I could help out with one of the "classroom pets." The classroom pet was a rat, and when I called her back, she gave me the details. She said that this rat had a *huge* tumor, but the school wasn't willing to pay for any veterinary care and wouldn't even pay to have the rat euthanized. She said she had called the local Humane Society, and a woman there had given her my phone number, as word had gotten out that I rescue rats. The young woman told me she would be leaving the school and moving out of town the following week, so she wanted to make sure the rat was taken care of before she left.

Upon further questioning, I learned that the rat's tumor was nearly the size of the rat herself, and her arm was embedded in it. She was living in a small aquarium on improper bedding (cedar shavings, which are unhealthful for rats), together with another rat. Both of them had labored breathing and didn't look very healthy, according to the young woman.

"We've got to get this rat out of here," she said. "This just isn't good for the children." When she said this, I got the strong sense that she was just repeating what the other teachers had said. As we spoke further and I voiced my opinion about how cruel and unacceptable the situation was, she quietly agreed. It was obvious that she was the only one there who cared. Yet another case of an animal whose only purpose was to serve the whims of humans—humans who weren't willing to lift a finger when the animal then needed help.

When I agreed to take the rats and pay for their veterinary care, the young woman then disclosed that there was another rat in a different classroom who *also* had a tumor, though it was smaller. This rat lived all by herself, which meant long, dark, lonely nights, weekends, and holidays. So, upon my prodding, she went to go ask that teacher if I could take *her* rat for surgery as well; the teacher agreed, as long as *I* paid for it.

Then she mentioned a guinea pig in yet another classroom with some sort of "huge, gaping sore" (the diameter of an orange) that had gone untreated for quite some time; and she ran to ask *that* teacher if I could take the guinea pig for veterinary care, too. Of course, none of them was willing to contribute a dime, and the young woman informed me that if I hadn't stepped in, they would have just left the animals untreated in their prison cells, where they had been for much too long already. If compassion is something that is taught, then the children in *this* school weren't off to a very good start.

Still juggling too many tasks to complete in a day myself, I called my dad and informed him that I had yet another rescue mission for him, if he had the time. He rushed right over. I helped him load up his car with cages and asked him to please get as many animals out of there as he could. He returned with three rats and a guinea pig. They were all in horrendous condition and smelled as if they had been living in dirty cages for years.

I was told that the school *definitely* wanted the rat with the smaller tumor back after I had her tumor removed. She was a very beautiful, fluffy beige-and-white rat with a teddy bear face, so *of course* they wanted *her* back. The other two rats were dark gray, old and thin, so they wouldn't be missed at all. Although I had no intentions of returning *any* of these rats to that prison, I instructed my dad to tell the people whatever they wanted to hear to ensure that they would relinquish the animals to him.

When my dad returned from picking up the animals, he was visibly shaken. I had been involved in many rescues over the years, so I had grown accustomed to such cases of senseless suffering. However, my dad was new at this, so I now realized I hadn't adequately prepared him, and I apologized for having put him in that position. He assured me that he was glad to have been able to help out, that it had been a very eye-opening experience for him.

He reported that he had gotten out with all of the animals there except one remaining rat, a six-month-old living by herself in a small aquarium, surrounded by noisy children who were not yet old enough to treat such fragile animals with the sensitivity they require . . . and whose teachers had clearly left compassion out of their curriculum. They wouldn't let him take this particular rat because she was still "young and healthy."

That night, I did my best to apologize to the animals for the way they had been treated by my fellow humans, who obviously didn't know better. I assured them that not all humans were like that, and that we would take good care of them. I scheduled the surgeries for the very next day. So, the three rats (Jane Doe 1, Jane Doe 2, and Jane Doe 3) and Mr. Guinea Pig headed off to the vet with Dad.

The vet, Dr. Mabley, said that these animals were in the worst condition he had seen in quite some time. We were all amazed and appalled at the size of the tumor on one of the rats, which she and her companion literally slept atop. She had to use all of her force to drag the giant tumor across the aquarium to get to the water bottle for a drink. The bottom of the tumor was scabbed and bloody from being dragged around, and the rat was extreme-ly thin, as she was unable to eat enough to support herself *and* the huge mass. Because her right arm was embedded in the tumor, she ate and groomed herself with her left hand only. It was heart-breaking to watch her struggle. As Dr. Mabley said, the most heartbreaking part of all was the fact that it was so *unnecessary*. A tumor such as this would have been so simple to remove had they only sought veterinary care before it got so big.

While Jane Doe 1 (the one with the enormous tumor) was being prepared for surgery, her cage mate literally leapt up out of the aquarium and onto my dad's shoulder. As soon as she arrived there, she began to make the joyful chattering sound that rats make when they are happy. After all that they had been through, here she was, trusting a human and expressing affection. He was deeply moved.

Much to everyone's amazement, Jane (she kept the name) survived her surgery, and over time, made a complete recovery. When the tumor was weighed after it was removed, it was discovered that it weighed just about the same as she did. She was overjoyed at no longer having to cart around the excess baggage of human indifference.

Happily, Mr. Guinea Pig had a successful surgery as well. It was cancer, but Dr. Mabley was successful at removing it completely. My friend and fellow animal rescuer, an exceptional woman named Fenella Speece (founder of Wee Companions Small Animal Rescue and Adoptions), offered to take Mr. Guinea Pig, whom she named Nelson. Fenella has a family to care for and also works as a nurse caring for *humans*, yet she somehow finds the time to take good care of countless *animals* in need as well. Under her care, Nelson made a complete recovery.

Sadly, one of the rats had inoperable cancer that had spread to the lungs, and she died shortly thereafter; but at least she died peacefully, in the presence of humans who respected her and cared about her well-being. The other two rats, Jane and Sarabeth, are living happily here at the Rat Refuge to this day. It still warms my heart to see them running freely around the Rat Room, while memories of their years in that filthy prison have faded away.

When I called the preschool to let them know that one of the rats had died but the other animals were all doing great, I also politely told the woman who answered the phone that I really didn't think their preschool was an appropriate environment for animals. She was noticeably perturbed at my intrusion into their business.

"I appreciate your opinion," she said coldly and curtly, obviously not appreciating it at all. "Thanks for all you've done. Good-bye." And I knew that the suffering would continue, as more "classroom pets" replaced those whose neglected bodies had been discarded.

The worst sin towards our fellow creatures is not to hate them, but to be indifferent to them. That is the essence of inhumanity.
— GEORGE BERNARD SHAW

Despite my best efforts, I find it difficult to stop such cruelty, because as of this writing, certain animals—including rats, mice and birds—do not have any legal protection. (Even those animals who *are* "protected" by the law are protected by laws that aren't always enforced.) Ultimately, there are *no* laws that protect them, other than the laws of conscience.

In my rescue work, I have seen the worst of humanity, and I've also seen the best of humanity. It is heartbreaking to see the tremendous unnecessary suffering that occurs at the hands of humans who are indifferent to the feelings of animals and treat them as nothing more than showpieces, or worse. On the bright side, it is heartwarming to see the kind acts of those who are working tirelessly to make things right.

It is not enough to be compassionate; you must act.
— THE DALAI LAMA

ANIMALS AS SAINTS—ANIMALS AS TEACHERS

OVER THE YEARS as I spoke with countless people about their own departed companion animals, I noticed a very common theme. As they spoke of these animals, it was almost as if they were speaking of an angel or a saint. These animals hadn't just brought them love and companionship; these animals had acted as spiritual teachers, bringing incredible amounts of insight and inspiration.

KATHLEEN DEMETZ, an attorney in Cleveland Heights, Ohio, had the following to say about her beloved dog, Sammy:

I always felt that there was something more about him, that in many ways he was much more than a dog. There was a wiseness about him, and a gentleness. I felt that he was almost some kind of an advanced spirit . . . there was something about him. I always called him my angel dog— my guardian angel. He had the sweetest disposition. When I looked in his eyes, I almost saw the face of God because he was totally good.

One day he was in the yard and he ran up to something and stopped. I was in the kitchen doing the dishes and he looked at me and he started barking. This was a dog who almost never barked. I said, "What's he barking at? He doesn't bark." And then he looked at the ground, he looked back at me, and he barked again. And he kept it up. He wanted something. I couldn't figure out what it was. I went outside and there was a little injured bird in the yard. He was calling me to help the bird. When I went over to the bird, he stopped barking.

A year later, I adopted another dog, Harry, who was on his way to the pound. Sammy accepted him right away. Harry had seizures. The first time this happened I was lying in bed sleeping, and all of a sudden Sammy was jumping on me. He didn't normally wake me up like this. I woke up and he kept jumping on me, so I sat up. Then he jumped off the bed and I ran over and Harry was having a seizure. Sammy always woke me up to alert me when Harry was having a seizure. He was always doing very kind things like that.

When I was in labor with my son, Sammy was on my stomach. When I adopted my daughter, I brought her home from the adoption agency and he went right up and gave her a kiss. He didn't have a jealous bone. He was total unconditional love.

I've only ever gone to a meditation class once in my life. It was very interesting because when I went into the meditation, it involved *him*. In the meditation, I was walking in the woods with Sammy and I came to a clearing; there was an ancient circle of wisdom. Sammy stopped, and I went on to the circle of wisdom. There were all these people in white robes and they said, "You have to learn to love as he loves. He has total unconditional love. Your purpose is to learn to love as he does. He does not care what anyone looks like, if you are rich or poor, your race, your nationality, your wealth, your education; he just loves totally and completely, and that is how you are to learn to love, as Sammy loves." Then, in the meditation, I walked back to him and we walked out.

Years ago I took Sammy to an animal communicator. I didn't tell her anything about him. She told me he was very empathic and altruistic. She said he told our other dog not to do bad things because the other dog was always getting into trouble. She said Sammy was very sensitive, and if we weren't home, he would worry; he worried about us because he cared so much about us.

He was always just pure love. He had a very empathic quality. He also taught me so many things. I saw the love and the caring and the emotions that he had, and I started feeling that way about other animals. I thought, *If he has these emotions, how do other animals feel? And how do they feel about being eaten?* and he actually got me to stop eating meat. I used to eat meat—in fact, I didn't even *like* vegetables—I loved meat, and he got me to quit eating it. He got me to respect all life and all creation, even little insects. If there is an ant or a moth in my house, I gently take them and let them outside. If I see a worm on the ground and it's raining, I'll move it out of the way so people don't step on it. Sammy got me to do all that. It was all him. That's why I say he was my guide, my life lesson, my angel. I revere all creation now, and it's all because of him.

It's amazing how it spreads, because now I teach my kids; and they tell kids at school not to hurt the insects, and it really multiplies. When somebody goes to smash an insect, they will say, "No, I'll let him out." Now even some of their teachers are starting to let them out—and other kids—it's amazing how it spreads.

So many people say animals don't have souls, and I say God is such a wonderful God there is no way that could be true. At least my dogs have a wonderful life, but look at all those animals that have a horrible life—look at all those animals in the factory farms. There is no way God would let

those animals live a life of total misery and then just have
them rot in the ground. A good God is not going to do that.

TIME AND AGAIN, I heard similar comments by people from all
walks of life. They had looked upon their beloved companions as
spiritual guides or teachers. Many people had been so touched by
an animal that they changed their thinking, their life direction,
even their diet, and all were better for it.

Another wonderful example of this is an exceptional man
named Eddie Lama whose whole perspective changed as a result
of the love of a cat. He now devotes himself to the welfare of animals and has made a tremendous difference in the world. Among
other things, he founded Oasis: A Sanctuary for People and Animals. His moving story is told in the award-winning documentary *The Witness,* by Tribe of Heart Productions (**www.Tribe
OfHeart.org**). I highly recommend this eye-opening film.

I, too, am leading a completely different life than I would
otherwise be leading if not for the love of animals. I, too, changed
my diet as a result of their love and inspiration. I decided at a
young age that I wanted to become a vegetarian when I grew up.
And that I did. My only regret is that I didn't do it sooner. In
college, I became a vegan, and I've never looked back.

For me, it was a decision based solely on the desire not to cause
suffering to my fellow beings. I later learned that this decision
also had a powerful beneficial impact on our environment and
world hunger, issues that are also very important to me (for more
information on this, I highly recommend the book *Diet for a New
America* by John Robbins, and the video documentary with the
same title). An added and unexpected bonus was that my health
benefited dramatically when I changed my diet. I was a relatively
sickly child and young adult, but because of a decision that was
solely inspired by the animals themselves, my health improved
tremendously. I am ever grateful to them.

When I later changed majors, studied nutrition, and went on
to become a practicing naturopath and health researcher, I discovered the solid scientific explanations as to *why* my health had
improved so dramatically due to changing my diet. (Jameth had

originally made the decision to adopt a vegan diet exclusively for its health benefits. However, once he learned of the ethical reasons for such a diet, these reasons became even *more* important to him as well.)

When people came to Jameth and me for nutritional guidance during the many years that we practiced together as naturopaths (Jameth still does), we—and they—were always amazed at the dramatic healings that took place due to this simple change in diet, regardless of blood type, body type, or any other factor (when done healthfully, of course). Because of my own blood type and body type, I am not "supposed to" be able to thrive on such a diet according to the popular fad theory of the day, but nothing could be further from the truth. My personal blood work and long-term research—and that of countless others—put such theories to rest long ago.

Over time, I've observed as conflicting theories and trends have come and gone (often due to the common resistance that so often flares up when humans and industries feel threatened by change), but the actual data—and more importantly, the results themselves—have remained steadfast; and more and more people are changing their diets similarly. As grateful as we all are for the improved health that accompanies this dietary decision, I think the animals are the most grateful of all.

One farmer says to me, "You cannot live on vegetable food solely, for it furnishes nothing to make bones with," and . . . all the while he walks behind his oxen, which, with vegetable-made bones, jerk him and his lumbering plow along in spite of every obstacle.
— HENRY DAVID THOREAU

Nuclear power, starvation, cruelty— we must make a statement against these things. Vegetarianism is my statement. And I think it's a strong one.
— ISAAC BASHEVIS SINGER,
NOBEL PRIZE WINNER AND HOLOCAUST HISTORIAN

When non-vegetarians say that "human problems come first,"
I cannot help wondering what exactly it is that they are doing
for human beings that compels them to continue to support
the wasteful, ruthless exploitation of farmed animals.
— Dr. Peter Singer (Princeton Bioethicist),
Animal Liberation

I FEEL FORTUNATE to have known and loved many different types of animals as a child. In fact, cows and chickens were my friends long before I realized they were my food. Spending my summers on thousands of pristine acres of wilderness at The Ranch gave me an opportunity early on to commune with a wide assortment of incredible beings; it gave me the opportunity to get to know the animals who, unbeknownst to me at the time, were destined for my plate.

Something that always struck me as odd was the fact that the cows at The Ranch, with whom I spent a lot of time, always had a distinct air of caution and fear. They were my friends and clearly trusted me, but I always noticed their lack of trust toward—and fear of—the adults on The Ranch. When I communed with them, I always felt an impending sense of doom. It was almost as if they were awaiting some horrible fate, every day wondering if this would be the day their peaceful life would end—the day it would all change.

At the time, it struck me as odd. They were living on this beautiful ranch and grazing on the natural grasses of the land, surrounded by thousands of acres of wilderness, taken care of by these wonderful people known as Grandmother and Grandaddy, and protected by a saintly border collie named Duffy. It was an unusually large ranch, and an incredibly magical place; these were unusually lucky cows. They had it so good, and as far as I could tell, this was where they would remain for the rest of their lives. Yet, every day they lived with a feeling of despair and hopelessness. I felt it in their presence, and it made absolutely no sense to me. I felt sad for them, and I did my best to reassure and comfort them.

I was so confused at their seemingly inappropriate demeanor, given their lot in life, that I spent long hours just trying to understand. I tried to ask them what was wrong—*why* did they feel this way, when they had such a wonderful life. I got the sense that they knew something I didn't, something so terrible that they didn't even want to think about it—yet they couldn't get it out of their minds. Something in such stark contrast to their current idyllic lifestyle that it was unimaginable. And every day for them began with the thought, *Is this the day? Please don't let this be the day.*

The day for what? I wondered to myself. *Why are they so afraid? What do they dread?*

That answer came the day I found out that some of my friends had been sent off to the slaughterhouse. Well, that was the *first* part of the answer, anyway. I didn't get the full answer until years later, when I learned what a slaughterhouse was really like. When I learned of the poking, prodding, crowding, pain, and deprivation of their long, terrifying journey to that ultimate fate. When I learned of the assembly line of horrors (or rather, *disassembly* line) that awaited them, assuming they survived the torturous journey.

I felt horrible when I realized that my friends had been sent there. That I hadn't done something to help them. My realization that "meat" was actually the flesh of my friends was a turning point in my life. That was the understanding that led me to become a vegetarian. To take "Thou shalt not kill" quite literally.

I find it interesting that the terms "free-range" or "organic" or "grass-fed" are terms often used to assure us that "no, there was no suffering involved in the production of *this* product." If only that were true. Not only do these terms conjure up images that are often quite different than the reality behind the scenes, but ironically, it was the fate of animals who actually *did* live the epitome of a free-range, organic, grass-fed lifestyle that originally led me to give up meat. I learned from the animals themselves that no amount of grass or land could take away their fear and doom and dread of the undignified death that awaited them at the end of the line.

> *The time will come when men such as I will look upon the*
> *murder of animals as now they look upon the murder of men.*
> — LEONARDO DA VINCI

I THINK WE ALL HAVE CERTAIN KEY MOMENTS in our lives that we see as pivotal. For me, one such moment took place when I was in college and went fishing with my boyfriend at that time. I had previously joined him on several afternoon trips to a nearby creek where he enjoyed catching crayfish (basically, miniature lobsters), which he intended to cook for dinner. He collected them in a bucket of water, and I quietly helped them back to safety whenever he had his back turned. (He thought they kept escaping on their own; little did he know, I was their guilty accomplice.)

Having had little success at crayfish hunting, he had now purchased his first fishing pole and decided to become a "real" fisherman. I had no intention of actually *joining* him in his new hobby; I merely went along for the peaceful scenery and the relaxing ride in a rowboat. It seemed like a nice way to spend a sunny Sunday afternoon. However, all illusions of tranquility quickly vanished for me when I found myself face-to-face with the struggling, terrified victim of my boyfriend's new source of "relaxation," who was dangling from his fishing hook.

As I looked into the fish's eyes, I *literally felt* the terror—and understood the excruciating pain—that this helpless creature was now enduring, having been violently pulled out of his world and into the foreign, suffocating world of what must have appeared to him as monsters or aliens who had no mercy. It was one of those moments when my direct connection with an animal was undeniable . . . and completely overwhelming. The fish was asking me—*begging* me—for help.

I began to cry and scream to my boyfriend to *please* let the poor creature go. For the first time, I really understood how *unnecessary* such suffering was. My boyfriend wasn't *intentionally* abusing an animal, of course; he was simply unable to *hear* that animal's cries. But I heard them loud and clear, and I've never forgotten them. After much struggling, the fish's life reached a tragic end, and

I understood—for the first time, perhaps—the meaning of the phrase, "Ignorance is bliss."

Up until that point, it hadn't fully registered what an incredible amount of suffering takes place to land *any* animal on our dinner plates—not only a cow or a chicken or a lamb—but also a fish. It was then that it first fully hit me that *all* animals are sentient beings worthy of our compassion; and when we choose to eat them, a tremendous amount of suffering takes place, whether we are the ones who do the killing or not.

Our human-crafted devices of killing—whether they be hooks or nets or slaughterhouse production lines—are so outside of the laws of nature, so outside of the laws of compassion, that if a *human* were to be subjected to any one of them, the perpetrator would undoubtedly receive maximum punishment.

To a man whose mind is free there is something even more intolerable in the sufferings of animals than in the sufferings of man. For with the latter it is at least admitted that suffering is evil and that the man who causes it is a criminal. But thousands of animals are uselessly butchered every day without a shadow of remorse. If any man were to refer to it, he would be thought ridiculous. And that is the unpardonable.
— ROMAIN ROLLAND (1866–1944)

ANOTHER SUCH PIVOTAL MOMENT in my life took place when I received some literature in the mail from the organization People for the Ethical Treatment of Animals. It was then that I first learned of the *tremendous* amount of unimaginable animal suffering that goes on in our world, often behind closed doors and with our unwitting approval . . . and usually with our own dollars.

I could hardly believe it and wanted to *do* something about it, so I sent for additional educational materials right away. I'll never forget the day they arrived. I sat and read every word of every page they sent. I learned of the horrors of factory farming and animal testing; of fur farms and leather production; of animals of all types used for food, clothing, and more. I learned of chickens and pigs being literally boiled alive in "scalding tanks"; of animals having their throats slit and their limbs cut off while fully conscious. I learned of such "routine" practices as "debeaking" and castration—and countless other unthinkable acts—all done without anesthesia. I learned of the tremendous suffering that countless animals endure at the hands of humanity twenty-four hours a day, seven days a week—due to a dangerous combination of greed, arrogance, and ignorance. *If people knew what was really going on,* I thought to myself, *they'd revolt.*

When I finished reading, I was angry and upset—not at the organization that had sent the information (I admired and appreciated what they were doing on behalf of animals)—but at humanity, for allowing such things to happen and then labeling those who attempted to *do* something about it as "radicals" trying to mess up the status quo. I didn't blame the messenger, but it occurred to me that, for some reason in our world, we often *do* get angry at the messenger rather than the message. It was then that I first began to realize that, *sometimes,* that which is deemed good and decent in our world can be, *behind the scenes,* anything but; and those who work to change things for the better are often ostracized, punished, or vilified. It seems that this is the way it has been throughout human history.

That night, I quietly wept as I deeply empathized with all of the helpless animals who were suffering unnecessarily at the hands of human beings, for the sake of products we don't even need and would be better off without. It was then that it occurred to me that the only reason more people weren't concerned was because they didn't know they had anything to be concerned *about.* I vowed that I would henceforth refrain from contributing to such senseless suffering, and that I would do everything in my power to make things right in my lifetime. And I felt in my heart that most people—if they only knew the *truth*—would undoubtedly do the same.

Cowardice asks the question—is it safe?
Expediency asks the question—is it politic?
Vanity asks the question—is it popular?
But conscience asks the question—is it right?
And there comes a time when one must take a position that
is neither safe, nor politic, nor popular; but one must take it
because it is right.
— THE REVEREND DR. MARTIN LUTHER KING, JR.

I began to think about humanity and our bloody history here on Earth. I began to wonder if perhaps we were missing the lesson, over and over, and were repeatedly being given the opportunity to do things differently . . . to expand our minds and our hearts to love unconditionally. The many colors and creeds within our own species have given us abundant opportunities to expand our circle of love and compassion, and it seems that we have failed at almost every turn. Here on classroom Earth, history tends to repeat itself *until we get the lesson.*

The animal kingdom provides us perhaps an even bigger opportunity to get the lesson, for the animals we oppress don't have the means—or the voice—to fight back. So, this time it's entirely up to *us* to speak up for *them.*

First they came for the socialists,
and I did not speak out because I was not a socialist.
Then they came for the trade-unionists,
and I did not speak out because I was not a trade-unionist.
Then they came for the Jews,
and I did not speak out because I was not a Jew.
Then they came for me—and there was no one left to speak for me.
— REVEREND MARTIN NIEMOLLER

I'VE ALWAYS BEEN a relatively low-key person, not wanting to offend others and constantly concerned about what people think of me, often biting my tongue instead of speaking up for fear of creating conflict or controversy. However, the one area in which I've always spoken up is the issue of injustice—whether it be social injustice or environmental injustice or interspecies injustice. As a child, I often spoke up for other children who were teased, and in so doing, I myself became the target of much abuse. Even so, I always felt in my heart that I had done the right thing and would do it again if need be.

The issue of unnecessary suffering of my fellow beings, whether they be humans *or* other animals, is simply more important than what people think of me. Any offense that anyone might take in my voicing these issues is *nothing* compared to the offenses that will continue to be committed against the innocent if we *don't* voice these issues. To me, the oppression of others is so blatantly wrong and, unfortunately, so often overlooked or misunderstood in our world, that I simply cannot remain silent. I've seen too much, and in knowing what I do, I feel I simply *must* give voice to these issues.

> *Our lives begin to end the day we*
> *become silent about things that matter.*
> — THE REVEREND DR. MARTIN LUTHER KING, JR.

Early on, I naively thought that *everyone* would be supportive of my decision to stop eating animals, but over time I've come to realize that such is not always the case. Some people actually become defensive upon hearing that I don't eat meat, and I do understand that defensiveness can be a very normal reaction to that which is different or unfamiliar. I've been exposed to information and life experiences that have inspired me to take this step, yet there was a time when I, too, ate meat, and I certainly don't hold judgment over those who do. Nevertheless, there are those who seem to take my dietary choice as some sort of personal attack and grounds for an argument, though I go out of my way to never position it as such. For me, it is a choice of compassion, not of confrontation. So, rather than argue, my personal philosophy is to lead by example and education.* I find that one of the many excellent resources for this is "Veganism in a Nutshell" by Bruce Friedrich, available on audio tape, CD, and online at **www.GoVeg.com**. (Bruce is a wonderful example of compassion for *all* beings. He spent many years working in a shelter for home-less families and the largest soup kitchen in Washington, D.C.) He does a wonderful job of fielding many of the questions that come up surrounding this dietary choice, including the ever pop-ular, "But you eat plants! Don't plants feel pain?" In his words:

> This also is sometimes posed as, "Where do you draw the line? Rights for roaches?" So far, as best we can determine biologically and physiologically, plants do not feel pain. They are alive and have some sort of response to light, water, etc., but they don't feel pain. Pain requires a brain, a central nervous system, pain receptors, and so on. All mammals, birds, and fish have these things. No plants do. We all know this to be true: We all understand that there is a fundamental difference between cutting your lawn and lighting a cat's tail on fire, and between breaking up a head of lettuce and bashing a dog's head in. Birds, mammals, and fish are made of flesh, bones, and fat, just as we are. They feel pain, just as we do. I may not know quite where to draw the line. For example, I'm not sure what a roach or an ant experiences. But I do know with 100 percent certainty that intentionally inflicting suffering because of tradition, custom, convenience, or a palate preference is unethical. [***Kim's note:*** I feel it's important to mention here that the key word is "intentionally." Most people certainly do not do so intentionally.]

The day may come when the rest of animal creation may acquire those rights which could never have been withheld from them but by the hand of tyranny. . . . The question is not, can they reason? Nor can they talk? But can they suffer? Why should the law refuse its protection to any sensitive being? The time will come when humanity will extend its mantle over everything which breathes . . .
— JEREMY BENTHAM (1748–1832)

We, as a society, agree that cruelty to animals is wrong; yet, sadly, we support unimaginable animal cruelty every time we purchase products from industries that exploit animals. The good news is, cruelty-free alternatives exist. The other good news is, cruelty-free products tend to be more natural, and therefore, nontoxic, in the first place. Not only is this choice better for the animals—and better for the environment—it's also better for *us*. (For more information on this, visit **www.CompassionCircle. org**.)

Every time we shop, we vote with our dollars. Our purchases send the message—for better or for worse, whether intentional or not—that we support the practices of the industries that manufacture the products we buy. What message are we sending? If we confirm that the products we buy do not involve animal suffering in their manufacture, we are casting our vote for a cruelty-free world.

If a product *doesn't* state on the label that it is "cruelty-free" or "not tested on animals," then it is up to us to ask the right people the right questions before we buy that product. Any minor inconvenience of checking out the products we intend to buy is *nothing* compared to the injustices imposed upon countless innocent animals behind the scenes.

If the products we buy—whether they be cosmetics, household cleaners, foods, supplements, or other items—*do* involve animal suffering and, therefore, we choose to *no longer purchase* these products, or to switch brands, we are taking a very deliberate step in making our world a more compassionate place. If we demand change of those industries or companies that *do* include the exploitation of animals, we are taking yet another step on the path to peace.

> *We must be the change we wish to see in the world.*
> — GANDHI

Of course, the animals will be taken care of in the afterlife, and their ultimate destiny is the same as ours. However, it's the journey that counts. The animals have been born onto this Earth, just as we have—and they have a right to be here, just as we do, without suffering needlessly at our hands. Just as passing from the physical world into the world of spirit is a major event (known to us as "death"), I find that those who come to Earth from spirit are faced with an equally major transition. The birthing of spirit into physical form is no small task and one that must be respected. All life is sacred.

If chimpanzees have consciousness, if they are capable of abstractions, do they not have what until now has been described as "human rights"? How smart does a chimp have to be before killing him constitutes murder?
— CARL SAGAN

For as long as men massacre animals, they will kill each other. Indeed, he who sows the seed of murder and pain cannot reap joy and love.
— PYTHAGORAS

Until he extends the circle of compassion to all living things, Man will not himself find peace.
— ALBERT SCHWEITZER

Non-violence leads to the highest ethics, which is the goal of all evolution. Until we stop harming all other living beings, we are still savages.
— THOMAS EDISON

ONE OF MY FAVORITE BUMPER STICKERS says, "Ignorance is the most dangerous thing in society." One of the dangers of ignorance is the fact that it prevents good people from demanding change where change is needed, simply because they *do not know* that anything is wrong. Another danger of ignorance is the vulnerability that enables us to be swayed by impressive-sounding belief systems, whether they actually hold truth or not.

There is an underlying belief system in our culture that seems to imply that a problem isn't a problem unless it affects us *personally*. In reality, part of the problem in our world is that we are often looking to solve problems only within our *own* lives—or our own race or our own species.

There is also a danger in belief systems that reflect the idea that everything external that upsets us does so *only* because it brings up something *else* within us—our *own* past hurts and traumas—rather than because we care about someone *else's* suffering and simply want to do something about it.

There are those who claim that animals "sacrifice themselves" for us and are "okay" with it, and that their purpose here on Earth is to serve us. This is a convenient explanation that enables us to overlook some uncomfortable realities in our world. Unfortunately, this explanation is sometimes touted by those who honestly believe they are in touch with the animals themselves, presenting this idea as a higher spiritual truth. As a result, it is all too easily swallowed by those who want to believe that all is well in the world.

When those of our *own* species are harmed or killed, it's much more difficult for us to believe that it's because they've *chosen* to sacrifice themselves or that they are *okay* with it. We're less likely to make such convenient claims and more likely to jump to the aid of our fellow humans and to punish the perpetrators. Herein lies a clue that such claims are based in speciesism and not in higher spirituality.

I feel it's important that we question belief systems that condone the suffering of animals on the grounds of "spirituality." Some spiritual philosophies dictate that there is truly no "right or wrong"—that we must learn to accept *everything* without judgment, without differentiation. In my opinion, this is dangerous thinking. This is the type of thinking that has led many people astray throughout history, as it breeds complacency and creates a space for cruelty and oppression to thrive unchallenged.

Take sides. Neutrality helps the oppressor, never the victim.
Silence encourages the tormentor, never the tormented.
— ELIE WIESEL

The only thing necessary for the triumph of evil
is for good men to do nothing.
— EDMUND BURKE

Many people have asked me about animals who suffer and die the most horrific deaths at the hands of humans. They ask me *why* such things happen. People sometimes use karma as an excuse, implying that the animals somehow deserve it for some past wrongdoing. In my opinion, this, too, is dangerous thinking and often nothing more than an excuse for complacency.

Throughout most of my life, I've studied various spiritual philosophies and teachings in-depth and am well versed in such belief systems. I do believe in karma in that we do reap that which we sow. In other words, if we do good, good will come back to us in the end; and if we do harm, that is something we will also have to answer to eventually, in one way or another. However, in my understanding, just *because* something bad happens to us, it doesn't *necessarily* mean we're paying off a debt from a prior transgression.

What I've come to understand is that some people and animals come here to Earth *not* to work out bad karma—or even to learn a lesson—but simply to teach others. And if they suffer in the process, it's *not* because they did something wrong. Sometimes, it's because they are here to express innocence in a world that hasn't yet fully embraced compassion. Sometimes, it's because they are here to initiate change in a world that doesn't always take kindly to that which upsets the status quo. Few, if any, would contend that Jesus of Nazareth was crucified because of some wrongdoing in his own past. Few, if any, would contend that those who die for *any* good cause do so because they did something wrong. One of my heroes is Martin Luther King, Jr., and few, if any, would contend that he was killed because he had "bad karma." Quite the contrary, he was a very compassionate and enlightened soul who came here, stood up, spoke out, and demanded change because he saw injustice and sought to make things right. He died for a cause, and God bless him for it.

When people turn their backs on the suffering of animals and explain it away with so-called spiritual talk about how it's the animals' destiny or karma and we should just accept it, I simply remind them that people once said that about slavery—and then there were those who took a stand and *did something* about it.

*The hottest places in hell are reserved for those who,
in times of great moral crisis, maintain their neutrality.*
— Dante

*In the end, we will remember not the words of our enemies,
but the silence of our friends.*
— The Reverend Dr. Martin Luther King, Jr.

Those who promote *any* cause in our world are often accused of having an "agenda," as if that label somehow makes their cause less valid. Someone once told me that *everyone* has an agenda. Perhaps that's true. In my opinion, you can tell a *lot* about a person based on their agenda. Is it an agenda of selfishness, or an agenda of service? To me, that makes all the difference. All truly good causes seem to elicit controversy when they run counter to the accepted societal norm, but they are good nonetheless. We must never forget this.

Those who fight for the rights of the oppressed are often called self-righteous, "holier than thou," or preachy. More often then not, they are none of the above; rather, they are humbly but boldly listening to their hearts and choosing a path far more difficult than that of conformity. It's not about comfort, profit, or reputation—in fact, it's often about giving up those very things for the sake of a higher cause.

In my opinion, there is no greater cause than that which stems purely from love and compassion for one's fellow beings. Not from a perspective of, "What's in it for me?" but rather, "How can I help others? How can I make a difference in the world around me?" My philosophy is simple: Care deeply, feel strongly, and act accordingly.

My religion is kindness.
— The Dalai Lama

I am reminded of St. Francis of Assisi, who was known, among other things, for his ability to communicate with animals. He felt at one with all creation and was known to preach to the birds and the other animals about the love of God. The animals were drawn to him, listened to him, and responded accordingly. This included fish. Whenever a fish was caught and St. Francis was nearby, he returned the fish to the water and warned him or her not to be caught again. Sometimes the fish would linger awhile near the boat, listening to him preach, before swimming off.

Perhaps the most famous story about St. Francis involves a wolf who was known for terrorizing the people in the town of Gubbio. The wolf was killing and eating animals and humans alike; and those who tried to go after the wolf to fight back were killed as well. The people of Gubbio lived in fear, and the story of the infamous wolf was known throughout the land. So, despite warnings from the townspeople, St. Francis went to Gubbio to speak to the wolf.

"Come to me, Brother Wolf," he said. He ordered the wolf not to hurt anyone, and the formerly vicious wolf lowered his head and lay down at St. Francis's feet. St. Francis told the wolf he wanted to make peace. He explained that the people of Gubbio would no longer harm the wolf, and the wolf was no longer to harm them. He said that all past crimes were to be forgiven.

The wolf literally nodded his head in agreement. Then, as a crowd of people gathered and watched in amazement, St. Francis asked the wolf to make a pledge, and as he extended his hand, the wolf extended his front paw and placed it in St. Francis's hand.

St. Francis then commanded the wolf to follow him into the town square to make a "peace pact" with the people. The wolf followed St. Francis and remained at his side as he gave a sermon to the townspeople, who felt they were witnessing a miracle. St. Francis offered peace on the wolf's behalf, explaining that "Brother Wolf" would no longer be killing for his sustenance, and the townspeople promised to feed the wolf. When asked if he agreed to the terms of this peace pact, the wolf bowed his head and again placed his paw in St. Francis's hand.

For the rest of his life, the wolf lived peacefully among the townspeople, going from door to door for food and love. He harmed no one and no one harmed him. Not even dogs barked at him. When the wolf eventually died of old age, the people of

Gubbio were saddened at the loss. They had witnessed not only the gift of St. Francis, but the power of love, forgiveness, and understanding; and the possibility of interspecies peace.

MANY PROPHECIES SPEAK OF A TIME in our future here on Earth when we will have at last attained peace—a time when the lion will *literally* lie down with the lamb, and there will be no more killing. I am hearing more and more reports of biologically carnivorous animals who are mysteriously refusing to eat meat (even "organic" meat)—and are thriving regardless—and I can't help but wonder if this is a sign that a more peaceful future is in sight for *all* of us. Perhaps these animals are here to assist us in our *own* spiritual evolution—here to teach *us* a better way.

I do know many people whose beloved dogs and cats consume a vegetarian or vegan diet, and contrary to what one might think, these animals are living unusually long, healthy lives. In fact, as of this writing, to my knowledge, the oldest living dog in the world is a 27-year-old border collie who thrives on a vegan diet. (Please note: When making any dietary change, it's important to make sure all nutritional requirements are being properly met. For more information on vegan diets for animals, visit **www.VeganPets. com**.)

Perhaps one of the first cases of an animal refusing to eat meat took place in the 1940's. Little Tyke, a lioness, absolutely *refused* to eat flesh, despite her human caretakers' best attempts at getting her to do so. She was an exceptionally gentle being who lived harmoniously among many animal friends, including a lamb named Becky, with whom she did, indeed, lie down peacefully. (Her story is told in the book *Little Tyke,* by Georges Westbeau, as well as online at **www.CompassionCircle.org**.)

Little Tyke chose nonviolence as a way of life, even though it was supposed to go against her biology to do so—and she thrived. I wonder what it will take for humanity to likewise choose nonviolence as a way of life. I wonder what *our* excuse is, or if we even have one, for creating so much violence in our world. Animals such as Little Tyke have so much to teach us, if we only listen.

Likewise, our own companion animals have so much to teach

us. They bring us joy, they bring us unconditional love, and they teach us how very precious and sacred life is. There's something about fur that creates an external *and* internal warmth and softness. (And even if they don't have fur, they are soft and warm in their own special way.) We are lucky to touch them . . . and we are luckier when they touch us.

Everything I have learned on my journey with the animals has shown me that they truly are our spiritual brothers and sisters, and it is high time we start treating them as such. We are on this journey *together*.

- CHAPTER 21 -

Full Circle

True love is boundless like the ocean and,
swelling within one, spreads itself out and, crossing
all boundaries and frontiers, envelops the whole world.
— GANDHI

AS TIME WENT ON, more and more people found their way to me during times of tremendous grief over the loss of a beloved animal, and as I shared their pain, I realized how perfect it was that I should be endowed with the gift of experience. I had experienced so much loss in my own life, and I now saw the Divine plan in all of it, for it enabled me to truly relate to those who came to me for support.

Likewise, as time went on, more and more dying animals came to me when they had been discarded because they were not viewed as worthy of veterinary care or even euthanasia. Many of them had been abused, neglected, or abandoned, and I felt honored to be the one who got to help them release their pain and experience love for perhaps the first time in their lives. I was able to truly *be there* for them during their final hours on Earth, and I realized that this, too, was all part of the Divine plan.

Days became months and months became years, and one day, it suddenly occurred to me that over seven years had passed since that remarkable little being named June had opened a new chapter in my life, a chapter that had brought me so much growth and healing. My, how time had flown. As I grasped the reality of all that had happened since then, I found myself immersed in a feeling of total love and acceptance.

I had come such a long way since those final, desperate moments of June's life—those feelings of despair and of certainty that I could *never* love another animal again—and *certainly* not as much as I had loved *her*. Yet, time had taught me that love is not nearly so limited as I had once believed. Indeed, I *had* loved other animals after her. My heart had broken when she died, yet as my heart healed, it had become stronger than ever. It had become somehow capable of loving more fully and completely, in a more expansive and unlimited way than ever before.

Of course, I had been faced with a long, painful journey to the depths of despair before I had reached the bottom. Thankfully, when I got there, I found that the bottom was actually an illusion; and in time, it became a portal, a doorway that led out to a fresh beginning. And when I emerged out through this doorway, I still had June's love with me, yet I also had an understanding of the seasons of life and death, and an acceptance that brought me peace.

As I looked back upon the fragile, frightened person I had been when June left, I now realized how I had been transformed by the journey her leaving had sent me upon. I had become stronger, more okay with myself, more okay with loss, and more certain that death is by no means the end. And because of the doorway that she had opened, so many remarkable beings had entered my life since then.

One such being was that precious little rat named Allison, the one who died a mere six months after she entered my life, yet returned to me later and made it so clear that she was the same being (as told in Chapter 16, "Sweet Reunions"). Although June has yet to return to me, I have come to accept that all things happen in their own perfect Divine timing—and my experience with Allison has taught me that such things *do* happen.

In hindsight, I don't think it's a coincidence that I chose to name her Allison. When she first entered my life, she was a nameless, abandoned rat in a dirty cage. I just looked at her, wondering what to call her, and the name simply came to me. It just *felt* like the perfect name for her. Then, after she returned to me and I realized who she was, it felt fitting to call her Allison once again.

One day, just recently, it hit me that the name "Allison" sounds very much like, "A lesson." And she sure has been a lesson for me. She taught me, in a very literal way, that death is not the end; and that somehow, some way, when the time is right, we are truly reunited with those we love.

In many ways, her life was a parallel to June's life. The first time around, she actually *looked* very much like June. So much so, that when I had that magical dream in which Henry appeared (as told in Chapter 14, "Sweet Dreams"), at first I wasn't sure whether the rat in the background was Allison or June. When Jameth then shared that he had just had the same dream, he expressed that he, too, had been unsure at first whether the other rat in the dream was June or Allison.

The first time around, Allison hadn't been with us for very long, yet I had grown quite attached to her in a short time, just like June. The second time around, Allison was with us for much longer, and the bond she and I developed was just as close and deep and meaningful as the bond I had shared with June. And as she grew old and began to show signs that she wouldn't be around for much longer, I realized that I wasn't ready to say good-bye.

Allison had several nicknames. Not only was she known as Alligator, which eventually was shortened to Gator; she was also known as Sweet Pea, which, over time, became Sweetest Pea. And perhaps the most appropriate nickname of all was Angel Face. People often commented on her wise, sweet, angelic face.

As Allison grew old and frail, she needed help getting around. So I often picked her up, rocked her, and gently sang what came to be known as "her song," which I softly sang to the tune of "Edelweiss" (from *The Sound of Music*):

Angel Face
Angel Face
You are my little Angel Face
Soft and sweet
So petite
I love my little Angel Face . . .

Whenever I sang this and held her against my cheek, she softly chattered in contentment, and the love between us overflowed. As I held her, I was reminded of the love June and I had shared, and I realized that I was now doing what I had once considered impossible: I was loving other animals, and it was *okay*. It didn't mean I loved June any less; it just meant that I now had many other special little beings who filled my life with unconditional love and joy.

I loved *all* of the wonderful beings who had shared my life since June's passing, yet there was something extra-special about the connection I had with Allison.

"This is going to be perhaps the most difficult loss since June," I often told people who asked about Allison as she grew old and weary. There was something about her that was so remarkable, and it was so uplifting to have her near. She radiated such warmth and understanding. She was always the one who comforted other rats who were hurting. She was always the one who comforted *people* who were hurting, just as June had done. Allison was a little ambassador for ratkind, just as June had been. People often asked about her, just as they had once done with June. And she and I had a very strong connection and clear communication, always understanding each other's thoughts and feeling each other's feelings.

Toward the end of her life, Allison spent her days on my lap or in a little bed at my side as I worked on this book. She spent her nights in bed with Jameth and me, just as June had done. And when it became apparent that she didn't have much time left and that it would be her final night with us, I panicked, just as I had done when I knew that June was leaving.

Over time, I had learned how to let go, how to say good-bye. I had also learned how to help the *animals* to let go as they made their transition, often coaxing them to go to the Light and reassuring them that they would be fine. Animals had even begun coming to me with the request that I assist them in their transition, as they were having trouble leaving. And I had become amazed at how, time and time again, as they had struggled to remain alive, I had held them and lovingly reassured them, "It's okay. You can go." And more often than not, as soon as I had given them this reassurance, they had gone in peace. Even when they needed the additional assistance of euthanasia, the whole process became much more peaceful for them—and for me.

Yet now I found myself faced with having to say good-bye to little Allison, my precious Angel Face, who had become such a big and important part of my life. I always try not to play "favorites" with the animals in my life, and I truly love them all, yet there was no denying it: She was my extra-special little companion.

As her breath became more shallow and her time became more scarce, I took her to bed with me, knowing with certainty that this would be our final night together. I settled her fragile little body on the pillow next to me and spent hours just stroking her fur and looking into her soulful, loving eyes, reminiscing about our time together. I felt the connection of love between us. It was so full and deep and pure. It felt so eternal.

Then her breathing changed, and she began to show signs that the end was near. I began to cry and beg, *"No!* You *can't* leave! I just *can't* let you go! Not *again!* This *isn't fair!"* And I held her and rocked her as my tears soaked her soft coat.

And she listened. Her breathing steadied, and I realized it had been a false alarm—or perhaps she was giving me another chance to get it right. I apologized to her for begging her to stay—a habit I thought I had overcome by now—and I told her that I understood it was her time. I didn't *like* it, but I understood it.

It had become a regular practice of mine to play meaningful music during an animal's transition, whatever piece of music seemed to suit the particular animal. So I settled Allison back down on the pillow facing me, and we continued gazing at one another, exchanging feelings of love; then gently drifted off to sleep together to the tune of "Edelweiss" as I softly sang . . .

Angel Face
Angel Face
You are my little Angel Face
Soft and sweet
So petite
I love my little Angel Face . . .

She chattered in contentment, and I continued softly singing her song, the Angel Face song, until sleep overtook me.

When I awakened several hours later, Allison's little body was very still, and I knew it was over. I held her lifeless body and sobbed, telling her how much I loved her, telling her how much I'd miss her, telling her how special she was—and always would be— to me. I held her body against my cheek and cried, long and hard.

In that moment, I was suddenly reminded of the very similar scene that had taken place many years prior, when I had awakened to *June's* lifeless body. I now realized, for perhaps the first time ever, that Allison had indeed taught me a powerful lesson. She had taught me that, as difficult as it is to imagine when we are faced with a devastating loss, we truly *can* love again, just as fully and deeply as we did the first time. And that's what our loved ones *want* for us.

I couldn't help but notice the parallels between June's life and Allison's life, between June's death and Allison's death. Yet there was a difference. With June's death, I came away feeling totally lost and confused, completely helpless and hopeless—and feeling very much alone and abandoned. The path that had unfolded for me *since* June's death had, over time, taught me so much. And now, with Allison's death, along with the tears, I felt a sense of peace and understanding. Instead of feeling completely alone and abandoned, I knew that, among the seasons of life, fall had just turned into winter— but surely spring would come again. A feeling of unconditional love washed over me and I felt her say,

I love you—and I always will.

ABOUT THE AUTHOR

Kim Sheridan grew up in Southern California, surrounded by animals of various shapes and sizes. She also had psychic abilities she didn't understand, and from a very early age, she was fascinated with paranormal phenomena and the afterlife.

As an adult, Kim's life changed direction. First, she earned degrees in psychology and clinical hypnotherapy. Then, she studied health and nutrition; earned a degree in naturopathy; and became a respected health writer, researcher, and nutritional consultant. Along with her husband, she co-founded HealthForce Nutritionals, Inc., which offers nutritional supplements for both humans and animals (including the famous Green Mush™).

While grieving the loss of a beloved animal companion named June, Kim unexpectedly began to receive signs and messages from the Other Side. This led her on an incredible journey into the realm of animals and the afterlife, bringing her full circle to the path begun in childhood.

Today she is a highly respected and sought-after expert on life after death for animals, and her time is devoted not only to animals but to those who are left behind when they pass. Kim is a popular guest on radio and television; and she is an acclaimed lecturer and workshop leader, providing support to those whose beloved animal companions have passed. She is also the founder of Compassion Circle (www.CompassionCircle.org), with a mission to expand the circle of compassion to all beings. She lives in Southern California with her husband and their beloved animal family. Her goal is to make the world a better place, and to teach compassion and respect for all.

www.AnimalsandtheAfterlife.com

Resources

Kim's note: There are so many resources I'd like to recommend. However, with new resources coming up all the time—and ever-changing addresses—I've found it impossible to create what I consider a complete, up-to-date list. Therefore, rather than set myself up for errors of omission or outdated resources, I offer the following Websites, which comprise what I feel to be the most efficient list of resources I can offer.

For information on future books and upcoming events, as well as a photo gallery of the animals included in this book, please visit:

www.AnimalsAndTheAfterlife.com

For information on animal wellness, animal rescue, pet loss grief support, animal communicators, and more, please visit:

www.CompassionCircle.org

For information on Green Mush™ and other holistic nutritional products for animals and humans, please visit:

www.HealthForce.com

For information on health, longevity, nutrition, and optimal well-being for animals, with case histories and resources, please visit:

www.VeganPets.com

Have you had an experience suggesting life after death for animals?

The author's research into this subject is ongoing, and she is now compiling data for *Animals and the Afterlife: Book 2*.

If you have a story or other input you'd like to share, the preferred method of submission is via e-mail to:

StorySubmissions@AnimalsAndTheAfterlife.com

And if e-mail is not possible, good old-fashioned mail is still welcome:

Animals and the Afterlife™
c/o EnLighthouse
1835A S. Centre City Pkwy. #181
Escondido, CA 92025
U.S.A.

Due to a high volume of mail, it is not possible for the author to answer letters personally, but all submissions are greatly appreciated.

For more information, please visit:
www.AnimalsAndTheAfterlife.com

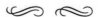

Hay House Titles of Related Interest

YOU CAN HEAL YOUR LIFE, the movie,
starring Louise L. Hay & Friends
(available as a 1-DVD program and an expanded 2-DVD set)
Watch the trailer at: **www.LouiseHayMovie.com**

THE SHIFT, the movie,
starring Dr. Wayne W. Dyer
(available as a 1-DVD program and an expanded 2-DVD set)
Watch the trailer at: **www.DyerMovie.com**

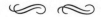

*POWER ANIMALS: How to Connect with Your
Animal Spirit Guide,* by Steven D. Farmer, Ph.D.

*SACRED CEREMONY: How to Create Ceremonies for
Healings, Transitions, and Celebrations,*
by Steven D. Farmer, Ph.D.

*PETS ARE FOREVER:
Amazing True Stories of Angelic Animals,*
by Jenny Smedley

PETS HAVE SOULS TOO by Jenny Smedley

THE AMAZING POWER OF ANIMALS
by Gordon Smith

*THE MYSTERY OF THE WHITE LIONS:
Children of the Sun God,* by Linda Tucker

*THE ANIMAL HEALER: A Unique Insight into the
Healing, Care and Wellbeing of Animals,*
by Elizabeth Whiter

All of the above are available at your local
bookstore, or may be ordered through Hay House.